Enterprise AI

Shazia Sadiq
Editor

Enterprise AI

Springer

Editor
Shazia Sadiq
School of Electrical Engineering and
Computer Science
The University of Queensland
St Lucia, QLD, Australia

ISBN 978-3-032-01939-4 ISBN 978-3-032-01940-0 (eBook)
https://doi.org/10.1007/978-3-032-01940-0

This Springer imprint is published by the registered company Springer Nature Switzerland AG
The registered company address is: Gewerbestrasse 11, 6330 Cham, Switzerland

Preface

Enterprise AI refers to artificial intelligence (AI) technologies developed to address business and organisational needs in both public and private enterprises. It is expected to be highly customisable to integrate with existing infrastructure and enterprise software systems while flexible enough to scale capabilities as demands shift. It puts a strong emphasis on trust, reliability, and security, as well as creating value for competitive advantage and social good. Enterprise AI contrasts with Consumer AI, which is designed for use by individuals, enhancing convenience in everyday tasks.

Advancements in AI valued at contributing trillions of dollars to the global economy are often dominated by Enterprise products and services. It is reasonable to envisage that the benefits of Enterprise AI will go beyond productivity gains and operational efficiencies and provide entirely new systems of value creation and a redefinition of competitive advantage.

However, progress is asymmetrical. While AI growth for consumer Internet companies has been phenomenal, other sectors have yet to harness the full potential current AI solutions can offer. There is an increasing recognition of the economic and social implications of this asymmetry, which could result in *AI privilege*, deepening economic inequality and social discontent. Specifically, small and medium-sized enterprises (SMEs) are exposed to a range of vulnerabilities due to limited control over critical technologies, diminished capacity to differentiate in the global marketplace, and increasing risks of data leakage, misuse, and privacy concerns.

Globally, most current approaches to Enterprise AI are focussed on solutions at a functional level that target single decisions, e.g., fraud detection in financial transactions. The diffusion of AI in enterprises is accelerating, and merely collecting a series of solutions will exasperate functional silos leading to organisational inefficiencies and redundancies, sub-optimal resource allocation, and hindered innovation. The inherent interconnectedness of decisions within and between enterprises needs to be recognised. Similar to historic technological disruptions, such as electricity markets, transformative outcomes take time: they reshape entire business models and create new theories, new solutions, new markets, and new industries. We are just entering this period for AI right now: the next decade will be critical for enterprises to adapt.

There are significant challenges that need to be addressed to achieve success from Enterprise AI so that benefits flow to a broader span of organisations while ensuring that the deployments are responsible in meeting stipulated risks and returns. These challenges include overcoming sustainability challenges of large-scale AI models, understanding how enterprise-wide scaling of AI will shape the structure and operations of the enterprise, what capability frameworks are needed to amplify employee capacity, improving trust in AI solutions by protecting developer and user communities, understanding the barriers to adoption that can potentially widen the gap of AI privilege, and developing authentic evaluation systems to realise and measure commercial and public value from AI at individual organisational and sectoral levels.

These challenges form the basis of the book, wherein experts in multiple socio-technical disciplines provide their perspectives and deliberations on the barriers and opportunities for Enterprise AI, as well as a range of state-of-the-art approaches that can facilitate AI adoption more widely. The contributions have been accordingly structured in three parts, namely:

Part I: Scalable and Sustainable Practices for Enterprise AI
Part II: Safe and Responsible Enterprise AI
Part III: Value Creation with Enterprise AI

The aim of this book is to provide a comprehensive and authoritative resource on Enterprise AI so that students, researchers, and practitioners have the benefit of accessing the full scope of the problem and approaches in one place, relating to the critical aspects of Enterprise AI projects. The contributions have been prepared to ensure the content is accessible to readers from a variety of backgrounds, including computer science and engineering, information systems, business, and management.

I would like to express my sincere gratitude to all the authors who have made valuable and comprehensive contributions. I am deeply thankful to many colleagues for their thought-leadership and guidance on various aspects of Enterprise AI: Lyria Bennett Moses, Andrew Burton-Jones, Shane Culpepper, Gianluca Demartini, Joshua Gans, Marta Indulska, Ramayya Krishnan, Tongliang Liu, Flavio Menezes, Divish Srivastava, Eduardo Velloso, Martie-Louise Verreynne, Mary-Anne Willims, Wenjie Zhang, Xiaofang Zhou, and Guido Zuccon. A big thanks to the fabulous K-team, Kate Aldridge and Kathleen Williamson, for your constant support and help.

I hope that the compilation of these diverse areas of Enterprise AI will provide readers with an appreciation of the full scope of Enterprise AI pitfalls and promises and will serve as a point of reference for students, researchers, practitioners, and professionals in this exciting and evolving area.

St Lucia, QLD, Australia — Shazia Sadiq
June 2025

Contents

Contributors

Agathe Balayn Microsoft Research, New York, NY, USA

Tong Chen The University of Queensland, Brisbane, QLD, Australia

Lisa Ehrlinger Information Systems, Hasso Plattner Institute, University of Potsdam, Potsdam, Germany

Lixin Fan Webank, Shenzhen, China

Shaoyang Fan The University of Queensland, Brisbane, QLD, Australia

Ujwal Gadiraju Delft University of Technology, Delft, The Netherlands

Nicole Gillespie Melbourne Business School, The University of Melbourne, Melbourne, VIC, Australia

Shengbo Gong Department of Computer Science, Emory University, Atlanta, GA, USA

Christian Janiesch TU Dortmund University, Dortmund, Germany

Wei Jin Department of Computer Science, Emory University, Atlanta, GA, USA

Yan Kang Webank, China

Marek Kowalkiewicz Centre for Future Enterprise, Queensland University of Technology, Brisbane, QLD, Australia

Steven Lockey Melbourne Business School, The University of Melbourne, Melbourne, VIC, Australia

Neil G. Marchant School of Computing and Information Systems, University of Melbourne, Parkville, VIC, Australia

Tim Miller School of Electrical Engineering and Computer Science, The University of Queensland, Brisbane, QLD, Australia

Felix Naumann Information Systems, Hasso Plattner Institute, University of Potsdam, Potsdam, Germany

Juntong Ni Department of Computer Science, Emory University, Atlanta, GA, USA

Olga Ohrimenko School of Computing and Information Systems, University of Melbourne, Parkville, VIC, Australia

Javad Pool The University of Queensland, Brisbane, QLD, Australia

Michael Rosemann Centre for Future Enterprise, Queensland University of Technology, Brisbane, QLD, Australia

Benjamin I. P. Rubinstein School of Computing and Information Systems, University of Melbourne, Parkville, VIC, Australia

Ida Someh Information Systems Discipline, UQ Business School, The University of Queensland, Brisbane, QLD, Australia

Francesco Sovrano Collegium Helveticum, ETH Zurich, Zurich, Switzerland

Department of Informatics, University of Zurich, Zurich, Switzerland

Ben Tan Webank, China

Barbara Wixom MIT Center for Information Systems Research, Massachusetts University of Technology, Cambridge, MA, USA

Hongzhi Yin The University of Queensland, Brisbane, QLD, Australia

Junliang Yu The University of Queensland, Brisbane, QLD, Australia

Ying Zhao School of Computing and Information Systems, University of Melbourne, Parkville, VIC, Australia

Vincent Zheng Webank, China

Part I
Scalable and Sustainable Practices for Enterprise AI

As artificial intelligence continues to mature, enterprises are increasingly eager to move beyond experimental prototypes and into full-scale production. Yet, despite the proliferation of powerful tools and frameworks, a persistent gap remains between proof-of-concept success and real-world deployment. This gap is often driven by the high computational and labour costs associated with data preparation, model training, and system maintenance.

This part explores emerging strategies that enable organizations to scale AI systems sustainably by maximizing performance while minimizing resource consumption. The chapters presented here offer a deep dive into three complementary approaches that address this challenge from different angles: data distillation, federated learning, and resource-efficient deployment.

The first chapter by Tong Chen, Junliang Yu, and Hongzhi Yin tackles the challenge of deploying advanced AI models, such as large language models, in environments with limited computational resources. The authors present a taxonomy of techniques for reducing model size and inference cost, including pruning, quantization, and knowledge distillation. Real-world examples illustrate how these methods can democratize access to cutting-edge AI, allowing smaller enterprises to benefit from powerful models without prohibitive infrastructure investments. This chapter underscores the importance of efficient AI deployment as an enabler of innovation in enterprise settings.

The second chapter by Juntong Ni, Shengbo Gong, and Wei Jin introduces dataset distillation as a powerful technique to reduce the data burden in enterprise AI workflows. By compressing large datasets into smaller, information-rich subsets, organizations can dramatically cut down on training time and memory usage without sacrificing model performance. The authors categorize and analyse four key distillation methods, namely, performance matching, gradient matching, trajectory matching, and distribution matching, and demonstrate their applicability across diverse data types, including images, graphs, and time-series. This approach directly supports scalable AI by enabling faster experimentation and deployment with fewer resources.

The final chapter by Ben Tan, Yan Kang, Lixin Fan, and Vincent Zheng focuses on Federated Learning (FL), which addresses a critical tension in enterprise AI: how to harness the value of distributed, sensitive data without compromising privacy or security. It provides a comprehensive overview of FL's foundational principles and practical implementations, which not only allows readers to gain a thorough understanding of FL but also allows them to analyse different approaches as relevant to their use-case. The chapter further provides a case study on federated recommendation systems to demonstrate how FL empowers enterprises to scale AI solutions while adhering to regulatory and ethical standards.

Together, these three chapters present a cohesive strategy for scaling enterprise AI sustainably. They explore efficient deployment, dataset distillation, and federated learning as complementary approaches to reduce resource demands while maintaining performance. Through practical techniques and real-world case studies, the section equips organizations to bridge the gap between prototypes and production in a secure and cost-effective manner.

Chapter 1
Resource-Efficient Model Deployment for Enterprise AI

Tong Chen, Junliang Yu, and Hongzhi Yin

Abstract While the rise of foundation models, like large language models, has brought immense opportunities for some enterprises to roll out new products and further optimize their operational logistics, the ever-expanding digitalization gap caused by the skewed ownership of computing power is also evident, preventing AI from realizing wider business benefits. This implies that democratizing AI among all enterprises requires addressing the key challenge of making the use of state-of-the-art AI technologies less dependent on the availability of computing resources. In this chapter, with a main focus on deploying advanced yet resource-intensive AI models in less resourceful enterprise environments, we will provide an in-depth analysis of the research and applications within this context. Firstly, we will review and taxonomize the main technical pathways for reducing the resource footprint of a bulky AI model while keeping the utility trade-off minimal. Then, we will associate each category of the solutions with real examples, so as to discuss when and how their advantages can be fully leveraged. Finally, by providing a roadmap that entails high-potential R&D areas, we will conclude this chapter by pointing out future directions for developing technologies for resource-efficient enterprise AI.

1.1 Introduction

In today's world, the integration with artificial intelligence (AI) is a highly anticipated move for enterprises of different sizes. AI's enterprise roles include improving customer service with individualized assistance, uplifting efficiency via automation in key business processes, and even "smartifying" their consumer products. Corresponding examples are personalized chatbots and recommender systems [1, 2], sales forecasting for inventory management [3, 4], as well as smart devices with embedded AI ecosystems like Apple Intelligence [5] and Google Gemini [6]. In short, the uptake of AI, or the willingness to engage AI, is showing an

T. Chen (✉) · J. Yu · H. Yin
The University of Queensland, Brisbane, QLD, Australia
e-mail: tong.chen@uq.edu.au; jl.yu@uq.edu.au; h.yin1@uq.edu.au

S. Sadiq (ed.), *Enterprise AI*, https://doi.org/10.1007/978-3-032-01940-0_1

exponentially upward trend. According to a 2023 survey published by IBM [7], over 80% of IT professionals at large organizations are active users or investigators of AI technologies. Furthermore, 59% of the IT professionals at companies deploying or exploring AI indicate that their company has accelerated their investments in or rollout of AI in the past 24 months [7].

However, on the flip side of the coin, the fast-evolving AI landscape has also been expanding the variation of technology readiness across enterprises. This is due mainly to the skewed resource availability at different enterprises. Those important resources include, but are not restricted to, computing facilities that enable the training and deployment of complex AI models; the feasibility of acquiring large-scale, application-specific data to facilitate model training and evaluation; human experts that are familiar with machine learning pipelines and can incorporate domain knowledge into machine learning algorithms; long-term support from end-users to guarantee market share; and continuous improvement of the AI system deployed. All the resources are indispensable for harnessing the full potential of AI for business applications, whereas an imbalance on any of the resources may enlarge the aforementioned **digitalization gap** between enterprises. Take the resource consumption as an example, where Fig. 1.1 shows an evolution trajectory of major AI models in terms of their training computational cost. Before the deep learning era (starting 2010), the amount of computation needed for training an AI model increases by 1.5 times per year. Meanwhile, as we enter the deep learning era, this number has started increasing by 4.6 times per year, due mainly to the heavy parameterization of deep neural networks including various foundation models.

In this chapter, we will specifically discuss the **resource** aspect of this digitalization gap, as this is usually the first practical challenge shared by a large body of enterprises when it comes to AI adoption. This challenge is amplified in the context of small- and medium-sized enterprises (SMEs) that have a strong demand for increasing competitiveness with AI but are highly resource constrained. Let us take the large language models (LLMs) as an example. On the one hand, despite the accessibility offered by companies like OpenAI (for ChatGPT) [10] and Anthropic PBC (for Claude) [11] via paid Application Programming Interfaces (APIs), the need for preserving the privacy of user data and building customized applications has lit the red light for such adoption channels. On the other hand, the prohibitive computational cost also limits the idea of building a customized LLM from the ground up to world-leading technical giants [12]. Even the direct deployment and fine-tuning, as a more resource-friendly option, is often deemed infeasible, given the computing environment required. For instance, Llama [13]—the open-source LLM released by Meta—requires a total of over 160GB of GPU memory to run its full version with 70 billion parameters, which is impossible without substantial upfront investments in building an advanced GPU cluster. Furthermore, in relation to computing resources, the exerted costs of energy consumption, dedicated personnel, and ongoing maintenance can create further overhead that bottlenecks scalable adoption of state-of-the-art AI technologies.

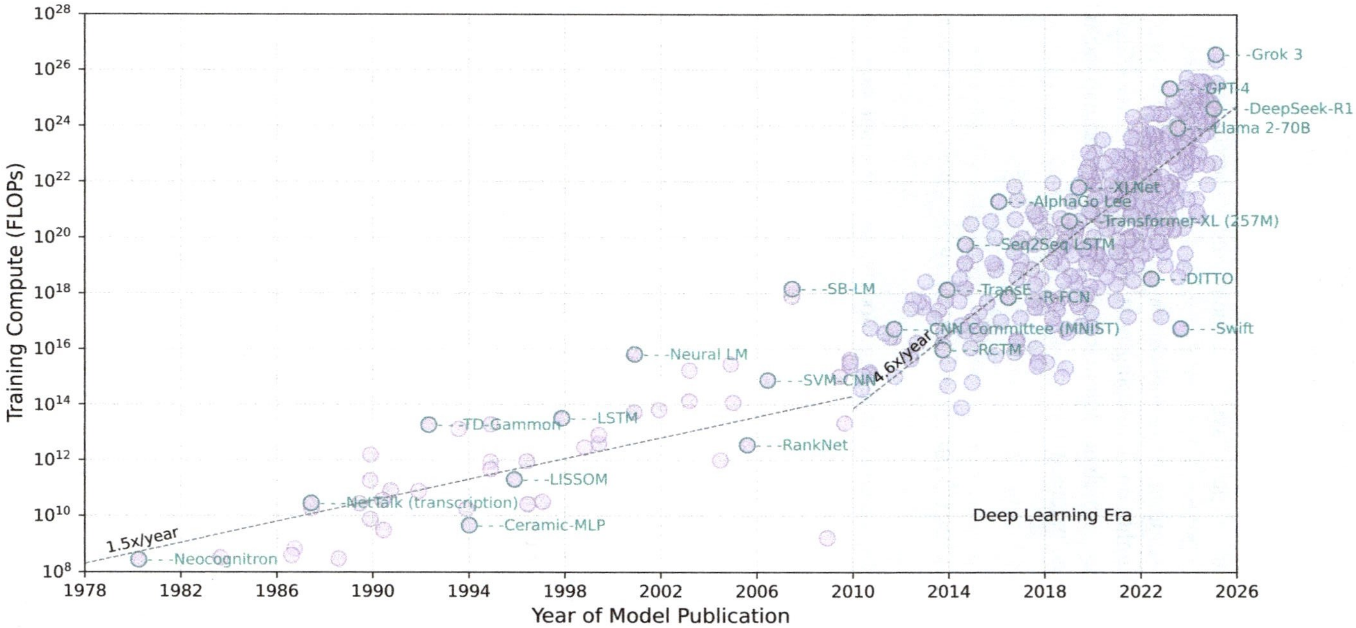

Fig. 1.1 The computational cost of different AI models throughout five decades up to 2025, measured by Floating Point Operations per Second (FLOPs). A quick reference is that, 10^{20} FLOPs translate to approximately four GPU days (measured with Nvidia A100). Since the deep learning era began in 2010, AI models' training cost has been increasing 4.6 times per year, and by February 2025, the Grok 3 [8] from xAI currently peaks at 4.6×10^{26} FLOPs. This visualization is generated with data from Epoch AI [9], which also provides a comprehensive list of model names and specifications

Organization of the Chapter Motivated by the resource-intensive nature of modern AI models, we aim to discuss existing research and development (R&D) practices in AI solutions that are less dependent on the computing resources, which can potentially pave the way for a variety of resource-efficient enterprise applications. We will start the discussion with Sect. 1.2 by taxonomizing and analyzing the main technical pathways for reducing the resource consumption for deploying and using AI. In Sect. 1.5, we will provide a real example for each type of resource-efficient AI solution in the application-oriented industrial setting. Then, we will outline our thoughts on developing next-generation resource-efficient AI for enterprise applications, which are summarized in an R&D roadmap in Sect. 1.6. Finally, remarks and conclusions will be covered in Sect. 1.7.

1.2 Resource-Efficient Machine Learning

Before designing efficient machine learning models, an important step is to first understand the desiderata of those models. In other words, we need to identify and define important efficiency aspects that should be achieved by those lightweight models. Without loss of generality, we have segmented those key efficiency requirements into two main categories:

- **Memory consumption.** A machine learning model, especially a deep learning–based one, commonly contains a certain number of parameters (e.g., weights and biases in feedforward networks) that numerically approximate a real-world function. In general, a more capable model encapsulates a larger set of parameters. This is especially true for foundation models like the Vision Transformer [14] (for computer vision) with 22 billion parameters and T5-XL [15] (for natural language understanding) with 11 billion parameters, which, respectively, translate into over 80 and 40 GB memory in a 32-bit floating point system. Consequently, memory consumption is usually the very first hurdle that prevents a high-performance model from being deployed in a resource-constrained environment. In this line of research, metrics including parameter count, peak runtime memory, and parameter reduction rate (a.k.a. sparsity) [16, 17] are popular choices for quantifying and comparing the memory consumption of different machine models.
- **Inference time.** The amount of time required for training the model is crucial for high-throughput, Web-scale applications. Meanwhile, compared with training that is mostly a "one-off" process and can be performed offline, inference is a more frequent action that requests a trained model to generate corresponding outputs (e.g., conversational responses, predictions, recommendations, etc.) based on end-users' inputs. In this regard, a model's capability of efficiently performing inference on-the-fly with minimal latency is of great importance. Notably, models having a smaller footprint in memory do not necessarily imply lower inference time, as inference time is predominately determined by the

complexity of layer-wise operations of the deep neural network [18]. As such, metrics like Multiply-Addition Counts (MACs) [19] and wall clock runtime [20, 21] are used to measure the time spent on model training and inference.

In short, the lowered memory consumption ensures that an AI solution is *deployable* in resource-constrained environments. For applications that do not run in a real-time manner, e.g., sales forecasting over long horizons [4] and document summarization [22], performing memory consumption optimization will suffice as it also allows the end-user to benefit from larger model capacity (and hence higher accuracy). Meanwhile, in applications that rely on *efficient decision support*, such as traffic monitoring [23] and autonomous driving [24], optimization on inference time seeks further trade-off between a model's complexity and performance. In the next two sections, we will provide detailed analyses on both technical aspects concerning resource-efficient AI.

1.3 Memory Consumption Reduction

In this section, we review the main technical choices for reducing a machine learning model's memory footprint. Essentially, this comes down to removing excessive parameters from the model while keeping the performance sacrifice minimal. Based on the types of data to be processed, the majority of parameter consumption can come from the feature representations (i.e., input embeddings [25]) or the main network architectures, or both. Reducing the memory footprint in each part of the AI system requires different techniques. As such, we introduce methodologies associated with lightweight feature representations and neural architectures in Sects. 1.3.1 and 1.3.2, respectively.

1.3.1 Lightweight Feature Representations

A machine learning model always needs to represent a given data sample by mapping it into a predefined feature space to support subsequent computations. If the input data contains discrete, categorical features like $country = \{Australia, Burma, Canada, \cdots\}$, then each possible feature value will correspond to a d-dimensional real-valued vector termed *embedding* [25, 26]. In large-scale applications where the discrete feature space is large, such feature embeddings are prone to become a significant hurdle on memory efficiency. A typical example is the billion-scale user/item IDs in recommendation services [27, 28], whereas the recommender system deployed by Meta consumes 12 trillion parameters and can demand up to 96TB memory to run [16, 29]. Next, we unfold the three major types of techniques used for lowering the memory consumption from feature representations, namely, low-precision feature embeddings, embedding

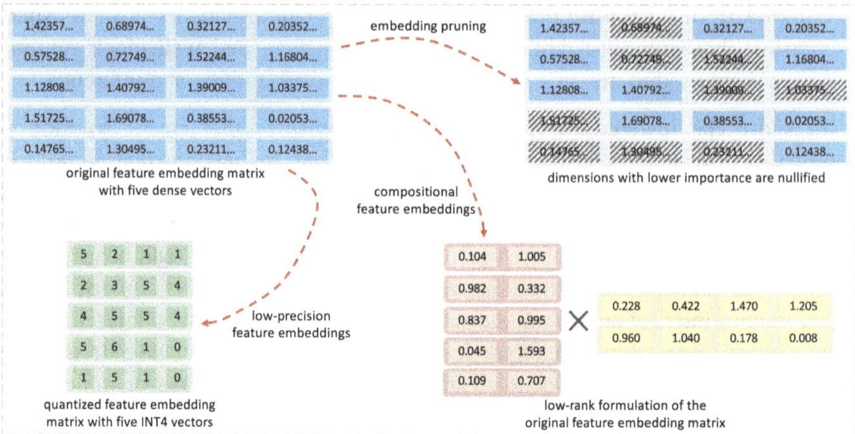

Fig. 1.2 A visualization of low-precision feature embeddings (bottom left), embedding pruning (top right), and compositional feature embeddings (bottom right)

pruning, as well as compositional feature embeddings. A visual comparison of the three types of techniques is also provided in Fig. 1.2.

Low-Precision Feature Embeddings A straightforward remedy to the excessive memory consumption of feature embeddings is to use a low-precision storage format instead of the default 32- or 64-bit precision, where binary codes are a typical choice. It compresses each real-valued embedding entry from full-precision as binary code of just one bit [30, 31], demanding significantly less memory for storage. However, compared with their original version, the expressiveness of the resulting binary codes is greatly impaired [32]. To better retain model performance, quantization is proposed as a middle ground that represents each embedding entry with a multi-bit (e.g., 4-bit) integer, which is achieved by mapping a full-precision floating point number to a quantized value with carefully designed clipping functions. Representative solutions include post-training quantization (PTQ) [33–35] that can adaptively determine the optimal clipping thresholds for trained feature embeddings, as well as the low-precision training [36, 37] that enables training the quantized feature embeddings from scratch in an end-to-end manner.

Embedding Pruning Alternatively, another widely used approach is to zero-out embedding entries with lower importance, such that the embedding weights become a sparse matrix. The resulting sparse matrix can then be managed by various sparse matrix storage techniques [38, 39] that bring negligible cost for storing zero-valued entries [40]. Some common practices include designing a reinforcement learning [40], reparameterization [41], or evolutionary search [42] framework to prune out less informative entries in the full embedding weight matrix. In a nutshell, these methods aim to learn a binary matrix termed pruning mask with the same dimensionality as the embedding matrix, where 1 and 0 are, respectively, used in the pruning mask to indicate embedding entries to be kept or pruned. During model inference, an element-wise multiplication between the pruning mask and embedding matrix is performed, thus producing a sparse, pruned embedding matrix for deployment. It is worth noting that, instead of using sparse embeddings, some methods [32, 43–45] allow for a set of embedding dimensions $d \in \{d_1, d_2, d_3, \cdots\}$ for each feature, where the best dimension per feature is searched based on a joint optimization objective that combines model accuracy and memory consumption. At the end of the search, each feature is assigned a dense embedding, while the average dimensionality (hence the overall memory footprint) of all feature embeddings is reduced [32, 46]. This resembles the core idea of pruning, which removes less informative parts of embeddings to cut the parameter size used in feature representations.

Compositional Feature Embeddings Low-precision feature embeddings reduce memory consumption by decreasing the bits needed for storing all dense embeddings, while embedding pruning achieves this by removing redundant embedding dimensions [47]. In contrast, compositional feature embeddings represent all features with shared parameters [48], thus effectively reducing the overall parameter count. Essentially, compositional feature embeddings define a pool of embedding vectors (termed *meta-embeddings* [49, 50]) to be shared by all features, whose size is significantly smaller than the number of features. Then, by assigning each feature a unique combination of meta-embeddings, a unique representation of each feature can be generated by combining these meta-embeddings via operations like vector concatenation, sum, or element-wise product [51]. Bearing a similar intuition of using a smaller parameter space to represent the full feature embedding matrix, decomposition methods like low-rank factorization [52] and tensor-train decomposition [53, 54] are also widely adopted to compress the feature representations in industry-scale applications.

1.3.2 Lightweight Neural Architectures

Given the complexity of real-world data, a neural network needs to be endowed with sufficient computational capacity to capture the subtle correlations between different data-driven patterns and the predicted outputs. Such computational capacity is commonly achieved by stacking multiple deep layers in a single neural network. As a consequence, this leads to the prosperity of large networks like ResNet-152 (115 million parameters) for image understanding [55] and BERT-Large (340 million parameters) for natural language processing [56]. More recently, the rise of foundation models further pushes the parameter sizes into billion level (see examples of T5-XL and Vision Transformer in Sect. 1.2). Being parallel to lightweight feature representations, simplifying the bulky network architectures has long been a focal point for resource-efficient AI solutions. As depicted by Fig. 1.3, network quantization, knowledge distillation, and network pruning are three widely adopted pathways to lightweight neural architectures. In what follows, we introduce these well-established methods for achieving lightweight neural architectures.

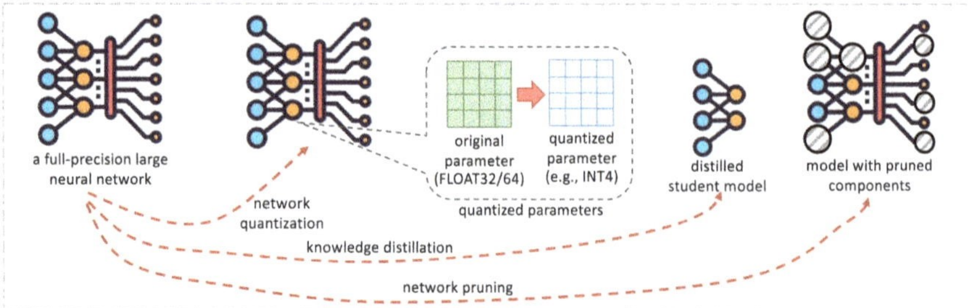

Fig. 1.3 A visualization of network quantization, knowledge distillation, and network pruning (respectively, presented from left to right)

Network Quantization Analogous to lightweight feature representations, quantization can also be applied to the deep layers inside a neural network, where the neural networks' parameters (i.e., weights and biases) are converted to a low-precision format to save memory space. As the key is to minimize the accuracy gap before the quantized and full-precision models, a broad collection of existing work is proposed to mitigate the possible performance drop brought by the quantization of model parameters [57]. Among those efforts, quantization-aware training [58, 59] and post-training quantization [60, 61] are currently the most popular choices. Quantization-aware training aims to re-calibrate quantized model by performing further training using gradient descent, where solutions like learned quantization networks [62], differentiable soft quantization [63], and straight-through estimator [64] are proposed to cope with the non-differentiable nature of quantization operations (e.g., rounding, clipping, etc.). In contrast, post-training quantization is a more efficient solution that directly quantizes a model's parameters and activations (i.e., intermediate outputs) [57], where strategies like layer-wise weight balance [65] and output reconstruction [66], as well as withholding a small unlabeled data as calibration set for quantization parameters [67], are in place to help maintain the original model's accuracy.

Knowledge Distillation Bearing a teacher-student interaction ethos, knowledge distillation is a model compression scheme that learns a compact student model by letting it mimic the behavior of a full teacher model [68]. In a nutshell, when given the same input data sample, a well-trained student model should be able to replicate the decision-making process of the teacher model, which is facilitated by transferring and distilling the teacher model's knowledge into the student model. To quantify such knowledge, a popular approach is response-based comparisons between teacher and student, where the outputs (i.e., *logits* such as predicted class distributions [69]) of the last deep layer of both models are compared during the distillation process [53, 70]. As such, the student model can be trained to generate decisions similar to the teacher model. The second approach is feature-based knowledge distillation [71–73], which uses the extracted latent representations of the input data as an additional supervision signal for training the student model. The third approach, namely, relation-based knowledge distillation [68], further extends the second approach by considering the correlations between model layers [74, 75] and/or data samples [76, 77] calculated with pairwise latent features, so as to further enhance the comprehensiveness of the knowledge a student model inherits from the teacher model.

Network Pruning Stripping away model components with lower performance contributions, i.e., network pruning [78], has been a well-established research direction for achieving lightweight neural architectures. In this line of work, the pruning principles can be divided into three main categories: unstructured pruning, structured pruning, and semi-structured pruning. Unstructured pruning focuses on sparsifying the weight matrices (e.g., the filters in convolution neural networks) [79–81] without modifying the workflow of the network. Thus, unstructured pruning on neural networks essentially resembles the idea of embedding pruning, as both of them cut the parameter consumption by obtaining sparsified parameter matrices. Compared with unstructured pruning, structured pruning happens at the network structure level, where the prunable components include filters and channels in convolution networks [82, 83], attention heads in Transformer networks [84], and various intermediate deep layers in a variety of fully connect networks [85]. With the goal of a better balance between memory efficiency and performance, semi-structured pruning has emerged as an extension to structured pruning, where substructures inside model components (instead of the entire components) are pruned out based on identified patterns [86, 87], offering more fine-grained pruning results compared with structured pruning [88].

1.4 Inference Time Optimization

Despite advances in memory consumption reduction, recent research has shown that in practicality, simply reducing these model parameters does not always lead to efficient on-device learning [16, 17, 89]. Hence, in this chapter, we discuss approaches that are specifically designed for reducing model complexity to shorten the inference time. Figure 1.4 shows three highly relevant solutions, namely, adaptive model selection, parallelization, and hardware-software co-design, of which the details will be presented in the rest of this section.

1.4.1 Adaptive Model Selection

For various machine learning tasks, if accuracy is the main target, then a heavily parameterized neural network usually needs to be designed and trained. In the meantime, when inference efficiency is added to the requirement list, adaptive model selection [18] comes into play to disable some components of the network such

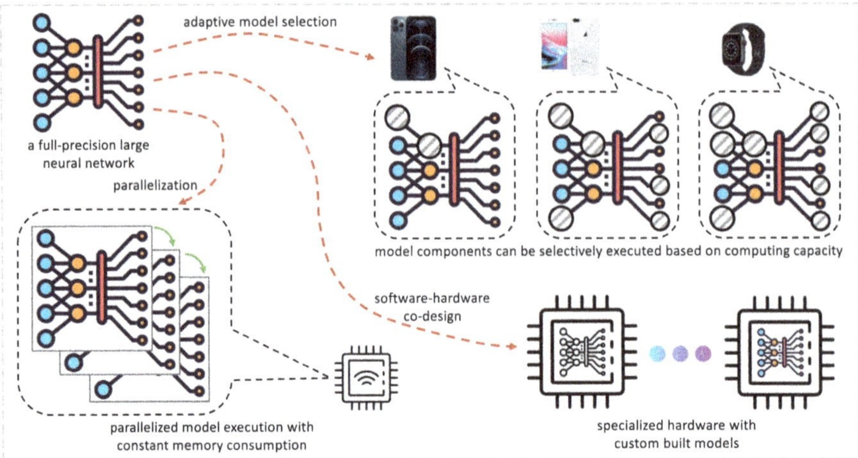

Fig. 1.4 A visualization of adaptive model selection (top right), parallelization (bottom left), as well as hardware-software co-design (bottom right)

that the inference process can be simplified with some accuracy compromises. This approach shares a similar underlying principle with the structured pruning method introduced in Sect. 1.3.2, where a smaller network can be constructed by selecting trained components of the full-size network based on the accuracy-efficiency trade-off allowed [19, 90] and then deployed on resource-constrained environments. In settings where a deployed model needs to meet the dynamic on-device resource availability, adaptive inference methods [20, 91–93] are able to flexibly decide the model components needed based on the levels of complexity associated with each specific input data sample. In a nutshell, by measuring the confidence of intermediate layers' outputs, the inference router can determine whether or not to skip subsequent network layers in the inference process [94], so as to reduce the inference overhead of a deployed model in an adaptive fashion.

1.4.2 Parallelization

In addition to adaptive model selection, another widely used approach to speed up model inference is to design efficient parallelization schemes. Parallelization allows a larger amount of input to be processed by the same model within the memory constraint, thus boosting inference efficiency w.r.t. the same data size by increasing the throughput of the model. A typical example is the development trajectory of natural language processing methods, where the early versions of recurrent neural networks [95] are known to be inefficient for handling long sequences, as the next tokens in the sequence can only be processed one after the other. Afterward, Transformer networks [96], whose self-attention blocks allow all tokens to be processed in the same forward pass, are proposed, followed by various efforts in further parallelizing its self-attention blocks [97, 98]. Similar efforts in parallelization are also witnessed in computer vision models, including layer parallelization in deep residual networks [99], vision Transformers [100], and diffusion models [101].

1.4.3 Software-Hardware Co-design

In many situations, the model-centric solutions alone are insufficient for specialized applications. Consequently, this calls for the co-design and joint optimization from both software and hardware perspectives. On the one hand, for the same neural network architecture, the way it is implemented—which is usually facilitated by different deep learning packages like Caffe [102], TensorFlow [103], and PyTorch [104])—can largely impact the inference efficiency [18]. On the other hand, software-level optimizations are still bounded by the inherent limitation of the hardware, where certain types of machine learning models are found to benefit from dedicated improvements involving storage, I/O, tensor operations, etc. [105–107]. As such, co-designing software and hardware offers an opportunity to jointly optimize both heavily entangled aspects, where real applications can be seen in Meta's recommendation services [29], Tesla's full self-driving computer [108], and Apple's neural engine [109].

1.5 Enterprise Applications of Resource-Efficient AI

In this section, we provide some real-world examples w.r.t. memory consumption reduction and inference time optimization, so as to strengthen the link between resource-efficient machine learning and enterprise AI. Specifically, we will discuss how memory consumption reduction is achieved in Apple's core techniques for on-device multimodal data analysis (e.g., object recognition from images) and what the core tricks are for inference time optimization in Taobao's on-device recommender systems.

1.5.1 Apple's On-Device Multimodal Data Analysis Solutions

Apple's OpenELM and Ferret-v2 represent significant advancements in on-device machine learning and multimodal processing within Apple's ecosystem. Its efficient language model named OpenELM [110] is a high-capacity language model embedded into iOS, functioning as a core system utility comparable to location services. With its layer-wise scaling architecture, OpenELM efficiently leverages its 1.1 billion parameters to deliver a 2.36% improvement in accuracy over previous models, despite utilizing only half the pre-training data. Moreover, its integration with MLX (Apple's efficient machine learning library) enables seamless fine-tuning directly on Apple devices, optimizing model adaptability for diverse applications.

In parallel, Ferret-v2 [111] introduces a significant upgrade over its predecessor Ferret [112], designed for enhanced multimodal data-processing capabilities. Key innovations include support for arbitrary-resolution grounding, multi-granular visual encoding via the DINOv2 [113] encoder, and a rigorous three-stage training process. These advancements bolster Ferret-v2's ability to process high-resolution images and enrich its visual understanding, delivering state-of-the-art, on-device visual intelligence tailored for iOS users.

The Upward Trend of On-Device Foundation Models Since Apple reinterpreted "AI" as "Apple Intelligence" in mid-2024, the race for integrating AI into portable personal devices as a fully personalized assistant became unprecedentedly competitive among various manufacturers. And yet, this has further promoted the upward trend of deploying high-performance foundation models from vision, language, and multimodality domains on resource-constrained devices. From an industry practitioner's perspective, recent advances in algorithmic optimization, including Apple's OpenELM and Ferret-v2 in this example, as well as DeepSeek's dynamic resource allocation strategies [114], have provided solid, production-ready backend foundations for embedding the intelligence of foundation models into a wider range of devices (e.g., home appliances, digital cameras, medical equipment).

1.5.2 EdgeRec: The Edge-Based Recommender System from Taobao

Traditional recommender systems often operate in a cloud-to-edge paradigm, where recommendations are precomputed on cloud servers and then delivered to user devices. This paradigm can suffer from network latency and bandwidth limitations, leading to delays in system feedback and diminished user experience [32]. To address these challenges, Taobao, a leading e-commerce company, has rolled out EdgeRec [115], a recommender system designed to perform computations on edge devices—specifically, on users' mobile devices. When deployed on user devices, EdgeRec processes diverse user behavior sequences (e.g., browsing, searching, adding items to cart, paying, etc.) by separating different behavioral categories, encoding them in parallel, and then encoding them with a lightweight behavior attention network. As a recurrent neural network is in use for modelling the sequential user behaviors, to further ensure inference efficiency, EdgeRec caches the model outputs for previously processed user behaviors and only processes the newly received user behavior. In this way, EdgeRec avoids performing inferences from the start of a long sequence and instead can focus on the most recent user behavior to dramatically boost on-device inference efficiency. As an exciting note, in Taobao's online testing, EdgeRec has been proven to contribute up to 8.87% increased number of user clicks and an impressive 10.92% profit gain [115] and is now a core service component deployed by Taobao to serve the main traffic.

Preventing User Privacy Breaches in Large-Scale Cloud Services An additional advantage of EdgeRec is its stronger privacy guarantee. When rolling out Web-scale services like personalized recommendation, privacy concerns tend to become a major obstacle for ensuring trust among end-users and establishing a loyal customer base. Moving cloud-based services to edge devices helps users retain their sensitive data (e.g., user profile, browsing history, location, etc.), where all the personalized results can be provided by the on-device model deployed. As such, for industry sectors that frequently deal with private user information, such as e-health, banking, and online trading, an on-device service paradigm provides a new opportunity to counteract the privacy threats that are rapidly emerging in today's online environment.

1.6 Roadmap Toward Practical Resource-Efficient AI

After providing an overview on the existing research landscape, we use this section to provide an outlook on potential research directions that can further promote practical resource-efficient AI for enterprise applications.

We summarize those high-potential areas in the bullet points below:

- **Breaking the Machine Learning Silos.** Because the use case is closely related to individual users or enterprises, resource-efficient AI systems are subject to limitations in both model capacity and training data availability. Hence, collaborative machine learning can provide a possible remedy to those limitations by allowing isolated on-device models to communicate with each other and exchange knowledge [116, 117], thus improving model performance. In the meantime, to bypass the privacy hurdles brought by sharing sensitive data or personalized model parameters in the communication process, encryption methods like differential privacy [118] and secure knowledge exchanging schemes like the use of reference data [119] are highly recommended.
- **Moving from Model-Centric AI to Data-Centric AI.** Existing efforts on resource-efficient AI are mainly around more advanced model designs in pursuit of stronger model performance under tight computational resource budgets. However, it is worth pointing out that real-world data used for model training is prone to noise and biases, thus constraining the accuracy and generalizability of the trained model [120]. In fact, when trained with a small set of high-quality data samples, a structurally simpler machine learning model is likely to outperform sophisticated models trained with large-scale but noisy data [121, 122]. In this regard, devising approaches that can enhance the inherent quality of data [123, 124], or generate synthetic high-quality data [125, 126], can provide an alternative to training a competitive model without sophisticated designs.

- **Model Lifespan Matters.** A trained machine learning model, once deployed, can face performance degradation over time. This is due mainly to the streaming nature of real-world data, which produces distribution shifts that challenge the generalizability of models trained with historical observations [127]. However, given the constraints w.r.t. resources, engineering cost, and service downtime, many enterprise-level applications do not have the luxury of frequently retraining a machine learning model to keep it up to date. As such, witnessed by existing efforts on causal inference [128], efficient domain adaptation [129], and patch learning [130], it is worth developing methods to extend the lifespan of a deployed model with minimal overheads.

1.7 Final Remarks and Conclusions

The integration of AI into enterprise operations has been proven transformative, offering unprecedented opportunities to enhance efficiency, personalization, and automation. However, the rapid evolution of AI technologies has highlighted a pronounced disparity in technology readiness among organizations, driven largely by unequal access to critical resources such as computational infrastructure, large-scale datasets, and skilled personnel. This disparity, particularly detrimental to small- and medium-sized enterprises (SMEs), threatens to widen the digitalization gap and limit the democratization of AI benefits.

In this chapter, we have addressed the resource-intensive nature of modern AI systems by exploring the current research landscape regarding resource-efficient AI solutions. Through our taxonomy and analysis of technical approaches in Sects. 1.2, 1.3, and 1.4, we demonstrated how advances such as lightweight feature representations, model compression, knowledge distillation, and hardware-software co-design can significantly lower the computational and financial barriers to AI adoption in enterprises. Section 1.5 has illustrated these concepts with real-world examples, showcasing how resource-efficient AI is already being utilized in diverse industrial applications. Finally, Sect. 1.6 laid out a forward-looking R&D roadmap, identifying key priorities for developing scalable and sustainable AI solutions.

By focusing on resource-efficient AI, we can empower a broader range of enterprises to leverage cutting-edge technologies, fostering innovation and competitiveness across industries. Continued research and collaboration will be essential to realize this vision, ensuring that AI remains an inclusive tool for economic and societal progress.

References

1. Ren, X., Yin, H., Chen, T., Wang, H., Huang, Z., Zheng, K.: Learning to ask appropriate questions in conversational recommendation. In: Proceedings of the 44th International ACM SIGIR Conference on Research and Development in Information Retrieval, pp. 808–817 (2021)

2. Ren, X., Chen, T., Nguyen, Q.V.H., Cui, L., Huang, Z., Yin, H.: Explicit knowledge graph reasoning for conversational recommendation. ACM Trans. Intell. Syst. Technol. **15**(4), 1–21 (2024)
3. Chen, T., Yin, H., Chen, H., Wang, H., Zhou, X., Li, X.: Online sales prediction via trend alignment-based multitask recurrent neural networks. Knowl. Inform. Syst. **62**(6), 2139–2167 (2020)
4. Chen, T., Yin, H., Chen, H., Wu, L., Wang, H., Zhou, X., Li, X.: Tada: trend alignment with dual-attention multi-task recurrent neural networks for sales prediction. In: 2018 IEEE International Conference on Data Mining (ICDM), pp. 49–58 (2018). IEEE, Piscataway
5. Gunter, T., Wang, Z., Wang, C., Pang, R., Narayanan, A., Zhang, A., Zhang, B., Chen, C., Chiu, C.-C., Qiu, D., et al.: Apple intelligence foundation language models (2024). arXiv preprint arXiv:2407.21075
6. Google AI: Introducing Gemini, Google's Next-Generation AI (2023). Accessed 10 Nov 2024. https://blog.google/technology/ai/google-gemini-ai/
7. IBM Newsroom: Data Suggests Growth in Enterprise Adoption of AI is Due to Widespread Deployment by Early Adopters (2024). Accessed 10 Nov 2024. https://newsroom.ibm.com/2024-01-10-Data-Suggests-Growth-in-Enterprise-Adoption-of-AI-is-Due-to-Widespread-Deployment-by-Early-Adopters
8. xAI: Grok-3: Advanced Reasoning AI Model. https://grok.x.ai. Accessed: April 23, 2025 (2025)
9. Epoch AI: Data on Notable AI Models (2024). Accessed 23 Apr 2025. https://epoch.ai/data/notable-ai-models
10. OpenAI: ChatGPT: OpenAI Language Model (2023). https://openai.com/chatgpt. Accessed 23 Dec 2024
11. Anthropic PBC: Claude: Anthropic Language Model (2023). https://www.anthropic.com/index/claude. Accessed 23 Dec 2024
12. Buchholz, K.: The Extreme Cost of Training AI Models (2024). https://www.forbes.com/sites/katharinabuchholz/2024/08/23/the-extreme-cost-of-training-ai-models/. Accessed 23 Dec 2024
13. Touvron, H., Lavril, T., Izacard, G., Martinet, X., Lachaux, M.-A., Lacroix, T., Rozière, B., Goyal, N., Hambro, E., Azhar, F., Rodriguez, A., Joulin, A., Grave, E., Lample, G.: LLaMA: Open and Efficient Foundation Language Models (2023). https://arxiv.org/abs/2302.13971. Accessed 23 Dec 2024
14. Dosovitskiy, A., et al.: An Image Is Worth 16×16 Words: Transformers for Image Recognition at Scale. ICLR (2021)
15. Raffel, C., Shazeer, N., Roberts, A., Lee, K., Narang, S., Matena, M., Zhou, Y., Li, W., Liu, P.J.: Exploring the limits of transfer learning with a unified text-to-text transformer. In: Journal of Machine Learning Research, vol. 21, pp. 1–67 (2020)
16. Tran, H.V., Chen, T., Nguyen, Q.V.H., Huang, Z., Cui, L., Yin, H.: A thorough performance benchmarking on lightweight embedding-based recommender systems. TOIS (2025)
17. Cai, H., Gan, C., Zhu, L., Han, S.: Tinytl: Reduce memory, not parameters for efficient on-device learning. NeurIPS **33**, 11285–11297 (2020)
18. Dhar, S., Guo, J., Liu, J., Tripathi, S., Kurup, U., Shah, M.: A survey of on-device machine learning: An algorithms and learning theory perspective. ACM Trans. Internet Things **2**(3), 1–49 (2021)
19. Cai, H., Gan, C., Wang, T., Zhang, Z., Han, S.: Once-for-All: Train One Network and Specialize It for Efficient Deployment. ICLR (2020)
20. Bolukbasi, T., Wang, J., Dekel, O., Saligrama, V.: Adaptive neural networks for efficient inference. In: ICML, pp. 527–536 (2017)
21. Gao, X., Zhang, W., Yu, J., Shao, Y., Nguyen, Q.V.H., Cui, B., Yin, H.: Accelerating scalable graph neural network inference with node-adaptive propagation. In: ICDE, pp. 3042–3055 (2024)
22. Christensen, J., Soderland, S., Etzioni, O. et al.: Towards coherent multi-document summarization. In: NAACL, pp. 1163–1173 (2013)

23. Jiang, W., Chen, T., Ye, G., Zhang, W., Cui, L., Huang, Z., Yin, H.: Physics-guided active sample reweighting for urban flow prediction. In: CIKM, pp. 1004–1014 (2024)
24. Hu, Y., Yang, J., Chen, L., Li, K., Sima, C., Zhu, X., Chai, S., Du, S., Lin, T., Wang, W. et al.: Planning-oriented autonomous driving. In: CVPR, pp. 17853–17862 (2023)
25. Coleman, B., Kang, W.-C., Fahrbach, M., Wang, R., Hong, L., Chi, E., Cheng, D.: Unified embedding: Battle-tested feature representations for web-scale ML systems. NeurIPS **36**, 56234–56255 (2024)
26. Mnih, A., Kavukcuoglu, K.: Learning word embeddings efficiently with noise-contrastive estimation. NeurIPS **26** (2013)
27. Ying, R., He, R., Chen, K., Eksombatchai, P., Hamilton, W.L., Leskovec, J.: Graph convolutional neural networks for web-scale recommender systems. In: SIGKDD, pp. 974–983 (2018)
28. Wang, J., Huang, P., Zhao, H., Zhang, Z., Zhao, B., Lee, D.L.: Billion-scale commodity embedding for e-commerce recommendation in alibaba. In: SIGKDD, pp. 839–848 (2018)
29. Mudigere, D., et al.: Software-hardware co-design for fast and scalable training of deep learning recommendation models. In: Proceedings of the 49th Annual International Symposium on Computer Architecture, pp. 993–1011 (2022)
30. Liu, X., He, J., Deng, C., Lang, B.: Collaborative hashing. In: CVPR, pp. 2139–2146 (2014)
31. Zhang, Z., Wang, Q., Ruan, L., Si, L.: Preference preserving hashing for efficient recommendation. In: SIGIR, pp. 183–192 (2014)
32. Chen, T., Yin, H., Zheng, Y., Huang, Z., Wang, Y., Wang, M.: Learning elastic embeddings for customizing on-device recommenders. In: SIGKDD, pp. 138–147 (2021)
33. Guan, H., Malevich, A., Yang, J., Park, J., Yuen, H.: Post-training 4-bit quantization on embedding tables. MLSys-NeurIPS (2019)
34. Bai, H., Hou, L., Shang, L., Jiang, X., King, I., Lyu, M.R.: Towards efficient post-training quantization of pre-trained language models. NeurIPS **35**, 1405–1418 (2022)
35. Xiao, G., Lin, J., Seznec, M., Wu, H., Demouth, J., Han, S.: Smoothquant: accurate and efficient post-training quantization for large language models. In: ICML, pp. 38087–38099 (2023)
36. Li, S., Guo, H., Hou, L., Zhang, W., Tang, X., Tang, R., Zhang, R., Li, R.: Adaptive low-precision training for embeddings in click-through rate prediction. In: AAAI, vol. 37, pp. 4435–4443 (2023)
37. Chen, T., Li, L., Sun, Y.: Differentiable product quantization for end-to-end embedding compression. In: ICML, pp. 1617–1626 (2020)
38. Virtanen, P., et al.: Scipy 1.0: fundamental algorithms for scientific computing in python. Nature methods **17**(3), 261–272 (2020)
39. Sedaghati, N., Mu, T., Pouchet, L.-N., Parthasarathy, S., Sadayappan, P.: Automatic selection of sparse matrix representation on GPUs. In: Proceedings of the 29th ACM on International Conference on Supercomputing, pp. 99–108 (2015)
40. Qu, Y., Chen, T., Zhao, X., Cui, L., Zheng, K., Yin, H.: Continuous input embedding size search for recommender systems. In: SIGIR, pp. 708–717 (2023)
41. Liu, S., Gao, C., Chen, Y., Jin, D., Li, Y.: Learnable embedding sizes for recommender systems. ICLR (2021)
42. Qu, Y., Chen, T., Nguyen, Q.V.H., Yin, H.: Budgeted embedding table for recommender systems. In: WSDM, pp. 557–566 (2024)
43. Joglekar, M.R., Li, C., Chen, M., Xu, T., Wang, X., Adams, J.K., Khaitan, P., Liu, J., Le, Q.V.: Neural input search for large scale recommendation models. In: SIGKDD, pp. 2387–2397 (2020)
44. Zhao, X., et al.: Autoemb: Automated embedding dimensionality search in streaming recommendations. In: ICDM, pp. 896–905 (2021)
45. Zheng, R., Qu, L., Chen, T., Zheng, K., Shi, Y., Yin, H.: Personalized elastic embedding learning for on-device recommendation. TKDE (2024)
46. Zhao, M., Jiang, L., Yu, Y., Wang, X., Yuan, Y., Wei, Z., Niu, D.: Dimreg: embedding dimension search via regularization for recommender systems. In: SDM, pp. 562–570 (2024)

47. Yin, H., Qu, L., Chen, T., Yuan, W., Zheng, R., Long, J., Xia, X., Shi, Y., Zhang, C.: On-device recommender systems: a comprehensive survey. arXiv preprint arXiv:2401.11441 (2024)
48. Li, S., Guo, H., Tang, X., Tang, R., Hou, L., Li, R., Zhang, R.: Embedding compression in recommender systems: a survey. ACM Comput. Surv. **56**(5), 1–21 (2024)
49. Liang, X., Chen, T., Nguyen, Q.V.H., Li, J., Yin, H.: Learning compact compositional embeddings via regularized pruning for recommendation. In: ICDM, pp. 378–387 (2023)
50. Liang, X., Chen, T., Cui, L., Wang, Y., Wang, M., Yin, H.: Lightweight embeddings for graph collaborative filtering. In: SIGIR, pp. 1296–1306 (2024)
51. Shi, H.-J.M., Mudigere, D., Naumov, M., Yang, J.: Compositional embeddings using complementary partitions for memory-efficient recommendation systems. In: SIGKDD, pp. 165–175 (2020)
52. Acharya, A., Goel, R., Metallinou, A., Dhillon, I.: Online embedding compression for text classification using low rank matrix factorization. In: AAAI, vol. 33, pp. 6196–6203 (2019)
53. Wang, Q., Yin, H., Chen, T., Huang, Z., Wang, H., Zhao, Y., Viet Hung, N.Q.: Next point-of-interest recommendation on resource-constrained mobile devices. In: WWW, pp. 906–916 (2020)
54. Xia, X., Yin, H., Yu, J., Wang, Q., Xu, G., Nguyen, Q.V.H.: On-device next-item recommendation with self-supervised knowledge distillation. In: SIGIR, pp. 546–555 (2022)
55. He, K., Zhang, X., Ren, S., Sun, J.: Deep residual learning for image recognition. In: CVPR, pp. 770–778 (2016)
56. Kenton, J.D.M.-W.C., Toutanova, L.K.: Bert: Pre-training of deep bidirectional transformers for language understanding. In: NAACL, pp. 4171–4186 (2019)
57. Li, M., Huang, Z., Chen, L., Ren, J., Jiang, M., Li, F., Fu, J., Gao, C.: Contemporary advances in neural network quantization: a survey. In: IJCNN, pp. 1–10 (2024)
58. Nagel, M., Fournarakis, M., Bondarenko, Y., Blankevoort, T.: Overcoming oscillations in quantization-aware training. In: ICML, pp. 16318–16330 (2022)
59. Sakr, C., Dai, S., Venkatesan, R., Zimmer, B., Dally, W., Khailany, B.: Optimal clipping and magnitude-aware differentiation for improved quantization-aware training. In: ICML, pp. 19123–19138 (2022)
60. Ding, Y., Feng, W., Chen, C., Guo, J., Liu, X.: Reg-ptq: regression-specialized post-training quantization for fully quantized object detector. In: CVPR, pp. 16174–16184 (2024)
61. Shomron, G., Gabbay, F., Kurzum, S., Weiser, U.: Post-training sparsity-aware quantization. NeurIPS **34**, 17737–17748 (2021)
62. Zhang, D., Yang, J., Ye, D., Hua, G.: Lq-nets: learned quantization for highly accurate and compact deep neural networks. In: ECCV, pp. 365–382 (2018)
63. Gong, R., Liu, X., Jiang, S., Li, T., Hu, P., Lin, J., Yu, F., Yan, J.: Differentiable soft quantization: Bridging full-precision and low-bit neural networks. In: ICCV, pp. 4852–4861 (2019)
64. Bengio, Y., Léonard, N., Courville, A.: Estimating or propagating gradients through stochastic neurons for conditional computation (2013). arXiv preprint arXiv:1308.3432
65. Nagel, M., Baalen, M.v., Blankevoort, T., Welling, M.: Data-free quantization through weight equalization and bias correction. In: CVPR, pp. 1325–1334 (2019)
66. Meller, E., Finkelstein, A., Almog, U., Grobman, M.: Same, same but different: recovering neural network quantization error through weight factorization. In: ICML, pp. 4486–4495 (2019)
67. He, X., Cheng, J.: Learning compression from limited unlabeled data. In: ECCV, pp. 752–769 (2018)
68. Gou, J., Yu, B., Maybank, S.J., Tao, D.: Knowledge distillation: a survey. Int. J. Comput. Vision **129**(6), 1789–1819 (2021)
69. Ba, J., Caruana, R.: Do deep nets really need to be deep? NeurIPS **27** (2014)
70. Chen, G., Choi, W., Yu, X., Han, T., Chandraker, M.: Learning efficient object detection models with knowledge distillation. NeurIPS **30** (2017)
71. Chen, D., Mei, J.-P., Zhang, Y., Wang, C., Wang, Z., Feng, Y., Chen, C.: Cross-layer distillation with semantic calibration. In: AAAI, vol. 35, pp. 7028–7036 (2021)

72. Passalis, N., Tefas, A.: Learning deep representations with probabilistic knowledge transfer. In: ECCV, pp. 268–284 (2018)
73. Passban, P., Wu, Y., Rezagholizadeh, M., Liu, Q.: Alp-kd: attention-based layer projection for knowledge distillation. In: AAAI, vol. 35, pp. 13657–13665 (2021)
74. Mirzadeh, S.I., Farajtabar, M., Li, A., Levine, N., Matsukawa, A., Ghasemzadeh, H.: Improved knowledge distillation via teacher assistant. In: AAAI, vol. 34, pp. 5191–5198 (2020)
75. Chen, H., Wang, Y., Xu, C., Xu, C., Tao, D.: Learning student networks via feature embedding. TNNLS **32**(1), 25–35 (2020)
76. Park, W., Kim, D., Lu, Y., Cho, M.: Relational knowledge distillation. In: CVPR, pp. 3967–3976 (2019)
77. Peng, B., Jin, X., Liu, J., Li, D., Wu, Y., Liu, Y., Zhou, S., Zhang, Z.: Correlation congruence for knowledge distillation. In: ICCV, pp. 5007–5016 (2019)
78. Cheng, H., Zhang, M., Shi, J.Q.: A survey on deep neural network pruning: taxonomy, comparison, analysis, and recommendations. IEEE Trans. Pattern Anal. Mach. Intell. **46**(12), 10558–10578 (2024)
79. Lee, N., Ajanthan, T., Torr, P.: Snip: single-shot network pruning based on connection sensitivity. In: ICLR (2019)
80. Wang, C., Zhang, G., Grosse, R.: Picking winning tickets before training by preserving gradient flow. In: ICLR (2019)
81. Liu, L., Zhang, S., Kuang, Z., Zhou, A., Xue, J.-H., Wang, X., Chen, Y., Yang, W., Liao, Q., Zhang, W.: Group fisher pruning for practical network compression. In: ICML, pp. 7021–7032 (2021)
82. You, Z., Yan, K., Ye, J., Ma, M., Wang, P.: Gate decorator: global filter pruning method for accelerating deep convolutional neural networks. NeurIPS **32** (2019)
83. Ashkboos, S., Croci, M.L., Nascimento, M.G., Hoefler, T., Hensman, J.: Slicegpt: compress large language models by deleting rows and columns. In: ICLR (2024)
84. Ma, X., Fang, G., Wang, X.: Llm-pruner: on the structural pruning of large language models. NeurIPS **36**, 21702–21720 (2023)
85. Chen, S., Zhao, Q.: Shallowing deep networks: Layer-wise pruning based on feature representations. IEEE Trans. Pattern Anal. Mach. Intell. **41**(12), 3048–3056 (2018)
86. Meng, F., Cheng, H., Li, K., Luo, H., Guo, X., Lu, G., Sun, X.: Pruning filter in filter. NeurIPS **33**, 17629–17640 (2020)
87. Ma, X., et al.: An image enhancing pattern-based sparsity for real-time inference on mobile devices. In: ECCV, pp. 629–645 (2020). Springer
88. Li, Z., et al.: Npas: a compiler-aware framework of unified network pruning and architecture search for beyond real-time mobile acceleration. In: CVPR, pp. 14255–14266 (2021)
89. Yang, T.-J., Howard, A., Chen, B., Zhang, X., Go, A., Sandler, M., Sze, V., Adam, H.: Netadapt: platform-aware neural network adaptation for mobile applications. In: ECCV, pp. 285–300 (2018)
90. Marco, V.S., Taylor, B., Wang, Z., Elkhatib, Y.: Optimizing deep learning inference on embedded systems through adaptive model selection. ACM Trans. Embed. Comput. Syst. **19**(1), 1–28 (2020)
91. Huang, G., Chen, D., Li, T., Wu, F., Maaten, L., Weinberger, K.: Multi-scale dense networks for resource efficient image classification. In: ICLR (2018)
92. Wang, X., Yu, F., Dou, Z.-Y., Darrell, T., Gonzalez, J.E.: Skipnet: learning dynamic routing in convolutional networks. In: ECCV, pp. 409–424 (2018)
93. Zeng, Z., Hong, Y., Dai, H., Zhuang, H., Chen, C.: Consistentee: a consistent and hardness-guided early exiting method for accelerating language models inference. In: AAAI, vol. 38, pp. 19506–19514 (2024)
94. Tang, S., Wang, Y., Kong, Z., Zhang, T., Li, Y., Ding, C., Wang, Y., Liang, Y., Xu, D.: You need multiple exiting: dynamic early exiting for accelerating unified vision language model. In: CVPR, pp. 10781–10791 (2023)

95. Sutskever, I.: Training Recurrent Neural Networks. University of Toronto Toronto, ON, Canada (2013)
96. Vaswani, A., Shazeer, N., Parmar, N., Uszkoreit, J., Jones, L., Gomez, A.N., Kaiser, Ł., Polosukhin, I.: Attention is all you need. Advances in neural information processing systems. NeurIPS **30**(2017) (2017)
97. Dao, T., Fu, D., Ermon, S., Rudra, A., Ré, C.: Flashattention: fast and memory-efficient exact attention with IO-awareness. NeurIPS **35**, 16344–16359 (2022)
98. Dao, T.: Flashattention-2: faster attention with better parallelism and work partitioning. In: ICLR (2024)
99. Gunther, S., Ruthotto, L., Schroder, J.B., Cyr, E.C., Gauger, N.R.: Layer-parallel training of deep residual neural networks. SIAM J. Math. Data Sci. **2**(1), 1–23 (2020)
100. Touvron, H., Cord, M., El-Nouby, A., Verbeek, J., Jégou, H.: Three things everyone should know about vision transformers. In: ECCV, pp. 497–515 (2022)
101. Shih, A., Belkhale, S., Ermon, S., Sadigh, D., Anari, N.: Parallel sampling of diffusion models. NeurIPS **36** (2024)
102. Jia, Y., Shelhamer, E., Donahue, J., Karayev, S., Long, J., Girshick, R., Guadarrama, S., Darrell, T.: Caffe: convolutional architecture for fast feature embedding. In: Proceedings of the 22nd ACM International Conference on Multimedia, pp. 675–678 (2014)
103. Abadi, M., Barham, P., Chen, J., Chen, Z., Davis, A., Dean, J., Devin, M., Ghemawat, S., Irving, G., Isard, M., et al.: Tensorflow: a system for large-scale machine learning. In: Proceedings of the 12th USENIX Conference on Operating Systems Design and Implementation, pp. 265–283 (2016)
104. Paszke, A., Gross, S., Massa, F., Lerer, A., Bradbury, J., Chanan, G., Killeen, T., Lin, Z., Gimelshein, N., Antiga, L., et al.: Pytorch: An imperative style, high-performance deep learning library. NeurIPS **32** (2019)
105. Google: Coral Edge TPU Products (2024). https://coral.ai/products/. Accessed 23 Dec 2024
106. Intel Corporation: Intel® Movidius™ Myriad™ 2 Vision Processing Unit (2024). https://www.intel.com/content/www/us/en/products/details/processors/movidius-vpu.html. Accessed 23 Dec 2024
107. NVIDIA Corporation: NVIDIA Jetson Nano Developer Kit (2024). https://developer.nvidia.com/embedded/jetson-nano. Accessed 23 Dec 2024
108. Talpes, E., Sarma, D.D., Venkataramanan, G., Bannon, P., McGee, B., Floering, B., Jalote, A., Hsiong, C., Arora, S., Gorti, A., et al.: Compute solution for tesla's full self-driving computer. IEEE Micro **40**(2), 25–35 (2020)
109. Apple Machine Learning Research: Deploying Transformers on the Apple Neural Engine (2023). https://machinelearning.apple.com/research/neural-engine-transformers. Accessed 23 Dec 2024
110. Mehta, S., Sekhavat, M.H., Cao, Q., Horton, M., Jin, Y., Sun, C., Mirzadeh, S.I., Najibi, M., Belenko, D., Zatloukal, P., et al.: Openelm: an efficient language model family with open training and inference framework. In: Workshop on Efficient Systems for Foundation Models II@ ICML2024 (2024)
111. Zhang, H., You, H., Dufter, P., Zhang, B., Chen, C., Chen, H.-Y., Fu, T.-J., Wang, W.Y., Chang, S.-F., Gan, Z., et al.: Ferret-v2: an improved baseline for referring and grounding with large language models. COLM (2024)
112. You, H., Zhang, H., Gan, Z., Du, X., Zhang, B., Wang, Z., Cao, L., Chang, S.-F., Yang, Y.: Ferret: refer and ground anything anywhere at any granularity. In: ICLR (2024)
113. Oquab, M., Darcet, T., Moutakanni, T., Vo, H., Szafraniec, M., Khalidov, V., Fernandez, P., Haziza, D., Massa, F., El-Nouby, A., et al.: Dinov2: learning robust visual features without supervision. Trans. Mach. Learn. Res. J. 1–31 (2024)
114. Liu, A., Feng, B., Xue, B., Wang, B., Wu, B., Lu, C., Zhao, C., Deng, C., Zhang, C., Ruan, C., et al.: Deepseek-v3 technical report (2024). arXiv preprint arXiv:2412.19437
115. Gong, Y., Jiang, Z., Feng, Y., Hu, B., Zhao, K., Liu, Q., Ou, W.: Edgerec: recommender system on edge in mobile Taobao. In: CIKM, pp. 2477–2484 (2020)

116. Long, J., Chen, T., Nguyen, Q.V.H., Xu, G., Zheng, K., Yin, H.: Model-agnostic decentralized collaborative learning for on-device POI recommendation. In: SIGIR, pp. 423–432 (2023)
117. Ye, G., Yin, H., Chen, T., Xu, M., Nguyen, Q.V.H., Song, J.: Personalized on-device e-health analytics with decentralized block coordinate descent. IEEE J. Biomed. Health Inform. **26**(6), 2778–2786 (2022)
118. Zhang, S., Yin, H., Chen, T., Huang, Z., Cui, L., Zhang, X.: Graph embedding for recommendation against attribute inference attacks. In: Proceedings of the Web Conference 2021, pp. 3002–3014 (2021)
119. Zheng, R., Qu, L., Chen, T., Cui, L., Shi, Y., Yin, H.: Decentralized collaborative learning with adaptive reference data for on-device poi recommendation. In: Proceedings of the ACM on Web Conference 2024, pp. 3930–3939 (2024)
120. Whang, S.E., Roh, Y., Song, H., Lee, J.-G.: Data collection and quality challenges in deep learning: a data-centric ai perspective. VLDB J. **32**(4), 791–813 (2023)
121. Bhatt, N., Bhatt, N., Prajapati, P., Sorathiya, V., Alshathri, S., El-Shafai, W.: A data-centric approach to improve performance of deep learning models. Sci. Rep. **14**(1), 22329 (2024)
122. Wang, Q., Yin, H., Wang, H., Nguyen, Q.V.H., Huang, Z., Cui, L.: Enhancing collaborative filtering with generative augmentation. In: SIGKDD, pp. 548–556 (2019)
123. Jiang, W., Gao, X., Xu, G., Chen, T., Yin, H.: Challenging low homophily in social recommendation. In: Proceedings of the ACM on Web Conference 2024, pp. 3476–3484 (2024)
124. Tashiro, Y., Song, J., Song, Y., Ermon, S.: Csdi: conditional score-based diffusion models for probabilistic time series imputation. NeurIPS **34**, 24804–24816 (2021)
125. Gao, X., Chen, T., Zang, Y., Zhang, W., Nguyen, Q.V.H., Zheng, K., Yin, H.: Graph condensation for inductive node representation learning. In: ICDE, pp. 3056–3069 (2024)
126. Gao, X., Chen, T., Zhang, W., Li, Y., Sun, X., Yin, H.: Graph condensation for open-world graph learning. In: SIGKDD, pp. 851–862 (2024)
127. Hoi, S.C., Sahoo, D., Lu, J., Zhao, P.: Online learning: a comprehensive survey. Neurocomputing **459**, 249–289 (2021)
128. Wen, H., Chen, T., Chai, L.K., Sadiq, S., Gao, J., Yin, H.: Variational counterfactual prediction under runtime domain corruption. IEEE Trans. Knowl. Data Eng. **36**(5), 2271–2284 (2024)
129. Jiang, J., Wang, X., Long, M., Wang, J.: Resource efficient domain adaptation. In: Proceedings of the 28th ACM International Conference on Multimedia, pp. 2220–2228 (2020)
130. Xia, X., Yu, J., Xu, G., Yin, H.: Towards communication-efficient model updating for on-device session-based recommendation. In: CIKM, pp. 2795–2804 (2023)

Tong Chen is currently an Associate Professor with the Data Science Discipline, School of Electrical Engineering and Computer Science, The University of Queensland. His research has been focused on developing accurate, efficient, and trustworthy data mining solutions to discover actionable patterns and intelligence from large-scale user data to facilitate prediction and recommendation in a wide range of domains. To date, his publications in relevant fields have attracted over 6500 citations and an H-index of 40 on Google Scholar. In addition, his research has received various recognitions including the Brisbane Lord Mayor's Trailblazer Award in 2025, Best Student Paper Award of CIKM in 2024, and ARC Discovery Early Career Researcher Award in 2023.

Junliang Yu is an ARC DECRA Fellow in the Data Science discipline at The University of Queensland, where he completed his PhD in Computer Science in 2023. His research focuses on recommender systems, graph learning, LLM-based agents, and trustworthy AI. His work has been widely cited and recognized, with multiple papers selected as Most Influential by *Paper Digest* and others highlighted as ESI Hot or Highly Cited Papers. He has delivered tutorials at leading international conferences and actively contributes to community knowledge sharing. He is also listed among the World's Top 2% Scientists by Stanford University and was named a Rising Star in Information Retrieval and Recommender Systems by AI Open Index.

Hongzhi Yin is an ARC Future Fellow and Full Professor at The University of Queensland, Australia. He has made significant contributions to on-device learning, decentralized intelligence, recommender systems, graph learning, and spatio-temporal predictive analytics. His research excellence has been widely recognized through numerous prestigious awards and honours, including IEEE Computer Society's "AI's 10 to Watch" (2022), Australian Young Tall Poppy Science Award (2023), Australian Research Council Future Fellowship (2021), DECRA (2016), Computer Science in Australia Leader Award (2024–2025), AI 2000 Most Influential Scholar Honorable Mention in Data Mining (2022–2024), and ScholarGPS Highly Ranked Scholar 2025 (Top 0.05% of all scholars). He has published over 350 peer-reviewed papers in the leading venues and holds an H-index of 84 with more than 22,600 citations.

Chapter 2
Dataset Distillation for Enterprise Applications

Juntong Ni, Shengbo Gong, and Wei Jin

Abstract Deep learning has achieved remarkable success in recent decades, which is largely attributed to the sheer amount of data. However, the constraints of computing resources result in significant time and memory required to train deep learning models on large-scale data. To address this, dataset distillation has attracted increasing research attention in the community. Dataset distillation aims to derive informative small datasets that distill the most important knowledge from large datasets. These small curated datasets can replace the original large datasets to benefit scenarios such as efficient model training and inference, neural architecture search, and privacy protection. In this chapter, we aim to provide a comprehensive summary of dataset distillation. We first introduce the dataset distillation problem and group existing methods into four categories: performance matching, gradient matching, trajectory matching, and distribution matching. Specifically, we provide a formal task definition and establish a unified framework for these methods. Then, we systematically review the technical details of methods in each category and discuss the application of dataset distillation across various data modalities such as image, graph, text, and time-series data. Finally, we provide concluding remarks on the pitfalls and prospects of dataset distillation.

2.1 Introduction

Over the last decades, the application of artificial intelligence (AI) in enterprise settings, commonly referred to as Enterprise AI, has expanded rapidly, with successful deployment across various business domains. For instance, JPMorgan Chase employs an AI system called COiN (Contract Intelligence) to process legal documents using natural language processing (NLP), significantly reducing review time [1]. Amazon uses machine learning for demand forecasting and inventory optimization across its global supply chain [2]. Additionally, Siemens leverages AI

J. Ni · S. Gong · W. Jin (✉)
Department of Computer Science, Emory University, Atlanta, GA, USA
e-mail: juntong.ni@emory.edu; shengbo.gong@emory.edu; wei.jin@emory.edu

S. Sadiq (ed.), *Enterprise AI*, https://doi.org/10.1007/978-3-032-01940-0_2

for predictive maintenance in industrial systems, improving operational reliability and reducing downtime [3]. These applications illustrate how AI is being integrated into business operations to increase efficiency and improve service delivery.

However, many of these enterprise-grade AI solutions rely on large-scale machine learning models, whose development is heavily influenced by recent progress in foundational AI research in areas such as computer vision [4], NLP [5], and data mining [6]. Models like ChatGPT by OpenAI and Gemini by Google illustrate the increasing practicality of AI for diverse use cases. Despite their capabilities, the success of such models is largely dependent on training with massive datasets [7], leading to significant demands in terms of data storage, processing, and energy consumption. While large technology firms such as Google, Meta, and OpenAI possess sufficient computing resources, small- to medium-sized enterprises often struggle to meet these requirements. For instance, GPT-3, with 175 billion parameters and trained on 45 terabytes of text data using thousands of GPUs [8], remains far beyond the reach of most businesses. This imbalance restricts broader access to advanced AI technologies and raises concerns about eco-sustainability [9]. Additionally, resource-intensive tasks such as continual learning [10], hyperparameter optimization [11], and neural architecture search (NAS) [12] pose further challenges. This creates a clear tension between the increasing power of AI models and the limited resources available to many enterprises. A promising direction to mitigate this issue is dataset compression, which aims to reduce dataset size while preserving task-relevant information. This approach helps reduce storage, memory, and compute costs, making advanced AI development more accessible to a wider range of organizations.

An intuitively straightforward way to obtain such a smaller dataset is to select the most representative samples for original dataset, namely, *Coreset Selection* [13–16]. Coreset selection involves choosing a subset based on heuristic criteria to maintain essential information, thus reducing training costs. However, coreset selection is limited because (1) it heavily depends on heuristic criteria and often lacks guidance from downstream task performance and (2) it requires the presence of representative samples in the dataset to approximate it effectively. As a result, recent studies point out that the efficacy of coreset selection methods rarely and irregularly transfers to practical scenarios [17].

An alternative approach to coreset is *Dataset Distillation*, which aims to synthesize a much smaller and more informative data summary with little performance drops [19–22]. The overall pipeline of dataset distillation is shown in Fig. 2.1. Dataset distillation has a range of advantages. First, the data summary can serve as an effective replacement for original datasets for scenarios like model training, hyperparameter search, architecture search, etc. Second, dataset distillation can help save computing costs and then accelerate research iterations, i.e., more ideas can be experimented. Third, dataset distillation may contribute to privacy preservation since it alters the original datasets, making them challenging to recover [23].

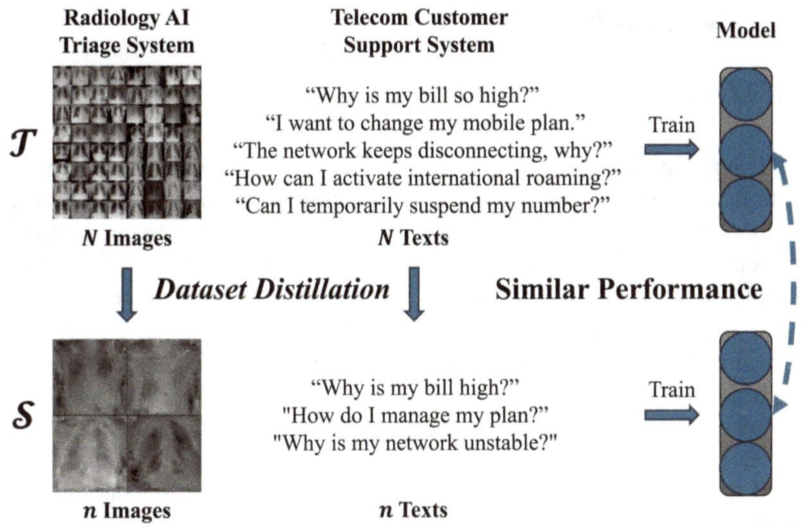

Fig. 2.1 An illustration of the dataset distillation pipeline, where $n \ll N$. Dataset distillation aims to synthesize a much smaller and more informative data summary $\mathcal{S}$ with minimal performance drops compared to the original dataset $\mathcal{T}$. Left: Chest X-ray images used in a hospital's automated radiology triage system for pneumonia risk screening [18]. Right: Customer query examples from a telecom company's service logs for question answering

Given the importance of dataset distillation, various algorithms have been proposed, falling into four distinct strategies: performance matching, gradient matching, trajectory matching, and distribution matching based on the objectives applied to match target data. With the development of these algorithms, the real-world performance of models trained on data summaries is approaching those trained on original datasets. Besides, while the earliest dataset distillation techniques are designed for the image domain, a variety of works have extended the application of dataset distillation to other data modalities such as text and graph domains.

In this chapter, we intend to provide a comprehensive overview of various dataset distillation frameworks across different data modalities. The rest of this chapter is organized as follows. We will begin with the definition of dataset distillation task formally in Sect. 2.2. Based on this, various methods will be systematically classified into categories. We classify all dataset distillation techniques into four categories. Then in Sect. 2.3, we will discuss dataset distillation for synthesizing data of different modalities, shedding light on real-world expertise scenarios where these techniques prove valuable. Implications with dataset distillation are shown in Sect. 2.4. In Sect. 2.5, we conclude by presenting common pitfalls in existing dataset distillation methods and identifying key challenges and promising future research directions, guiding the continued advancement of dataset distillation.

2.2 Dataset Distillation Methods

2.2.1 Task Definition

We first introduce the notations used in this chapter. For the sake of uniformity, we refer to the data synthesized by dataset distillation techniques as a *data summary* henceforth. Given a real dataset consisting of $|\mathcal{T}|$ pairs of training images and corresponding labels, denoted as $\mathcal{T} = (\mathbf{X}_t, \mathbf{Y}_t)$, where $\mathbf{X}_t \in \mathbb{R}^{N \times d}$, N is the number of samples, d is the number of features, $\mathbf{Y}_t \in \mathbb{R}^{N \times C}$ are one-hot label vectors, and C is the number of classes. Let $\mathcal{T}_c = \{(\mathbf{X}_t, \mathbf{Y}_t) | \mathbf{Y}_t = c\}_{t=1}^{|\mathcal{T}|}$ be the subset of $\mathcal{T}$ with class c. The synthesized data summary is denoted as $\mathcal{S} = (\mathbf{X}_s, \mathbf{Y}_s)$, where $\mathbf{X}_s \in \mathbb{R}^{n \times d}$, $n \ll N$. We define $\mathcal{S}_c$ similarly as defined for $\mathcal{T}_c$. For typical image classification tasks, d is $height \times width \times channels$. Let ϕ_θ represent a learning algorithm parameterized by θ. Then we define $\mathcal{L}_{\mathcal{T}}(\theta) = \mathbb{E}_{(\mathbf{X},\mathbf{Y}) \sim \mathcal{T}}[l(\phi_\theta(\mathbf{X}), \mathbf{Y})]$, where l denotes a twice-differentiable loss function, e.g., cross-entropy loss for classification. The objective of dataset distillation is to make performance gap smaller between the model trained on $\mathcal{T}$ and the model trained on $\mathcal{S}$.

Based on the matching objectives between $\mathcal{S}$ and $\mathcal{T}$, we classify dataset distillation methods into four categories: performance matching, gradient matching, trajectory matching, and distribution matching. Each method defines a distinct notion of similarity between the original dataset $\mathcal{T}$ and the synthesized data summary $\mathcal{S}$. Performance matching directly minimizes the loss on the original dataset using models trained on the data summary. Gradient matching instead aligns the gradients obtained from training on $\mathcal{S}$ with those from $\mathcal{T}$. Trajectory matching aligns entire sequences of parameter updates (training trajectories) between the real and synthetic data. Distribution matching optimizes the statistical similarity between the embedded representations of $\mathcal{T}$ and $\mathcal{S}$ in a feature space, typically without explicitly training a model during optimization.

looseness-1These four dataset distillation approaches present different trade-offs between performance and efficiency, making them suitable for different industrial scenarios. Performance matching and trajectory matching often yield the best downstream accuracy but require expensive bilevel optimization and significant memory consumption, especially when unrolling long training trajectories. These methods are well suited for offline training in domains where accuracy is critical and training resources are available, such as medical imaging diagnostics, financial risk modeling, or defect detection in manufacturing pipelines. On the other hand, gradient matching and distribution matching are more computationally efficient, often requiring fewer training steps or avoiding model training altogether during distillation. While they may achieve slightly lower performance, they are particularly advantageous in settings with limited compute or memory. This includes customer service systems deployed on edge devices, cold-start scenarios in personalized recommendation systems, or lightweight AI models for embedded IoT applications. The choice of distillation strategy should therefore be guided not only by accuracy requirements but also by system constraints and the practical deployment environment.

2.2.2 *Dataset Distillation by Performance Matching*

Performance matching is the most straightforward method because its loss function directly minimizes the error on the original dataset $\mathcal{T}$ of the model trained on the data summary $\mathcal{S}$. The loss function is backpropagated to update the data summary $\mathcal{S}$. Thus, $\mathcal{S}$ can be viewed as the meta-data of the model, and the method can be considered a meta learning–based approach. To further improve the efficiency of meta learning–based performance matching, the kernel ridge regression–based performance matching has been proposed. In this section, we first introduce meta learning–based performance matching and then introduce kernel ridge regression–based performance matching.

2.2.2.1 Meta Learning–Based Performance Matching

Meta learning–based performance matching is first proposed in the seminal work by Wang et al. [19]. This method aims to optimize a synthetic data summary such that neural networks trained by it could have the lowest loss on the original dataset, and thus the performance of models trained by synthetic and real dataset is matched. S is updated by the outer loop, and the inner loop solves the conventional supervised learning problem w.r.t. S as follows:

$$\arg\min_{\mathcal{S}} \mathbb{E}_{\theta^0 \sim \Theta}[\mathcal{L}_{\mathcal{T}}(\theta^T)] \text{ (outer loop)}, \tag{2.1}$$

$$\theta^t = \theta^{t-1} - \eta \nabla \mathcal{L}_{\mathcal{S}}(\theta^{t-1}) \text{ (inner loop)}, \tag{2.2}$$

where Θ is the distribution for initialization of network parameters. Because the inner loop is determined by data summary $\mathcal{S}$ and the initialized network parameter θ^0, to improve the robustness and generalization of data summary $\mathcal{S}$ to a different parameter initialization, many dataset distillation algorithms will take expectation on $\mathcal{S}$ $w.r.t.$ θ^0, and the objective function has form of $\theta^0 \sim \Theta$. T denotes the number of inner iterations, and η is the learning rate for inner loop. The objective of meta learning–based performance matching indicates a bilevel optimization algorithm. In inner loops, weights of a differentiable model with parameter θ are updated with $\mathcal{S}$ via gradient descent. However, in the inner loop of Eq. (2.2), the neural network is trained by iterative gradient descent, which yields a series of intermediate parameter states of $\{\theta^0, \theta^1, \cdots, \theta^T\}$; backpropagation through time (BPTT) [24] is required to recursively compute the gradient $\nabla_{\mathcal{S}} \mathcal{L}_{\mathcal{T}}(\theta^T)$ in the outer loop:

Algorithm 1: Dataset distillation by performance matching

Input: Original dataset $\mathcal{T}$, outer-loop iterations K, parameter initialization distribution Θ, inner-loop iterations T (For TBPTT, $T = 1$), learning rate η

Initialize: $(\mathbf{X}_s^0, \mathbf{Y}_s) \sim \mathcal{T}$; // Random, real, or coreset
for $k = 1, \ldots, K$; // **Outer loop:** optimize $\mathcal{S}$
do
  Initialize $\theta_0 \sim \Theta$ **for** $t = 1, \ldots, T$; // **Inner loop:** optimize θ on $\mathcal{S}^{k-1}$
  do
    $\theta^t \leftarrow \theta^{t-1} - \eta \nabla \mathcal{L}_{\mathcal{S}^{k-1}}(\theta^{t-1})$
  $\mathbf{X}_s^k \leftarrow \mathbf{X}_s^{k-1} - \eta \nabla_{\mathbf{X}_s} \mathcal{L}_{\mathcal{T}}(\theta^T)$; // Update $\mathbf{X}_s$ by unrolled gradient decent

Output: $\mathcal{S}^K = (\mathbf{X}_s^K, \mathbf{Y}_s)$

$$\nabla_{\mathcal{S}} \mathcal{L}_{\mathcal{T}}(\theta^T) = \frac{\partial \mathcal{L}}{\partial \mathcal{S}} = \frac{\partial \mathcal{L}}{\partial \theta^T} \left(\sum_{k=0}^{k=T} \frac{\partial \theta^T}{\partial \theta^k} \cdot \frac{\partial \theta^k}{\partial \mathcal{S}} \right), \tag{2.3}$$

$$\frac{\partial \theta^T}{\partial \theta^k} = \prod_{i=k+1}^{T} \frac{\partial \theta^i}{\partial \theta^{i-1}}. \tag{2.4}$$

Due to the requirement of unrolling the recursive computation graph, BPTT is both computationally expensive and memory demanding, which also severely affects the final distillation performance. To make the implementation of Eq. (2.3) feasible, Wang et al. [19] suggest using the Truncated Back-Propagation Through Time (TBPTT) method, which involves unrolling the inner-loop optimization steps as a single step of gradient descent optimization:

$$\theta^1 = \theta^0 - \eta \nabla \mathcal{L}_{\mathcal{S}}(\theta^0) \text{ (inner loop)}, \tag{2.5}$$

We also elucidate the dataset distillation method for performance matching in Algorithm 1 for reference. Firstly, S is initialized before the optimization loop, which plays an important role in accelerating the convergence of dataset distillation algorithms [25]. Prior dataset distillation methods typically initialize the dataset from either random Gaussian noise or selected real images. Since advanced coreset selection methods such as K-Center [26] outperform random selection by a large margin, a natural way is to use images from K-Center to initialize distillation methods. In the iterative loop for synthetic data summary optimization, parameters of neural networks θ and data summary $\mathcal{S}$ are updated alternately. The parameters θ are periodically fetched at the beginning of the loop, which is optimized via $\mathcal{S}$ in the inner loop. Then the data summary $\mathcal{S}$ is updated via BPTT or TBPTT through the outer loop. However, BPTT has disadvantages such as computationally expensive inner-loop unrolling, gradients exploding or vanishing in long unrolls, and chaotic conditioned loss landscapes. TBPTT is associated with drawbacks involving bias with short truncated unrolling [27].

2.2.2.2 Variants of Meta Learning–Based Performance Matching

Sucholutsky and Schonlau [28] extend the work of Wang et al. [19] by learning a soft label in the dataset summary $\mathcal{S}$ instead of freezing distilled labels. Specifically, for better information distillation, the label Y_s in the data summary is trainable:

$$\mathbf{Y}_s^k \leftarrow \mathbf{Y}_s^{k-1} - \eta \nabla_{\mathbf{Y}_s} \mathcal{L}_{\mathcal{T}}(\theta^T) \tag{2.6}$$

Similarly, Bohdal et al. [29] extend standard feature distillation to label distillation by exclusively optimizing the labels of the data summary $\mathcal{S}$. These researchers also provide enhancements in the efficiency of long inner loop optimization through (1) iteratively updating the model parameters θ and the distilled labels $\mathbf{Y}_s$, with one outer step followed by only one inner step for faster convergence, and (2) fixing the feature extractor of neural networks and solely updating the last linear layer with ridge regression to avoid second-order gradient computation. Although the BPTT framework has been shown to underperform compared to other algorithms, Deng and Russakovsky [30] empirically demonstrate that adding a momentum term and extending the length of unrolled trajectories (to 200 steps) in the inner loop optimization can consistently improve performance. They find that longer unrolled trajectories lead to better model parameters that produce more efficient gradients for compressed representation learning. Consequently, the inner loop of model training becomes

$$\theta^t = \theta^{t-1} - \eta m^t, \tag{2.7}$$

where

$$m^t = \beta m^{t-1} + \nabla \mathcal{L}_{\mathcal{T}}(\theta^{t-1}) \; s.t. \; m^0 = 0. \tag{2.8}$$

2.2.2.3 Kernel Ridge Regression–Based Performance Matching

Above methods involve bilevel optimization to compute the unrolled gradients by backpropagating through time and the whole training graph. Thus, the computation cost of outer loops is extremely high, and the usage of GPU memory depends on the number of inner loops. The number of inner loops is limited due to limited GPU memory, resulting in insufficient inner optimization and poor distillation performance. To solve this issue, a separate line of work focuses on using Kernel Ridge Regression (KRR)–based algorithms [31], simplifying the optimization objective into a single-level problem by substituting the closed-form solution of the lower-level problem into the upper-level objective. KRR projects samples into a high-dimensional feature space with a non-linear neural network ϕ parameterized by θ; the objective of dataset distillation for performance matching can be rewritten as:

$$\arg\min_{\mathcal{S}} \mathbb{E}_{\theta \sim \Theta}[||\mathbf{Y}_t - \phi_\theta(\mathbf{X}_t) W^*_{\mathcal{S},\theta}||^2], \tag{2.9}$$

where $W^*_{\mathcal{S},\theta}$ can be solved as follows:

$$
\begin{aligned}
W^*_{\mathcal{S},\theta} &= \arg\min_{W_{\mathcal{S},\theta}} ||\mathbf{Y}_s - \phi_\theta(\mathbf{X}_s)W_{\mathcal{S},\theta}||^2 + \lambda||W_{\mathcal{S},\theta}||^2 \\
&= \phi_\theta(\mathbf{X}_s)^T(\phi_\theta(\mathbf{X}_s)\phi_\theta(\mathbf{X}_s)^T + \lambda\mathbf{I})^{-1}\mathbf{Y}_s.
\end{aligned}
\tag{2.10}
$$

The second term is for regularization, and λ is a fixed regularization hyperparameter [32]. We can rewrite the above two equations in kernel version as follows:

$$
\arg\min_{\mathcal{S}} \mathbb{E}_{\theta\sim\Theta}[||\mathbf{Y}_t - \mathbf{K}^\theta_{\mathbf{X}_t\mathbf{X}_s}(\mathbf{K}^\theta_{\mathbf{X}_s\mathbf{X}_s} + \lambda\mathbf{I})^{-1}\mathbf{Y}_s||^2],
\tag{2.11}
$$

where $\mathbf{K}^\theta_{\mathbf{X}_1\mathbf{X}_2} = \phi_\theta(\mathbf{X}_1)\phi_\theta(\mathbf{X}_2)^T$, $\mathbf{K}^\theta_{\mathbf{X}_t\mathbf{X}_s} \in \mathbb{R}^{N\times n}$ and $\mathbf{K}^\theta_{\mathbf{X}_s\mathbf{X}_s} \in \mathbb{R}^{n\times n}$. Then the data summary $\mathcal{S}$ can be directly updated via the single-level gradient of the above kernel function-based loss. As KRR is a closed-form solution to the previous objective, there is no need to backpropagate through time and the recursive gradient graph.

2.2.2.4 Variants of Kernel Ridge Regression–Based Performance Matching

However, the above KRR-based dataset distillation algorithm only employs simple kernels and is not specifically designed for dataset distillation scenarios, which makes the data summary hard to train neural networks. Thus, the Kernel-Inducing Point (KIP) algorithm is proposed [31], which utilizes a more powerful kernel named Neural Tangent Kernel (NTK) [33]. The infinite-width correspondence states that performing KRR using the NTK of a given neural network is equivalent to training the same ∞-width neural network with L2 reconstruction loss for ∞ SGD steps. Thus, with this equivalence, KIP employs ∞-width neural network as the kernel for dataset distillation [34], which narrows the gap between KRR and deep learning.

However, to obtain a kernel matrix, i.e., K, we have to calculate every entry in K separately via the kernel function. Thus, KIP has an $O(N \cdot n \cdot \dim(X))$ time and memory cost, limiting its scalability to large-scale datasets with a huge number of samples. To tackle this problem, RFAD [35] proposes replacing NTK with the lightweight Empirical Neural Network Gaussian Process (NNGP) kernel [36]. RFAD uses a random feature approximation (RFA) of the NNGP kernel by instantiating random neural networks. By adopting this approach, random features $\phi(X)$ can be explicitly derived through repeated sampling from a Gaussian process. Consequently, the computation of the kernel matrix is broken down into the calculation of random features and the multiplication of the random feature matrix. Given that matrix multiplication is nearly instantaneous for small data summary, the time complexity for computing the kernel matrix is reduced to $O(N + n)$. Also, RFAD explores two issues of Mean Square Mean (MSE) loss in Eq. (2.11): (1)

overinfluence of already correctly classified data points and (2) unclear probabilistic interpretation of MSE for classification. Thus, RFAD proposes Platt Scaling [37] by using cross-entropy loss instead of the MSE loss for the outer loop as follows:

$$\mathcal{L}_{platt} = CE(\mathbf{Y}_t, \mathbf{K}^{\theta}_{\mathbf{X}_t\mathbf{X}_s}(\mathbf{K}^{\theta}_{\mathbf{X}_s\mathbf{X}_s} + \lambda\mathbf{I})^{-1}\mathbf{Y}_s/\tau) \tag{2.12}$$

where τ is a positive learned temperature scaling parameter and CE denotes cross-entropy loss.

Similarly, FRePO [27] decouples the feature extractor and a linear classifier in ϕ. FRePo fixes the feature extractor at each gradient computation and trains the linear classifier to convergence before updating $\mathcal{S}$. After that, FRePo adjusts the feature extractor by training the whole network ϕ on the updated data summary $\mathcal{S}$. Notably, (1) FRePo randomly samples a model from a pool at each outer loop and updates it using the current data summary $\mathcal{S}$ to prevent overfitting to small $\mathcal{S}$, and (2) FRePo achieves better performance and scalability compared to previous KRR-based methods because the backpropagation only conduct on the classifier and KRR sidesteps the recursive computation graph of feature extractor.

2.2.3 Dataset Distillation by Gradient Matching

2.2.3.1 Gradient Matching

The approach of gradient parameters of neural networks in dataset distillation is first proposed by Zhao et al. [38]. Different from performance matching, which optimizes a model's performance trained on the data summary, the most important principle of gradient matching is to encourage the model trained on the data summary to approximate the model trained on the original dataset in the gradient space. If we fix the parameter initialization θ^0, we can obtain a training trajectory of $\{\theta^0, \theta^1, \cdots, \theta^T\}$. Then, we can derive a series of gradients corresponding to the training trajectory. When the distance between gradients trained on the synthetic dataset and the real dataset is consistently close, the data summary $\mathcal{S}$ can be considered a good alternative to the original whole dataset $\mathcal{T}$. Thus, it's an intuitive way to match the gradients induced by $\mathcal{S}$ and $\mathcal{T}$. The objective function of gradient matching can be expressed as:

$$\min_{\mathcal{S}} \mathbb{E}_{\theta^0 \sim \Theta}\left[\sum_{t=0}^{T} D\left(\nabla\mathcal{L}_{\mathcal{S}}(\theta^t),\ \nabla\mathcal{L}_{\mathcal{T}}(\theta^t)\right)\right], \tag{2.13}$$

$$\theta^{t+1} \leftarrow \theta^t - \eta\nabla_{\theta}\mathcal{L}_{\mathcal{S}}(\theta^t), \tag{2.14}$$

where $D(\cdot,\cdot)$ is a distance function (typically cosine distance). The distance function can be decomposed into a sum of layer-wise losses:

$$D(\nabla\mathcal{L}_{\mathcal{S}}(\theta^t), \nabla\mathcal{L}_{\mathcal{T}}(\theta^t)) = \sum_{l=1}^{L} d(\nabla\mathcal{L}_{\mathcal{S}}(\theta_l^t), \nabla\mathcal{L}_{\mathcal{T}}(\theta_l^t)), \tag{2.15}$$

where l is the layer index, L is the number of layers with weights, and

$$d(\mathbf{A}, \mathbf{B}) = \sum_{i=1}^{\text{out}} (1 - \frac{\mathbf{A}_i \cdot \mathbf{B}_i}{||\mathbf{A}_i||||\mathbf{B}_i||}), \tag{2.16}$$

where $\mathbf{A}_i$ and $\mathbf{B}_i$ are flattened vectors of gradients corresponding to each output node i, which is in dimensional for FC weights and $in \times height \times width$ dimensional for convolutional weights.

This approach is memory-efficient compared with performance matching because only a single-step gradient is necessary instead of the expensive unrolling of the recursive computation graph over the previous parameters. Particularly, to improve the convergence speed in practical implementation, when updating the data summary $\mathcal{S}$, Zhao et al. [38] sample each synthetic and real batch pair $\mathcal{S}_c$ and $\mathcal{T}_c$ from $\mathcal{S}$ and $\mathcal{T}$, respectively, containing samples from the c-th class, and each class of data summary is updated separately in each iteration:

$$\min_{\mathcal{S}} \mathbb{E}_{\theta^0 \sim \Theta} \left[\sum_{c=1}^{C} \sum_{t=0}^{T} D\left(\nabla\mathcal{L}_{\mathcal{S}_c}(\theta^t),\ \nabla\mathcal{L}_{\mathcal{T}_c}(\theta^t)\right) \right], \tag{2.17}$$

where C is the total number of classes. We depict the optimization details in Algorithm 2. At the outer level, it contains a loop over random weight initializations, as we want to obtain condensed images that can later be used to train previously unseen models. One θ is randomly initialized; it first computes the gradient distance over $\mathcal{S}$ and $\mathcal{S}$ and then optimizes the data summary $\mathcal{S}$ to match these gradients. Next, it trains θ on the updated data summary. Note that it samples each real and synthetic batch pair from $\mathcal{T}$ and $\mathcal{S}$ containing samples from a single class, and the synthetic data for each class are separately (or parallelly) updated at each iteration (t).

2.2.3.2 Variants of Gradient Matching

Subsequently, various other methods have been developed based on this framework, incorporating subtle modifications and enhancements. For instance, the distance metric between two gradients treats each class independently, ignoring the class-discriminative features of the target dataset. To address this limitation, DCC [39]

Algorithm 2: Dataset distillation by gradient matching

Input: Original dataset $\mathcal{T}$, outer-loop iterations K, parameter initialization distribution Θ, inner-loop iterations T, learning rate η

Initialize: $\mathcal{S} \sim \mathcal{T}$; `// Random, real, or coreset`
for $k = 1, \ldots, K$ **do**
  Initialize $\theta_0 \sim \Theta$
  for $t = 1, \ldots, T$ **do**
    for $c = 1, \ldots, C$ **do**
      Sample a minibatch pair $\mathcal{S}_c \sim \mathcal{S}$ and $\mathcal{T}_c \sim \mathcal{T}$
      Compute $D\left(\nabla \mathcal{L}_{\mathcal{S}_c}(\theta^t),\ \nabla \mathcal{L}_{\mathcal{T}_c}(\theta^t)\right)$
      $S_c \leftarrow S_c - \eta \nabla_{S_c} D(\nabla \mathcal{L}_{\mathcal{S}_c}(\theta^t), \nabla \mathcal{L}_{\mathcal{T}_c}(\theta^t))$
    $\theta^t \leftarrow \theta^{t-1} - \eta \nabla \mathcal{L}_{\mathcal{S}}(\theta^{t-1})$; `// Use the whole` $\mathcal{S}$

Output: $\mathcal{S}$

enhances the gradient-matching objective by integrating class contrastive signals into each gradient-matching step, leading to improved stability and performance. With θ^t evolving in a manner similar to Eq. (2.17), the revised optimization objective for DCC can be expressed as follows:

$$\min_{\mathcal{S}} \mathbb{E}_{\theta^0 \sim \Theta} \left[\sum_{t=0}^{T} D \left(\sum_{c=1}^{C} \nabla \mathcal{L}_{\mathcal{S}_c}(\theta^t),\ \sum_{c=1}^{C} \nabla \mathcal{L}_{\mathcal{T}_c}(\theta^t) \right) \right], \tag{2.18}$$

To simultaneously account for both intra-class and inter-class features, Jiang et al. [40] propose combining Eqs. (2.17) and (2.18). This is achieved by introducing a hyperparameter λ that balances the significance of the two equations. Furthermore, they not only measure the angle between gradients using cosine distance but also consider the magnitude. This leads to a modification of the distance function in Eq. (2.16) to:

$$D(\mathbf{A}, \mathbf{B}) = \sum_{i=1}^{\text{out}} \left(1 - \frac{\mathbf{A}_i \cdot \mathbf{B}_i}{||\mathbf{A}_i||, ||\mathbf{B}_i||} + ||\mathbf{A}_i - \mathbf{B}_i|| \right). \tag{2.19}$$

To incorporate data augmentation into the dataset distillation, DSA [41] enhances dataset distillation by applying identical image augmentations (such as scale, flip, crop, rotate, color jitters, and cutout) to both $\mathcal{T}$ and $\mathcal{S}$ while optimizing Eq. (2.17). This approach allows the transfer of knowledge from the augmentation of target images to the corresponding synthetic images. Importantly, these augmentations must be differentiable with respect to the data summary $\mathcal{S}$ to enable backpropagation. Given that these augmentations are universally applicable across dataset distillation frameworks, the augmentations performed by DSA have become a standard component of all subsequent methods.

2.2.4 *Dataset Distillation by Trajectory Matching*

2.2.4.1 Trajectory Matching

The first trajectory matching-based dataset distillation method is introduced by Cazenavette et al. [42]. Trajectory matching directly mimics the long-range training dynamics of networks trained on real datasets, rather than focusing on short-range behaviors such as gradients, to avoid error accumulation during evaluation. In this method, the data summary is applied over multiple steps. Specifically, trajectory matching aligns segments of parameter trajectories $\theta_{\mathcal{S}}^{t}, \theta_{\mathcal{S}}^{t+1}, \cdots, \theta_{\mathcal{S}}^{t+N}$, trained on the data summary $\mathcal{S}$, with segments of pre-computed trajectories $\theta_{\mathcal{T}}^{t}, \theta_{\mathcal{T}}^{t+1}, \cdots, \theta_{\mathcal{T}}^{t+M}$ from models trained on the original dataset $\mathcal{T}$. Here, M denotes the number of update steps between the starting and target parameters on the expert trajectory, and N denotes the number of update steps applied to the student network at each distillation step. This approach avoids the pitfalls of being either short-sighted (i.e., focusing on single steps) or too difficult to optimize (i.e., modeling the full trajectories).

Trajectory matching treats the resulting sequence of network parameters as an *expert trajectory*. The key idea is that if the data summary can induce the network's training dynamics to follow such expert trajectories, then the resulting model will converge to a similar solution as one trained on the full dataset, thereby achieving comparable test performance. At each distillation step, trajectory matching samples a set of parameters from one of the expert trajectories at a random time step $\theta_{\mathcal{T}}^{t}$ and uses it to initialize the student network with $\theta_{\mathcal{S}}^{t} = \theta_{\mathcal{T}}^{t}$. The objective is formulated as follows:

$$\arg\min_{\mathcal{S}} \quad \mathbb{E}_{\theta_0 \sim \Theta} \left[\sum_{t=0}^{T-M} \frac{D\left(\theta_{\mathcal{T}}^{t+M}, \theta_{\mathcal{S}}^{t+N}\right)}{D\left(\theta_{\mathcal{T}}^{t+M}, \theta_{\mathcal{T}}^{t}\right)} \right], \tag{2.20}$$

$$\theta_{\mathcal{S}}^{t+i+1} \leftarrow \theta_{\mathcal{S}}^{t+i} - \eta \cdot \nabla \mathcal{L}_{\mathcal{S}}(\theta_{\mathcal{S}}^{t+i}), \quad \theta_{\mathcal{S}}^{t} = \theta_{\mathcal{T}}^{t}, \tag{2.21}$$

where D is a distance metric of choice, typically the L2 distance. Equation (2.20) normalizes the distance by the expert distance traveled, ensuring a strong signal from later training epochs where the expert does not move as much. This normalization also helps self-calibrate the magnitude differences across neurons and layers. Algorithm 3 illustrates the main algorithm.

2.2.4.2 Variants of Trajectory Matching

Although trajectory matching has shown empirical success, FTD [43] points out that $\theta_{\mathcal{S}}^{t}$ is typically derived from training on $\mathcal{S}$ for t epochs during the actual training process. However, in the previously mentioned trajectory matching algorithm, it is

Algorithm 3: Dataset distillation by trajectory matching

Input: Original dataset $\mathcal{T}$, distillation steps K, parameter initialization distribution Θ, updates steps between starting and target expert params M, updates iterations to student network per distillation step N, learning rate η

Initialize: $\mathcal{S} \sim \mathcal{T}$; // Random, real, or coreset

Pre-compute expert trajectories by training a large number of networks initialized by $\theta \sim \Theta$ on the original dataset.

for $k = 1, \ldots, K$ **do**

  Sample an expert trajectory $\{\theta_{\mathcal{T}}^0, \theta_{\mathcal{T}}^1, \cdots, \theta_{\mathcal{T}}^T\}$

  Randomly choose a start epoch $t < T$

  Initialize student network with expert params $\theta_{\mathcal{S}}^t = \theta_{\mathcal{T}}^t$

  for $n = 1, \ldots, N$ **do**

    $\theta_{\mathcal{S}}^{t+n+1} \leftarrow \theta_{\mathcal{S}}^{t+n} - \eta \cdot \nabla \mathcal{L}_{\mathcal{S}}(\theta_{\mathcal{S}}^{t+n})$

  Compute loss $\mathcal{L}$ between ending student and expert params using Eq. (2.20)

  Update data summary $S \leftarrow S - \eta \nabla_S \mathcal{L}$

Output: $\mathcal{S}$

directly initialized with $\theta_{\mathcal{T}}^t$, leading to accumulated trajectory errors. To mitigate this issue, FTD introduces flat regularization during the initialization of $\theta_{\mathcal{S}}^t$ to enhance robustness to the perturbation of the weights.

Compared to gradient matching-based algorithms, trajectory matching-based algorithms require unrolling N SGD updates due to the existence of $\theta_{\mathcal{S}}^{t+N}$ in Eq. (2.20), while it also sidesteps second-order gradient computation. Thus, back-propagating requires expanding and storing N gradient computational graphs in GPU memory and is prohibitive in large-scale problems. By a procedure to cache and rearrange the gradient computation of the trajectory matching loss, TESLA [44] greatly reduces the memory required by trajectory matching and successfully scaled trajectory matching approach to the large ImageNet-1K dataset.

2.2.5 Dataset Distillation by Distribution Matching

2.2.5.1 Distribution Matching

Despite the advancements brought by the aforementioned algorithms, dataset condensation still involves solving an expensive bilevel optimization problem. This requirement undermines the goal of reducing training time due to the costly image synthesis process. Moreover, these algorithms necessitate tuning multiple hyper-parameters for both the outer and inner loop optimizations, such as determining the number of steps to update the data summary $\mathcal{S}$ and the network parameters in each iteration. These hyperparameters can vary depending on different settings, such as the sizes of $\mathcal{S}$. To overcome these limitations, distribution matching [45] frames dataset distillation as a distribution matching problem, where the data summary is optimized to align with the original data distribution. Given that training

Algorithm 4: Dataset distillation by distribution matching

Input: Original dataset $\mathcal{T}$, distillation steps K, parameter initialization distribution Θ, learning rate η

Initialize: $\mathcal{S} \sim \mathcal{T}$; `// Random, real, or coreset`

for $k = 1, \ldots, K$ **do**

  Randomly initialize embedding function $\theta \sim \Theta$

  Compute loss $\mathcal{L}$ using Eq. (2.23)

  Update data summary $S \leftarrow S - \eta \nabla_S \mathcal{L}$

Output: $\mathcal{S}$

images in the original dataset are typically high dimensional, estimating the original data distribution directly can be expensive and inaccurate. Instead, they propose embedding each training image into a lower-dimensional space using a family of parametric functions. In other words, each embedding function ϕ provides a partial interpretation of its input, and their combination delivers a comprehensive representation. The family of embedding functions ϕ can be efficiently obtained by sampling randomly initialized deep neural networks. The distance between the distributions of the original dataset and the data summary can then be measured using the commonly employed maximum mean discrepancy (MMD) [46] metric:

$$\mathbb{E}_{\theta \sim \Theta} \left\| \frac{1}{|\mathcal{T}|} \sum_{t=1}^{|\mathcal{T}|} \phi_\theta(\mathbf{X}_t) - \frac{1}{|\mathcal{S}|} \sum_{s=1}^{|\mathcal{S}|} \phi_\theta(\mathbf{X}_s) \right\|^2, \tag{2.22}$$

Importantly, Eq. (2.22) can be efficiently solved, as it requires only optimizing $\mathcal{S}$ but no model parameters and thus avoids expensive bilevel optimization and involves tuning only one hyperparameter (i.e., learning rate for data summary). Note that, as targeting at image classification problems, distribution matching minimizes the discrepancy between the real and synthetic samples of the same class only, which can be formulated as follows:

$$\mathbb{E}_{\theta \sim \Theta} \left[\sum_{c=1}^{C} \left\| \frac{1}{|\mathcal{T}_c|} \sum_{t=1}^{|\mathcal{T}_c|} \phi_\theta(\mathbf{X}_t) - \frac{1}{|\mathcal{S}_c|} \sum_{s=1}^{|\mathcal{S}_c|} \phi_\theta(\mathbf{X}_s) \right\|^2 \right], \tag{2.23}$$

Algorithm 4 illustrates the training procedure for distribution matching. The data summary $\mathcal{S}$ is trained over K iterations. In each iteration, distribution matching randomly samples a model θ with parameters $\theta \sim \Theta$. The mean discrepancy between the original dataset and the data summary for each class is then calculated and summed to form the loss $\mathcal{L}$. The data summary $\mathcal{S}$ is updated by minimizing $\mathcal{L}$ using stochastic gradient descent with a learning rate η.

2.2.5.2 Variants of Distribution Matching

CAFE [47] enhances the distribution consistency between the data summary and original dataset by aligning the embeddings from all intermediary layers, rather than just the final embeddings as in the previous algorithm, which further improves the distribution alignment:

$$\mathbb{E}_{\theta\sim\Theta}\left[\sum_{c=1}^{C}\sum_{l=1}^{L}\left\|\frac{1}{|\mathcal{T}_c|}\sum_{t=1}^{|\mathcal{T}_c|}\phi_{\theta,l}(\mathbf{X}_t)-\frac{1}{|\mathcal{S}_c|}\sum_{s=1}^{|\mathcal{S}_c|}\phi_{\theta,l}(\mathbf{X}_s)\right\|^2\right], \tag{2.24}$$

where L is the number of intermediary layers. Additionally, the synthetic samples from one class should accurately represent the corresponding clusters of real samples. To achieve this, CAFE treats each real sample as a test sample and classifies it based on its affinity to the synthetic clusters. This approach ensures that the synthetic samples are not only representative of their classes but also distinguishable.

2.3 Dataset Distillation for Data Modalities

A large portion of existing dataset distillation techniques are designed for image data, primarily because images exist in a real-valued, continuous data domain. This characteristic allows for SGD-based optimization directly on the data, which is treated as a set of free parameters. Incrementally changing each pixel value can be considered as slight perturbations in the color space, enabling naive optimization using SGD given a suitable dataset distillation loss. Beyond image data, which the majority of dataset distillation works focus on, dataset distillation has since been extended to various other data modalities such as text, graph, and time series. In this section, we categorize existing works based on the data modality they distill and discuss some of the associated challenges.

2.3.1 Text Data

Textual data is abundantly available from sources such as Web sites, news articles, and academic manuscripts, with datasets like Common Crawl[1] reaching sizes of nearly 541TB. The rise of large language models (LLMs) has made training these models from scratch on such massive datasets increasingly costly. For instance, GPT-3, which is trained on 45TB of data, comprises approximately 175 billion

[1] https://commoncrawl.org/the-data/

parameters [8]. This sheer scale presents challenges in both training and fine-tuning the model. Although recent advancements, such as those by Geiping and Goldstein [48], aim to accelerate LLMs training, the effective dataset distillation of large-scale textual data as a data-centric solution remains an underexplored area. The primary challenge of textual dataset distillation lies in the inherently discrete nature of text data, where tokens must belong to a limited vocabulary of words. To address this, two works [28, 49] extend dataset distillation to text by using embedding vectors as inputs instead of discrete text. They assume access to a latent space defined by a fixed text encoder, such as pretrained GloVe embeddings [50] or BERT [5], allowing each sentence to be treated like a single-channel image with dimensions corresponding to sentence length $\times$ embedding size. Thus, the data summary $\mathcal{S}$ is conceptualized as a learnable embedding matrix. The continuous embeddings of each word in the matrix are optimized using the TBPTT dataset distillation framework proposed by Wang et al. [19]. Despite remaining in the embedding space, the data summary can be mapped back to the nearest sentences corresponding to the distilled embeddings. To achieve this, each column vector in the embedding matrix is matched to its closest embedding vector from the original vocabulary. These vectors are then converted back into their respective words, which are combined to form sentences. While the aforementioned studies apply text dataset distillation to model architectures based on convolutional neural networks (CNNs) and recurrent neural networks (RNNs), Maekawa et al. [51] aim to distill few-shot datasets specifically for fine-tuning pretrained transformers like BERT for NLP tasks. In addition to optimizing text embeddings and soft labels within the data summary, they introduce the concept of distilling attention labels. This involves supervising the attention scores by minimizing the KL divergence between the attention scores of the data summary and those of the model during the distillation process.

To tackle the challenges posed by the discrete nature of text, the above text dataset distillation methods employ an embedding technique. They optimize data summary as continuous word embeddings matrix instead of discrete text. However, these approaches present a significant issue: the distilled synthetic data summary, represented as embeddings, cannot be used to train models with different word embedding weights, limiting its practical applications. Additionally, the distilled word embedding sequences are unreadable to humans, making it difficult to interpret and analyze the original training dataset through the synthetic samples. Although converting embeddings to sentences by finding the nearest neighbor embeddings can be done, the resulting sentences often consist of unrelated words, rendering them nonsensical and challenging to interpret. To address these shortcomings, DiLM [52] proposes using a language model as a surrogate continuous optimization target rather than directly optimizing synthetic text samples. Specifically, DiLM trains a language model to minimize the gradient matching loss [38] of generated synthetic samples, using this as the dataset distillation objective. To enable backpropagation of the gradient matching loss to the language model, they design a differentiable backward pass. This is achieved by weighting the loss with generation probabilities, thereby circumventing the non-differentiable nature of text. This method offers a more practical and interpretable approach to text dataset distillation.

2.3.2 Graph Data

Graphs are prevalent data structures that describe relationships between entities, and they are used in various domains such as recommendation systems [53], chemistry [54], epidemiology [55], and e-commerce [56]. The intrinsic relational structure of graph data makes it a potent representation for modeling complex interactions and dependencies. However, large-scale graphs, often comprising millions of nodes and edges, are common in real-world applications [57], presenting significant computational challenges for training graph neural networks (GNNs). Inspired by dataset distillation, which generates a small set of images to train deep neural networks for downstream tasks, dataset distillation for graphs aims to condense a given graph by learning a synthetic graph structure and node attributes.

In this context, Jin et al. [58] introduce the concept of graph condensation (or graph distillation). The goal is to minimize the performance gap between GNN models trained on a synthetic, simplified graph and those trained on the original, more complex training graph. This approach seeks to retain the essential properties and performance characteristics of the original graph while significantly reducing its size and complexity.

Significant research has been dedicated to graph condensation [59]. Inspired by the impressive results of gradient matching-based dataset distillation in the image domain [38], the pioneering work in graph condensation, GCond [58], adopts this gradient matching approach for node classification tasks. Specifically, GCond aligns the gradients of GNN parameters concerning both the condensed graph and the original graph, formulating it as a bilevel optimization problem similar to Eq. (2.13). One fundamental challenge in graph condensation is modeling the condensed graph structure and managing node dependencies. Let $\mathbf{A}_t \in \mathbb{R}^{N\times N}$ and $\mathbf{A}_s \in \mathbb{R}^{n\times n}$ represent the adjacency matrices of the original and synthetic graphs, respectively. In image dataset distillation, X_s is treated as a set of free parameters. Similarly, the straightforward approach for graph condensation is to treat both $\mathbf{A}_s$ and $\mathbf{X}_s$ as free parameters. However, the number of parameters in $\mathbf{A}_s$ grows quadratically with n, increasing the model complexity and the risk of overfitting, which complicates the optimization process. Therefore, it is preferable to parameterize the condensed adjacency matrix in a manner that limits the growth of parameters. Additionally, treating $\mathbf{A}_s$ and $\mathbf{X}_s$ as independent parameters ignores the inherent correlations between graph structure and node features. For example, in social networks, user interactions are influenced by shared interests, while in e-commerce, product purchases are driven by product attributes. To address this, GCond proposes modeling the condensed graph structure as a function of the condensed node features:

$$\mathbf{A}_{s,ij} = \sigma\left(\left[\mathrm{MLP}_\phi\left(\left[\mathbf{X}_{s,i}; \mathbf{X}_{s,j}\right]\right) + \mathrm{MLP}_\phi\left(\left[\mathbf{X}_{s,j}; \mathbf{X}_{s,i}\right]\right)\right]/2\right) \tag{2.25}$$

where MLP_ϕ is a multi-layer perception (MLP) parameterized with ϕ and $[\cdot;\cdot]$ indicates concatenation. GCond employs an alternating optimization approach for $\mathbf{X}_s$ and ϕ, iteratively updating ϕ for several epochs before updating $\mathbf{X}_s$. However, the nested loop structure of this optimization process, as outlined in Eq. (2.13), limits the scalability of the method. To address this limitation, DosCond [60] introduces a one-step gradient matching scheme. This approach simplifies the process by matching the network gradients only at the model initialization θ_0, thus avoiding the need to track the entire training trajectory θ_t and eliminating the summation in Eq. (2.13). In DosCond, the graph structure $\mathbf{A}_s$ is treated as a probabilistic model, learning a discretized graph structure by modeling a Bernoulli distribution over the edge set. This method not only simplifies the optimization but also provides theoretical insights into the gradient matching scheme in graph condensation. Specifically, DosCond demonstrates that the smallest gap between the resulting loss (from training on synthetic graphs) and the optimal loss is upper bounded by the gradient matching loss. Moreover, DosCond is notable for being the first graph condensation method to focus on graph classification, aiming to reduce the number of multiple graphs. This shift in focus marks a significant advancement in the practical application of graph condensation techniques.

Similar to dataset distillation in the image domain, graph condensation techniques can be divided into four main categories: performance matching [61, 62], gradient matching [58, 60, 63, 64], trajectory matching [61, 65], and distribution matching [66, 67]. While the fundamental concepts are analogous to those in dataset distillation, each method incorporates specific designs tailored to the unique characteristics of graph datasets.

In recommendation systems, the user-item interaction matrix can be seen as a graph, making recommendation dataset distillation a specific case of graph distillation. The heterogeneity, sparsity, and semi-structured nature of recommendation data present additional challenges. To address these, DISTILL-CF [68], a gradient matching-based dataset distillation framework for collaborative filtering (CF) datasets, has been introduced. This framework utilizes ∞-AE within a bilevel optimization objective to generate data summaries. DISTILL-CF leverages efficient multi-step differentiable Gumbel sampling [69] at each optimization step to manage the heterogeneity, sparsity, and semi-structured characteristics of recommendation data.

2.3.3 Time Series Data

Most existing dataset distillation methods have focused on classification tasks, such as image classification, where synthetic data are optimized to preserve decision boundaries across discrete classes. In such tasks, gradient matching and performance matching have shown notable success [38, 58]. Time series classification, which often resembles image classification in structure, has also seen progress. For example, CondTSC [70] extends gradient matching to the time series domain by aligning surrogate losses in both the time and frequency domains.

However, time series forecasting introduces additional complexity. Unlike classification, it is inherently a regression problem, where the model predicts continuous future values instead of discrete labels [71, 72]. This difference in task formulation makes it nontrivial to apply existing classification-based condensation methods directly. Moreover, the temporal continuity and autocorrelation in time series demand specialized treatment during data synthesis.

To address these challenges, CondTSF [73] redefines the objective of dataset condensation for forecasting tasks. Rather than focusing on class-based losses, CondTSF minimizes a composite objective that includes a gradient term to align training dynamics and a value term to ensure numerical similarity in predictions between the original and synthetic time series. This approach falls under the gradient matching category and offers a tailored solution for compressing large-scale time series datasets for efficient fine-tuning of foundation models [74, 75].

2.3.4 *Other Modalities*

There are also a few works studying other modalities. Video data has an extra time dimension compared to image data, which can significantly enhance the complexity of both time and space in dataset distillation methods. To tackle this issue, video distillation [76] can either decrease the number of synthetic frames or trim the bipartite correspondence graph between real and synthetic frames. In this method, both real and synthetic videos are divided into multiple segments, and distillation methods are applied to each real-synthetic segment pair. The synthetic videos are subsequently interpolated to match the target video length.

For multimodal data like vision-language datasets, distillation faces several challenges. First, as illustrated in text modality, text data is inherently non-differentiable, making direct SGD-based optimization on discrete text tokens impossible. Second, these vision-language datasets cannot be treated as a classification task because they only contain image and text pairs. Third, the complexity of cross-modal features and vision-language models introduces computational difficulties. To tackle these challenges, vision-language dataset distillation [77] has been proposed, based on the idea of trajectory matching. Specifically, given a dataset of images with corresponding text descriptions, this method generates a much smaller data summary of (image, text embedding) pairs such as image-text retrieval tasks [78], which can then be used to efficiently train a model for image-text alignment. Additionally, Low-Rank Adaptation (LoRA) matching [118] is employed to enable more efficient and effective trajectory matching in complex modern vision-language models.

2.4 Implications of Dataset Distillation

The distilled dataset is commonly viewed as a condensed and informative representation of the original training data, allowing it to serve as the original data in many applications. This capability is particularly valuable for enterprise AI, where efficiency, scalability, and privacy are paramount. We first categorize these applications into two major categories below and briefly introduce them.

2.4.1 *Computationally Intensive Tasks*

Computationally intensive methods, such as continual learning (CL) [79] and Neural Architecture Search (NAS) [80], require multiple accesses to the dataset throughout the algorithm. In these scenarios, replacing the original dataset with a distilled dataset of comparable performance and essential information can significantly enhance the efficiency of these algorithms.

2.4.1.1 Continual Learning

Continual Learning (CL) [81] studies the problem of learning from an infinite stream of data, with the challenge of gradually extending learned knowledge and using it for unseen tasks. CL typically uses a small dataset called replay memory to review essential knowledge, thereby avoiding catastrophic forgetting [82] when new data or task comes. However, this technique faces the problem of rapidly enlarging memory, making the replay process increasingly time-consuming as the learning history grows. Therefore, reducing the size of the dataset for replay can significantly enhance the efficiency of CL algorithms. Since dataset distillation can reduce the size while keeping the essential knowledge, leveraging it to generate the memory bank has been widely used in CL in the image [30, 83, 84] and graph [85] domain. These methods have been empirically demonstrated to be superior to traditional CL methods that use a coreset as the replay memory.

2.4.1.2 Neural Architecture Search

Neural Architecture Search (NAS) is proposed to automatically and efficiently find state-of-the-art architectures from complex neural network designs, avoiding exhaustive traversal or manual tuning based on domain knowledge [80]. Similar to CL, NAS also requires accessing the dataset multiple times to find the best architecture for the given dataset or tasks. To improve efficiency and avoid trying all parameter combinations (i.e., grid search), a major direction in NAS is to design heuristic [86] or learnable [87] methods to determine the optimal parameter combination. However, these methods cannot guarantee finding the best combination with the highest test accuracy. Another promising direction is to apply dataset distillation to NAS by conducting grid search on a distilled dataset instead of the original dataset and choosing the architecture according to the best performance on the distilled dataset. In the image domain, two empirical studies [25, 41] investigated this approach using a toy NAS bench with 720 variations of the ConvNet architecture, and the much larger NAS-Bench-201 [88], respectively, reached opposite conclusions. The former study concluded that dataset distillation can be directly used in NAS, while the latter argued that current dataset distillation methods perform poorly in NAS and should be specifically designed for it. In the graph domain, recent work [89] empirically finds that graph dataset distillation (or condensation) methods based on trajectory matching or with an inner loop have high NAS performance.

2.4.2 *Privacy Preservation*

Since the synthetic data is distorted from original data and hard to understand for human, dataset distillation has the potential to preserve the privacy. We introduce the privacy preservation of dataset distillation from theoretical view-differential privacy and empirical studies-federated learning.

2.4.2.1 Differential Privacy

Differential Privacy (DP) is now one of the golden criteria for evaluating the privacy preservation ability of an algorithm. It is defined as the influence of a single sample change in the input on the output distribution [90]. Dong et al. [23] theoretically prove that distilled datasets can provide a tighter differential privacy (DP) constraint as $O(m/n)$ than the original dataset with $O(n)$ [90] to both downstream linear and non-linear feature extractors, where m is the number of distilled samples and n is the number of original samples. They further demonstrate the membership and visual privacy of distilled datasets under real attacks. To guarantee the DP on the dataset distillation algorithm itself as well as downstream tasks, Chen et al. [91] add white noise to the gradients calculated from the original datasets, achieving a significantly better trade-off between utility and privacy preservation.

2.4.2.2 Federated Learning

Federated Learning (FL) is an emerging research area where the training data is held separately by different clients who collaborate to train the model without directly sharing their private data [92]. Current FL methods primarily train local models on private data and then share the model parameters and calculate the gradient in a server. However, these methods face many issues, such as model heterogeneity [93], when different clients adopt different architectures for their local models. In such scenarios, collaboration in terms of model parameters becomes difficult to achieve. Hopefully, the privacy-preserving nature of distilled datasets can satisfy the privacy requirements of FL and allow it to work in a more straightforward way—by collecting all distilled data from each client and training a model on a central server. Many works have implemented such dataset distillation-based FL methods in the image [94, 95], language [28, 96], and graph domains [97]. These methods have been empirically demonstrated to be better than parameter-sharing-based FL methods and also more efficient. This distilled-data-sharing paradigm has been applied in medical imaging [98], demonstrating effectiveness in constructing high-accuracy AI-aided diagnosis systems and helping preserve patient privacy.

2.5 Pitfalls and Future Directions

Though dataset distillation has rapidly developed in recent years, some pitfalls remain, especially for enterprise use, such as efficiency and robustness. Addressing these pitfalls also sheds light on future directions for this area.

2.5.1 Efficiency of Dataset Distillation Methods

The main objective of dataset distillation is to produce a smaller yet highly informative dataset that enables models to achieve similar performance as if they are trained on the original dataset, thus saving GPU time. However, creating this synthetic dataset is usually resource intensive, with the time required increasing significantly for large-scale datasets. For instance, when distilling ImageNet-1K with an input resolution of 224×224 and an IPC of 100, a total of $224 \times 224 \times 1000 \times 100 = 5$ billion learnable parameters (pixels) need to be optimized simultaneously. This presents a significant computational challenge, which is mainly due to the necessity of backpropagating through unrolled computational graphs to update the synthetic datasets. To tackle this issue, various approaches have been proposed to reduce computational costs across different dataset distillation frameworks. One straightforward strategy is to eliminate the inner-loop network training. In performance matching, KRR-based methods [27, 31, 34, 35] enhance computational efficiency by performing convex optimization, resulting in a closed-form solution for linear models and avoiding extensive inner-loop training. For distribution matching, distribution matching [45] improves efficiency by using random initialized networks as feature extractors without training, thus avoiding costly bilevel optimization. However, this increase in efficiency often comes at the expense of performance. Regarding trajectory matching, Cui et al. [44] have reorganized the computation flow for gradients, reducing the memory cost to a constant complexity. Despite this improvement, it still requires pretraining hundreds of teacher models on the original datasets, which negatively impacts both time and memory efficiency. These efforts illustrate ongoing attempts to balance computational efficiency with maintaining high performance in dataset distillation. If made more efficient, dataset distillation could support rapid retraining in enterprise MLOps workflows, enabling frequent updates of models such as fraud detection or customer behavior prediction without large compute overhead.

2.5.2 Scalability of Dataset Distillation Methods

Current dataset distillation methods typically evaluate the performance of the synthetic dataset with an Image Per Class (IPC) of around 50 [99]. In real-world applications, it may be necessary to increase the compression ratio to capture more information from the entire dataset. Additionally, the datasets and networks used may be larger and more complex. However, as noted by Cui et al. [25], existing dataset distillation methods tend to perform well only when the IPC is relatively low. As the IPC increases, the performance of most distillation methods declines and starts to resemble that of random sampling. Things get worse in the graph domain, as they usually require prohibitive memory consumption when attempting the same extent of reduction rate as in the image domain [89]. Therefore, it is crucial to investigate whether dataset distillation can overcome this limitation and maintain high performance on larger datasets. Scalable distillation would allow enterprises to compress large-scale datasets, such as product catalogs or nationwide medical records, into reusable training subsets for fine-tuning task-specific models across business units.

2.5.3 Dataset Distillation Methods Extension to New Data Modalities

Existing dataset distillation techniques have predominantly focused on image datasets due to the continuous pixel domain's suitability for data optimization. Applications of these techniques to other data modalities remain largely underexplored. Although recent efforts have extended dataset distillation to other modalities such as graphs [58], text [52], time series [73], and multimodal data [77], each modality presents unique challenges that require further research. For instance, in modalities like video [76], where rich spatial and temporal information are intertwined, it remains difficult for dataset distillation algorithms to distill both spatial and temporal features into a compact dataset simultaneously. Additional modalities, including data used in tabular data [100] and speech data [101], remain unexplored and require pioneering work. Extending distillation to modalities like time series, speech, or multimodal data could improve AI adoption in telecom monitoring, voice-based interfaces, and sensor-driven manufacturing processes.

2.5.4 Dataset Distillation Methods for New Tasks

Another limitation of current dataset distillation techniques is that their underlying optimization is primarily designed for classification scenarios. However, many popular tasks do not fit neatly into the existing supervised dataset distillation framework, such as object detection [102, 103], semantic segmentation [104], and machine translation [105], as their label spaces are located in much higher-dimensional spaces. Unlike single-label classification in dataset distillation, where a specific number of synthetic images (IPC) are pre-assigned for each class, enumerated assignment becomes impractical when dealing with highly dimensional label spaces. Consequently, representing the rich label space requires careful adjustment of high-dimensional labels of synthetic data, significantly hindering dataset distillation efficiency, especially when optimized jointly with the input data. Supporting tasks beyond classification, such as object detection or translation, would enable compact training sets for enterprise applications like automated checkout, logistics tracking, or multilingual customer support.

2.5.5 Robust Dataset Distillation

Robustness is a critical concern in enterprise AI, as noise, adversarial attacks, and out-of-distribution data frequently occur in real-world environments. Jia et al. [106] made the first attempt to combine dataset distillation with adversarial training in CL to enhance robustness memory. Zheng and Li [107] focus on poisoning attacks and propose the concept of poisoned deviation to quantify the poisoning effect on dataset distillation. They further propose a poisoning-resilient dataset distillation algorithm with a calibration method to reduce the poisoned deviation. Ma et al. [108] first distill both in-distribution samples and outliers to enable the distilled datasets to be competent in both in-distribution classification and out-of-distribution detection. In the graph domain, similar attempts are made by Gao et al. [109] and Gao et al. [110] with respect to denoising and out-of-distribution detection, respectively. Robust distillation methods can improve AI reliability in the face of noisy or adversarial inputs, which is essential for deploying models in critical areas like customer service, healthcare, or finance.

2.5.6 Model Augmentation for Dataset Distillation

During dataset distillation, the learned data summary is highly related to the initialized neural network parameter θ_0. The process introduces a concern that the distillation performance may drop when training the neural network with significantly different initialized parameters. To improve the robustness and generalization of data summary to different parameter initialization, many dataset distillation methods use models with a diverse set of initialized parameters to train the data summary. Zhang et al. [111] demonstrate that using early-stage models trained for only a few epochs as initialization parameters can improve distillation performance. They further propose weight perturbation methods to efficiently generate early-stage models for calculating the distillation loss. Therefore, it is essential to explore model augmentation methods to reduce the sensitivity of data summary to model parameters and improve overall dataset distillation generalization performance. Generalizing across model initializations would let companies reuse a single distilled dataset across diverse deployment environments, reducing retraining costs and simplifying the distribution of foundation models.

2.5.7 Explainability for Dataset Distillation

To make algorithms more trustworthy, an area named explainability [112] is rising with the goal of identifying the most important samples or patterns and explaining the mechanism of the algorithm by analyzing these selected samples or patterns. In the image domain, Loo et al. [35] innovated a new method to explain why the model made a wrong prediction by calculating the influence of certain distilled samples on the prediction of specific test samples. This approach shows a more significant explanation compared to the influence from training samples. In the graph domain, EXGC [113] prioritizes the most informative nodes in synthetic graphs and iteratively prunes the redundant nodes during the distillation process. To extract patterns with the highest fidelity in graph classification, Nian et al. [114] synthesize interpretive graphs by matching the edge and feature distribution of the original, demonstrating that it contains both data and model fidelity, i.e., the synthetic graph can achieve comparable performance and train a similar model as the original dataset. Explainable distillation would improve transparency and traceability in enterprise AI, aiding in model debugging, compliance, and user trust—especially in regulated sectors like banking or insurance.

2.6 Conclusion

In this chapter, we highlight the significance of developing dataset distillation methods and their application in enterprise AI. These techniques can broaden AI accessibility for various businesses and industry sectors. We offer a systematic taxonomy of current dataset distillation methods, dividing them into four main categories based on optimization objectives: performance matching, gradient matching, trajectory matching, and distribution matching. Additionally, we examine dataset distillation across different modalities, such as image, text, and graph, and underscore the related challenges. These methods should be adaptable to multiple modalities. Furthermore, we delve into the applications of dataset distillation in areas like computationally intensive tasks, privacy preservation, and robustness. Finally, we point out the pitfalls of existing dataset distillation methods and propose potential future research directions.

For readers interested in learning more about dataset distillation, several comprehensive surveys are available in the image domain [99, 115–117] and the graph domain [59]. An open-source benchmark repository for the image domain, called DC-Bench [25], has been developed and includes most of the popular dataset distillation methods.[2] Similarly, a corresponding open-source benchmark repository for the graph domain, named GC4NC [89], contains many of the well-known graph condensation methods.[3] For a comprehensive and up-to-date summary of dataset distillation publications, we recommend readers to refer to the GitHub repository named Awesome-Dataset-Distillation[4] and Awesome-Graph-Reduction.[5]

References

1. Galeon, D.: An ai completed 360,000 hours of finance work in just seconds (2017)
2. Shah, A.: Addressing industry-specific supply chain challenges with AWS supply chain (2024)
3. Johnson, E.: Leveraging ai for predictive maintenance: the future of industrial efficiency (2024)
4. Krizhevsky, A., Sutskever, I., Hinton, G.E.: Imagenet classification with deep convolutional neural networks. In: Advances in Neural Information Processing Systems, vol. 25 (2012)
5. Devlin, J., Chang, M.W., Lee, K., Toutanova, K.: Bert: pre-training of deep bidirectional transformers for language understanding (2018). arXiv preprint arXiv:1810.04805
6. Han, J., Pei, J., Tong, H.: Data Mining: Concepts and Techniques. Morgan Kaufmann, Los Altos (2022)
7. Ghorbani, B., Firat, O., Freitag, M., Bapna, A., Krikun, M., Garcia, X., Chelba, C., Cherry, C.: Scaling laws for neural machine translation (2021). arXiv preprint arXiv:2109.07740
8. Brown, T., Mann, B., Ryder, N., Subbiah, M., Kaplan, J.D., Dhariwal, P., Neelakantan, A., Shyam, P., Sastry, G., Askell, A., et al.: Language models are few-shot learners. In: Advances in Neural Information Processing Systems, vol. 33, 1877–1901 (2020)
9. Gupta, U., Kim, Y.G., Lee, S., Tse, J., Lee, H.H.S., Wei, G.Y., Brooks, D., Wu, C.J.: Chasing carbon: the elusive environmental footprint of computing. In: 2021 IEEE International Symposium on High-Performance Computer Architecture (HPCA), pp. 854–867. IEEE, Piscataway (2021)
10. Castro, F.M., Marín-Jiménez, M.J., Guil, N., Schmid, C., Alahari, K.: End-to-end incremental learning. In: Proceedings of the European Conference on Computer Vision (ECCV), pp. 233–248 (2018)
11. Maclaurin, D., Duvenaud, D., Adams, R.: Gradient-based hyperparameter optimization through reversible learning. In: International Conference on Machine Learning, pp. 2113–2122. PMLR (2015)
12. Liu, H., Simonyan, K., Yang, Y.: Darts: differentiable architecture search (2018). arXiv preprint arXiv:1806.09055
13. Nalepa, J., Kawulok, M.: Selecting training sets for support vector machines: a review. Artif. Intell. Rev. **52**(2), 857–900 (2019)
14. Mirzasoleiman, B., Bilmes, J., Leskovec, J.: Coresets for data-efficient training of machine learning models. In: International Conference on Machine Learning, pp. 6950–6960. PMLR (2020)

[2] https://github.com/justincui03/dc_benchmark

[3] https://github.com/Emory-Melody/GraphSlim/tree/main/benchmark

[4] https://github.com/Guang000/Awesome-Dataset-Distillation

[5] https://github.com/Emory-Melody/awesome-graph-reduction

15. Coleman, C., Yeh, C., Mussmann, S., Mirzasoleiman, B., Bailis, P., Liang, P., Leskovec, J., Zaharia, M.: Selection via proxy: efficient data selection for deep learning (2019). arXiv preprint arXiv:1906.11829
16. Killamsetty, K., Durga, S., Ramakrishnan, G., De, A., Iyer, R.: Grad-match: gradient matching based data subset selection for efficient deep model training. In: International Conference on Machine Learning, pp. 5464–5474. PMLR (2021)
17. Guo, C., Zhao, B., Bai, Y.: Deepcore: a comprehensive library for coreset selection in deep learning. In: International Conference on Database and Expert Systems Applications, pp. 181–195. Springer, Berlin (2022)
18. Li, G., Togo, R., Ogawa, T., Haseyama, M.: Dataset distillation for medical dataset sharing (2022). arXiv preprint arXiv:2209.14603
19. Wang, T., Zhu, J.Y., Torralba, A., Efros, A.A.: Dataset distillation (2018). arXiv preprint arXiv:1811.10959
20. Tran, M.T., Le, T., Le, X.M., Do, T.T., Phung, D.: Enhancing dataset distillation via non-critical region refinement (2025). arXiv preprint arXiv:2503.18267
21. Shen, Z., Sherif, A., Yin, Z., Shao, S.: Delt: a simple diversity-driven early-late training for dataset distillation (2024). arXiv preprint arXiv:2411.19946
22. Zhong, W., Tang, H., Zheng, Q., Xu, M., Hu, Y., Nie, L.: Towards stable and storage-efficient dataset distillation: Matching convexified trajectory (2024). arXiv preprint arXiv:2406.19827
23. Dong, T., Zhao, B., Lyu, L.: Privacy for free: how does dataset condensation help privacy? In: International Conference on Machine Learning, pp. 5378–5396. PMLR (2022)
24. Werbos, P.J.: Backpropagation through time: what it does and how to do it. Proc. IEEE **78**(10), 1550–1560 (1990)
25. Cui, J., Wang, R., Si, S., Hsieh, C.J.: Dc-bench: Dataset condensation benchmark. In: Advances in Neural Information Processing Systems, vol. 35, 810–822 (2022)
26. Sener, O., Savarese, S.: Active learning for convolutional neural networks: a core-set approach (2017). arXiv preprint arXiv:1708.00489
27. Zhou, Y., Nezhadarya, E., Ba, J.: Dataset distillation using neural feature regression. In: Advances in Neural Information Processing Systems, vol. 35, 9813–9827 (2022)
28. Sucholutsky, I., Schonlau, M.: Soft-label dataset distillation and text dataset distillation. In: 2021 International Joint Conference on Neural Networks (IJCNN), pp. 1–8. IEEE, Piscataway (2021)
29. Bohdal, O., Yang, Y., Hospedales, T.: Flexible dataset distillation: learn labels instead of images (2020). arXiv preprint arXiv:2006.08572
30. Deng, Z., Russakovsky, O.: Remember the past: Distilling datasets into addressable memories for neural networks. In: Advances in Neural Information Processing Systems, vol. 35, 34391–34404 (2022)
31. Nguyen, T., Chen, Z., Lee, J.: Dataset meta-learning from kernel ridge-regression (2020). arXiv preprint arXiv:2011.00050
32. Petersen, K.B., Pedersen, M.S., et al.: The matrix cookbook. Tech. Univ. Denmark **7**(15), 510 (2008)
33. Jacot, A., Gabriel, F., Hongler, C.: Neural tangent kernel: convergence and generalization in neural networks. In: Advances in Neural Information Processing Systems, vol. 31 (2018)
34. Nguyen, T., Novak, R., Xiao, L., Lee, J.: Dataset distillation with infinitely wide convolutional networks. In: Advances in Neural Information Processing Systems, vol. 34, 5186–5198 (2021)
35. Loo, N., Hasani, R., Amini, A., Rus, D.: Efficient dataset distillation using random feature approximation. In: Advances in Neural Information Processing Systems, vol. 35, 13877–13891 (2022)
36. Neal, R.M.: Bayesian Learning for Neural Networks, vol. 118. Springer, Berlin (2012)
37. Platt, J., et al.: Probabilistic outputs for support vector machines and comparisons to regularized likelihood methods. Adv. Large Margin Classif. **10**(3), 61–74 (1999)
38. Zhao, B., Mopuri, K.R., Bilen, H.: Dataset condensation with gradient matching (2020). arXiv preprint arXiv:2006.05929

39. Lee, S., Chun, S., Jung, S., Yun, S., Yoon, S.: Dataset condensation with contrastive signals. In: International Conference on Machine Learning, pp. 12352–12364. PMLR (2022)
40. Jiang, Z., Gu, J., Liu, M., Pan, D.Z.: Delving into effective gradient matching for dataset condensation. In: 2023 IEEE International Conference on Omni-layer Intelligent Systems (COINS), pp. 1–6. IEEE, Piscataway (2023)
41. Zhao, B., Bilen, H.: Dataset condensation with differentiable Siamese augmentation. In: International Conference on Machine Learning, pp. 12674–12685. PMLR (2021)
42. Cazenavette, G., Wang, T., Torralba, A., Efros, A.A., Zhu, J.Y.: Dataset distillation by matching training trajectories. In: Proceedings of the IEEE/CVF Conference on Computer Vision and Pattern Recognition, pp. 4750–4759 (2022)
43. Du, J., Jiang, Y., Tan, V.Y., Zhou, J.T., Li, H.: Minimizing the accumulated trajectory error to improve dataset distillation. In: Proceedings of the IEEE/CVF Conference on Computer Vision and Pattern Recognition, pp. 3749–3758 (2023)
44. Cui, J., Wang, R., Si, S., Hsieh, C.J.: Scaling up dataset distillation to imagenet-1k with constant memory. In: International Conference on Machine Learning, pp. 6565–6590. PMLR (2023)
45. Zhao, B., Bilen, H.: Dataset condensation with distribution matching. In: Proceedings of the IEEE/CVF Winter Conference on Applications of Computer Vision, pp. 6514–6523 (2023)
46. Gretton, A., Borgwardt, K.M., Rasch, M.J., Schölkopf, B., Smola, A.: A kernel two-sample test. J. Mach. Learn. Res. **13**(1), 723–773 (2012)
47. Wang, K., Zhao, B., Peng, X., Zhu, Z., Yang, S., Wang, S., Huang, G., Bilen, H., Wang, X., You, Y.: Cafe: learning to condense dataset by aligning features. In: Proceedings of the IEEE/CVF Conference on Computer Vision and Pattern Recognition, pp. 12196–12205 (2022)
48. Geiping, J., Goldstein, T.: Cramming: training a language model on a single GPU in one day. In: International Conference on Machine Learning, pp. 11117–11143. PMLR (2023)
49. Li, Y., Li, W.: Data distillation for text classification (2021). arXiv preprint arXiv:2104.08448
50. Pennington, J., Socher, R., Manning, C.D.: Glove: global vectors for word representation. In: Proceedings of the 2014 Conference on Empirical Methods in Natural Language Processing (EMNLP), pp. 1532–1543 (2014)
51. Maekawa, A., Kobayashi, N., Funakoshi, K., Okumura, M.: Dataset distillation with attention labels for fine-tuning bert. In: Proceedings of the 61st Annual Meeting of the Association for Computational Linguistics (Volume 2: Short Papers), pp. 119–127 (2023)
52. Maekawa, A., Kosugi, S., Funakoshi, K., Okumura, M.: Dilm: distilling dataset into language model for text-level dataset distillation (2024). arXiv preprint arXiv:2404.00264
53. Fan, W., Ma, Y., Li, Q., He, Y., Zhao, E., Tang, J., Yin, D.: Graph neural networks for social recommendation. In: The World Wide Web Conference, pp. 417–426 (2019)
54. Reiser, P., Neubert, M., Eberhard, A., Torresi, L., Zhou, C., Shao, C., Metni, H., van Hoesel, C., Schopmans, H., Sommer, T., et al.: Graph neural networks for materials science and chemistry. Commun. Mater. **3**(1), 93 (2022)
55. Liu, Z., Wan, G., Prakash, B.A., Lau, M.S., Jin, W.: A review of graph neural networks in epidemic modeling (2024). arXiv preprint arXiv:2403.19852
56. Wang, Y., Zhao, Y., Zhang, Y., Derr, T.: Collaboration-aware graph convolutional network for recommender systems. In: Proceedings of the ACM Web Conference 2023, pp. 91–101 (2023)
57. Hu, W., Fey, M., Ren, H., Nakata, M., Dong, Y., Leskovec, J.: Ogb-lsc: a large-scale challenge for machine learning on graphs (2021). arXiv preprint arXiv:2103.09430
58. Jin, W., Zhao, L., Zhang, S., Liu, Y., Tang, J., Shah, N.: Graph condensation for graph neural networks (2021). arXiv preprint arXiv:2110.07580
59. Hashemi, M., Gong, S., Ni, J., Fan, W., Prakash, B.A., Jin, W.: A comprehensive survey on graph reduction: sparsification, coarsening, and condensation (2024). arXiv preprint arXiv:2402.03358
60. Jin, W., Tang, X., Jiang, H., Li, Z., Zhang, D., Tang, J., Yin, B.: Condensing graphs via one-step gradient matching. In: Proceedings of the 28th ACM SIGKDD Conference on Knowledge Discovery and Data Mining, pp. 720–730 (2022)

61. Zheng, X., Zhang, M., Chen, C., Nguyen, Q.V.H., Zhu, X., Pan, S.: Structure-free graph condensation: From large-scale graphs to condensed graph-free data. In: Advances in Neural Information Processing Systems, vol. 36 (2024)
62. Wang, L., Fan, W., Li, J., Ma, Y., Li, Q.: Fast graph condensation with structure-based neural tangent kernel (2023). arXiv preprint arXiv:2310.11046
63. Gao, J., Wu, J.: Multiple sparse graphs condensation. Knowl.-Based Syst. **278**, 110904 (2023)
64. Yang, B., Wang, K., Sun, Q., Ji, C., Fu, X., Tang, H., You, Y., Li, J.: Does graph distillation see like vision dataset counterpart? In Advances in Neural Information Processing Systems, vol. 36 (2024)
65. Zhang, Y., Zhang, T., Wang, K., Guo, Z., Liang, Y., Bresson, X., Jin, W., You, Y.: Navigating complexity: toward lossless graph condensation via expanding window matching (2024). arXiv preprint arXiv:2402.05011
66. Liu, M., Li, S., Chen, X., Song, L.: Graph condensation via receptive field distribution matching (2022). arXiv preprint arXiv:2206.13697
67. Gong, S., Hashemi, M., Ni, J., Yang, C., Jin, W.: Scalable graph condensation with evolving capabilities (2025). arXiv preprint arXiv:2502.17614
68. Sachdeva, N., Dhaliwal, M., Wu, C.J., McAuley, J.: Infinite recommendation networks: A data-centric approach. In: Advances in Neural Information Processing Systems, vol. 35, 31292–31305 (2022)
69. Jang, E., Gu, S., Poole, B.: Categorical reparameterization with gumbel-softmax (2016). arXiv preprint arXiv:1611.01144
70. Liu, Z., Hao, K., Zheng, G., Yu, Y.: Dataset condensation for time series classification via dual domain matching (2024). arXiv preprint arXiv:2403.07245
71. Ni, J., Liu, Z., Wang, S., Jin, M., Jin, W.: Timedistill: efficient long-term time series forecasting with mlp via cross-architecture distillation (2025). arXiv preprint arXiv:2502.15016
72. Liu, Z., Ni, J., Lau, M.S., Jin, W.: Cape: covariate-adjusted pre-training for epidemic time series forecasting (2025). arXiv preprint arXiv:2502.03393
73. Ding, J., Liu, Z., Zheng, G., Jin, H., Kong, L.: Condtsf: One-line plugin of dataset condensation for time series forecasting (2024). arXiv preprint arXiv:2406.02131
74. Jin, M., Wen, Q., Liang, Y., Zhang, C., Xue, S., Wang, X., Zhang, J., Wang, Y., Chen, H., Li, X., et al.: Large models for time series and spatio-temporal data: a survey and outlook (2023). arXiv preprint arXiv:2310.10196
75. Liang, Y., Wen, H., Nie, Y., Jiang, Y., Jin, M., Song, D., Pan, S., Wen, Q.: Foundation models for time series analysis: a tutorial and survey (2024). arXiv preprint arXiv:2403.14735
76. Wang, Z., Xu, Y., Lu, C., Li, Y.L.: Dancing with still images: video distillation via static-dynamic disentanglement. In: Proceedings of the IEEE/CVF Conference on Computer Vision and Pattern Recognition, pp. 6296–6304 (2024)
77. Wu, X., Zhang, B., Deng, Z., Russakovsky, O.: Vision-language dataset distillation (2023)
78. Cao, M., Li, S., Li, J., Nie, L., Zhang, M.: Image-text retrieval: a survey on recent research and development (2022). arXiv preprint arXiv:2203.14713
79. De Lange, M., Aljundi, R., Masana, M., Parisot, S., Jia, X., Leonardis, A., Slabaugh, G., Tuytelaars, T.: A continual learning survey: defying forgetting in classification tasks. IEEE Trans. Pattern Anal. Mach. Intell. **44**(7), 3366–3385 (2021)
80. White, C., Safari, M., Sukthanker, R., Ru, B., Elsken, T., Zela, A., Dey, D., Hutter, F.: Neural architecture search: insights from 1000 papers (2023). arXiv preprint arXiv:2301.08727
81. Chen, Z., Liu, B.: Lifelong Machine Learning. Springer, Berlin (2022)
82. French, R.M.: Catastrophic forgetting in connectionist networks. Trends Cogn. Sci. **3**(4), 128–135 (1999)
83. Rosasco, A., Carta, A., Cossu, A., Lomonaco, V., Bacciu, D.: Distilled replay: overcoming forgetting through synthetic samples. In: International Workshop on Continual Semi-Supervised Learning, pp. 104–117. Springer, Berlin (2021)
84. Yang, E., Shen, L., Wang, Z., Liu, T., Guo, G.: An efficient dataset condensation plugin and its application to continual learning. In: Advances in Neural Information Processing Systems, vol. 36 (2023)

85. Liu, Y., Qiu, R., Huang, Z.: Cat: Balanced continual graph learning with graph condensation. In: 2023 IEEE International Conference on Data Mining (ICDM), pp. 1157–1162. IEEE, Piscataway (2023)
86. White, C., Neiswanger, W., Savani, Y.: Bananas: Bayesian optimization with neural architectures for neural architecture search. In: Proceedings of the AAAI Conference on Artificial Intelligence, vol. 35, pp. 10293–10301 (2021)
87. Yan, S., Zheng, Y., Ao, W., Zeng, X., Zhang, M.: Does unsupervised architecture representation learning help neural architecture search? In: Advances in Neural Information Processing Systems, vol. 33, 12486–12498 (2020)
88. Dong, X., Yang, Y.: Nas-bench-201: extending the scope of reproducible neural architecture search (2020). arXiv preprint arXiv:2001.00326
89. Gong, S., Ni, J., Sachdeva, N., Yang, C., Jin, W.: Gc-bench: a benchmark framework for graph condensation with new insights (2024). https://arxiv.org/abs/2406.16715
90. Dwork, C.: Differential privacy: a survey of results. In: International conference on theory and applications of models of computation, pp. 1–19. Springer, Berlin (2008)
91. Chen, D., Kerkouche, R., Fritz, M.: Private set generation with discriminative information. In Advances in Neural Information Processing Systems, vol. 35, 14678–14690 (2022)
92. Liu, B., Lv, N., Guo, Y., Li, Y.: Recent advances on federated learning: a systematic survey. Neurocomputing **597**, 128019 (2024)
93. Pei, J., Liu, W., Li, J., Wang, L., Liu, C.: A review of federated learning methods in heterogeneous scenarios. IEEE Trans. Consum. Electron. **70**(3), 5983–5999 (2024)
94. Goetz, J., Tewari, A.: Federated learning via synthetic data (2020). https://arxiv.org/abs/2008.04489
95. Hu, S., Goetz, J., Malik, K., Zhan, H., Liu, Z., Liu, Y.: Fedsynth: gradient compression via synthetic data in federated learning (2022). https://arxiv.org/abs/2204.01273
96. Zhou, Y., Pu, G., Ma, X., Li, X., Wu, D.: Distilled one-shot federated learning (2020). arXiv preprint arXiv:2009.07999
97. Pan, Q., Wu, R., Tengfei, L., Zhang, T., Zhu, Y., Wang, W.: Fedgkd: unleashing the power of collaboration in federated graph neural networks. In: NeurIPS 2023 Workshop: New Frontiers in Graph Learning (2023)
98. Li, G., Togo, R., Ogawa, T., Haseyama, M.: Compressed gastric image generation based on soft-label dataset distillation for medical data sharing. Comput. Methods Progr. Biomed. **227**, 107189 (2022)
99. Yu, R., Liu, S., Wang, X.: Dataset distillation: a comprehensive review. IEEE Trans. Pattern Anal. Mach. Intell. **46**, 150–170 (2024)
100. Medvedev, D., D'yakonov, A.: New properties of the data distillation method when working with tabular data. In: Analysis of Images, Social Networks and Texts: 9th International Conference, AIST 2020, Skolkovo, Moscow, Russia, October 15–16, 2020, Revised Selected Papers 9, pp. 379–390. Springer, Berlin (2021)
101. Ritter-Gutierrez, F., Huang, K.P., Wong, J.H., Ng, D., Lee, H.y., Chen, N.F., Chng, E.S.: Dataset-distillation generative model for speech emotion recognition (2024). arXiv preprint arXiv:2406.02963
102. Zhao, Z.Q., Zheng, P., Xu, S.t., Wu, X.: Object detection with deep learning: a review. IEEE Trans. Neural Netw. Learn. Syst. **30**(11), 3212–3232 (2019)
103. Qi, D., Li, J., Peng, J., Zhao, B., Dou, S., Li, J., Zhang, J., Wang, Y., Wang, C., Zhao, C.: Fetch and forge: efficient dataset condensation for object detection. In: Proceedings of the Advances in Neural Information Processing Systems (NeurIPS) (2024)
104. Long, J., Shelhamer, E., Darrell, T.: Fully convolutional networks for semantic segmentation. In: Proceedings of the IEEE Conference on Computer Vision and Pattern Recognition, pp. 3431–3440 (2015)
105. Bahdanau, D., Cho, K., Bengio, Y.: Neural machine translation by jointly learning to align and translate (2014). arXiv preprint arXiv:1409.0473
106. Jia, J., Zhang, Y., Song, D., Liu, S., Hero, A.: Robustness-preserving lifelong learning via dataset condensation. In: ICASSP 2023-2023 IEEE International Conference on Acoustics, Speech and Signal Processing (ICASSP), pp. 1–5. IEEE, Piscataway (2023)

107. Zheng, T., Li, B.: Rdm-dc: poisoning resilient dataset condensation with robust distribution matching. In: Uncertainty in Artificial Intelligence, pp. 2541–2550. PMLR (2023)
108. Ma, S., Zhu, F., Cheng, Z., Zhang, X.Y.: Towards trustworthy dataset distillation (2023). arXiv preprint arXiv:2307.09165
109. Gao, X., Yin, H., Chen, T., Ye, G., Zhang, W., Cui, B.: Robgc: towards robust graph condensation (2024). https://arxiv.org/abs/2406.13200
110. Gao, X., Chen, T., Zhang, W., Li, Y., Sun, X., Yin, H.: Graph condensation for open-world graph learning (2024). https://arxiv.org/abs/2405.17003
111. Zhang, L., Zhang, J., Lei, B., Mukherjee, S., Pan, X., Zhao, B., Ding, C., Li, Y., Xu, D.: Accelerating dataset distillation via model augmentation. In: Proceedings of the IEEE/CVF Conference on Computer Vision and Pattern Recognition, pp. 11950–11959 (2023)
112. Došilović, F.K., Brčić, M., Hlupić, N.: Explainable artificial intelligence: a survey. In: 2018 41st International Convention on Information and Communication Technology, Electronics And Microelectronics (MIPRO), pp. 0210–0215. IEEE, Piscataway (2018)
113. Fang, J., Li, X., Sui, Y., Gao, Y., Zhang, G., Wang, K., Wang, X., He, X.: Exgc: bridging efficiency and explainability in graph condensation. In: Proceedings of the ACM on Web Conference 2024, pp. 721–732 (2024)
114. Nian, Y., Chang, Y., Jin, W., Lin, L.: Globally interpretable graph learning via distribution matching. In: Proceedings of the ACM on Web Conference 2024, WWW '24. ACM, New York (2024). https://doi.org/10.1145/3589334.3645674
115. Geng, J., Chen, Z., Wang, Y., Woisetschlaeger, H., Schimmler, S., Mayer, R., Zhao, Z., Rong, C.: A survey on dataset distillation: approaches, applications and future directions (2023). arXiv preprint arXiv:2305.01975
116. Lei, S., Tao, D.: A comprehensive survey of dataset distillation. IEEE Trans. Pattern Anal. Mach. Intell. **46**, 17–32 (2024)
117. Sachdeva, N., McAuley, J.: Data distillation: a survey (2023). arXiv preprint arXiv:2301.04272
118. Hu, E.J., Shen, Y., Wallis, P., Allen-Zhu, Z., Li, Y., Wang, S., Wang, L., Chen, W.: Lora: low-rank adaptation of large language models (2021). arXiv preprint arXiv:2106.09685

Juntong Ni is a PhD student in the Department of Computer Science at Emory University. His research focuses on dataset distillation, time series analysis, and multimodal foundation models. He has published in top-tier conferences such as KDD, IJCAI, and ACM MM, including notable work on dataset distillation for graph data. He also regularly serves as a program committee member for leading conferences, including KDD, NeurIPS, WWW, AAAI, and ICLR.

Shengbo Gong is a PhD student in the Department of Computer Science at Emory University. His research interests include dataset distillation, graph neural networks, and representation learning. He has published in top-tier venues such as *TPAMI*, IJCAI, and CIKM, with notable work on dataset distillation for graph data. He also regularly serves as a program committee member for leading conferences including KDD, NeurIPS, WWW, AAAI, ICLR, CIKM, and WWW.

Wei Jin is an Assistant Professor at Emory University. His research centres on graph machine learning and efficient machine learning, with significant contributions to dataset distillation through several signature works. His accomplishments include the NIH R01Award, KAUST Rising Stars in AI, INNS Doctoral Dissertation Runner-up Award, Snap Research Fellowship, Most Influential Papers in KDD and WWW by *Paper Digest*, the Fitch H. Beach Award, and top finishes in three NeurIPS competitions. He has also organized multiple workshops at leading conferences including WWW, KDD, ECCV, and CIKM and has published extensively in premier venues such as KDD, ICLR, ICML, NeurIPS, WWW, and AAAI.

Chapter 3
Federated Learning for Enterprise AI

Ben Tan, Yan Kang, Lixin Fan, and Vincent Zheng

Abstract Modern enterprises operate in a data-driven world where sensitive data (e.g., customer information, intellectual property, financial records) are both a critical asset and a significant liability. Although leveraging these data can unlock innovation, improve decision-making, and personalize customer experiences, mishandling it risks breaches, regulatory penalties, and loss of trust. How to maximize data utility while ensuring privacy and security is a core challenge in enterprise AI. Federated learning (FL) has emerged as a groundbreaking paradigm in the realm, effectively addressing critical data privacy and security concerns while facilitating the collaborative development of robust AI models. Its versatility and effectiveness have been demonstrated across various industries, including healthcare, finance, advertising, and personalized recommendations, where it has been successfully employed to address data heterogeneity and privacy concerns. This chapter aims to provide a comprehensive introduction to the fundamental concepts of FL, encompassing categorization, formulation, and challenges. We will also utilize a federated recommendation system as a case study to illustrate the application of FL in real-world scenarios with diverse settings. Furthermore, we will explore the role of federated learning in refining and adapting large foundation models to meet industrial requirements. By grasping the fundamental concepts and applications of FL, readers can gain a thorough understanding of this approach and select the most suitable techniques for their specific use cases.

3.1 Introduction

Data is one of the most fundamental components of enterprise AI. It enables organizations to uncover patterns, predict trends, and automate complex tasks at scale. For instance, retail giants leverage customer behavior data to personalized

B. Tan (✉) · Y. Kang · L. Fan · V. Zheng
Webank, China
e-mail: btan@connect.ust.hk; yangkang@webank.com; lixinfan@webank.com; vincentz@webank.com

S. Sadiq (ed.), *Enterprise AI*, https://doi.org/10.1007/978-3-032-01940-0_3

recommendations, while financial institutions rely on transactional data to detect fraud. In healthcare, patient data drives diagnostic accuracy, and in manufacturing, sensor data optimizes supply chains. The more comprehensive and representative the dataset, the more accurate and generalizable the AI model becomes. Yet enterprises often operate in data-rich but fragmented environments, where information resides across departments, institutes, regions, or devices. Aggregating this data into centralized repositories for model training exposes organizations to risks such as breaches, unauthorized access, and regulatory noncompliance, raising significant privacy, legal, and security concerns. Regulations like the General Data Protection Regulation (GDPR) and the California Consumer Privacy Act (CCPA) impose strict requirements on data handling, mandating transparency, user consent, and stringent safeguards. Furthermore, even internal data sharing can create vulnerabilities, as centralized storage becomes a high-value target for attacks. These concerns often force enterprises to silo their data and limit collaboration. Traditional cloud-based AI approaches, which require raw data to be uploaded to third-party servers, exacerbate these risks.

Federated learning (FL) emerges as a groundbreaking privacy-preserving collaborative machine learning paradigm that enables multiple entities (e.g., devices, organizations) to collaboratively develop robust machine learning models without the need to collect or centrally store their raw data. FL was initially introduced by Google in 2016 [1, 2]. It was designed for cross-device scenarios, where thousands to millions of mobile devices collaboratively train a shared model under the coordination of a central server. In this setup, each device computes model updates using its local data (e.g., typing patterns, app usage), which are then securely aggregated at the server to refine the global model. This approach addressed critical challenges in mobile ecosystems, such as data privacy regulations, bandwidth constraints, and the impracticality of transmitting sensitive user data to a central repository. Over time, FL has evolved beyond its original scope to encompass cross-silo learning scenarios among organizations [3]. In cross-silo FL, trusted organizations, such as hospitals, banks, or smart retails, jointly train a model while keeping their data within their own infrastructure. For example, in this setup, multiple hospitals collaborate to improve a disease prediction model using patient records that cannot leave their respective institutions. Banks can collaborate on fraud detection models without exposing proprietary transaction details, while smart retails jointly optimize product recommendations using users' preference in different markets.

This chapter is structured to provide readers with a comprehensive picture of federated learning. We begin by laying the groundwork in Sect. 3.2, where we introduce the fundamental concepts and categories of federated learning, as well as the challenges it encounters. Next, in Sect. 3.3, we venture into the practical use case of this innovative paradigm. FL's ability to address privacy and security concerns while enhancing model performance has significant implications for various industries. In this section, we illuminate the practical deployment of FL in recommendation systems, which suggest relevant items to users by using user preferences data. We explain how FL can provide personalized services without compromising user privacy. This section will explore the nuances of federated recommender systems (FedRec), which include horizontal, vertical, and transfer FedRec, and discuss their respective roles in shaping modern e-commerce strategies. Finally, in Sect. 3.4, we broaden our perspective to encompass the integration of FL with large-scale foundation models, such as those used in language processing and computer vision. This section will elucidate the mechanisms by which FL is applied to refine and adapt large foundation models to specific industrial needs, thereby enhancing their applicability and effectiveness. The discussion will include the optimization of domain models, foundation models, and both through federated transfer learning, highlighting the synergistic relationship between general and specialized machine learning models in solving complex, real-world problems.

3.2 Basics of Federated Learning

Federated learning is delineated into three categories based on the distribution of data across samples and features [3], as shown in Fig. 3.1. They are horizontal federated learning (HFL), vertical federated learning (VFL), and federated transfer

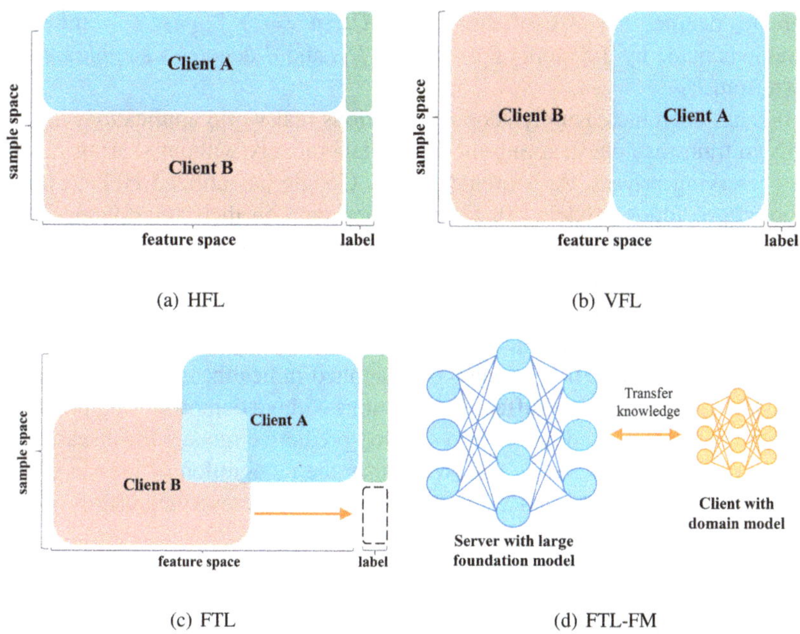

Fig. 3.1 Four settings of federated learning. The HFL, VFL, and FTL are traditional categories as defined in [3]. FTL-FM denotes the FTL paradigm in the Large Model Era, which essentially involves grounding foundation models (FM) through FTL, as discussed in [4]

learning (FTL). In this section, we introduce the fundamental concepts of federated learning and also summarize the challenges that federated learning faces.

3.2.1 Horizontal Federated Learning

In horizontal federated learning (HFL) [1], participating clients contribute to the model training process by utilizing a common set of features despite having distinct data samples. An illustrative example of this is Google's application to enable mobile phone users to train a predictive model for next-word suggestions collaboratively as illustrated in Fig. 3.1a. The objective of the K participating clients in HFL is to collaboratively build a global model, θ, based on their respective private datasets. As formulated by McMahan et al. [1], the federated optimization problem in HFL can be expressed as:

$$\arg\min_{\theta} L(\theta, \mathcal{D}_{i\in\{1,\ldots,K\}}) = \sum_{k=1}^{K} \frac{n_k}{n} \mathbb{E}_{d\sim\mathcal{D}_k} \ell(\theta, d), \tag{3.1}$$

where n_k denotes the size of the dataset $\mathcal{D}_k$, $n = \sum_{k=1}^{K} n_k$, ℓ is the loss of predictions made by the model θ on dataset $\mathcal{D}_k$, and d denotes a sample randomly drawn from $\mathcal{D}_k$.

HFL has been increasingly adopted in various real-world applications due to its ability to train machine learning models collaboratively without sharing raw data, thus preserving privacy. As aforementioned, Google has utilized HFL to improve keyboard prediction models [5]. Users' typing data on their smartphones is used to train the model, with the learning happening locally on the device to ensure privacy. With the proliferation of IoT devices, HFL is used to train models on data collected from these devices without the need to aggregate the data centrally. This is particularly useful for applications like smart home systems, wearable devices, and industrial IoT [6]. HFL has also been applied in healthcare to train models on sensitive patient data across different institutions without compromising privacy. For instance, hospitals can collaborate to develop predictive models for diseases while keeping patient records secure and to enhance the recognition of human activities using data from wearable devices, with an emphasis on preserving user privacy [7].

3.2.2 Vertical Federated Learning

Vertical federated learning (VFL) [8], on the other hand, involves a scenario where the datasets from different participants include the same set of samples or users. But the set of samples or users has different feature attributes. A case in point is a bank of VFL to partner with an invoice company in the development of financial risk assessment models tailored for their corporate clients. In this setting, all participating clients can be regarded as leveraging a virtual dataset, denoted by $\mathcal{D} = \{(\mathbf{x}_i, y_i)\}_{i=1}^N$, comprising N samples, to collaboratively train a joint machine learning model, Θ, while maintaining the privacy of their local data.

Following [8], each feature vector $\mathbf{x}_i \in \mathbb{R}^{1\times m}$ in $\mathcal{D}$ is distributed among K parties $\{\mathbf{x}_{i,k} \in \mathbb{R}^{1\times m_k}\}_{k=1}^K$, where m_k is the feature dimension of party k, for $k \in [K-1]$, and the Kth party has the label information $y_i = y_{i,K}$, as illustrated in Fig. 3.1b. The Kth party who owns the labels is typically referred to as the *active party*, while the rest of the clients are referred to as *passive parties*. Each passive party k has dataset $\mathcal{D}_k = \{\mathbf{x}_{i,k}\}_{i=1}^N$, while the active party has dataset $\mathcal{D}_K = \{\mathbf{x}_{i,K}, y_{i,K}\}_{i=1}^N$.

To precisely formulate the optimization problem of VFL, we decompose Θ into local models $\mathcal{G}_k$ parameterized by θ_k, $k \in \{1, \cdots, K\}$, which operates only on local data, and a global model $\mathcal{F}_K$ parameterized by ψ_K, accessible only to the active party K. The optimization problem of VFL can thus be formally expressed as follows:

$$\arg\min_{\Theta} L(\Theta; \mathcal{D}) = \mathbb{E}_{(\mathbf{x}, y_K)\sim\mathcal{D}} \ell\left(\mathcal{F}_K\left(\psi_K; \mathcal{G}_1(\mathbf{x}_1, \theta_1), \ldots, \mathcal{G}_K(\mathbf{x}_K, \theta_K)\right), y_K\right) \tag{3.2}$$

where Θ denotes the joint ML model, $\ell(\cdot)$ denotes the loss function, and L denotes the task objective (e.g., mean squared error loss for regression tasks and cross-entropy loss for classification tasks).

In the financial field, VFL has found widespread application in areas such as marketing and risk management. Due to the limited availability of high-quality data, financial institutions often rely on external sources to enhance their risk assessment models. However, the growing emphasis on data privacy and the implementation of stringent regulations in many countries have made it increasingly challenging to access alternative data, including sensitive information about individuals' creditworthiness, purchasing habits, and preferences, which are typically held by e-commerce platforms and social media companies. In response, VFL has emerged as a solution to facilitate collaborative modeling across institutions while respecting data privacy constraints. For example, Secureboost [9, 10], a novel VFL version of XGboost [11] and LightGBM [12], has been widely used in risk assessment applications by banks and financial institutions.

In conventional vertical federated learning (VFL), the alignment of all parties' training data referencing identical entities is a prerequisite for model training. However, in many real-world applications, aligned training data is in short supply, and labeled data is often scarce. To address these limitations, researchers have turned to self-supervised and semi-supervised VFL approaches. Self-supervised VFL methods such as VFed-SSD [13], FedHSSL [14], and SS-VFNAS [15] leverage contrastive learning and autoencoders to pretrain parties' local models using unlabeled data, which are then fine-tuned with labeled data. Semi-supervised VFL methods, including FedCVT [16] and FedMC [17], seek to improve VFL model performance by expanding labeled and aligned samples through pseudo-labeling or estimating labeled samples.

3.2.3 *Federated Transfer Learning*

Federated transfer learning (FTL) [3] is originally characterized by datasets that are varied in both the sample and feature dimensions, with only minimal overlaps. An example of FTL is the collaborative construction of Brain-Computer Interface (BCI) models using EEG data from various subjects with diverse distributions facilitated by FTL. With the advent of large foundation models, the concept of FTL is extended to include transferring knowledge between foundation models and domain-specific models [4]. FTL seeks to transfer knowledge from source domain parties to target domain parties, thereby enabling the target parties to develop improved machine learning models without compromising the privacy of all parties' local data.

Traditional FTL is characterized by its capacity to accommodate datasets that exhibit significant heterogeneity in both sample size and feature dimensions [3], as illustrated in Fig. 3.1c. Specifically, in traditional FTL, a source domain party with a substantial corpus of labeled data is utilized to augment the performance of a target domain party with limited or no labeled data, thereby enhancing the machine learning model owned by the target party. These traditional approaches involve the learning of a shared latent representation space, which facilitates the transfer of knowledge from the source domain to the target domain.

The advent of large language and vision models has expanded the purview of FTL, enabling the transfer of knowledge from a large language or vision model owned by a server to much smaller domain-specific models of clients, with the ultimate goal of enhancing the performance of domain models on specific tasks by harnessing the capabilities of large models [4], as illustrated in Fig. 3.1d.

3.2.3.1 Traditional Federated Transfer Learning

Traditional federated transfer learning (FTL) typically involves an active party from the source domain possessing a substantial collection of labeled data, and a passive party from the target domain usually has access to a limited number of labeled samples or solely unlabeled data. Traditional FTL methods often rely on VFL as a bridge to facilitate knowledge transfer from the active to the passive party. According to [8], the objective of traditional FTL can be formally defined as follows:

$$\min_{\phi_B,\theta_B} \ell_B(\phi_B;\theta_B;\mathcal{D}_B) + \lambda_1\ell_A(\psi_A,\theta_A,\theta_B;\mathcal{D}_A) + \lambda_2\ell_{\text{TL}}(\theta_A,\theta_B;\mathcal{D}_A,\mathcal{D}_B) \tag{3.3}$$

where ψ_A and ϕ_B are the predictors of the active party A and passive party B, respectively. θ_A and θ_B are the backbone models of the active party A and passive party B, respectively. The transfer learning loss, ℓ_{TL}, is designed to mitigate the discrepancy between the source and target domains. In parallel, party A's loss function, ℓ_A, is employed to train models using labeled samples from the source domain. The synergy between these two losses facilitates the transfer of knowledge from the source domain to the target domain. Furthermore, party B leverages its task-specific loss, ℓ_B, to adapt the transferred knowledge to its local task, utilizing target domain samples, $\mathcal{D}_B$, if available. The involvement of party A' in the inference process depends on the specific requirements of the application.

3.2.3.2 Federated Transfer Learning in the Era of Large Models

With the advent of large foundation models, the concept of FTL is extended to include transferring knowledge from large language or vision models to domain-specific models, as illustrated in Fig. 3.1d. FTL enables domain-specific models to leverage the knowledge and expertise gained from large-scale models such as ChatGPT, which are pre-trained on a massive corpus of text data, to train a smaller, domain-specific NLP model for a specific task, such as sentiment analysis or named entity recognition.

For example, small- or medium-sized companies can use ChatGPT as a teacher to train a smaller domain model that is specifically designed to analyze customer reviews and sentiment. The domain model can learn to recognize patterns and relationships in customer feedback, such as identifying common complaints or praising phrases, without having to be trained on the entire corpus of text data. This approach significantly reduces data volume and computational resources needed for training domain-specific models. Crucially, it still maintains high accuracy and preserves the privacy of companies' sensitive proprietary data. Transfer and adapt the knowledge of a large foundation model θ_{FM}^S (FM strands for foundation model) hosted by a server to help enhance clients' DMs for their specific tasks [4].

$$\begin{aligned} &\underset{\theta_1,\ldots,\theta_K}{\arg\min}\, \mathcal{L}(\theta_{\mathrm{FM}}^S, \theta_1, \ldots, \theta_K) = \sum_{k=1}^{K} p_k \ell_k(\theta_{\mathrm{FM}}^S, \theta_k), \\ &\text{where} \quad \ell_k(\theta_{\mathrm{FM}}^S, \theta_k) = \mathbb{E}_{d\sim\mathcal{D}_k}[\ell_k(\theta_{\mathrm{FM}}^S, \theta_k; d)], k \in \{1, ..., K\} \end{aligned} \tag{3.4}$$

where $\ell_k(\theta_{\mathrm{FM}}^S, \theta_k)$ is the expected loss over the dataset $\mathcal{D}_k$, aiming to transfer and adapt the general knowledge and abilities of θ_{FM}^S to client k's domain model θ_k for a domain-specific task; p_k is preference toward the loss of client k.

The benefits of leveraging FTL to ground domain-specific models are numerous. For example, FTL allows for faster and more efficient training of domain-specific models while also enabling the reuse of knowledge and expertise gained from large models; FTL can also help reduce the risk of overfitting, as the smaller model learns from a larger, more generalizable model; FTL can facilitate the development of more specialized and accurate models for specific domains, leading to improved performance and decision-making in those domains.

3.2.4 Challenges in Federated Learning

The primary driver behind the adoption of federated learning (FL) is its capacity to enable the collaborative training of a machine learning model that outperforms those trained by individual participants while maintaining the privacy of their data. As FL research and applications continue to evolve, new challenges have arisen. Notably, unprotected FL algorithms have been found to be susceptible to gradient-based privacy attacks, such as deep leakage from gradients [18]. To develop a trustworthy FL system, it is imperative to consider a range of factors beyond mere model performance. The literature has identified several essential criteria that a trustworthy FL system should satisfy [19–21]. From an algorithmic standpoint, we distill the key aspects that are critical to ensuring trustworthy FL as privacy, utility, efficiency, robustness, fairness, and intellectual property.

The first is privacy. The protection of participants' private data is essential to thwart privacy attacks by adversaries, as privacy is a fundamental requirement for trustworthy federated learning. To ensure data privacy in FL, techniques such as differential privacy (DP), secure multi-party computation (MPC), and homomorphic encryption are being used to protect data during the training process. For instance, Google's system employs DP and secure aggregation to enhance privacy [22].

The second is utility. Optimizing the performance of the federated learning model on test data is crucial, as any protection mechanism employed may compromise utility. This may lead to a trade-off between preserving privacy and minimizing utility loss [23, 24]. To optimize model performance without compromising privacy, approaches like adaptive randomization, model compression, quantization, and knowledge distillation are being explored.

The third is efficiency. Federated learning models should be trained and make inferences within a reasonable and controlled computational and communication cost. However, implementing protection mechanisms may decrease efficiency, potentially leading to a trade-off between privacy protection and efficiency. In the era of large models, efficiency is critical to the success of grounding large foundation models. To improve efficiency, research has investigated a range of areas, including asynchronous coordination, one-shot communication, compression, and client selection, with the aim of reducing the communication and computational costs associated with FL. In recent years, with the growing popularity of large language and vision models, the focus of research has shifted toward parameter-efficient fine-tuning methods, such as LoRA [25], which enable the conservation of resources during the training or fine-tuning of large models.

The fourth is robustness. A robust federated learning system should withstand extreme conditions, including malicious attacks and heterogeneous data distributions among participating parties. To build robust FL systems, research is being conducted on defense mechanisms against adversarial attacks and strategies to handle heterogeneous data distributions. This includes the development of robust aggregation methods that can identify and mitigate the effects of compromised or biased data [26].

The fifth is fairness. It is a crucial aspect of federated learning, as it directly impacts participants' willingness to engage in the process. Fairness in FL is mainly defined from two angles: firstly, the performance of the federated learning model should be optimized on each participant's test data, and secondly, the payoff should be distributed fairly among participants based on their contributions to the federation, as highlighted in previous research [27, 28]. Fairness in FL is being addressed by designing algorithms that ensure the model performs well across all participants' data and by developing incentive mechanisms that reward participants based on their contributions. For example, q-Fair Federated Learning (q-FFL) [29] is an optimization algorithm that adjusts weights to ensure a fair distribution of model accuracy across devices.

The last is intellectual property. The intellectual property rights associated with private models must be safeguarded, traced, and audited to prevent valuable model assets from being stolen or breached, thereby ensuring IP-right security. Protecting intellectual property in FL is achieved through techniques that allow for model traceability and auditing. Watermarking [30] technology is being explored for its potential to provide a secure and transparent record of model contributions and usage, thus protecting IP rights.

3.3 Federated Recommendation Systems

Recommender systems (RecSys) are essential tools for tackling information overload across various real-world applications. In the context of e-commerce, for instance, a RecSys meticulously analyzes user preferences by examining their past behaviors and interactions with products. By doing so, the system can accurately identify and select the most appropriate items from a vast pool of products, ensuring that users' personalized requirements are met with precision. Given the potentially enormous number of users and products involved in online transactions, RecSys not only enhances the overall user experience but also significantly reduces the costs of product selection, saving both time and effort for users.

In order to provide accurate and tailored recommendations, RecSys needs to gather as much information as possible about users. This often includes collecting various types of private user data, such as behavioral information, contextual details, item metadata, purchase history, recommendation feedback, social data, and more. In the quest for delivering superior recommendations, some systems go a step further by integrating multiple data sources from different organizations. This approach allows the system to gain a more comprehensive understanding of users' preferences and needs, ultimately enhancing the quality of recommendations. To support various recommendation services, all this valuable user data is typically stored in a centralized database managed by one organization.

Despite the advantages of data centralization in RecSys, it can also give rise to significant privacy and security concerns. For instance, some organizations may collect users' private data without consent and share this information with third parties for profit. Additionally, there is a risk of privacy leaks during data transmission. In recent years, several regulations have been enacted to protect privacy and security, such as the General Data Protection Regulation (GDPR). In response to these concerns, the federated recommender system (FedRec) has been introduced. FedRec employs a decentralized data architecture, allowing participants to retain their private data locally while collaboratively training recommendation models in a secure and privacy-preserving manner. Each participant could be a RecSys or a data provider. A RecSys participant typically holds rating/purchasing information, user profiles, and item attributes, while a data provider participant possesses additional user profiles or item attributes.

In this section, we define the FedRec concept and then categorize it based on its data structure. For each category, we describe typical real-world scenarios and discuss related solutions. By exploring these aspects, we aim to provide a comprehensive understanding of Federated Recommender Systems and their potential applications in addressing privacy and security concerns.

3.3.1 Definition of Federated Recommender System

Define n participants, k of whom are recommender systems, and let $\mathcal{S}_{i\in\{1,\ldots,k\}} = \{\mathcal{U}_i, \mathcal{P}_i, \boldsymbol{R}_i, \boldsymbol{X}_i, \boldsymbol{X}_i^{'}\}$. $\mathcal{U}_i = \{u_i^1, u_i^2, \ldots, u_i^{t_i}\}$ and $\mathcal{P}_i = \{p_i^1, p_i^2, \ldots, p_i^{w_i}\}$ stand for the user set and item set, respectively. $\boldsymbol{R}_i \in \mathbb{R}^{t_i \times w_i}$ is the rating matrix that contains the interaction information of users and products. $\boldsymbol{X}_i \in \mathbb{R}^{t_i \times d_i}$ and $\boldsymbol{X}_i' \in \mathbb{R}^{w_i \times d_i^{'}}$ represent the user profiles and item attributes, respectively. The other m participants are data providers containing user profiles, i.e., $\mathcal{D}_{i\in\{1,\ldots,m\}} = \{\mathcal{U}_i, \boldsymbol{X}_i\}$, or item attributes, i.e., $\mathcal{D}_{i\in\{1,\ldots,m\}} = \{\mathcal{P}_i, \boldsymbol{X}_i^{'}\}$.

Definition 3.1 FedRec aims to collaboratively train the recommendation model(s) among multiple participants without direct access to the private data of each other:

$$\arg\min_{\tilde{\boldsymbol{\theta}}_i} \sum_{i=1}^{k} L(\boldsymbol{R}_i, f_{\tilde{\boldsymbol{\theta}}_i}^{fed}(\mathcal{U}_i, \mathcal{P}_i | \mathcal{S}_i, z(\mathcal{S}_{i'\in\{1,\ldots,k\}\setminus\{i\}}), z(\mathcal{D}_{h\in\{1,\ldots,m\}}))), \tag{3.5}$$

where $L(\cdot, \cdot)$ is a loss function, $f_{\tilde{\boldsymbol{\theta}}_i}^{fed}(\cdot, \cdot)$ is the prediction model for the ith FedRec, and $z(\cdot)$ stands for the data processing technique that exchanges intermediate results between participants instead of the raw data.

We anticipate that the performance of FedRec surpasses that of individual RecSys trained on their own data. At the same time, its performance should closely approach that of a system where all participants' data is simply aggregated together without taking privacy and security concerns into account. Formally, we have:

$$|V(f_{\tilde{\boldsymbol{\theta}}_i}^{fed}) - V(f_{\boldsymbol{\theta}_i})| > \delta \quad \text{and} \quad |V(f_{\bar{\boldsymbol{\theta}}_i}^{sum}) - V(f_{\tilde{\boldsymbol{\theta}}_i}^{fed})| \leq \epsilon, \tag{3.6}$$

where $\delta \in \mathbb{R}^+$, $\epsilon \in \mathbb{R}^*$, and $V(\cdot)$ is the evaluation function utilized by RecSys. The prediction model $f_{\boldsymbol{\theta}_i}$ is obtained via separately training the model with the recommender's own data:

$$\arg\min_{\boldsymbol{\theta}_i} L(\boldsymbol{R}_i, f_{\boldsymbol{\theta}_i}(\mathcal{U}_i, \mathcal{P}_i|\mathcal{S}_i)). \tag{3.7}$$

The recommender $f_{\bar{\boldsymbol{\theta}}_i}^{sum}$ is obtained via training the recommendation model with all parties' data simply consolidated together:

$$\arg\min_{\bar{\boldsymbol{\theta}}_i} \sum_{i=1}^{k} L(\boldsymbol{R}_i, f_{\bar{\boldsymbol{\theta}}_i}^{sum}(\mathcal{U}_i, \mathcal{P}_i|\mathcal{S}_{i' \in \{1,\ldots,k\}}, \mathcal{D}_{h \in \{1,\ldots,m\}})). \tag{3.8}$$

3.3.2 *Categorization of Federated Recommender System*

A RecSys primarily comprises two types of data entities: users and items. Building upon the principles of federated learning, we can classify typical scenarios of Federated Recommender Systems (FedRec) based on its data structure. We divide FedRec into three distinct types, horizontal FedRec, vertical FedRec, and transfer FedRec, depending on the sharing situation of users and items. In this subsection, we describe the details of each category and provide typical scenarios for illustration. Related works about FedRec are discussed under the corresponding categories.

3.3.2.1 Horizontal Federated Recommender System

In horizontal FedRec, the items of all participants are shared, but users are different between participants. Under this setting, the participants could be in the form of individual users or sets of users.

Definition 3.2 Given n participants and each participant containing a set of users or an individual user, i.e., $\mathcal{S}_{i \in \{1,\ldots,n\}} = \{\mathcal{U}_i, \mathcal{P}_i, \boldsymbol{R}_i, \boldsymbol{X}_i, \boldsymbol{X}_i'\}$, $\mathcal{U}_i \neq \mathcal{U}_j, \mathcal{P}_i = \mathcal{P}_j, \forall \mathcal{S}_i, \mathcal{S}_j,\ i \neq j$, horizontal FedRec aims to train a recommender model by integrating users' historical behaviors on shared items from different participants, without revealing user's privacy:

$$\arg\min_{\tilde{\boldsymbol{\theta}}} \sum_{i=1}^{n} L(\boldsymbol{R}_i, f_{\tilde{\boldsymbol{\theta}}}^{fed}(\mathcal{U}_i, \mathcal{P}_i|z(\mathcal{S}_{i' \in \{1,\ldots,n\} \setminus \{i\}}))). \tag{3.9}$$

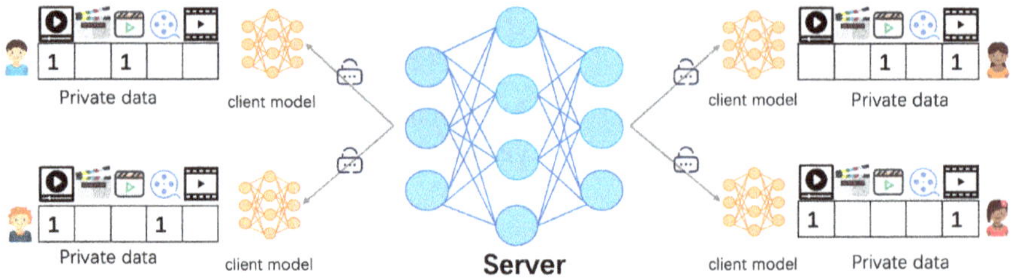

Fig. 3.2 The typical scenario of horizontal FedRec. Each participant is the device of an individual user. The participants share the same products but have different users

Typical Scenario of Horizontal FedRec

As shown in Fig. 3.2, users appreciate personalized movie recommendations provided by a movie recommender system, but they are often concerned about the collection of their private data. In horizontal FedRec, each user device is regarded as a participant containing the rating information between one specific user and all items. Those devices can build a RecSys together to achieve both personalization and privacy requirements.

A number of studies have focused on this scenario. For instance, the Federated Collaborative Filtering (FCF) algorithm is proposed in [31], which is based on matrix factorization. In the traditional RecSys, the matrix factorization algorithms work by decomposing the user-item rating matrix into the product of two lower-dimensional matrices, namely, the user latent factors matrix and the item latent factors matrix. In the FedRec setting, FCF introduces a central server to maintain the shared item latent factors; meanwhile, the user latent factors are stored locally on each device. In each iteration of training, the central server distributes the item latent factors to each participant. Then, participants update their user latent factor by local rating data and send the item latent factor updates back to the server for aggregation. During the training process, FCF algorithm ensures that only model updates are transmitted between participants, and no user's private data is collected or shared. To further enhance privacy and reduce reliance on a third-party central server, a fully decentralized matrix factorization approach without central server is introduced in [32]. The participants communicate directly with each other to update the model. Additionally, [33] proposed another decentralized method of matrix factorization, where local models are exchanged between neighborhood participants, not with an arbitrary party. The neighboring participants are selected by calculating the cosine similarities over rated items between users. This approach further improves the performance of the algorithm. Moreover, [34] proposed a federated meta-learning framework for the recommendation. This framework treats the recommendation for each user as a separate task and designs a meta-learner to generate task-specific parameters. The framework utilizes a support set to generate the recommendation model on each party and computes the loss gradient on a query set. In addition, [35] offered another federated meta-learning algorithm for recommendation. It needs no separate support and query sets. The latter one performs relatively well within considerably fewer episodes in the experiments.

While the aforementioned works offer privacy advantages compared to data centralized approaches, they do not employ additional security methods, leaving some privacy risks when transferring plain-text model parameters. To address these risks, a few studies have explored the use of obfuscation methods based on data-centralized architectures. These obfuscation methods include anonymization, randomization, and differential privacy techniques. For instance, [36] proposed the private social recommendation (PrivSR) algorithm by utilizing the DP technique. This approach is based on a matrix factorization method with the friends-impacting regularizer. Since an inference attack can be conducted from the contribution of one particular user, the DP noise is added into the objective function to perturb the individual's involvement. Kharitonov [37] proposed the federated online learning to the rank algorithm by using users' online feedback. It trains the ranking model on local devices in a way that respects the users' privacy and utilizes the DP technique to protect model privacy on the server. DP noise is injected into the communicated values before it is transmitted to the server, which is different from the PrivSR. However, DP also introduces additional noise. These works involve a trade-off between performance and privacy. A secure federated matrix factorization algorithm (FedMF) with HE schemes is proposed in [38]. Each user encrypts the item latent factor updates with HE before transmitting. Besides, the item latent factor is aggregated and maintained by the central server under the encrypted form. No information of latent factors and updates will be leaked to the introduced server. Li et al. [39] provided an efficient privacy-preserving item-based collaborative filtering algorithm. An SMC protocol is designed to compute the summation of private values of each party without revealing them. Then with this protocol, the PrivateCosine and PrivatePearson algorithm are implemented to calculate the item correlations. Final recommendations are generated using the correlations without revealing privacy.

3.3.2.2 Vertical Federated Recommender System

In vertical FedRec, two participants shared the same user set but have different item sets or feature spaces. Under this setting, the participants could be different recommenders or data providers.

Definition 3.3 Given two participants, one of whom is a RecSys, i.e., $\mathcal{S}_A = \{\mathcal{U}_A, \mathcal{P}_A, \boldsymbol{R}_A, \boldsymbol{X}_A, \boldsymbol{X}'_A\}$; the other one is a data provider or the other recommender. Taking a data provider as an example, we have $\mathcal{D}_B = \{\mathcal{U}_B, \boldsymbol{X}_B\}$, and $\mathcal{U}_A = \mathcal{U}_B = \mathcal{U}$. The vertical FedRec aims to train a recommender model by exploiting the side information of users from the data provider or other recommenders. The training process is completed in a secure and privacy-preserving manner:

$$\arg\min_{\tilde{\theta}} L(\boldsymbol{R}_A, f_{\tilde{\theta}}^{fed}(\mathcal{U}, \mathcal{P}_A, z(\boldsymbol{X}_B)|z(\mathcal{D}_B))). \tag{3.10}$$

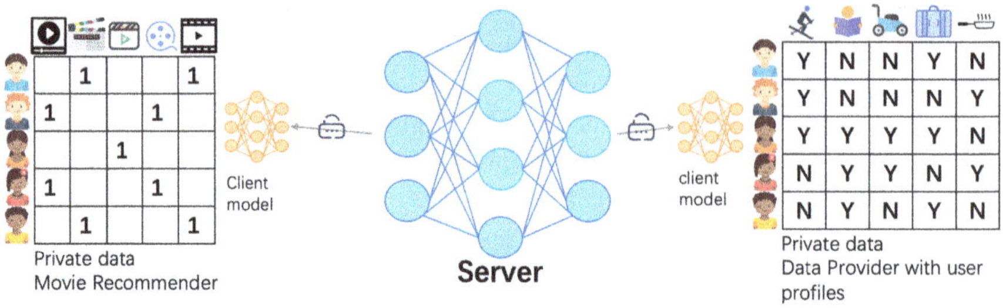

Fig. 3.3 The typical scenario of Vertical FedRec. One participant is a movie recommender, while the other one is a data provider with user profiles. They share the same users

Typical Scenario of Vertical FedRec

As illustrated in Fig. 3.3, the participants include a RecSys and a data provider. For example, one participant could be a movie RecSys, while the other participant is a data provider that is capable of offering comprehensive user profiles. These participants share a large set of common users. The application of vertical FedRec is to enhance the quality of the book recommendation service while avoiding the risk of data privacy leakage.

Several existing works have been designed for such a feature distributed learning problem where participant A and B hold different feature sets. Hu et al. [40] proposed an asynchronous stochastic gradient descent algorithm in which each participant could use an arbitrary model to map its local features to a local prediction. These local predictions from different are aggregated into a final output using linear and nonlinear transformations. The training procedure of each party is allowed to be at various iterations up to a bounded delay. This approach ensures that no raw data or local models are shared, thereby minimizing privacy risks. Besides, for a higher level of privacy, it can easily incorporate the DP technique. Similar to horizontal FedRec, there are also works that further utilize cryptography techniques. Cheng et al. [9] presented a secure gradient-tree boosting algorithm. This algorithm adopts HE methods to provide lossless performance as well as preserving privacy. And [41] proposed a secure linear regression algorithm. MPC protocols are designed using garbled circuits to obtain a highly scalable solution.

The participants of vertical FedRec could also be two recommenders with different item sets. For instance, a movie RecSys and a book RecSys have a large user overlapping but different items to recommend. It is assumed that users share a similar taste in movies and books. With FedRec, the two participants want to train better recommendation algorithms together in a secure and privacy-preserving way. Shmueli and Tassa [42] proposed a secure, distributed item-based CF method. It jointly improves the effect of several RecSys, which offer different subsets of items to the same underlying population of users. Both the predicted ratings of items and their predicted rankings could be computed without compromising privacy nor predictions' accuracy.

3.3.2.3 Transfer Federated Recommender System

In the transfer FedRec, users and items could be different from participants. In most cases, the participants are different recommender systems. For instance, participants are movie and music recommender systems, respectively. Their item catalogs and primary users may differ entirely; we assume that a small subset of overlapping users exists across these systems. Although these systems have different items and users, users who exhibit preferences for action movies might gravitate toward high-energy music genres, reflecting latent correlations in their behavioral patterns. By identifying and modeling these cross-domain correlations, participants can collaboratively enhance their recommendation models without directly sharing raw user-item interaction data. This enables platforms to leverage complementary insights from other domains while preserving user privacy.

Definition 3.4 Given two participants, who are different RecSys, i.e., $\mathcal{S}_i = \{\mathcal{U}_i, \mathcal{P}_i, \boldsymbol{R}_i, \boldsymbol{X}_i, \boldsymbol{X}_i'\}$ as the source-domain participant, $\mathcal{S}_j = \{\mathcal{U}_j, \mathcal{P}_j, \boldsymbol{R}_j, \boldsymbol{X}_j, \boldsymbol{X}_j'\}$ as the target-domain participant, and $\mathcal{U}_i \neq \mathcal{U}_j, \mathcal{P}_i \neq \mathcal{P}_j$. Generally, $\boldsymbol{R}_i$ contains much more rating information than $\boldsymbol{R}_j$. Transfer FedRec aims to train a recommender model by transferring knowledge from the source-domain participant to the target-domain participant, without revealing user privacy:

$$\arg\min_{\tilde{\boldsymbol{\theta}}} \sum_{k \in \{i,j\}}^{N} \lambda_k L(\boldsymbol{R}_k, f_{\tilde{\boldsymbol{\theta}}_k}^{fed}(\mathcal{U}_k, \mathcal{P}_k | z(\mathcal{S}_{k' \in \{i,j\} \setminus \{k\}})), \tag{3.11}$$

where λ_k is the weight for balancing the performance of two participants.

Typical Scenario of Transfer FedRec

As shown in Fig. 3.4, a popular movie recommender system in region A wants to help another new music recommender system in region B to collaboratively learn a music recommendation model.

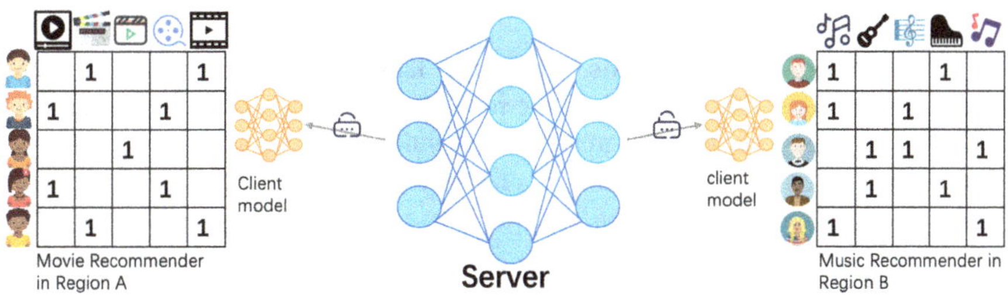

Fig. 3.4 The typical scenario of Transfer FedRec. One participant is a movie recommender, while the other one is a music recommender in the different region. They share neither users nor items

Since both users and items are different between participants, constructing a federated recommender system directly can be quite challenging. However, federated transfer learning [43] offers a feasible solution. In this approach, a limited set of co-occurrence samples is used as a "bridge" to transfer knowledge from the source domain to the target domain. At first, parties update their neural networks using local data. Then, they together optimize the loss on the co-occurrence samples. The secret sharing technique is employed to design a secure and efficient algorithm. This algorithm can be similarly applied in the transfer FedRec scenario via co-occurrence users or items, serving as a potential solution for scenarios where both users and items differ between participants.

3.3.3 Summary

In this section, we explore FedRec, a paradigm that applies federated learning to recommendation scenarios. FedRec addresses critical challenges of user privacy and data security in traditional RecSys. It allows multiple parties to collaboratively train enhanced recommendation models while retaining users' private data locally. We classify FedRec based on the data structure of RecSys. As we have reviewed, horizontal FedRec, which manages recommender systems across individuals or sets of users, is a significant area that has attracted considerable research attention. On the other hand, vertical FedRec and transfer FedRec, which involve building recommender systems among organizations, are typical tasks in recommendation businesses. However, despite their relevance and potential, vertical and transfer FedRec remain relatively underexplored areas in the research community. These areas present numerous opportunities for further investigation and development. Additionally, many popular recommendation algorithms have not been applied to FedRec. As a result, FedRec presents a promising direction with numerous potential opportunities.

3.4 Emerging Trends in Federated Learning

Large foundation models (LFMs, e.g., large language models like GPT-4 and large vision models like Florence-2) are revolutionizing enterprise AI by enabling advanced automation, decision-making, and innovation across industries. These models, trained on vast datasets, excel in tasks such as natural language processing, image analysis, code generation, and predictive analytics. For enterprises, they unlock efficiencies in customer service, supply chain optimization, and personalized marketing while reducing operational costs. Open-source models including Llama and Deepseek further enable more smaller enterprises to deploy advanced foundation models without prohibitive investments. It breaks proprietary barriers by open-sourcing its models, allowing more enterprises to customize and innovate without relying on closed ecosystems.

Although large foundation models excel at general-purpose tasks, they struggle with industry-specific terminology, workflows, and compliance requirements. For instance, medical diagnostics demand precise anatomical knowledge and regulatory adherence. Therefore, enterprises still require domain-specific models to address challenges in specialized fields. In enterprise AI, the integration of foundation models is paramount for addressing complex, domain-specific challenges. One of the pivotal advancements in this direction is the concept of grounding foundation models (FM) through Federated Transfer Learning (FTL), coined FTL-FM, which is particularly adept at grounding foundation models in various industrial contexts. This section delves into the intricacies of the FTL-FM framework, as proposed by a consortium of researchers, which serves as a versatile and secure paradigm for model adaptation and enhancement within the constraints of enterprise environments. The FTL-FM framework is designed to overcome the limitations typically encountered when applying FMs to specialized tasks. These limitations arise from FMs' pre-training on vast amounts of datasets, which often results in a lack of industry-specific insights and an inability to keep pace with the rapidly evolving knowledge required for certain industry-specific applications. To bridge this gap, the FTL-FM framework introduces a systematic approach to integrate domain-specific knowledge into FMs, leveraging the principles of federated learning and transfer learning. At the crux of the FTL-FM framework are three distinct yet interconnected settings, each targeting a unique aspect of the grounding process. Three settings are defined within the FTL-FM framework [4]:

- Optimize Clients' Domain Models (Setting 1): This setting involves leveraging the knowledge of the server's foundation model to enhance the clients' domain models for accomplishing specific tasks.
- Optimize Server's Foundation Model (Setting 2): This setting focuses on using domain-specific knowledge of one or more clients to augment the server's foundation model.
- Co-optimize Foundation and Domain Models (Setting 3): This setting aims to enhance both the server's foundation model and clients' domain models by leveraging mutual knowledge transfer.

In the following three subsections, we will elaborate on the three settings through a collaboration between one server and one or more clients. We assume that a client possesses a local dataset $\mathcal{D} = \{(x_i, y_i)\}_{i=1}^N$, comprising N samples, where x_i represents an input, while y_i represents the corresponding output of x_i.

3.4.1 Foundation Models to Domain Models

The first setting focuses on optimizing the client's domain model (DM) by leveraging the knowledge encoded within the server's foundation model (FM). The knowledge transferred from the FM to the DM can be data-level and representation-level knowledge. Federated knowledge distillation [44, 45], federated prompt

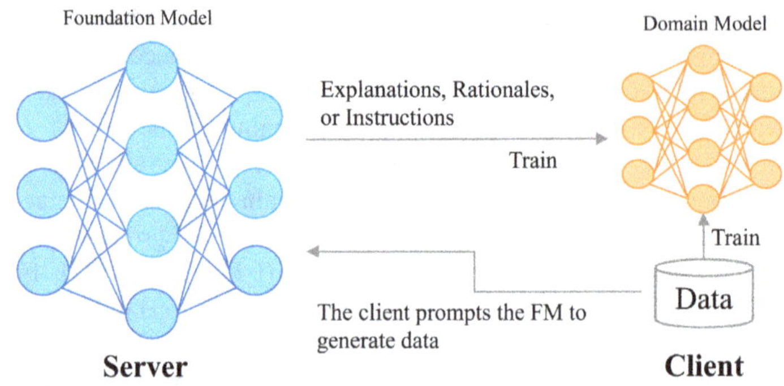

Fig. 3.5 Federated knowledge distillation. The knowledge of FM hosted by the server is transferred to the client by fine-tuning the client's domain model with knowledge generated by the foundation model (e.g., LLMs). Knowledge generated by the FM can be reasoning explanations, rationals, and instructions

tuning [46, 47], and federated split learning [48, 49] are three representative approaches.

Federated Knowledge Distillation typically involves a server hosting a large foundation model and a client owning a much smaller domain model for accomplishing a domain-specific task, and its goal is to transfer the knowledge of the FM to the DM to enhance the performance of the DM on the domain-specific task.

A typical way of transferring knowledge from the FM to the DM is to prompt the FM to generate data such as reasoning explanations, rationals, and instructions based on the client's local data and then leverage these generated data (together with the client's local data) to train the client's domain model. Specifically, a general workflow for each communication round between the server and the client of a federated knowledge distillation is as follows (see Fig. 3.5 for illustration):

1. The client randomly draws a mini-batch $\mathcal{D}' = \{(x_i, y_i)\}_{i=1}^{N'}$ with N' data points from $\mathcal{D}$. Then, the client sends $\mathcal{D}'$ to the server.
2. Upon receiving $\mathcal{D}' = \{(x_i, y_i)\}_{i=1}^{N'}$, the sever leverages the Chain-of-Thought (CoT) prompting technique [50] to generate data from its FM. These generated data, for example, can be reasoning rationales that explain why each x_i leads to y_i. Subsequently, the server transmits these generated data to the client.
3. Upon receiving generated data from the server, the client trains its local domain models using both generated data and its local data.

The federated knowledge distillation algorithm iterates through the aforementioned four steps until convergence is achieved or predetermined stopping criteria are satisfied.

It is worth noting that the local data sent from the client to the server may leak the privacy of the client's sensitive data. Therefore, certain privacy-preserving mechanisms should be utilized to protect the data sent from the client to the server to mitigate possible privacy leakage. To this end, Fan et al. [44] leverage randomization

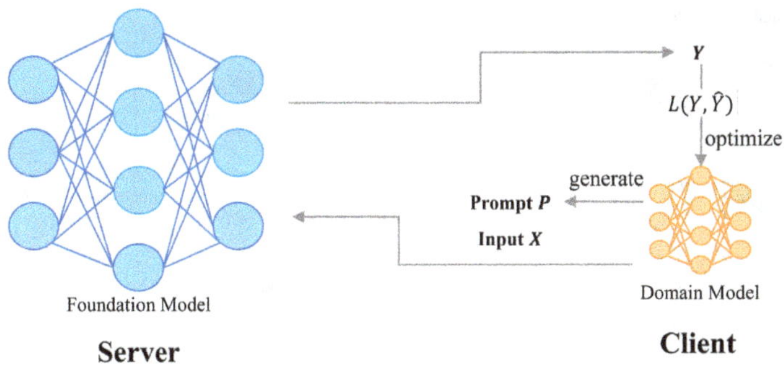

Fig. 3.6 Federated continuous prompt optimization. The knowledge of FM hosted by the server is adapted to the client by training a prompt generator that generates continuous prompts based on the responses from the FM

to perturb the data sent to the server, and Li et al. [45] proposed to train a local privacy-preserving generator to generate fake data from the original one and send the fake data to the server.

In **Federated Prompt Optimization**, the client aims to learn a local prompt generator, the primary function of which is to produce prompts that can effectively steer a black box FM hosted on the server toward generating the desired responses.

Federated prompt optimization research can be divided into two primary categories. One category concentrates on optimizing continuous or soft prompts using gradient-free or zero-order optimization techniques. Notably, BBT [51] and BBTv2 [52] employ the Covariance Matrix Adaptation Evolution Strategy (CMA-ES) [53] to optimize the client-side local prompt generator, while BlackVIP [54] leverages Simultaneous Perturbation Stochastic Approximation (SPSA) [55] to efficiently approximate high-dimensional gradients, which are subsequently used to optimize the prompt generator. A federated continuous prompt optimization (FedCPO) approach generally involves the following steps (see Fig. 3.6 for illustration):

1. The client randomly draws a mini-batch $\mathcal{D}' = \{(x_i, y_i)\}_{i=1}^{N'}$ from $\mathcal{D}$, comprising N' data points. The client then generates continuous prompts using its local prompt generator and prepends them to $\{(x_i)\}_{i=1}^{N'}$. Next, the client sends these continuous prompts with $\{(x_i)\}_{i=1}^{N'}$ to the server.
2. Upon receiving $\{(x_i)\}_{i=1}^{N'}$ prepended with continuous prompts, the server feeds them to its FM to generate responses and sends responses back to the client.
3. The client receives the responses from the server and subsequently computes the loss based on these generated responses and ground truth ones to optimize its local prompt generator.

A notable constraint of these FedCPO methods is that they necessitate continuous prompts, which are incompatible with FM APIs that only accept discrete inputs. To address this limitation, researchers have explored the second category: federated discrete prompt optimization, FedDPO for short.

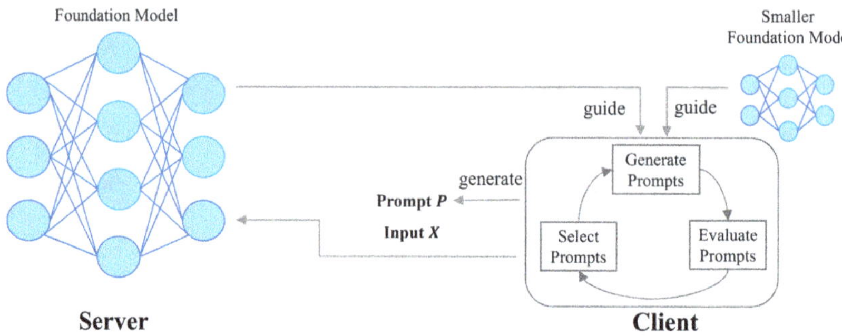

Fig. 3.7 Federated discrete prompt optimization. The knowledge of FM is adapted to the client by optimizing discrete prompts through a three-stage process: assessing the efficacy of existing prompts, identifying the top-performing prompts, and generating new candidate prompts. The three stages iterate until the process converges. Throughout the iterations, the client repeats queries with the server's FM and, if necessary, a supplementary local FM to inform its prompt optimization strategy

Figure 3.7 offers a high-level workflow of FedDPO. At its core, the process of FedDPO entails a three-stage cycle: assessing the efficacy of existing prompts, identifying the top-performing prompts, and generating new candidate prompts. This iterative process continues until convergence is achieved. Throughout the iterations, the client engages in repeated queries with the server's FM and, if necessary, a supplementary local FM to inform its prompt optimization strategy. A range of approaches has been developed to operationalize FedDPO, including BDPL [56] and DSP [57], which involve learning a discrete prompt generator (DPG) on the client side to customize FM responses. Specifically, BDPL leverages a variance-reduced policy gradient algorithm to optimize the DPG, whereas DSP adopts a hybrid approach that combines supervised fine-tuning with reinforcement learning for optimization.

The aforementioned federated prompt optimization methods have been confined to a single-client, single-server framework. More recent approaches, such as Fed-BBPT [46] and FedBPT [47], have successfully extended this framework to accommodate multiple clients. These methods rely on a dual-server architecture comprising a foundation model (FM) server and a federated server. The FM server hosts the large foundation model to be prompted, whereas the federated server facilitates the federated tuning of clients' local prompt generators. Specifically, in Fed-BBPT, clients leverage simultaneous perturbation stochastic approximation (SPSA) to train their prompt generators using local data together with predictions generated by the FM, and the federated server aggregates these local generators to form a global prompt generator. In FedBPT, by contrast, clients employ the covariance matrix adaptation evolution strategy (CMA-ES) to optimize the distribution of prompts generated by their local prompt generators, and the server derives the global prompt generator by aggregating these local distributions.

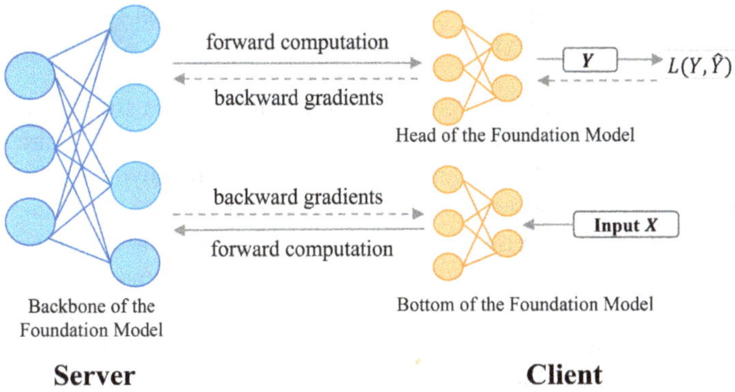

Fig. 3.8 Federated split learning. The FM is split into an FM backbone model, an FM bottom model, and an FM head model. The FM backbone is deployed on the server, while the FM head and bottom models are deployed on the client. The federated split learning follows the conventional stochastic gradient descent procedure, but each portion of FM is trained by a different party (i.e., client and server)

In **federated split learning**, a server and a client collaborate, each possessing a distinct segment of a large FM. This FM is typically divided into a computationally intensive backbone and several smaller components, typically an FM head and an FM bottom. The backbone, being the most resource-demanding part, is usually hosted on a server with ample computing power, while the remaining components are deployed on the client's side. The primary goal of this approach is to tailor the foundation model's knowledge to the client's specific domain by fine-tuning the distributed FM using the client's local data.

The training protocol for federated split learning builds upon the conventional split learning approach [8], leveraging stochastic gradient descent to train the model. In federated split learning, each component of the FM is trained independently by separate parties, specifically the client and the server. We illustrate the workflow for each communication round between the server and the client in Fig. 3.8 and elaborate on a general workflow of federated split learning as follows:

1. Given a local dataset $\mathcal{D} = \{(x_i, y_i)\}_{i=1}^{N}$, consisting of N samples, where each sample is represented by an input, x_i, and its corresponding output, y_i, the client randomly draws a mini-batch $\mathcal{D}' = \{(x_i, y_i)\}_{i=1}^{N'}$ from $\mathcal{D}$, comprising N' data points. The client then feeds $\{(x_i)\}_{i=1}^{N'}$ to its local FM bottom model and forwards the resulting intermediate outputs to the server.
2. Upon receiving the intermediate outputs from the client, the server processes them using its local FM backbone and returns the results to the client.
3. The client subsequently receives the intermediate outputs from the server and inputs them into its FM head to calculate the loss with respect to the corresponding outputs $\{(y_i)\}_{i=1}^{N'}$.
4. The client then computes the backward gradients to update its FM head and transmits the resulting gradients to the server to train the FM backbone. In

response, the server calculates the backward gradients and sends them back to the client to update the FM bottom model.

The federated split learning algorithm iterates through the aforementioned four steps until convergence is achieved or predetermined stopping criteria are satisfied.

SAP [48] and Shuffled Transformer [58] adopt the deployment strategy illustrated in Fig. 3.8. To ensure the privacy of sensitive data, SAP implemented d_χ-privacy [59], a differential privacy mechanism, to obfuscate representation vectors prior to transmission to the server. In a similar manner, the Shuffled Transformer approach designed a transformer-based network that exhibits weight permutation invariance, thereby preventing the server from inferring client data without compromising model performance. Moreover, SAP investigated the impact of splitting the FM at different positions on the privacy-preserving capacity and model performance of the SAP framework. The empirical results revealed that as the number of layers in the bottom model increases, the model's utility decreases, whereas its ability to preserve privacy is enhanced, underscoring the inherent trade-off between utility and privacy when partitioning the FM.

FedBERT [49] extends the federated split learning from one client to multiple clients. In FedBERT, a pre-specified FM is split into three parts: FM backbone, FM head, and FM bottom. The FM backbone is deployed on the server, while the FM head and FM bottom are deployed on each client. Clients in FedBERT collaborate with the server to train the FM backbone and their corresponding FM bottoms and heads following conventional split learning protocol [8].

3.4.2 Domain Knowledge to Foundation Models

The objective of fine-tuning a server's foundation model (FM) by integrating clients' domain-specific expertise through federated learning is to create a versatile FM that can accurately and reliably tackle a wide range of domain-specific tasks. Notwithstanding the scarcity of solutions for fine-tuning an FM in a federated manner, Xiao et al. [60] have pioneered an innovative approach, dubbed offsite tuning, to accomplish this goal.

In the offsite-tuning approach, the server selects two small subsets of its full FM, designated as top and bottom adapters, and compresses its full FM into an emulator. The two adapters and emulator are then transmitted to the client, where the two adapters are fine-tuned using the client's private data, with the emulator providing guidance. The refined adapters are subsequently returned to the server, where they are integrated into the original FM to create an adapted FM. This approach mitigates privacy leakage of the client's local data and protects the ownership of the server's FM, as neither party shares their full FM or private data. Figure 3.9 illustrates the workflow of the offsite-tuning approach.

The offsite-tuning approach has two significant drawbacks. First, it lacks explicit mechanisms to protect the privacy of the client's local data, leaving the client's

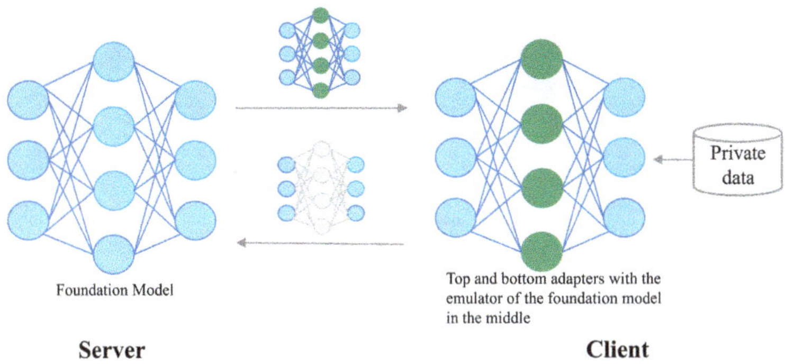

Fig. 3.9 Offsite tuning. The server selects two small subsets of its full FM to form top and bottom adapters (in blue) and compresses its full FM into an emulator (in green). The adapters and emulator are then transmitted to the client, where the adapters are fine-tuned using the client's private data, with the emulator providing guidance. The refined adapters are subsequently returned to the server, which integrates adapters into the original FM to form an adapted FM

sensitive information vulnerable to being recovered by the server, who might be malicious. Second, offsite tuning is limited to a single client, which restricts its applicability. To address these limitations, Fan et al. introduced FedOST [61], a federated learning variant of offsite tuning. In FedOST, the server initially distributes the emulator and two adapters derived from the foundation model to all participating clients. Each client then fine-tunes the adapters using their private data, assisted by the emulator. The clients subsequently transmit their adapters to the server, which aggregates them securely through secure aggregation [1] and integrates the resulting adapters into the foundation model. FedOST ensures the protection of clients' private data and enables the development of a fine-tuned foundation model with improved generalization capabilities. Note that the FedOST has already been integrated into the FATE, an industrial-grade federated learning framework [62].

3.4.3 *Co-optimize Foundation and Domain Models*

The concurrent optimization of the server's foundation model (FM) and the clients' domain models (DMs) creates a self-reinforcing cycle, enabling the continuous refinement of both foundation and domain models [63]. This process begins with the server sharing its FM's general knowledge and capabilities with the clients' DMs, which are then fine-tuned using domain-specific data for specific downstream applications. In return, the clients' DMs convey industry-specific insights that augment the server's FM. Ultimately, the server's FM is enriched with domain-specific knowledge, while each client's DM is enhanced with the FM's general knowledge and capabilities.

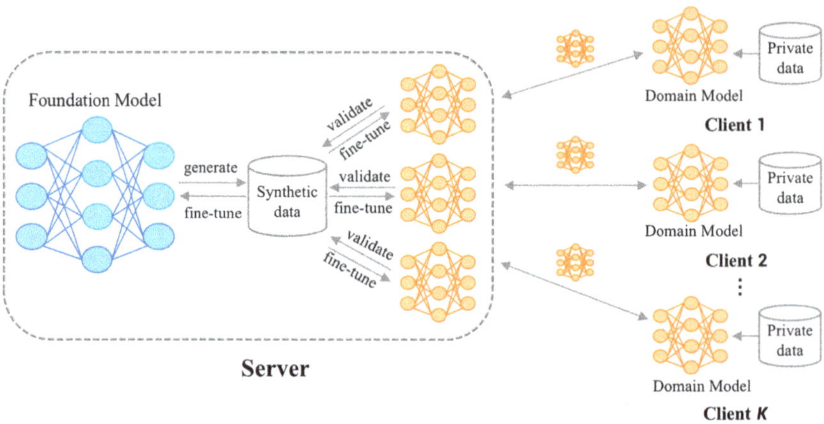

Fig. 3.10 CrossLM. During each communication round, clients train their domain models using their private data and then send them to the server. The server, in turn, fine-tunes its FM and clients' DMs using the synthetic data, which are generated by the FM and validated by clients' DMs, respectively. Next, the server dispatches DMs to their corresponding clients

The CrossLM, introduced by Deng et al. [64], is a pioneering method that simultaneously optimizes the server's FM and clients' DMs by leveraging synthetic data generated by the server's FM, as depicted in Fig. 3.10. During each communication round, clients train their local DMs using their local data and send them to the server asynchronously. The server generates synthetic data and utilizes the received DMs to evaluate the quality of the synthetic data. The server then refines its FM based on the validation feedback from the DMs and the validated synthetic data. Following this, the server fine-tunes each client's DM using the validated synthetic data and dispatches the updated DMs to the corresponding clients for further training.

CrossLM is subject to two limitations. Firstly, it necessitates substantial communication bandwidth to transmit clients' DMs between the server and clients. Secondly, it poses a risk of privacy leakage, as a malicious server may potentially infer sensitive information about clients from the DMs it observes. To mitigate these limitations, FedMKT was proposed to transfer knowledge between the server's FM and clients' DMs in a parameter-efficient way. In FedMKT, the server is deployed with an LLM, while clients utilize smaller, heterogeneous language models (SLMs). During each communication round, clients train their local SLMs using LoRA [25] and transmit the resulting output logits to the server using a shared public dataset. The server then aggregates and refines the knowledge embedded in these logins, incorporating the domain-specific knowledge gained by clients into its LLM. This process enhances the server's comprehensive capabilities. Furthermore, the server's LLM selectively shares its knowledge with clients' SLMs, facilitating a bidirectional knowledge transfer. Figure 3.11 illustrates the workflow of FedMKT.

Mutually enhancing the server's FM and clients' DMs is rarely exploited in literature and real-world applications. A large amount of research on the federated

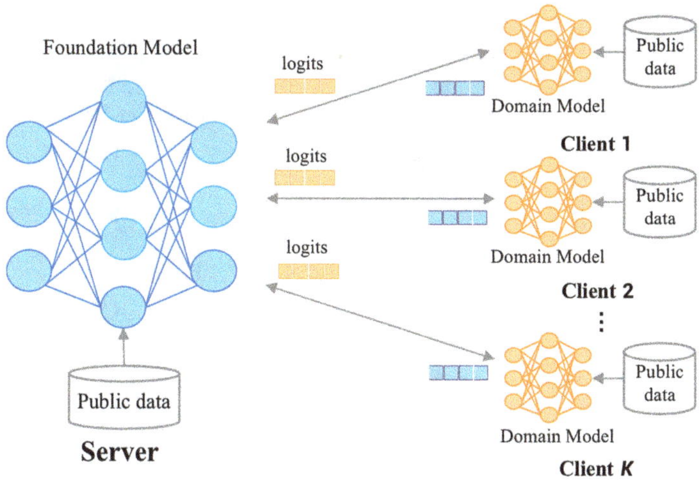

Fig. 3.11 FedMKT. The server and K clients exchange their logits to fine-tune the server's foundation model and clients' domain models based on a shared public dataset

foundation model has been focused on designing parameter-efficient fine-tuning (PEFT) mechanisms for clients to collaboratively fine-tune their DMs.

These federated parameter-efficient fine-tuning methods, which essentially fall under the purview of horizontal federated learning [1], typically involve clients whose DMs are initialized with pre-trained large FMs. During training, each client only uploads a PEFT module to the server for aggregation. The PEFT module can be an adapter, LoRA model, or prompt model that contributes to a small portion of the parameters of the original FM, thereby saving computational and communication overheads. A general workflow of federated parameter-efficient fine-tuning is illustrated in Fig. 3.12 and described as follows:

1. Each client trains a lightweight PEFT module comprising a small number of trainable parameters that augment or are integrated into its local FM. This PEFT module may take the form of an adapter, a low-rank matrix (such as LoRA), or a continuous prompt.
2. All clients send their PEFT modules to the server, which in turn aggregates these PEFT modules to form a global PEFT module and dispatches the global PEFT module back to clients.
3. Upon receiving the global PEFT module, each client integrates the global PEFT module into its original FM and fine-tunes the global PEFT module (while keeping other parameters of the FM frozen) using its local data.

A federated PEFT algorithm iterates through the aforementioned three steps until convergence is achieved or predetermined stopping criteria are satisfied. Compared to full fine-tuning, federated PEFT algorithms generally reduce the computational and communication overhead while still allowing for task-specific adaptations. For

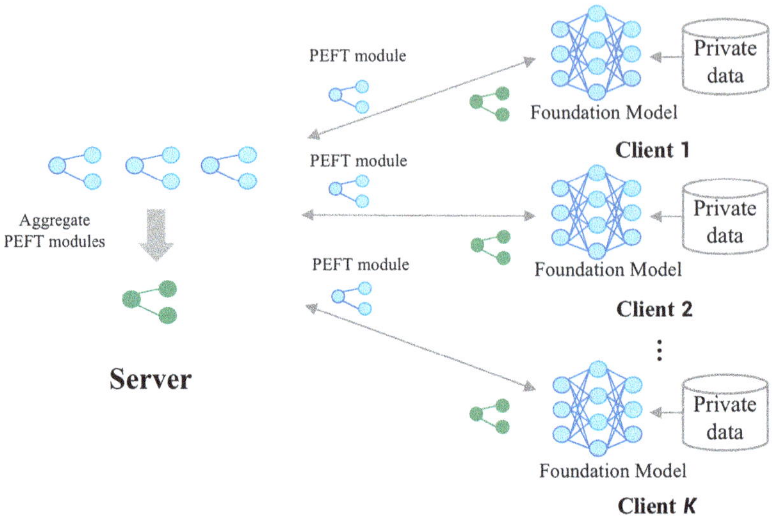

Fig. 3.12 Federated PEFT. Clients' DMs are initialized with pre-trained FMs. During each communication round, each client only uploads a lightweight PEFT module to the server for aggregation. The server then dispatches the aggregated PEFT module to each client. The PEFT module can be an adapter, LoRA model, or prompt model that contributes to a small portion of the parameters of the original FM, thereby saving computational and communication overheads

examples, the FedPETuning [65] integrates four techniques—adapter tuning, prefix tuning, LoRA, and BitFit—to fine-tune clients' DMs and has demonstrated optimal privacy-preserving outcomes when combined with federated learning and LoRA. In a similar vein, DP-LoRA [66] and PEU+LoRA [67] employ LoRA with differential privacy to fine-tune clients' DMs, seeking to achieve a more favorable balance between privacy, utility, and resource allocation. Notably, PEU+LoRA incorporates Partial Embedding Updates to minimize the noise required for privacy protection. Moreover, Zhao et al. proposed FedPrompt [68], which leverages federated learning and soft prompt tuning to fine-tune clients' DMs, such as T5, with the goal of reducing communication costs while maintaining model accuracy.

3.5 Conclusion

In conclusion, federated learning has emerged as a pioneering distributed machine learning paradigm, effectively bridging data silos and facilitating the development of machine learning models without compromising data privacy and security. In this chapter, we have provided a comprehensive overview of the various forms of federated learning, including horizontal federated learning, vertical federated learning, and federated transfer learning. Furthermore, we have discussed the challenges faced in implementing federated learning techniques.

Federated learning has been widely used in numerous applications across multiple industries like healthcare, finance, natural language processing, and personalized recommendations. We have specifically introduced federated recommendation systems as a key application and also explored FL's role in advancing large foundation models. By understanding the categorizations, applications, novel algorithms, and challenges, one can choose the most suitable federated learning techniques for their specific use cases. Moreover, one can gain a holistic view of the federated learning landscape and be in a better position to contribute to the evolution and enhancement of federated learning.

References

1. McMahan, B., Moore, E., Ramage, D., Hampson, S., y Arcas, B.A.: Communication-efficient learning of deep networks from decentralized data. In: Artificial Intelligence and Statistics, pp. 1273–1282. PMLR, Cambridge (2017)
2. Konečný, J., McMahan, H.B., Ramage, D., Richtárik, P.: Federated optimization: Distributed machine learning for on-device intelligence. arXiv preprint arXiv:1610.02527 (2016)
3. Yang, Q., Liu, Y., Chen, T., Tong, Y.: Federated machine learning: concept and applications. ACM Trans. Intell. Syst. Technol. **10**, 1–19 (2019)
4. Kang, Y., Fan, T., Gu, H., Fan, L., Yang, Q.: Grounding foundation models through federated transfer learning: A general framework. arXiv preprint (2023)
5. Hard, A., Rao, K., Mathews, R., Ramaswamy, S., Beaufays, F., Augenstein, S., Eichner, H., Kiddon, C., Ramage, D.: Federated learning for mobile keyboard prediction. arXiv preprint arXiv:1811.03604 (2018)
6. Nguyen, D.C., Ding, M., Pathirana, P.N., Seneviratne, A., Li, J., Poor, H.V.: Federated learning for internet of things: a comprehensive survey. IEEE Commun. Surv. Tutor. **23**(3), 1622–1658 (2021)
7. Antunes, R.S., da Costa, C.A., Küderle, A., Yari, I.A., Eskofier, B.: Federated learning for healthcare: systematic review and architecture proposal. ACM Trans. Intell. Syst. Technol. **13**(4), 1–23 (2022)
8. Liu, Y., Kang, Y., Zou, T., Pu, Y., He, Y., Ye, X., Ouyang, Y., Zhang, Y.-Q., Yang, Q.: Vertical federated learning: concepts, advances, and challenges. IEEE Trans. Knowl. Data Eng. **36**, 3615–3634 (2024)
9. Cheng, K., Fan, T., Jin, Y., Liu, Y., Chen, T., Yang, Q.: Secureboost: A lossless federated learning framework. arXiv preprint arXiv:1901.08755 (2019)
10. Fan, T., Chen, W., Ma, G., Kang, Y., Fan, L., Yang, Q.: Secureboost+: Large scale and high-performance vertical federated gradient boosting decision tree. In: Advances in Knowledge Discovery and Data Mining: 28th Pacific-Asia Conference on Knowledge Discovery and Data Mining, PAKDD 2024, Taipei, May 7–10, 2024, Proceedings, Part III, pp. 237–249 (2024)
11. Chen, T., Guestrin, C.: Xgboost: A scalable tree boosting system. In: Proceedings of the 22nd ACM SIGKDD International Conference on Knowledge Discovery and Data Mining, KDD '16. ACM (2016)
12. Ke, G., Meng, Q., Finley, T., Wang, T., Chen, W., Ma, W., Ye, Q., Liu, T.-Y.: Lightgbm: A highly efficient gradient boosting decision tree. In: Advances in Neural Information Processing Systems, vol. 30. Curran Associates, Red Hook (2017)
13. Li, W., Xia, Q., Deng, J., Cheng, H., Liu, J., Xue, K., Cheng, Y., Xia, S.: VFed-SSD: Towards practical vertical federated advertising. In: International Workshop on Trustworthy Federated Learning in Conjunction with IJCAI (2022)

14. He, Y., Kang, Y., Zhao, X., Luo, J., Fan, L., Han, Y., Yang, Q.: A hybrid self-supervised learning framework for vertical federated learning. IEEE Trans. Big Data **11**(5), 2210–2223 (2025). https://doi.org/10.1109/TBDATA.2024.3403386
15. Liu, Y., Liang, X., Luo, J., He, Y., Chen, T., Yao, Q., Yang, Q.: Cross-silo federated neural architecture search for heterogeneous and cooperative systems. In: Federated and Transfer Learning, pp. 57–86. Springer International Publishing, Cham (2023)
16. Kang, Y., Liu, Y., Liang, X.: FedCVT: Semi-supervised vertical federated learning with cross-view training. ACM Trans. Intell. Syst. Technol. **13**, 1–16 (2022)
17. Yang, Y., Ye, X., Sakurai, T.: Multi-view federated learning with data collaboration. In: ICMLC 2022, pp. 178–183. Association for Computing Machinery, New York (2022)
18. Zhu, L., Liu, Z., Han, S.: Deep leakage from gradients. In: Advances in Neural Information Processing Systems, 32 (2019)
19. Zhang, Y., Zeng, D., Luo, J., Xu, Z., King, I.: A survey of trustworthy federated learning with perspectives on security, robustness and privacy. In: Companion Proceedings of the ACM Web Conference 2023, pp. 1167–1176 (2023)
20. Kang, Y., Gu, H., Tang, X., He, Y., Zhang, Y., He, J., Han, Y., Fan, L., Chen, K., Yang, Q.: Optimizing privacy, utility and efficiency in constrained multi-objective federated learning. arXiv preprint arXiv:2305.00312 (2023)
21. Chen, D., Jiang, X., Zhong, H., Cui, J.: Building trusted federated learning: key technologies and challenges. J. Sensor Actuator Netw. **12**(1), 13 (2023)
22. Bonawitz, K.A., Ivanov, V., Kreuter, B., Marcedone, A., McMahan, H.B., Patel, S., Ramage, D., Segal, A., Seth, K.: Practical secure aggregation for federated learning on user-held data. In: NIPS Workshop on Private Multi-Party Machine Learning (2016)
23. Zhang, X., Kang, Y., Chen, K., Fan, L., Yang, Q.: Trading off privacy, utility, and efficiency in federated learning. ACM Trans. Intell. Syst. Technol. **14**(6), 1–32 (2023)
24. Kang, Y., Luo, J., He, Y., Zhang, X., Fan, L., Yang, Q.: A framework for evaluating privacy-utility trade-off in vertical federated learning. arXiv preprint arXiv:2209.03885 (2022)
25. Hu, E.J., Shen, Y., Wallis, P., Allen-Zhu, Z., Li, Y., Wang, S., Wang, L., Chen, W.: LoRA: Low-rank adaptation of large language models. In: International Conference on Learning Representations (2022)
26. Lu, Z., Pan, H., Dai, Y., Si, X., Zhang, Y.: Federated learning with non-iid data: a survey. IEEE Int. Things J. **11**(11), 19188–19209 (2024)
27. Lim, W.Y.B., Xiong, Z., Miao, C., Niyato, D., Yang, Q., Leung, C., Poor, H.V.: Hierarchical incentive mechanism design for federated machine learning in mobile networks. IEEE Int. Things J. **7**(10), 9575–9588 (2020)
28. Yu, H., Liu, Z., Liu, Y., Chen, T., Cong, M., Weng, X., Niyato, D., Yang, Q.: A fairness-aware incentive scheme for federated learning. In: Proceedings of the AAAI/ACM Conference on AI, Ethics, and Society, AIES '20, pp. 393–399. Association for Computing Machinery, New York, NY (2020).
29. Li, T., Sanjabi, M., Beirami, A., Smith, V.: Fair resource allocation in federated learning. In: International Conference on Learning Representations (2020)
30. Li, B., Fan, L., Gu, H., Li, J., Yang, Q.: Fedipr: Ownership verification for federated deep neural network models. IEEE Trans. Pattern Analy. Mach. Intell. **45**(4), 4521–4536 (2023)
31. Ammad-Ud-Din, M., Ivannikova, E., Khan, S.A., Oyomno, W., Fu, Q., Tan, K.E., Flanagan, A.: Federated collaborative filtering for privacy-preserving personalized recommendation system. arXiv preprint arXiv:1901.09888 (2019)
32. Hegedűs, I., Danner, G., Jelasity, M.: Decentralized recommendation based on matrix factorization: A comparison of gossip and federated learning. In: Proceedings of the 2nd Workshop on Decentralized Machine Learning at the Edge (2019)
33. Duriakova, E., Tragos, E.Z., Smyth, B., Hurley, N., Peña, F.J., Symeonidis, P., Geraci, J., Lawlor, A.: Pdmfrec: A decentralised matrix factorisation with tunable user-centric privacy. In: Proceedings of the 13th ACM Conference on Recommender Systems (2019)
34. Chen, F., Dong, Z., Li, Z., He, X.: Federated meta-learning for recommendation. arXiv preprint arXiv:1802.07876 (2018)

35. Jalalirad, A., Scavuzzo, M., Capota, C., Sprague, M.: A simple and efficient federated recommender system. In: Proceedings of the 6th IEEE/ACM International Conference on Big Data Computing, Applications and Technologies (2019)
36. Meng, X., Wang, S., Shu, K., Li, J., Chen, B., Liu, H., Zhang, Y.: Personalized privacy-preserving social recommendation. In: Proceedings of the 32nd AAAI Conference on Artificial Intelligence (2018)
37. Kharitonov, E.: Federated online learning to rank with evolution strategies. In: Proceedings of the 20th ACM International Conference on Web Search and Data Mining (2019)
38. Chai, D., Wang, L., Chen, K., Yang, Q.: Secure federated matrix factorization. arXiv preprint arXiv:1906.05108 (2019)
39. Li, D., Chen, C., Lv, Q., Shang, L., Zhao, Y., Lu, T., Gu, N.: An algorithm for efficient privacy-preserving item-based collaborative filtering. Future Gener. Comput. Syst. **55**, 311–320 (2016)
40. Hu, Y., Niu, D., Yang, J., Zhou, S.: Fdml: A collaborative machine learning framework for distributed features. In: Proceedings of the 25th ACM SIGKDD International Conference on Knowledge Discovery & Data Mining (2019)
41. Gascón, A., Schoppmann, P., Balle, B., Raykova, M., Doerner, J., Zahur, S., Evans, D.: Secure linear regression on vertically partitioned datasets. IACR Cryptol. ePrint Archi. **2016**, 892 (2016)
42. Shmueli, E., Tassa, T.: Secure multi-party protocols for item-based collaborative filtering. In: Proceedings of the 11st ACM Conference on Recommender Systems (2017)
43. Sharma, S., Xing, C., Liu, Y., Kang, Y.: Secure and efficient federated transfer learning. In: 2019 IEEE International Conference on Big Data, pp. 2569–2576 (2019)
44. Fan, T., Kang, Y., Chen, W., Gu, H., Song, Y., Fan, L., Chen, K., Yang, Q.: Pdss: A privacy-preserving framework for step-by-step distillation of large language models. arXiv preprint arXiv:2406.12403 (2024)
45. Li, H., Zhao, X., Guo, D., Gu, H., Zeng, Z., Han, Y., Song, Y., Fan, L., Yang, Q.: Federated domain-specific knowledge transfer on large language models using synthetic data. arXiv preprint arXiv:2405.14212 (2024)
46. Lin, Z., Sun, Y., Shi, Y., Wang, X., Huang, L., Shen, L., Tao, D.: Efficient federated prompt tuning for black-box large pre-trained models. arXiv preprint arXiv:2310.03123 (2023).
47. Sun, J., Xu, Z., Yin, H., Yang, D., Xu, D., Chen, Y., Roth, H.R.: Fedbpt: Efficient federated black-box prompt tuning for large language models. arXiv preprint arXiv:2310.01467 (2023)
48. Shen, X., Liu, Y., Liu, H., Hong, J., Duan, B., Huang, Z., Mao, Y., Wu, Y., Wu, D.: A split-and-privatize framework for large language model fine-tuning. arXiv preprint arXiv:2312.15603 (2023)
49. Tian, Y., Wan, Y., Lyu, L., Yao, D., Jin, H., Sun, L.: Fedbert: When federated learning meets pre-training. ACM Trans. Intell. Syst. Technol. **13**(4), 1–26 (2022)
50. Wei, J., Wang, X., Schuurmans, D., Bosma, M., Xia, F., Chi, E., Le, Q.V., Zhou, D., et al.: Chain-of-thought prompting elicits reasoning in large language models. Adv. Neural Inf. Process. Syst. **35**, 24824–24837 (2022)
51. Sun, T., Shao, Y., Qian, H., Huang, X., Qiu, X.: Black-box tuning for language-model-as-a-service. In: International Conference on Machine Learning, pp. 20841–20855. PMLR (2022)
52. Sun, T., He, Z., Qian, H., Zhou, Y., Huang, X., Qiu, X.: BBTv2: Towards a gradient-free future with large language models. In: Proceedings of the 2022 Conference on Empirical Methods in Natural Language Processing, Abu Dhabi. Association for Computational Linguistics (2022)
53. Hansen, N.: The cma evolution strategy: A tutorial. arXiv preprint arXiv:1604.00772 (2016)
54. Oh, C., Hwang, H., Lee, H.-y., Lim, Y., Jung, G., Jung, J., Choi, H., Song, K.: Blackvip: Black-box visual prompting for robust transfer learning. In: Proceedings of the IEEE/CVF Conference on Computer Vision and Pattern Recognition, pp. 24224–24235 (2023)
55. Spall, J.C.: Multivariate stochastic approximation using a simultaneous perturbation gradient approximation. IEEE Trans. Autom. Control **37**(3), 332–341 (1992)
56. Diao, S., Huang, Z., Xu, R., Li, X., Lin, Y., Zhou, X., Zhang, T.: Black-box prompt learning for pre-trained language models. arXiv preprint arXiv:2201.08531 (2022)

57. Li, Z., Peng, B., He, P., Galley, M., Gao, J., Yan, X.: Guiding large language models via directional stimulus prompting. Adv. Neural Inf. Process. Syst. **36**, 62630–62656 (2023)
58. Xu, H., Xiang, L., Ye, H., Yao, D., Chu, P., Li, B.: Shuffled transformer for privacy-preserving split learning. arXiv preprint arXiv:2304.07735 (2023)
59. Chatzikokolakis, K., Andrés, M.E., Bordenabe, N.E., Palamidessi, C.: Broadening the scope of differential privacy using metrics. In: International Symposium on Privacy Enhancing Technologies Symposium, pp. 82–102. Springer (2013)
60. Xiao, G., Lin, J., Han, S.: Offsite-tuning: Transfer learning without full model. arXiv preprint arXiv:2302.04870 (2023)
61. Fan, T., Kang, Y., Ma, G., Chen, W., Wei, W., Fan, L., Yang, Q.: Fate-llm: A industrial grade federated learning framework for large language models. arXiv preprint arXiv:2310.10049 (2023)
62. WeBank: Offsite-tuning with federated learning. https://github.com/FederatedAI/FATE-LLM/blob/main/doc/tutorial/offsite_tuning/README.md
63. DAMO: Co-evolution of large- and small-scale ai models. https://damo.alibaba.com/techtrends/2022/co-evolution-of-large-and-small-scale-ai-models?lang=en"
64. Deng, Y., Qiao, Z., Ren, J., Liu, Y., Zhang, Y.: Mutual enhancement of large and small language models with cross-silo knowledge transfer. arXiv preprint arXiv:2312.05842 (2023)
65. Zhang, Z., Yang, Y., Dai, Y., Wang, Q., Yu, Y., Qu, L., Xu, Z.: FedPETuning: When federated learning meets the parameter-efficient tuning methods of pre-trained language models. In: Findings of the Association for Computational Linguistics: ACL 2023, pp. 9963–9977 (2023)
66. Liu, X.-Y., Zhu, R., Zha, D., Gao, J., Zhong, S., White, M., Qiu, M.: Differentially private low-rank adaptation of large language model using federated learning. ACM Trans. Manag. Inf. Syst. **16**(2), 1–24 (2025)
67. Xu, M., Song, C., Tian, Y., Agrawal, N., Granqvist, F., van Dalen, R., Zhang, X., Argueta, A., Han, S., Deng, Y., Liu, L., Walia, A., Jin, A.: Training large-vocabulary neural language models by private federated learning for resource-constrained devices. In: 2023 IEEE International Conference on Acoustics, Speech and Signal Processing (ICASSP) (2023)
68. Zhao, H., Du, W., Li, F., Li, P., Liu, G.: Fedprompt: Communication-efficient and privacy-preserving prompt tuning in federated learning. In: ICASSP 2023 - 2023 IEEE International Conference on Acoustics, Speech and Signal Processing (ICASSP), pp. 1–5 (2023)

Ben Tan is currently a Senior Researcher at Tencent in Shenzhen, China. Prior to this, he served as a Senior Researcher at WeBank. He earned his Ph.D from Hong Kong University of Science and Technology. His re-search focuses on machine learning, federated learning, and their applications in recommendation systems and online advertising. His work has been published in top-tier conferences (e.g., KDD, AAAI, RecSys, SDM) and renowned journals (e.g., *ACM TIST*, *IEEE TITS*, *Pattern Recognition*).

Yan Kang is currently a Principal AI Engineer in the AI Platform Department at Honor in Shenzhen, China, conducting R&D on various aspects of mobile user behaviour. Previously, he was an AI Researcher at WeBank in Shenzhen, China, focusing on research in privacy-preserving machine learning and federated learning. His re-search has been published in well-known conferences and journals, including IEEE ISP, IEEE TBD, IJCAI, ICDE, and IEEE TKDE.

Lixin Fan is Chief AI Scientist at WeBank (Shenzhen), specializing in machine learning, privacy computing, federated learning, and computer vision. An author of 90+ publications, he previously worked at Nokia and Xerox research centres. He actively contributes as area chair and workshop organizer at top AI conferences (NeurIPS, ICML, CVPR, etc.). Dr. Fan holds 100+ patents globally and chairs the IEEE Computational Intelli-gence Society's Standards Committee. His expertise drives innovation in AI technologies and industry standards.

Vincent Zheng joined WeBank in 2018 and is now Deputy General Manager in charge of digital marketing for MSME banking business. His main business interests include prompting inclusive finance and building AI native banking services for MSMEs. In WeBank, he builds online B2B advertising system and digital campaign system that currently serve over 50 million MSMEs. He is also building next-generation financial products with new AI-native designs, ranging from insurance pricing to micro-loan user experience etc. He obtained PhD from Hong Kong University of Science and Technology in 2011.

Part II
Safe and Responsible Enterprise AI

As artificial intelligence becomes increasingly embedded in enterprise systems, the urgency to ensure its safe and responsible use has never been greater. The opaque nature of many AI models, the rapid pace of innovation driven by commercial incentives, and the potential for unintended harms ranging from bias and discrimination to privacy violations demand new knowledge, theories, frameworks, and safeguards. This part brings together leading research and practical insights that address the critical aspects of AI safety in the enterprise context.

The first chapter by Lisa Ehrlinger and Felix Naumann focuses on the foundational issue of data quality. Enterprises are appreciating the benefits of shifting from model-centric to data-centric AI, as the need to ensure that data is accurate, consistent, and fit for purpose becomes essential. The authors explore data quality from both technical and managerial perspectives, offering concrete methods for data preprocessing and long-term quality assurance. With a primary focus on the technical perspective, this chapter highlights the importance of embedding data quality practices into enterprise systems to support reliable and trustworthy AI outcomes.

The second chapter by Neil G. Marchant, Ying Zhao, Benjamin I. P. Rubinstein, and Olga Ohrimenko addresses data privacy, a foundational aspect of responsible AI deployment. Enterprise AI systems often process sensitive personal and organizational data, making them vulnerable to misuse and regulatory breaches. The authors provide a comprehensive guide to privacy-preserving techniques and highlight the risks of model inversion and data leakage. Their insights equip enterprises with the tools needed to protect data integrity and foster trust among stakeholders, enabling broader and more secure AI adoption.

The third chapter by Francesco Sovrano and Tim Miller introduces a unified framework for explainable AI (XAI) tailored to enterprise needs. While XAI has been promoted as a way to mitigate issues such as bias, opacity, and poor decision-making, the authors argue that progress has been uneven due to misconceptions about how AI is used in practice. Their framework reorients XAI toward real-world enterprise decision-making, emphasizing the need for transparency, accountability, and user understanding. This chapter reinforces the role of explainability as a critical enabler of responsible AI.

The final chapter by Ujwal Gadiraju and Agathe Balayn explores the evolving landscape of human-AI collaboration. As generative and agentic AI systems become more capable, enterprises face new opportunities and challenges in designing systems that augment rather than replace human capabilities. Drawing on empirical research, the authors examine the human, task, and system factors that influence trust and reliance in collaborative settings. They advocate for a broader evaluation framework that incorporates stakeholder values and organizational context, ensuring that human-AI configurations are designed to ensure that computational power and scalability of AI systems are complementing and amplifying human strengths.

Together, these chapters provide a comprehensive set of resources for individuals and enterprises seeking to implement AI systems that are not only powerful but also principled. By addressing data quality, privacy, explainability, and human-AI collaboration, this part lays the groundwork for building AI systems that are safe, transparent, and aligned with human and organizational values.

Chapter 4
Data Quality for Enterprise AI

Lisa Ehrlinger and Felix Naumann

Abstract The predominant shift from model-centric AI to data-centric AI matches well the needs of enterprises seeking to use and improve AI applications. Several studies show the large amount of time that data scientists spend on searching and cleaning datasets in practical scenarios, instead of designing and training machine learning (ML) models. This imbalance is partially caused by the fact that data is often distributed over different locations in enterprises, is stored in different formats, is heterogeneous, and has varying information quality. The form and speed of data ingestion also influence the types of ML models required for analysis. To ensure high-quality results by ML models, one must first ensure that the data at hand is fit for the intended purpose, i.e., that it is of high quality relative to the task at hand.

After introducing general concepts of data quality, this book chapter reviews data quality for enterprise AI from two perspectives: (1) the *data scientist perspective* covering concrete methods for data preprocessing to check and improve the quality of a specific dataset at hand and (2) the *management perspective* covering the implementation of a continuous data quality assurance pipeline within an enterprise that accounts for long-term monitoring and root cause analysis. Although the focus will be on the first perspective, the second perspective is essential for a comprehensive AI strategy within a company. We conclude this chapter with an outlook on open challenges in the area of data quality for AI for both researchers and practitioners.

4.1 Data and Information Quality

Data is the basis for almost all decisions taken in enterprises—its quality is therefore of high relevance. A few years ago, decision-makers were still able to manually assess and interpret the quality of data at hand. As digitalization and the productive

L. Ehrlinger (✉) · F. Naumann
Information Systems, Hasso Plattner Institute, University of Potsdam, Potsdam, Germany
e-mail: lisa.ehrlinger@hpi.de; felix.naumann@hpi.de

S. Sadiq (ed.), *Enterprise AI*, https://doi.org/10.1007/978-3-032-01940-0_4

use of artificial intelligence (AI) in enterprises became more prevalent, the amount of data being collected, stored, and consequently used for automated decision-making exceeds the capabilities of humans to process it. Hence, the need for automated approaches to assess and improve data quality has been recognized [1–3].

Poor data quality (DQ) impedes the operational excellence of enterprises; it can lead to effects like cost increase (both internally or loss of revenues), customer dissatisfaction, or organizational mistrust [4, 5]. According to Gartner, organizations believe that poor DQ is responsible for an average loss of $15 million per year and organization in the USA [6]. In a US market survey by Experian [7], 85% of the organizations report that poor-quality customer data negatively impacts their operational processes and therefore efficiency. Thus, DQ is nowadays perceived as the greatest challenge in corporate data management [8] and identified as one of the key challenges for applying AI in enterprises [9, 10].

At an abstract level, data quality is typically defined as "fitness for use" [11, 12] or, with its extended version, "fitness for all purposes made of the data, including the likely future uses" [13]. These definitions emphasize the fact that DQ cannot be assessed without the context, in which the data is used. While *data* is defined as "facts and statistics collected together for reference or analysis" [14], *information* describes the extension of data (i.e., facts) with context and semantics [13]. Despite the distinction between data and information in research, *information quality* is often used as a synonym for *data quality* [15, 16]. Sebastian-Coleman [17] points out that this ambiguity has its roots in the different usage of the terms *data* and *information*, e.g., information is described as "facts provided or learned about something or someone" in the New Oxford American dictionary [14]. In this chapter, we discuss both, the assessment and cleaning of data and information quality.

Over the last decades, data quality research has been conducted by different communities. Dasu and Johnson [18] identified four complementary approaches toward DQ research, stemming from (1) process management, (2) statistics, (3) the database community, and (4) domain specification. Seminal work in the process management community has been conducted by Wang et al., who proposed managing data as a product by drawing from quality research in the manufacturing domain and introduced the concept of DQ dimensions [15].

In the statistics community, the awareness of DQ has increased with the amount of data being analyzed. Here, the focus is on the identification and cleaning of specific data errors (cf. Sect. 4.1.2), such as missing values, suspicious (abnormal) data, and issues of the fit between data and analysis [18]. Note that the statistics community heavily overlaps with the fields of data mining, machine learning, data science, and artificial intelligence (see [19] for a distinction between these terms). The focus in all these communities is on the analysis of datasets to draw conclusions or to learn algorithmic behavior; hence, a clean and error-free dataset is required.

Research in the database community has historically focused on duplicate detection and data cleaning, including name and address correction [18]. More recent approaches cover the profiling of data, including the discovery and validation of functional dependencies, keys, and join paths, as discussed in Sect. 4.2. A few more recent approaches also attempt holistic data cleaning [20, 21], i.e., eliminating data error under minimal overall changes.

The fourth approach toward DQ research has emerged from specific application domains that record, transmit, or update data. It aims to encode quality requirements available as domain expertise in metadata. An example is the Common Data Model (CDM) developed by the Observational Medical Outcomes Partnership (OMOP), which is an open data standard to exchange electronic health record data that can be used to annotate DQ checks (cf. [22]).

In addition to research, there have also been endeavors to *standardize* the assessment of data quality. The ISO/IEC 25000 (SQuaRE—Software product Quality Requirements and Evaluation) series of international standards aims at general definition of quality management and evaluation for different parts of an information system. The most relevant standards with respect to DQ assessment in this series are ISO/IEC 25012 ISO/IEC [23] and ISO/IEC 25024 ISO/IEC [24]. ISO/IEC 25012:2008 ISO/IEC [23] defines a DQ model for structured data, categorizing quality attributes into fifteen "characteristics" (used as synonym to DQ dimensions) from both inherent and system-dependent perspectives. ISO/IEC 25024:2015 ISO/IEC [23] defines specific measures to quantify each characteristic outlined in ISO/IEC 25012 and includes guidance on how to apply these measures. More recently, the ISO/IEC 5259 [25] series have been developed, focusing on DQ for analytics and machine learning (ML). This standard establishes the framework for assessing and enhancing DQ across different phases of the data life cycle, crucial for reliable analytics and ML outcomes. Although there is research using these standards (e.g., [26, 27]) so far, widespread adoption can be observed neither in research nor in industry.

In the following sections, we introduce the notion of DQ dimensions in Sect. 4.1.1, discuss common DQ problems in Sect. 4.1.2, and give an overview of DQ management approaches in Sect. 4.1.3. In the remainder of the chapter, Sect. 4.2 introduces basic methods to extract quality-relevant metadata from large datasets. Then, Sect. 4.3 discusses specific methods to assess the quality of data in its various facets. Methods for the preparation and cleaning of datasets are discussed in Sect. 4.4, and solutions on how to manage and govern data quality in specific domains are provided in Sect. 4.5. We close this chapter with an outlook and open challenges in Sect. 4.6.

4.1.1 Data Quality Dimensions

Data quality is often perceived as a multidimensional concept that is characterized by different *DQ dimensions* [12, 28]. Each of these dimensions describes a specific aspect of high-quality data, such as accuracy, completeness, or timeliness. Although there is a general agreement on the concept of DQ dimensions, a wide variety of dimensions (more than 200 according to Berti-Équille [29]) and classifications have been proposed [30–34]. There is also an attempt to create an open standard of conformed DQ dimensions [33]. Consequently, there is much disparity in the definition and interpretation of DQ dimensions, hindering the systematic development of standardized measures. In this chapter, we discuss the measurement and assessment of DQ dimensions along with example metrics in Sect. 4.3.

While DQ dimensions describe the characteristics of high-quality data (e.g., completeness), data quality can also be investigated from the viewpoint of poor-quality data, that is, errors in the data, such as missing values. Although there is an intuitive mapping from some DQ problems to dimensions (e.g., missing values to the completeness dimension), Laranjeiro et al. [31] indicate that the mapping is not always straightforward or even possible due to different interpretations for both concepts. We argue that it is time to investigate the two perspectives jointly: developing methods for the detection of data errors (and their indicators) that can be used to develop meaningful metrics for DQ dimensions. For practical implementation in enterprises and organizations, domain-specific context can inform the selection, interpretation, and concrete implementation of specific DQ dimensions.

4.1.2 Data Quality Problems

Throughout the literature, data errors are also termed DQ problems, DQ issues, data defects, glitches, or dirty data. While single data erorrs (e.g., incorrect formats, missing key constraints, or spelling mistakes) might be easily detected in a specific context, real-world data typically contains multiple error types that can influence each other and make it difficult to consistently define, detect, and clean them. We discuss the (1) detection of data errors in Sect. 4.4.3.1, the (2) cleaning in Sect. 4.4.3.2, and (3) error generation for benchmarking in Sect. 4.4.3.3.

Over the years, there have been many attempts to list data errors and classify them into taxonomies [35–40]. While Rahm and Do [39] distinguish between single-source and multi-source errors, as well as between schema-level and instance-level errors, Ge and Helfert [36] review different data error classifications and distinguish between context-dependent and context-independent problems, as well as between a user perspective and the data perspective. Ilyas and Chu [41] perceive data errors as violations of rules or patterns, such as denial constraints. Notably, there are only two works that provide formal definitions to describe data errors: Oliveira et al. [42] and Josko et al. [43]. Oliveira et al. [42] provide formal definitions for a list of data errors grouped by the granularity level (attribute/tuple, single relation, multiple relations, multiple data sources) with the aim to enable automatic error detection. Josko et al. [43] propose a taxonomy that distinguishes between (1) data constraints and (2) fact representation deviations on the highest level. It is further sub-divided into four hierarchy levels, also including the granularity of the data.

We follow the understanding of Abedjan et al. [40] and define an error in a dataset as an atomic value (or cell) that deviates from its given real-world value (i.e., ground truth). The most common data error types mentioned throughout these surveys are missing values, outliers, duplicates, rule violations, and pattern violations.

4.1.3 Data Quality Management

According to the Data Management Association (DAMA), "data quality management" is the analysis, improvement, and assurance of data quality [8]. Over the years, a number of different DQ management methodologies (also declared as "frameworks," "programs," or "methods") have been proposed. Examples include the Total Data Quality Management (TDQM) by Wang [15], A Methodology for Information Quality Assessment (AIMQ) by Lee et al. [44], and the DQ assessment methods by Pipino et al. [45] and Maydanchik [46]. An overview of these DQ methodologies is provided by Batini et al. [47] and Cichy and Rass [32]. Although these methodologies have different emphases, they share four core activities or steps [13, 32, 46, 48]: (1) state reconstruction, (2) DQ measurement or assessment, (3) data cleaning or improvement, and (4) the establishment of a DQ governance strategy to ensure continuous monitoring. The following sections describe these four steps in detail. Step (1), the state reconstruction, describes the collection of contextual information on the observed data (e.g., database schemas, data flows between organizations) as well as on the organization (e.g., business processes, involved stakeholders) where a DQ project is carried out [47]. Since the focus of this chapter is on the technical background of DQ assessment and improvement, Step (1) is restricted to the data part (i.e., data profiling described in Sect. 4.2), and no detailed discussion on the gathering of contextual information within an organization is provided. Following, DQ assessment is discussed in Sect. 4.3, data cleaning in Sect. 4.4, and DQ governance in Sect. 4.5.

4.2 Data Profiling

Metadata is the foundation of any undertaking related to data quality. In fact, data quality is one type of metadata to describe a given dataset. In general, metadata is defined as "data that defines or describes other data" [49] and, thus, covers a very broad range of information. In this section, we focus on traditional metadata for relational (tabular) data, including statistics, dependencies, and other constraints, which form a basis to more advanced metadata concerning data quality. Data profiling for other data models is discussed at the end of the section.

Metadata can have two sources: (i) expert developers formulate metadata constraints on the data or (ii) the constraints can be discovered from the data itself. The former describes how the data should be, for instance, in the form of a database schema with data types, keys, and assertions, while the latter describes which form the data actually takes. *Data profiling* is the process of analyzing a dataset to collect metadata using a broad range of techniques [50]. It is thus an essential task prior to any DQ assessment or cleaning task to obtain insight into a given dataset. Often, data quality is assessed by comparing desired metadata values with actual metadata values. For instance, the database schema might demand a certain column to be a key, while data profiling might detect a non-perfect uniqueness.

The following sections list the types of metadata to consider, how to discover them from data, and, finally, how to distinguish spurious metadata, which can be ignored, from genuine metadata, which are relevant for data quality assessment.

4.2.1 Types of Metadata

Metadata can range from simple counting-based statistics to more involved aggregated values and all the way to complex dependencies, such as denial constraints. Metadata can cover individual columns, multiple columns, a whole table, or even an entire database. While an implicit annotation to the entire range of a table is very common (e.g., sum of sales or accuracy of temperature measurement), metadata annotations can also make sense on certain parts of a table (e.g., phone number is unique only for US citizens). In this section, we list important types of metadata and discuss how they are relevant to data quality.

4.2.1.1 Statistics and Patterns

The simplest forms of metadata are various counts on single columns, such as the number of values, the number of distinct values, or value distributions stored in histograms. Typically, such statistics are used for query optimization in a database or exploratory data analysis. Slightly more advanced metadata concern the characterization of values in a column, such as determining their data type, their domain, or their value patterns. Such metadata are already closer related to data quality concerns, as they can be used to identify outliers, incorrectly formatted data, or invalid data. Table 4.1 (from [50]) provides a list of basic metadata that can be assessed for individual columns grouped by category.

4.2.1.2 Dependencies

Data dependencies are metadata that generally affect multiple columns within a table or even columns across tables. Rather than prescribing the shape of individual data values, they describe valid relationships among values in a database.

Among the most useful dependencies are *unique column combinations* (UCCs), *functional dependencies* (FDs), *inclusion dependencies* (INDs), and *denial constraints* (DCs). A UCC specifies that each value combination in the specified set of columns appears only once. Typical examples of UCCs are primary and secondary keys in database tables, for instance, ensuring that data about a customer is not stored multiple times.

Table 4.1 Overview of single-column metadata (Taken from [50])

Category	Task	Description
Cardinalities	num-rows	Number of rows
	null values	Number or percentage of null values
	distinct	Number of distinct values
	uniqueness	Number of distinct values divided by number of rows
Value distributions	histogram	Frequency histograms (equi-width, equi-depth, etc.)
	extremes	Minimum and maximum values in a numeric column
	constancy	Frequency of most frequent value divided by number of rows
	quartiles	Three points that divide (numeric) values into four equal groups
	first digit	Distribution of first digit in numeric values; to check Benford's law
Data types, patterns, and domains	basic type	numeric, alphanumeric, date, time, etc.
	data type	DBMS-specific data type (varchar, timestamp, etc.)
	lengths	Minimum, maximum, median, and average lengths of values within a column
	size	Maximum number of digits in numeric values
	decimals	Maximum number of decimals in numeric values
	patterns	Histogram of value patterns (Aa9...)
	data class	Generic semantic data type, such as code, indicator, text, date/time, quantity, identifier
	domain	Semantic domain, such as credit card, first name, city, phenotype

A functional dependency describes a dependency between a set of determinant columns and a single dependent column: records with same values in the determinant columns must also have same values in the dependent column. For instance, addresses with the same zip code must also have the same city values. Thus, FDs can be used for both data quality assessment (i.e., error detection) and data cleaning (i.e., error correction).

An inclusion dependency prescribes that the values of one column (or column combination) shall be included in the values of another column (or column combination of the same size). In particular, INDs are prerequisites for foreign keys in databases. Again, such dependencies can be used to detect errors, such as dangling references, but also support schema discovery by explaining how different tables in a database might be related.

Finally, denial constraints are powerful expressions to encode complex business rules [51]. The DC formalism can express UCCs and FDs but also rules that might express that a manager shall not earn less than their employees. Detecting violations of such DCs is a complex task [52, 53] but can reveal data errors and thus serve DQ assessment.

4.2.1.3 Other Data Models

While we focus on relational (or tabular) data for our discussion of data profiling, other data models are equally affected by poor data quality and therefore deserve data profiling methods to uncover patterns and dependencies. Examples include textual data, for which additional linguistic measures [54] and semantic measures [55] can be applied; image and other multimedia data, for which media-specific measures like resolution or color depth can be profiled [56]; or hierarchical data models like XML (Extensible Markup Language) or JSON (JavaScript Object Notation), for which features like the nesting-depth can be profiled [57] as basis to identify malformed documents.

A large amount of Web data and linked open data is stored with the RDF[1] (Resource Description Framework) data model, which models facts as subject-predicate-object triples (e.g., ⟨*Shazia Sadiq, employer, UQ*⟩). The systematic survey by Ben Ellefi et al. [58] identified 85 publications and various software tools in this area, categorizing their profiling tasks by DQ dimensions. Beyond the typical metadata that is applicable to data of any model, so-called link features measure how much and how well a given dataset is linked to other datasets—an important principle for the linked data vision.[2] In general, a frequent approach for profiling graph data is to translate concepts from relational data to the new data model. As one example, Fan et al. propose graph functional dependencies [59] and provide a discovery method [60] for property graphs [61] (another popular graph data model besides RDF).

4.2.2 *Discovering Metadata*

Traditionally, constraints such as data types, keys, foreign keys, and functional dependencies are defined for a database schema at design time by domain experts and database experts. However, many datasets do not come with such dependencies explicitly: they might not be known in advance, database designers are reluctant to specify them fearing runtime penalties, or the DBMS might simply not be able to express them. When metadata are not known in advance, for instance, because it is not enforced by the database, they can be determined by analyzing the data at hand, motivating metadata discovery algorithms. Note that in contrast to metadata and dependencies that are defined at design time, each discovered dependency only holds for the given relational instance at hand. The next Sect. 4.2.3 discusses this important distinction in more detail.

Numerous methods have been developed to discover or extract metadata from a given table or entire database. This process is generally called *data profiling*. For

[1] https://www.w3.org/TR/PR-rdf-syntax/Overview.html

[2] https://www.w3.org/DesignIssues/LinkedData.html

simple metadata, such as cardinalities and value distributions, the discovery algorithms are equally simple and already a core component of most data management systems. Database systems, for instance, routinely collect such information as input to their query optimizers [62]. Discovery of data types and domains is more difficult, as these types of metadata go beyond the mere syntactic properties of data and need to understand the semantics of the data at hand. Such methods are commonly known as *semantic data type discovery* methods [63] and can make use of knowledge bases and large language models.

Discovering dependencies, as outlined in Sect. 4.2.1.2 is usually computationally complex: by definition, dependencies involve column combinations, for instance, multiple columns together functionally determining another column. Thus, the search space of all dependencies is of exponential size wrt. the number of columns in the table or database. To address this complexity, many advanced algorithms have been developed, which are able to effectively prune the search space and efficiently validate remaining dependency candidates [50].

Data profiling discovers metadata from some given data and therefore describes this data but passes no judgment about its quality. Only metadata that is specified or confirmed by an expert can help assess and maintain data quality. This can happen in two ways. First, given some metadata, such as data types or dependencies, a data system can help guarantee that this metadata remain valid despite changes in the data. Such data (quality) governance is one of the main objectives of database management systems, which enforce constraints such as keys, foreign keys, or data types. Second, confirmed metadata that does not hold for certain parts of the data can indicate violations in the data and thus targets for data cleaning (see Sect. 4.4.3).

4.2.3 Relaxing Metadata

Data profiling is important for data quality management, as it can extract yet unknown or unspecified constraints on the data, which can serve to measure data quality or clean the data. However, any metadata discovered from the data itself is not necessarily true metadata that is expected to hold for any real-world instance of the database. Thus, we distinguish *genuine* metadata from *spurious* metadata. The former is metadata that is confirmed by an expert; the latter just happens to be true for the given data instance. For instance, discovering eleven distinct values in a month column might be true for the data at hand, but should not be generalized to restricting the column domain. Likewise, dependency discovery algorithms tend to discover thousands or even hundreds of thousands of dependencies in a given dataset. Clearly, not all express real-world constraints on the data. For instance, one might discover that the combination ⟨first-name, street, zip⟩ is a unique column combination in a customer dataset. Yet this should not be turned into a data quality constraint, but rather it is a coincidence. Further, discovered dependencies can be rather large: in realistic scenarios, key constraints or functional dependencies should, perhaps, not exceed six columns. These are examples of spurious metadata, which can be discovered automatically, but need to be verified by human experts regarding their genuineness.

To support this verification task, automated methods exist to classify dependencies, for instance based on attribute names, their position in the schema [64], or their likelihood of being coincidental [51, 65]. Once established as being genuine, the discovered metadata can be turned into database constraints, such as data types, keys and foreign keys, or business rules during data import.

In many cases, however, the datasets at hand already contain dirty data, rendering the discovery of exact metadata moot. For instance, a phone number misplaced into a name column can prevent data profiling to extract a proper pattern for that column; a duplicated row prevents any unique column combination to be found; or an incorrectly entered zip code violates the otherwise true dependency between zip and city. To account for such dirty data, some data profiling approaches propose relaxed variants [66]: *partial* dependencies allow for a certain number or percentage of violating records, while *matching* dependencies relax the implied equality of dependencies, replacing it with similarity. For instance, the city values for a given zip code, if not the same, must at least all be similar. Thus, both "New York" and "New York City" might be valid for a zip code 10001.

4.2.4 Managing Metadata in Enterprises and Organizations

Having discovered many metadata, it can be a challenge to manage, maintain, and analyze them [67]. The management of simple metadata is commonplace in data management solutions. Commercial vendors, such as Viadotto,[3] offer specialized products to also support many kinds of dependencies. In addition, query languages for metadata were proposed, including the declarative domain-specific query language DPQL [68].

The metadata discussed in this section can be described as *technical metadata* as it can be collected automatically from a dataset or the database infrastructure. According to Quimbert et al. [69], technical metadata can also be subdivided into (1) descriptive metadata, e.g., a title or author of a table; (2) administrative metadata, e.g., file format, encoding, or access rights; and (3) structural metadata, e.g., describing foreign key relationships between tables. However, in the enterprise context, the collection of technical metadata for a central repository is not sufficient to add value to business users. In addition to verifying the genuineness of spurious technical metadata, also the annotation of domain knowledge (*business metadata*) is required as human input. Domain knowledge in the context of DQ can, for example, be the known minimum and maximum value of a specific sensor or the typical distribution that is expected from a measurement value.

[3] https://www.viadotto.tech/

For the joint management of technical and business metadata, data catalog tools have received increasing attention in enterprises [70, 71]. Note that the type of technical metadata collected by data catalogs is usually restricted to schema information and simple forms of metadata as discussed in Sect. 4.2.1.1.

In governmental and non-profit organizations, metadata management is as important as in closed enterprise settings but yields different challenges. For many initiatives, such as `data.gov`[4] by the US government or the knowledge organization system for the United Nations Sustainable Development Goals (SDGs) [72], metadata management is crucial. The main challenges in such enterprise settings are the integration of data from different sources with different formats and the unclear dataset responsibilities. Specifically in the context of non-governmental organizations (NGOs), organizations face challenges due to volunteers collecting, integrating, and publishing data of varying quality. One of the most popular data and metadata management systems for such applications is CKAN (Comprehensive Knowledge Archive Network)[5] since its code base is open source and has many plug-ins for various extensions [73].

In the context of AI, business metadata is crucial for datasets, not only because of their relevance to assess data quality but also to ensure proper and ethical use of the respective datasets. In recent years, several standards for annotating contextual metadata have been established, such as datasheets for datasets [74], Data Cards [75], the FAIR principles [76], or the Dataset Nutrition Label [77].

To summarize, data profiling is the task of extracting metadata of all kinds from a given dataset. Especially extracted constraints and dependencies are useful input to data quality assessment: whenever a constraint is violated, a data error has occurred, and data quality is lowered. Table 4.2 lists some of the discussed constraints, along with their possible violations. Such violations and their quantity in a dataset can affect different data quality dimensions, as we discuss in the next section.

Table 4.2 Constraints and errors

Constraint	Violation	Example
Data type	Value of incorrect type	`'today'` in a column of `date` type
Value pattern	Incorrect formatting	`012 345 6789` for a pattern `+dd ddd dddd`
Not-null	Missing value	Unknown `lastname` left empty
Unique	Duplicate value	Same `cust_id` given to different customers
Foreign key	Missing reference	Order referencing a non-existing `cust_id`
Functional dependency	Different dependent values for same determinant	Different `city` values for same `zip` value

[4] https://data.gov

[5] https://ckan.org

4.3 Data Quality Assessment

DQ cannot be improved if it cannot be measured [78]. Following this axiom, it is necessary to define meaningful measures (i.e., metrics) for data quality. In 2013, Sebastian-Coleman [17] pointed out that it was not clear on how to measure data quality and therefore considered this lack to be one of the greatest challenges for DQ practitioners. We believe that this statement still holds true for the age of AI.

Assessment is the "evaluation or estimation of the nature, ability, or quality of something" [14] and extends the concept of measurement by evaluating the measurement results and drawing a conclusion about the object of assessment [17]. The ISO standard 8000 [49] distinguishes between the following three categories in which DQ can be assessed [49]:

- *Syntactic quality* is the degree to which data conforms to a specified syntax, e.g., requirements defined by metadata.
- *Semantic quality* is the degree to which data corresponds to its real representation.
- *Pragmatic quality* is the degree to which data is suitable for a specific purpose.

While syntactic quality can be measured with a set of rules, for semantic quality, a (machine-readable) conceptual model of the universe of discourse is required to ensure that the investigated data can be compared to its real representation [49]. Pragmatic quality covers all perspectives that are not covered by the former two categories and therefore requires interaction with the users validating the data [49]. Consequently, automated DQ assessment is restricted to syntactic and semantic DQ aspects.

Since high-level DQ dimensions do not provide quantitative measures to automate DQ assessment, the definition and assignment of DQ metrics (i.e., measurement functions) are required [48, 79]. DQ metrics are functions that map a DQ dimension to a numerical value to allow an interpretation of the respective dimension's fulfillment [80]. Heinrich et al. [81] proposed five requirements (partially based on Even and Shankaranarayanan [82] and Pipino et al. [45]) that should be considered when developing DQ metrics:

1. *Existence of minimum and maximum metric values.* DQ metrics have to take values within a given range. In practice, DQ metrics are often provided as ratios with a result value between 0 (metric not fulfilled) and 1 (metric perfectly fulfilled).
2. *Interval-scaled metric values.* Differences and intervals of a metric should be able to be determined and be meaningful. In other words, a metric result must have identical differences in all ranges (e.g., between 0.2 and 0.3 or 0.9 and 1.0).
3. *Quality of the configuration parameters and the determination of the metric values.* To adjust a DQ metric to a different context, a number of quality criteria for the respective metric must be satisfied. Heinrich et al. [81] summarize this requirement to the easy and unambiguous retrieval and interpretation of configuration parameters and metric values.

4. *Sound aggregation of the metric values.* It should be possible to consistently aggregate the metric values on different granularity level of the data (e.g., from value level, row level, or column level to table level).
5. *Economic efficiency of the metric.* The last requirement describes the importance to consider the cost-benefit perspective when designing a DQ metric, as discussed in detail by Laney [83].

Note that there are different perspectives on the meaningfulness of these requirements. Bronselaer et al. [84] point out that even the interpretation of normalized (being in the unit interval [0, 1]) and interval-scaled DQ metrics is not always clear in practice and that the aggregatability does not always make sense [84].

In this section, we discuss the assessment of the four DQ dimensions that are explicitly mentioned by the AI Act [85]: representativity, accuracy (free of errors), completeness, and relevancy. Note that there are many additional and equally interesting DQ dimensions that should be considered for specific AI use cases and application scenarios. For example, the notion of duplicate data plays a crucial role in customer and address data, which is why a measure for the "minimality" or "non-redundancy" in data might be of interest (cf. [86]). In the context of AI-based systems, also the "fairness" or representativity of the data can be assessed in addition to the fairness of a machine learning model. Since a detailed discussion of all DQ dimensions is out of scope for this book, we refer to the glossary by Mohammed et al. [34] for a comprehensive list of dimensions that are specifically relevant in the context of AI.

4.3.1 Accuracy

The title of the seminal work "Beyond Accuracy: What Data Quality Means to Data Consumers" [12] highlights the central role of this DQ dimension, which is, according to Wand and Wang [79], the most cited DQ dimension in DQ research at the time. Despite this pivotal role, Haegemans et al. [87] list a number of diverse definitions and metrics for accuracy. While DQ researchers often describe accuracy as the closeness or similarity between a data value represented in an information system and its real-world representation [48, 79], natural scientists usually define accuracy as the "magnitude of an error" [87]. The most common metric to measure accuracy is the fraction of correct data items:

$$accuracy = \frac{number\ of\ correct\ data\ items}{number\ of\ all\ data\ items}$$

where data items can be of any granularity level of data, e.g., cells, attributes, or records. When calculating accuracy on the cell level, it can usually be aggregated to higher levels easily.

While this understanding aligns with the general accuracy measure for machine learning tasks (where the number of correct predictions/classifications is compared to all predictions/classifications), accuracy for the evaluation of recommender systems is often defined as the mean absolute error (MAE) [88]. For binary classification, accuracy can also be calculated in terms of positives and negatives as follows:

$$accuracy = \frac{TP + TN}{TP + TN + FP + FN}$$

where TP is the number of true positives, TN the true negatives, FP the false positives, and FN the false negatives [89].

A key challenge in assessing accuracy is the determination whether a value is classified as *correct* or *incorrect*. To take this decision automatically without asking human experts, (external) reference data is required to compare the data at hand. Another possibility is the use of error detection or cleaning methods and tools (cf. Sect. 4.4) to identify and correct data errors.

4.3.2 Completeness

Completeness is very generally described as the "breadth, depth, and scope of information contained in the data" [12, 48] and covers the condition for data to exist. Although completeness is often put on the same level as the detection of missing values (cf. Sect. 4.4.3.1), in practice, more considerations are required for its assessment. To assess the completeness of a dataset, at least the following three properties need to be checked: (1) all desired attributes must be included, i.e., *schema completeness*; (2) the desired amount of data must be included, i.e., *column completeness*; and (3) the dataset must be populated to the extent desired, i.e., *population completeness* [17, 48]. Most existing completeness metrics (cf. [44, 90]) represent the ratio between the number of all present and all possible data items:

$$completeness = \frac{number\ of\ data\ items\ present}{number\ of\ all\ data\ items}$$

Counting the number of NULL values for a given row is an intuitive and easy way to determine the *column completeness*. However, the assumption that missing values are always explicitly modeled as NULL values does not hold in practice, where missing values can also be "disguised," such as "11111111" for a phone number of "-99" for an invalid sensor value [91]. Here, domain expert knowledge in form of metadata or (external) reference data might be required to determine possible default values for a given column. Since placeholders usually differ for each data source, comprehensive documentation is important. In the context of machine learning, the use of open metadata standards such as Data Cards [75] (detailed in Sect. 4.2.4) are especially recommended. Another challenge is to determine the total number of a given population when measuring *population completeness*, such as the number of product types that should appear in a table.

In the context of AI-based analysis, all three types of completeness must be considered: *schema completeness* because it impacts feature selection, *column completeness* because missing values distort the analysis, and *population completeness* because neglected parts of the population introduce bias into the results of a statistical model.

4.3.3 Relevancy

Relevancy is the degree to which data is in accordance to the task at hand and satisfies a user's need [12, 48, 92], which means it is inherently subjective. This is also a reason why relevancy is a standard criterion in information retrieval to indicate whether the content of a document is relevant to a specific query [48].

When searching data for AI-based analysis in a data lake or on the Web, e.g., from open data platforms, such as data.gov,[6] Google datasets,[7] or Kaggle,[8] it is essential to measure and judge the relevancy of the obtained data for the specific task. In closed-world settings, relevancy can be implicitly high [92]. For example, when querying a database of hydrogen engines to analyze their performance, most likely, only relevant results will be returned. While small companies might resemble to the closed-world settings, large enterprises often suffer from intransparent data quality across departments, creating a greater need to ensure relevancy.

Following the definition, the assessment of relevancy requires domain experts to first define and understand the respective task at hand. Second, the relevancy of the data that is used to perform the respective task can be assessed using, for example, statistical methods to determine the importance and contribution of a feature (i.e., attribute) to an ML model's prediction. Example methods for feature importance calculation are Shapley [93, 94] or LIME [95]. Since feature importance is computationally expensive, manual assessment might still be needed. Depending on the respective task, a larger user study can be helpful to reflect the perspective of different stakeholders in the assessment.

The manual assessment of relevancy requires the analysis of the data at hand to understand the structure and content, which can be supported with data profiling methods (see Sect. 4.2). Based on the collected metadata, experts can then define domain- and task-specific criteria to assess the relevancy of individual attributes and records in the data using a rating system (e.g., Likert scale).

---

[6] https://data.gov

[7] https://datasetsearch.research.google.com

[8] https://www.kaggle.com

4.3.4 Representativity

A dataset is statistically representative when each entity in the total population has an equal chance of being included [34]. While representativity is not discussed as a separate DQ dimension in seminal DQ research, it has received increasing attention with the advent of AI-based data analysis [85, 96]. Here, it is important to understand what the data that is being used to draw conclusions represents and which inferences can be made [96]. Clemmensen and Kjærsgaard [96] provide a comprehensive overview on the so-far neglected topic of representativity in AI and ML research. For example, it is important to consider the representativity of samples when drawing conclusions from selected data only. Assuming a dataset of bird sightings in a given area, including 800 bald eagles, 200 turkey vultures, and 200 mockingbirds, a sample should allow the same conclusions to be drawn as for the original population [97]. For our dataset, a representative sample could consist of 38 eagles, 10 vultures, and 11 mockingbirds spotted in a specific subarea, since it keeps the relative ratios between the single bird species.

Gebru et al. [74] also propose a question in their paper on "datasheets about datasets," which addresses the need for data to be representative: "Does the dataset contain all possible instances or is it a sample (not necessarily random) of instances from a larger set? If the dataset is a sample, then what is the larger set? Is the sample representative of the larger set (e.g., geographic coverage)?" [74].

Since the representativity of data has only recently been addressed within the AI context, there are neither widely adopted measurement approaches nor DQ metrics for this dimension. Developing a metric for representativity would need to include the comparison of distributions as key characteristics in the given data against a total population. Of course, the major challenge here is to determine and model the *total population*, which might not always be available as a complete dataset but in some cases only reflected as metadata to a specific dataset.

4.3.5 Further Challenges of DQ Assessment

For the development of concrete metrics and methods to assess DQ dimensions, at least the following challenges need to be taken into account:

- Definition: How is the respective DQ dimension defined and communicated within my enterprise context?
- Input: Which data or metadata is required for the measurement?
- Output: Which scores and explanations can be expected as measurement result?
- Data granularity: On which data structure can/should the metric be calculated?
- Soundness: Does the metric fulfill the requirements for DQ metrics by Heinrich et al. [81]?
- Runtime efficiency: Can the metric be computed in reasonable time, given the data volume and complexity in my organization?
- Customizable: Can the metric be adjusted to a specific use case?

In addition to the data and metadata as input for a DQ metric, Mohammed et al. [98] claim that the following aspects (called *facets* in [98]) need to be considered for the assessment of individual DQ dimensions: (1) the *humans* working with the data; (2) the *source* of the data; (3) the *system* to store, handle, and access the data; and (4) the *task* to be performed on the data. The extent to which input from one facet is required for the assessment of a specific DQ dimension depends on the definition of the dimension's measurement. However, the scientific investigation of a specific facet on its own allows all DQ dimensions that require input from this facet to benefit simultaneously from solving facet-specific challenges [98].

4.4 Data Preparation and Data Cleaning

Data preparation is the process of obtaining, cleaning, transforming, and storing raw data before serving them further to downstream applications. It is reported to be a labor-intensive and tedious work accounting for 50–80% of the time expenses in the whole data analysis life cycle [18, 99, 100]. In the enterprise context, technicians spend much time and budget supporting their data preparation work, reducing resources that should be devoted to interesting downstream applications. Also, the large volumes of data in data lakes are compelling and can generate valuable information, provided they are thoroughly pre-processed, cleaned, and prepared [101].

Data preparation is used as a blanket term to describe the many activities that precede the actual consumption of data for analytics or training machine learning models. Assuming access to data has already been established, for instance, in a data lake [102] or enterprise data lakehouse [103], data preparation is at times defined to involve both syntactic and semantic steps to align and clean the data. The authors of [104] further organize data preparation steps ("preparators") into the following categories, motivated by the features of dedicated data preparation tools:

- *Data discovery* analyzes and collects data from different sources, for instance, to find missing data and locate outliers. Typical properties to identify usable data sources are unionability and joinability [105].
- *Data structuring* modifies and restructures information, for instance, to update the schema, detect and change file encodings, and transform data by example [106].
- *Data filtering* enables manual inspection and removal of irregular data rows or values [107]. Examples include extracting text parts and keeping or deleting filtered rows.
- *Data validation* applies rules and constraints, manually specified or determined through data profiling or ML, to inspect the data, for instance, for correctness, completeness, and other data quality constraints [21, 108]. These steps correspond to DQ assessment as described in Sect. 4.3.

- *Data enrichment* adds supplementary information to existing data from separate sources [109]. Typically, it involves augmenting existing data with new or derived data values using data lookups, primary key generation, and inserting metadata.
- *Data cleaning* or *data repair* refers to the removal, addition, or replacement of inaccurate data values with more suitable, accurate, or representative values. This task is typically informed by rule or constraint violations obtained through data validation. Typical examples are deduplication, data imputation, and removing whitespace.

Here, we distinguish between three tasks that are discussed in the following subsections: *data preparation* (including the discovery, structuring, and validation of data), *data enrichment*, and *data cleaning*. Data preparation [104, 110–112] aims at resolving any formatting issues with the raw data, such as file encoding, column delimiters, representation of null values, and date formats. Only once datasets follow a common and readable standard representation can they be used as training data for AI systems or for other analysis purposes. Yet the ability to ingest data into an AI system is not sufficient. Dirty data can have a severe negative impact on the performance of a machine learning model [9]. Data enrichment adds additional information to existing data and therefore can inform both data preparation and data cleaning tasks. Data cleaning, also known as data cleansing, data repair, or data scrubbing, describes the process of detecting and then correcting erroneous data or glitches to improve the quality of data [18, 39, 113, 114]. Both broad steps, data preparation and data cleaning, serve to improve the quality of the data. We introduce the main challenges and solutions for each in the following sections.

4.4.1 Data Preparation

Preparing data can be considered as a concatenation of simpler atomic computational tasks composing a preparation pipeline—reflecting the steps a data engineer could manually undertake to prepare the data. Preparation pipelines are a concept similar to the established research area of "scientific workflows" [115]: both are examples of data-flow-oriented processes combining various, heterogeneous processing steps, even if at different scopes.

While in some cases all pertinent source data for the task at hand is readily available, *data discovery* can help find additional datasets to enrich the data, either by adding additional features or by adding additional instances. See Sect. 4.4.2 for more details on adding additional information to the data at hand. After discovery, data preparation overcomes structural and syntactic differences between raw data from the original source and expected input data for the task at hand. In addition, raw data might have inherent flaws, such as missing headers, inappropriate lines (titles, footnotes, aggregations), shifted columns, or incorrect escaping of delimiters. Thus, a very first *data structuring* step is manipulating raw data files to enable loading them into a data system. Surprisingly, large percentages of raw data files contain errors that prevent proper ingestion. The authors of [110] report 26 different error types, pertaining only to the structure of a file, including inconsistent number of values in a row, unquoted strings, and multiple header lines. They devise a benchmark to evaluate the ability of a system to ingest poorly structured raw data. At this stage, *data filtering* can help eliminate such data that is of irreparably poor data quality or that is not relevant for the task at hand. An additional source of information for filtering are the results of the data quality assessment, i.e., *data validation* (Sect. 4.3).

Having successfully ingested data, a traditional data preparation workflow involves two roles: business experts who specify data preparation expectations and data experts who implement and execute corresponding preparation scripts or pipelines. Communication overhead is the major bottleneck of agile data preparation [111]. As a consequence, more sophisticated data preparation systems, such as Open-Refine,[9] Tableau Prep Builder,[10] and Talend,[11] try to fill this gap and boost efficiency by providing users with interactive interfaces and menu-based transformation options. Equipped with these tools, even non-expert users are able to perform some self-service data preparation. Typical data preparation steps within these tools are pre-defined or user-configured operations that affect all values in a column. Examples include splitting values (`fullname` into `firstname` and `lastname`), homogenizing data formats, reducing the precision of measurement values, or validating data from well-known domains, such as address lookups.

4.4.2 Data Enrichment

Data enrichment is the task of adding additional information to existing data from external sources. Reasons for data enrichment include (i) too few data for specific downstream tasks like training deep learning models, (ii) anonymized data that limits effective analysis [116], or (iii) the need for enterprises to personalize product recommendations by enriching customer profile information. In the context of data quality, data enrichment can also provide reference data or help derive additional rules for DQ assessment, as demonstrated by Töpper et al. [117] who enrich the DBpedia ontology to detect inconsistencies.

At a high level, we can distinguish between the enrichment of data with further real-world data (e.g., from public knowledge bases or data lakes) or with synthetically generated data using ML models or large language models (i.e., data augmentation [116]). The latter type of data enrichment is mainly used to improve prediction accuracy of downstream tasks, and is not suited if factual knowledge is required for business-critical decisions.

---

[9] http://openrefine.org

[10] https://www.tableau.com/products/prep

[11] https://www.talend.com

A common scenario for discovering additional data involves access to a data lake and finding *joinable* and *unionable* datasets [102]. A joinable dataset contains at least one column with the same semantics as the source table and can thus be joined to enrich the column set. A unionable table, on the other hand, has a large overlap in its schema and can thus be unioned to the source table. Both tasks pose challenges due both to the often large number of datasets to search through and to the difficult-to-interpret semantics of tables in a data lake.

A rich source for external data are general-purpose knowledge graphs, such as DBpedia [118], Wikidata [119], or Yago [120]. In addition, there are many domain-specific ontologies that provide more detailed information about entities and their relationships, such as SNOMED CT [121], which stores clinical terms for the health domain. Such public data sources are frequently used to enrich enterprise knowledge graphs but also to add additional semantic information to enrich structured tabular data [122].

4.4.3 Data Cleaning

Traditionally, the task of data cleaning is divided into the two steps of *error detection* and *error correction* [41], and much research and development has focused on these two. Yet to improve data quality along all dimensions, it might not be sufficient to regard errors only *within* the dataset at hand: problems can occur already with the selection of the dataset, which might be incomplete, not representative or not relevant. Nevertheless, this section focuses on the work on concrete data, essentially targeting the accuracy and completeness dimensions of data quality.

4.4.3.1 Error Detection

In their book, Ilyas and Chu call the first step *outlier detection* in the sense that any error in the data is an anomaly or outlier [113]. In their taxonomy, they distinguish statistics-based, distance-based, and model-based outliers. Statistics-based outlier detection methods assume a stochastic model of the data and detect outliers through hypothesis testing methods or by fitting a distribution on the observed data. Distance-based outlier detection assumes a given distance measure and searches for data points that are far from all or from some group of other data points. Missing values also fall into this category, as exemplified in recent work to identify disguised missing values [91]. Finally, model-based outlier detection learns a model from the data and is trained to classify data points as outliers. These models can be based on complex neural networks but can also be simple dependencies, as described in Sect. 4.2. In general, almost all error detection methods are both computationally complex and require some level of human expertise for guidance.

Heidari et al. [123] proposed Holodetect, a weakly supervised data detection tool that can automatically learn different types and amounts of errors using neural networks. A comparable tool that focuses on explainable methods is DQ-MeeRKat, which automatically learns the ground truth (termed "data profile" in [124]) for each dataset using a set of statistics and explainable ML models to distinguish between correct and incorrect data [124]. Schelter et al. [125] define the ground truth via a set of common quality constraints and allow defining user-defined unit tests. The system proposed in [125] focuses on the deployment of such DQ constraints in real-world scenarios by using ML for enhancing constraint suggestions and can be executed in parallel on Apache Spark.

Abedjan et al. [40] classify error detection tools according to the following four types of errors they can detect: (1) outliers, (2) duplicates, (3) rule violations, and (4) pattern violations. The authors note that the categorization is neither exhaustive nor perfect, since some errors might fit into more than one category. Their work concludes that many tools focus on the detection and cleaning of specific errors, and there is no single tool that covers all error types [40].

4.4.3.2 Error Removal

Detecting an error, unfortunately, does not always help in correcting it. For instance, it is not immediately clear which value an outlier or a missing value should actually take. In fact, most automated data cleaning techniques cannot guarantee finding a correct value, but rely on probabilistic techniques to replace a missing or erroneous value with a new value. Most prominently, data *imputation* techniques replace missing values with new values making use of the distribution of present values in the column [126, 127]. Simple statistical methods fill in a missing value with the mean (or mode) value of that column or the mean of values for similar records. Machine learning-based imputation methods, on the other hand, train (deep) models to predict missing values.

Rule-based cleaning methods rely on pre-defined rules or constraints and their violations. These rules can be defined by domain experts or discovered by data profiling runs. For instance, a functional dependency might specify that two records with the same zip code must also have the same city. A violation would occur when two same zip codes have different cities. However, any of the four participating values could be the cause of the violation. Thus, data cleaning procedures must make use of additional context to decide upon the cleaning action. For instance, a gazetteer (geographical dictionary) might prescribe the city values for the given zip codes. This approach can be generalized to include different types of input to decide upon which value to prefer [128]. Another approach is to consider all violations holistically and then derive a minimal repair [20]. For instance, an incorrect city might violate multiple dependencies, and, thus, this single correction might resolve multiple violations. Finally, rules based on regular expressions can prescribe how to resolve incorrectly formatted values, for instance, normalizing data formats to a single preferred format.

4.4.3.3 Error Generation

For many AI use cases, the generation of errors in real or synthetic data is an important task to evaluate the developed models. Real-world data often are dirty but have no ground truth available, and existing benchmark datasets often do not reflect the intended use case sufficiently [129]. Thus, *data pollution* allows researchers and practitioners to systematically generate data errors to evaluate the impact of these errors on a selected ML model or on a DQ assessment method. Data polluters allow the creation of benchmark datasets that fit to a specific use case in alignment with the *fitness for use* principle of data quality [12].

A number of tools to pollute data with errors have been developed, such as BART (Benchmarking Algorithms for data Repairing and Translation) [130], DaPo (Data Polluter) [131], GouDa (Generation of universal Data Sets) [129], or Jenga [125].

4.4.4 Duplicate Elimination

Duplicate detection and elimination, also known as entity resolution, data matching, or data linkage, is the process of finding and eliminating multiple records in a table that refer to the same real-world entity [132–134]. The most prominent use case is the deduplication of customer records in the context of customer relationship management (CRM). Other use cases include product matching in catalogs or even recognizing duplicate invoices. Heavily duplicated data, for instance, after integrating multiple data sources, can also introduce bias into the training process of an AI system. Duplicate elimination consists of two tasks as shown in Fig. 4.1: (1) to identify all pairs or clusters of duplicate records in a dataset and (2) to clean the table by merging (or fusing) these records into a single "golden record."

The first task, identifying all duplicate records, must overcome two challenges. The first challenge is the ability to recognize whether two records in fact refer to the same real-world entity. Duplicate records are rarely exact duplicates but rather are fuzzy duplicates. Traditional approaches apply manually defined similarity measures to compare the attribute values of the records. Typical similarity measures include the Levenshtein distance (or edit distance) for words or the Jaccard distance

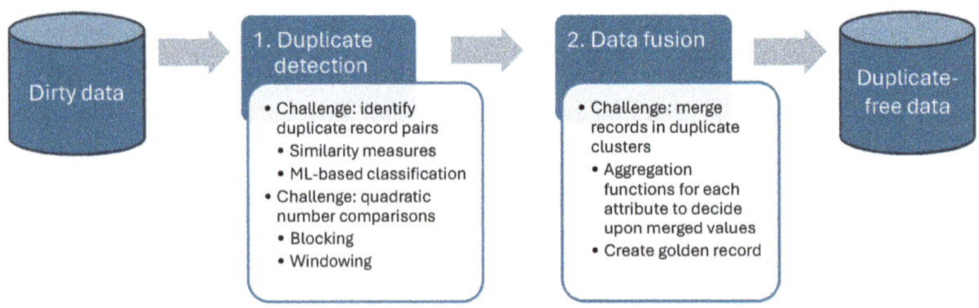

Fig. 4.1 The two steps of duplicate elimination and their challenges

for longer strings. Numeric values can be compared using simple distance metrics or alternatively treated as string [135]. If the overall similarity is higher than a given threshold, the records are declared to be duplicates.

More recent approaches train machine learning models [136, 137] or use pre-trained models [138] to either determine their similarity and then apply a threshold or to directly classify a record pair as duplicate or non-duplicate. A final issue arises when pairwise classification leads to inconsistent clusters. For instance, records A and B and records B and C might be identified as two duplicate pairs, while records A and C are not sufficiently similar. Then, the transitive nature of duplicity dictates that A and C should also represent the same entity. Various clustering algorithms exist to automatically resolve such inconsistencies [139].

The second challenge of duplicate detection is the quadratic complexity of the problem: in principle, to detect *all* duplicates, all pairs of records must be classified. For instance, to compare all pairs in a dataset of 100,000 customers, almost five billion comparisons would be needed, each involving complex calculations. To avoid such infeasible computations, blocking techniques are employed: the set of records is divided into separate blocks, and comparisons are performed only within each block [140, 141]. For instance, customer records could be blocked (partitioned) by their zip code or the first letter of their last name. Another technique is the sorted neighborhood method, which sorts by some criterion and then slides a window of fixed size along the data, comparing only records within the window [142]. To overcome errors in the partitioning or sorting attribute, multiple runs with different blocking criteria or sorting keys can be performed.

After successfully detecting duplicate record pairs or clusters, the second step to duplicate elimination is that of data fusion [143]: all records within a cluster should be merged to a single correct record. In typical scenarios, the old records are retained to ensure referential integrity, and the new (golden) record is stored separately, for instance, in a master data management (MDM) system. For each attribute in the schema, data fusion must decide with which aggregation function to merge values. Aggregation functions could be simple, for instance, choosing the longer string or the highest value, or involve more complex reasoning about the origin of the data values [144].

4.5 Data Quality Governance

In the previous sections, we have discussed the foundations of data profiling and how to assess and improve data quality in the context of AI. To implement these concepts in practice, further considerations are required.

Many companies face the challenge of choosing a suitable tool for their organization to support their DQ processes. We understand a data quality tool to be a software product that helps organizations to assess and improve the quality of data across various systems and databases. Before deploying a DQ tool in practice, it is however essential to build a comprehensive data quality governance strategy around it. This means that a DQ strategy (cf. Sect. 4.1.3) should be linked to a business' overall strategy in terms of data assets, processes, and data use (AI governance). For a deeper look into business process management, see [145]. Such a strategy is required to identify how users (employees, domain experts, customers) interact with the data assets. Based on the approach by Redman [146], the governance of data quality can be summarized with the following steps:

1. Identification and understanding of customers (i.e., consumers) and their most important requirements to data and its quality
2. Definition of measures against these requirements
3. Identification and elimination of root causes of data errors
4. Implementation of controls to ensure that DQ adheres to the expected standards over time

Following the first point, we discuss the importance of assigning data responsibility roles in Sect. 4.5.1. Since the execution of these tasks can be challenging for humans in the context of AI platforms (with huge amounts of data), we discuss available DQ tools and their scope of functionality in Sect. 4.5.2. The second and third points were already discussed in depth in Sects. 4.3 and 4.4, respectively.

4.5.1 Data Responsibility Roles

In addition to measuring DQ, its assessment requires the consideration of the sufficiency for a particular use case, i.e., whether the quality is "fit for use" [48]. Consequently, the definition and assignment of responsibility roles, that is, the people *judging* the fitness for use, is critical for the operative deployment of a DQ program.

In the context of DQ management, the most widely discussed role is the chief data officer (CDO) [147]. The CDO is an enterprise-wide role to manage the utilization of data as an asset through analysis (using AI or other techniques, such as business intelligence analysis) and usually directly reports to the chief executive officer (CEO) [147]. Despite different perceptions on which tasks should be assigned to the CDO role (see [146, 148–150]), the most important aspect is the overall management of an enterprise's DQ strategy. To develop and manage such a DQ strategy, the following tasks are required (amongst others):

- Collect knowledge about relevant stakeholders (e.g., domain experts, managers, data scientists) and their expectations to the data and its quality.
- Assign suitable roles to people and linking them with relevant data assets.
- Implement incentives to encourage people to report on DQ issues and to annotate business metadata.
- Establish a continuous evaluation of data responsibility role assignments.

Note that in addition to DQ management, Davenport and Bean [148] identified seven different roles in their study of CDO expectations, ranging from chief data and/or analytics officer (overseeing data management, data science, and analytics) to data ethicist (responsible for ethical guidelines on data management). This yearly study underlines the dependencies a DQ governance program has within a company, ranging from a comprehensive AI strategy, over privacy constraints, to ethical guidelines [98].

Only very recently has the perception that the CDO role is successfully deployed and well understood within an organization increased—two-thirds of the survey participants say that they have the primary responsibility for data, which is interpreted as clear effect of the generative AI movement by Davenport and Bean [151]. However, at the same time, the CDO role is still considered nascent and struggling with turnover for 43% of the respondents. Data quality remains a big challenge: only 37% of the respondents say that they have been able to improve it in 2024. The main barrier for becoming a data-driven enterprise are human factors (e.g., culture, people, process, organization) for 78% of the surveyed participants [151].

Apart from the executive role of the CDO, there are further more operational roles that need to be considered in the context of DQ strategies. Specific emphasis should be placed on the identification of *data producers* (also data collectors in [152]) and *data customers* (also consumers in [152]). While data customers, such as data scientists or business analysts, are the first to recognize errors in data since they work with it, data producers might know the cause behind the error due to their knowledge of the data production process and can possibly fix the problem. In practice, data producers are often assigned the role of data owners, and data customers are often assigned the role of data stewards. Note that different types of data stewards, such as business data steward or technical data steward, might be defined, depending on the size of the enterprise and its DQ program [153].

In the context of AI platforms with huge amounts of data and an increasing reliance on their high quality, monitoring and managing of all assigned data assets and their metadata become extremely difficult for humans, such as data stewards [76]. Hence, suitable tool support is critical to enable the execution of the role-inherent activities in practice, as we discuss next.

4.5.2 Data Quality Tools

Proper tool support is essential to allow persons with data responsibility roles to execute their tasks, such as allowing domain experts the specification of DQ rules and their automation (scheduling). This section examines DQ tools, which are software products (as opposed to management tools) that enable organizations to comprehensively assess and clean their data. Due to the large number of available DQ tools (667 tools are identified in [154]), practitioners and data leaders, such as CDOs, are often unsure which tool is best suited for their organizations' needs.

Note that data quality tools usually do not support all tasks required for a comprehensive DQ governance strategy. For example, tools such as Great Expectations[12] or Deequ [155] enable users to define and execute DQ rules, but do not allow assigning user roles to data assets as discussed in the previous section. The latter task is typically handled by dedicated data governance tools or platforms that include data governance functionalities, such as Ataccama ONE[13] or Informatica.[14] Hence, it is currently necessary to use a combination of tools to accomplish all of the tasks required for a DQ strategy as discussed in this chapter.

Following this need, several surveys investigate and compare DQ tools [35, 154, 156–159]. The Gartner "Magic Quadrant for Data Quality Tools" lists strengths and cautions of commercial DQ tools [156], which is a valuable source for practitioners in selecting a DQ tool for deployment. Ehrlinger and Wöß [154] investigated eight commercial and five open-source tools with respect to data profiling, DQ measurement, and DQ monitoring functionality. In [157–159], the functionalities of open-source DQ tools have been investigated in more detail. The main findings from these works are summarized in the following paragraphs.

Domain Specificity There is a large corpus of domain-specific DQ tools (in numbers, 339 or 51% of the total number of tools identified in [154]) that are typically excluded in surveys and not further investigated (cf. [154, 156]). This finding aligns with the "fitness for use" principle of DQ, demonstrating that specialized tools are often developed for specific data types (e.g., RDF or streams) or built on top of an existing data management platform. For practitioners, this means that it can be beneficial to look beyond mainstream solutions and investigate specialized tools when having very specific requirements or unique use cases.

Data Profiling Capabilities The majority of DQ tools support the most common single-column profiling functionalities, such as counting null values, extracting data types, or obtaining histograms, as summarized in Table 4.1. When considering the state of research [160], there is potential for the enhancement of multi-column profiling and dependency discovery as discussed in Sect. 4.2. Several tools use data profiling results to suggest DQ rules (e.g., Deequ, Great Expectations). These automated suggestions are considerably weaker than DQ rules generated by domain experts but allow for a higher degree of automation. In addition, several DQ tools perform data validation checks not only directly on the raw input data but also on the metadata obtained by data profiling [159].

Data Quality Assessment Interestingly, DQ tools rarely implement the conceptual framework of DQ dimensions and metrics advocated in academic research. When implemented, these concepts are mainly used to group data validation checks rather than as guiding principles [154]. Also, DQ metrics as proposed in scientific literature

[12] https://greatexpectations.io

[13] https://www.ataccama.com/platform

[14] https://www.informatica.com

face implementation barriers in practical settings. For instance, such metrics might require a gold standard that often does not exist in practice or lack aggregation capabilities beyond attribute-level measurements [84]. Papastergios and Gounaris [159] investigated the field from the reverse perspective, analyzing which data validation checks contribute to which DQ dimensions, thereby offering practical insights into how DQ dimensions could be effectively measured using current tool functionalities. To bridge this gap between theory and practice, we argue that a fresh look on DQ dimensions and metrics would be required to enable the practical implementation in tools.

Automation of Data Quality Functionalities While full automation of DQ assessment and improvement is limited by the need for human knowledge and liability concerns, specific tasks in the DQ pipeline can be successfully automated. Complete DQ automation requires both operational and analytical capabilities.

From an *operational* perspective, DQ tools should enable the scheduling of data profiling, DQ assessment, and cleaning tasks as well as the storage, retrieval, and comparison of the respective results. From an *analytical* perspective, DQ tools should support automatic learning of validation metrics and cleaning rules from existing data patterns. Most DQ tools support task scheduling and storage of profiling and DQ assessment results, yet many lack capabilities for importing previously stored results and visualizing quality trends over time. Only the most widely adopted enterprise DQ tools (e.g., Informatica, Ataccama, Experian) enable business users to schedule tasks and create DQ dashboards—other tools often require command-line knowledge.

The automatic learning of data validation and cleaning rules with machine learning has received increasing attention [1, 108, 161] with a recent focus on using large language models (LLMs) for these tasks [162]. For example, the systems Raha and Baran [161] are semi-supervised open-source tools to detect and clean data errors with traditional ML models (e.g., Gradient Boosting). While both perform well across various benchmarks [163], they are less capable of identifying complex contextual DQ issues than LLMs [162]. Interestingly, enterprise tools are relatively conservative in employing ML or LLMs for DQ management. Even tools that are classified as "leader" in the "Magic Quadrant for Augmented Data Quality Solutions" [156], such as Qlik Talend,[15] do not support ML techniques to generate DQ validation rules across multiple attributes nor to perform automated duplicate detection [156]. One reason for this gap may be the need for interpretable and explainable statistics and rules in critical domains, such as in healthcare. Another challenge is the non-trivial use of LLMs for data cleaning, as discussed in [162, 163]. While fully automated data cleaning is still a too complex task for current LLMs [162], they show potential in the identification of previously unseen data errors and suggestion of specific cleaning steps.

[15] https://www.qlik.com/us/products/qlik-talend-data-integration-and-quality

In summary, there is a clear trend toward the automation of DQ tasks with ML and LLMs [156, 162], and vendors that stick to the traditional rule-based solutions and do not plan to adopt these movements will likely be irrelevant soon. In addition, there is a trend that specialized DQ tools converge with other data management tools, such as data catalogs, data integration tools, or data governance tools [156]. This trend reflects the nature of DQ as being relevant across the entire data life cycle.

4.6 Outlook and Open Challenges

Despite much research into data quality over the last decades, the topic is far from being "solved." Especially in the era of AI, the consideration of data quality is essential to ensure trustworthy results when analyzing data or using them to train AI models.

The notion of data quality with its many dimensions, the variety of applications, their various application domains, the many different tasks, and finally the many different roles of individuals involved in data management are all themselves multidimensional, as shown in Fig. 4.2. The cross-product of all five dimensions spans an enormous space of research and development opportunities—in computer science, in information systems, in application domains, and many more. For instance, a data steward might notice that many patient records are missing phone numbers. This incompleteness could impact the organization's ability to send appointment reminders. To solve this data quality problem, they need to implement a systematic process to identify and fill in these gaps in the contact information.

Since each aspect can take one out of several forms, it is difficult to make a general statement about the suitability of specific DQ methods and tools. This is also one reason why DQ management is not yet widely adopted in practice: the subject cannot be easily grasped; it comes in many different flavors, and there is no single software package to solve all DQ issues at once. Individual research methods and prototypes often address only a single instance of this space, or they generalize only across one of its dimensions. DQ products, on the other hand, can cover a broader range of management tasks, but often do not make use of the most recent advances. Thus, there remain significant opportunities both in research and development, some of which we highlight here.

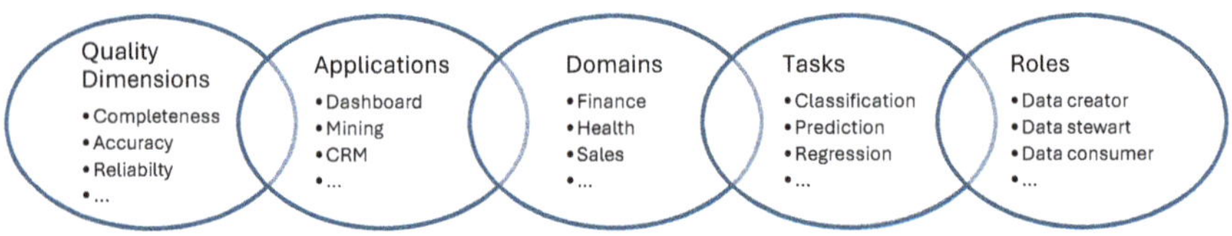

Fig. 4.2 Perspectives of data quality management

Metadata Management Invariably, data quality management in organizations produces large amounts of metadata. First, metadata is needed to actually assess data quality, and then the data quality measurements themselves form metadata that must be appropriately stored and analyzed. The former type of metadata comprises information about the origin of data, their schema, basic statistics about the data, transformations performed on the data, prior uses, data owners, etc. Such metadata is routinely collected, not just for data quality purposes. The latter type of metadata, DQ measurements, can also be complex to manage, due to different units, different subsets on which assessment was performed, the need to track DQ over time, etc. As DQ metadata often refers to specific subsets of a given database, a metadata system should be able to flexibly express the alignment between views on the data and DQ values, as envisioned, for instance, by Srivastava and Velegrakis [164].

Explainability of DQ Assessment Data quality dimensions are ambiguous by nature [165]. Thus, their definitions but in particular their assessment scores must be explainable to data consumers. DQ scores are useless without context and the ability to compare. Their context, such as the definition, the assessment environment, or the task at hand, should be documented and stored alongside the scores themselves. In addition, the actual assessment process, which itself can be complex, must also be explainable, traceable, and reproducible.

Data Quality Research for Specific Domains This book chapter provides an overview on data quality for enterprise AI without specific domains in mind. However, each application domain has different perspectives and needs regarding data and its quality. For instance, data quality assessment and data cleaning in manufacturing typically require different considerations than in healthcare or international organizations like the United Nations (UN). While much research has been conducted in the healthcare due to high standards and critical infrastructure (e.g., [166, 167]), data quality received less emphasis in other specialized domains.

Holistic DQ Governance Platform The number of DQ tools, data analytics tools, and data governance tools on the market is overwhelming, and it is often unclear which functionalities are covered in which tools. To truly support enterprises in the deployment of a comprehensive data quality governance strategy, we claim that a joint platform need to be developed that allows to model the entire strategy end to end. In other words, the platform must be able to integrate results from data profiling, manage metadata, and allow the measurement and assessment of DQ, the cleaning of data, and the definition and assignment of user roles responsible for these tasks.

References

1. Redyuk, S., Kaoudi, Z., Markl, V., Schelter, S.: Automating data quality validation for dynamic data ingestion. In: Proceedings of the International Conference on Extending Database Technology (EDBT), pp. 61–72 (2021). https://doi.org/10.5441/002/EDBT.2021.07
2. Ehrlinger, L., Wöß, W.: Automated data quality monitoring. In: Proceedings of the International Conference on Information Quality (ICIQ), pp. 15–1159 (2017)
3. Ilyas, I.F., Rekatsinas, T.: Machine learning and data cleaning: Which serves the other? J. Data Inf. Qual. **14**(3), 1–11 (2022)
4. Redman, T.C.: The impact of poor data quality on the typical enterprise. Commun. ACM **41**(2), 79–82 (1998)
5. Nagle, T., Redman, T., Sammon, D.: Assessing data quality: amanagerial call to action. Bus. Horiz. **63**(3), 325–337 https://doi.org/10.1016/j.bushor.2020.01.006
6. Moore, S.: How to Create a Business Case for Data Quality Improvement. Online. https://www.gartner.com/smarterwithgartner/how-to-create-a-business-case-for-data-quality-improvement (2018)
7. Global Data Management Research. Technical Report, Experian (2022)
8. Otto, B., Österle, H.: Corporate Data Quality: Prerequisite for Successful Business Models. Springer, Berlin (2016)
9. Mohammed, S., Budach, L., Feuerpfeil, M., Ihde, N., Nathansen, A., Noack, N., Patzlaff, H., Naumann, F., Harmouch, H.: The effects of data quality on machine learning performance. Inf. Syst. **132**, 102549 (2025) https://doi.org/10.1016/j.is.2025.102549
10. Polyzotis, N., Roy, S., Whang, S.E., Zinkevich, M.: Data lifecycle challenges in production machine learning: a survey. SIGMOD Record **47**(2), 17–28 (2018)
11. Chrisman, N.R.: The role of quality information in the long-term functioning of a geographic information system. Cartographica Int. J. Geograph. Inf. Geovisualiz. **21**(2), 79–88 (1983)
12. Wang, R.Y., Strong, D.M.: Beyond accuracy: what data quality means to data consumers. J. Manag. Inf. Syst. **12**(4), 5–33 (1996)
13. English, L.P.: Improving Data Warehouse and Business Information Quality: Methods for Reducing Costs and Increasing Profits. Wiley, New York, NY (1999)
14. McKean, E.: The New Oxford American Dictionary vol. 2. Oxford University Press, New York, Oxford (2005)
15. Wang, R.Y.: A product perspective on total data quality management. Commun. ACM **41**(2), 58–65 (1998)
16. Zhu, H., Madnick, S., Lee, Y., Wang, R.Y.: Data and information quality research: Its evolution and future. In: Computing Handbook: Information Systems and Information Technology, pp. 16–11620. Chapman and Hall/CRC, London (2014)
17. Sebastian-Coleman, L.: Measuring Data Quality for Ongoing Improvement: A Data Quality Assessment Framework. Elsevier, Waltham, MA (2013)
18. Dasu, T., Johnson, T.: Exploratory Data Mining and Data Cleaning vol. 479. Wiley, Hoboken, NJ (2003)
19. Van Der Aalst, W.: Process Mining – Data Science in Action. Springer, Berlin-Heidelberg (2016)
20. Rekatsinas, T., Chu, X., Ilyas, I.F., Ré, C.: Holoclean: Holistic data repairs with probabilistic inference. PVLDB **10**(11), 1190–1201 (2017)
21. Schelter, S., Lange, D., Schmidt, P., Celikel, M., Biessmann, F., Grafberger, A.: Automating large-scale data quality verification. PVLDB **11**(12), 1781–1794 (2018)
22. Blacketer, C., Voss, E.A., DeFalco, F., Hughes, N., Schuemie, M.J., Moinat, M., Rijnbeek, P.R.: Using the data quality dashboard to improve the EHDEN network. Appl. Sci. **11**(24), 11920 (2021)
23. ISO/IEC 25012 (2019). https://iso25000.com/index.php/en/iso-25000-standards/iso-25012

24. ISO/IEC 25024:2015 Systems and software engineering—Systems and software Quality Requirements and Evaluation (SQuaRE)—Measurement of data quality (2015). https://www.iso.org/standard/35749.html
25. ISO/IEC 5259 Artificial intelligence—Data quality for analytics and machine learning (ML) (2024). https://iso25000.com/index.php/en/iso-25000-standards/iso-25012
26. Gualo, F., Rodríguez, M., Verdugo, J., Caballero, I., Piattini, M.: Data quality certification using ISO/IEC 25012: Industrial experiences. J. Syst. Softw. **176**, 110938 (2021)
27. Caballero, I., Gualo, F., Rodríguez, M., Piattini, M.: Br4dq: a methodology for grouping business rules for data quality evaluation. Inf. Syst. **109**, 102058 (2022) https://doi.org/10.1016/j.is.2022.102058
28. Pipino, L., Wang, R., Kopcso, D., Rybolt, W.: Developing measurement scales for data-quality dimensions. Inf. Qual. **1**, 37–52 (2005)
29. Berti-Equille, L.: Measuring and modelling data quality for quality-awareness in data mining. In: Quality Measures in Data Mining, pp. 101–126. Springer, Berlin, Heidelberg (2007)
30. Scannapieco, M., Catarci, T.: Data quality under the computer science perspective. Archivi Comput. **2**, 1–15 (2002)
31. Laranjeiro, N., Soydemir, S.N., Bernardino, J.: A survey on data quality: Classifying poor data. In: Proceedings of the Pacific Rim International Symposium on Dependable Computing (PRDC), pp. 179–188. IEEE, Zhangjiajie (2015)
32. Cichy, C., Rass, S.: An overview of data quality frameworks. IEEE Access **7**, 24634–24648 (2019)
33. DQMatters.com: Conformed Dimensions of Data Quality (r4.3) (2024). http://dqmatters.com/alldimensions
34. Mohammed, S., Brandner, L.T., Burtscher, F., Hallensleben, S., Harmouch, H., Hauschke, A., Heesen, J., Hildebrandt, S., Hirsbrunner, S.D., Keselj, J., Mahlow, P., Massow, M., Naumann, F., Rostalski, F., Wilken, A., Wölke, A.: A data quality glossary (2024) https://doi.org/10.5281/ZENODO.10474880 . Zenodo Version Number: 1.0
35. Barateiro, J., Galhardas, H.: A survey of data quality tools. Datenbank-Spektrum **14**, 15–21 (2005)
36. Ge, M., Helfert, M.: A review of information quality research. In: Proceedings of the International Conference on Information Quality (ICIQ), pp. 76–91. MIT, Cambridge, MA (2007)
37. Kim, W., Choi, B.-J., Hong, E.-K., Kim, S.-K., Lee, D.: A taxonomy of dirty data. Data Min. Knowl. Discovery **7**(1), 81–99 (2003)
38. Müller, H., Freytag, J.-C.: Problems, Methods, and Challenges in Comprehensive Data Cleansing. Humboldt-Universität zu Berlin, Berlin (2005)
39. Rahm, E., Do, H.H.: Data cleaning: Problems and current approaches. IEEE Data Eng. Bull. **23**(4), 3–13 (2000)
40. Abedjan, Z., Chu, X., Deng, D., Fernandez, R.C., Ilyas, I.F., Ouzzani, M., Papotti, P., Stonebraker, M., Tang, N.: Detecting data errors: where are we and what needs to be done? PVLDB **9**(12), 993–1004 (2016) https://doi.org/10.14778/2994509.2994518
41. Ilyas, I.F., Chu, X.: Trends in cleaning relational data: consistency and deduplication. Found. Trends Databases **5**(4), 281–393 (2015)
42. Oliveira, P., Rodrigues, F., Henriques, P.R.: A formal definition of data quality problems. In: Proceedings of the International Conference on Information Quality (ICIQ) (2005)
43. Josko, J.M.B., Oikawa, M.K., Ferreira, J.E.: A formal taxonomy to improve data defect description. In: Database Systems for Advanced Applications (DASFAA), pp. 307–320. Springer, Heidelberg (2016)
44. Lee, Y.W., Pipino, L.L., Funk, J.D., Wang, R.Y.: Journey to Data Quality. The MIT Press, Cambridge, MA (2009)
45. Pipino, L.L., Lee, Y.W., Wang, R.Y.: Data quality assessment. Commun. ACM **45**(4), 211–218 (2002)
46. Maydanchik, A.: Data Quality Assessment. Technics Publications, LLC, Bradley Beach, NJ (2007)

47. Batini, C., Cappiello, C., Francalanci, C., Maurino, A.: Methodologies for data quality assessment and improvement. ACM Comput. Surv. **41**(3), 16–11652 (2009)
48. Batini, C., Scannapieco, M.: Data and Information Quality: Concepts, Methodologies and Techniques. Springer, Cham (2016)
49. Data Quality – Part 8: Information and data quality concepts and measuring. Standard, International Organization for Standardization, Geneva (2015)
50. Abedjan, Z., Golab, L., Naumann, F.: Profiling relational data: a survey. VLDB J. **24**(4), 557–581 (2015) https://doi.org/10.1007/s00778-015-0389-y
51. Chu, X., Ilyas, I.F., Papotti, P.: Discovering denial constraints. PVLDB **6**(13), 1498–1509 (2013) https://doi.org/10.14778/2536258.2536262
52. Pena, E.H.M., Almeida, E.C., Naumann, F.: Fast detection of denial constraint violations. PVLDB **15**(4), 859–871 (2021) https://doi.org/10.14778/3503585.3503595
53. Fan, W., Tian, C., Wang, Y., Yin, Q.: Parallel discrepancy detection and incremental detection. PVLDB **14**(8), 1351–1364 (2021) https://doi.org/10.14778/3457390.3457400
54. Keim, D.A., Oelke, D.: Literature fingerprinting: A new method for visual literary analysis. In: Symposium on Visual Analytics Science and Technology (VAST), pp. 115–122. IEEE Computer Society, Sacramento, CA (2007). https://doi.org/10.1109/VAST.2007.4389004
55. Hamborg, F., Donnay, K., Gipp, B.: Automated identification of media bias in news articles: an interdisciplinary literature review. Int. J. Digital Librar. **20**(4), 391–415 (2019) https://doi.org/10.1007/S00799-018-0261-Y
56. Wang, Z., Bovik, A.C.: Modern Image Quality Assessment. Synthesis Lectures on Image, Video, and Multimedia Processing. Morgan & Claypool Publishers, New York, NY (2006). https://doi.org/10.2200/S00010ED1V01Y200508IVM003
57. Möller, M.L., Berton, N., Klettke, M., Scherzinger, S., Störl, U.: jHound: Large-scale profiling of open JSON data. In: Proceedings of the Conference Datenbanksysteme in Business, Technologie und Web Technik (BTW). LNI, pp. 555–558. Gesellschaft für Informatik, Bonn (2019). https://doi.org/10.18420/btw2019-44
58. Ben Ellefi, M., Bellahsene, Z., Breslin, J.G., Demidova, E., Dietze, S., Szymański, J., Todorov, K.: RDF dataset profiling – a survey of features, methods, vocabularies and applications. Semantic Web **9**(5), 677–705 (2018) https://doi.org/10.3233/SW-180294
59. Fan, W.: Dependencies for graphs: challenges and opportunities. J. Data Inf. Qual. **11**(2), 1–12 (2019) https://doi.org/10.1145/3310230
60. Fan, W., Hu, C., Liu, X., Lu, P.: Discovering graph functional dependencies. In: Proceedings of the International Conference on Management of Data (SIGMOD), pp. 427–439. Association for Computing Machinery, New York, NY (2018). https://doi.org/10.1145/3183713.3196916
61. Maiolo, S., Etcheverry, L., Marotta, A.: Data profiling in property graph databases. J. Data Inf. Qual. **12**(4), 1–27 (2020) https://doi.org/10.1145/3409473
62. Graefe, G.: Query evaluation techniques for large databases. ACM Comput. Surv. **25**(2), 73–169 (1993) https://doi.org/10.1145/152610.152611
63. Hulsebos, M., Hu, K., Bakker, M., Zgraggen, E., Satyanarayan, A., Kraska, T., Demiralp, c., Hidalgo, C.: Sherlock: A deep learning approach to semantic data type detection. In: Proceedings of the International Conference on Knowledge Discovery and Data Mining (SIGKDD), pp. 1500–1508 (2019). https://doi.org/10.1145/3292500.3330993
64. Papenbrock, T., Naumann, F.: Data-driven schema normalization. In: Proceedings of the International Conference on Extending Database Technology (EDBT), pp. 342–353 (2017). https://doi.org/10.5441/002/EDBT.2017.31
65. Zhang, M., Hadjieleftheriou, M., Ooi, B.C., Procopiuc, C.M., Srivastava, D.: On multi-column foreign key discovery. PVLDB **3**(1), 805–814 (2010) https://doi.org/10.14778/1920841.1920944
66. Caruccio, L., Deufemia, V., Polese, G.: Relaxed functional dependencies - a survey of approaches. IEEE Trans. Knowl. Data Eng. **28**(1), 147–165 (2016) https://doi.org/10.1109/TKDE.2015.2472010

67. Kruse, S., Hahn, D., Walter, M., Naumann, F.: Metacrate: Organize and analyze millions of data profiles. In: Proceedings of the International Conference on Information and Knowledge Management (CIKM), pp. 2483–2486. Association for Computing Machinery, New York, NY (2017). https://doi.org/10.1145/3132847.3133180
68. Seeger, M., Schmidl, S., Vielhauer, A., Papenbrock, T.: DPQL: the data profiling query language. In: Proceedings of the Conference Datenbanksysteme in Business, Technologie und Web Technik (BTW). LNI, vol. P-331, pp. 391–415 (2023). https://doi.org/10.18420/BTW2023-19
69. Quimbert, E., Jeffery, K., Martens, C., Martin, P., Zhao, Z.: Data Cataloguing, pp. 140–161. Springer, Cham (2020)
70. Ehrlinger, L., Schrott, J., Melichar, M., Kirchmayr, N., Wöß, W.: Data catalogs: a systematic literature review and guidelines to implementation. In: Database and Expert Systems Applications-DEXA Workshops: BIOKDD, IWCFS, MLKgraphs, AI-CARES, ProTime, AISys, pp. 148–158. Springer, Berlin (2021).
71. Jahnke, N., Otto, B.: Data catalogs in the enterprise: Applications and integration. Datenbank-Spektrum **23**(2), 89–96 (2023) https://doi.org/10.1007/s13222-023-00445-2
72. Joshi, A., Morales, L.G., Klarman, S., Stellato, A., Helton, A., Lovell, S., Haczek, A.: A knowledge organization system for the united nations sustainable development goals. In: Proceedings of the Extended Semantic Web Conference (ESWC), pp. 548–564. Springer, Berlin (2021)
73. Macedo, J., Cacho, N., Lopes, F.: A comparative study of tools for smart cities open data publication and management. In: 2017 IEEE First Summer School on Smart Cities (S3C), pp. 79–84 (2017). https://doi.org/10.1109/S3C.2017.8501408
74. Gebru, T., Morgenstern, J., Vecchione, B., Vaughan, J.W., Wallach, H., Iii, H.D., Crawford, K.: Datasheets for datasets. Commun. ACM **64**(12), 86–92 (2021)
75. Pushkarna, M., Zaldivar, A., Kjartansson, O.: Data cards: Purposeful and transparent dataset documentation for responsible ai. In: Proceedings of the ACM Conference on Fairness, Accountability, and Transparency (FAccT), pp. 1776–1826. Association for Computing Machinery, New York, NY (2022). https://doi.org/10.1145/3531146.3533231
76. Wilkinson, M.D., Dumontier, M., Aalbersberg, I.J., Appleton, G., Axton, M., et al.: The FAIR guiding principles for scientific data management and stewardship. Sci. Data **3**(1), 160018 (2016) https://doi.org/10.1038/sdata.2016.18
77. Chmielinski, K.S., Newman, S., Taylor, M., Joseph, J., Thomas, K., Yurkofsky, J., Qiu, Y.C.: The dataset nutrition label (2nd gen): Leveraging context to mitigate harms in artificial intelligence. CoRR **abs/2201.03954** (2022) 2201.03954
78. Stvilia, B., Gasser, L., Twidale, M.B., Smith, L.C.: A framework for information quality assessment. J. Am. Soc. Inf. Sci. Technol. **58**(12), 1720–1733 (2007) https://doi.org/10.1002/ASI.20652
79. Wand, Y., Wang, R.Y.: Anchoring data quality dimensions in ontological foundations. Commun. ACM **39**(11), 86–95 (1996)
80. IEEE: Standard for a software quality metrics methodology. Technical Report 1061-1998, Institute of Electrical and Electronics Engineers (1998)
81. Heinrich, B., Hristova, D., Klier, M., Schiller, A., Szubartowicz, M.: Requirements for data quality metrics. J. Data Inf. Qual. **9**(2), 1–32 (2018)
82. Even, A., Shankaranarayanan, G.: Utility-driven assessment of data quality. SIGMIS Database **38**(2), 75–93 (2007)
83. Laney, D.B.: Infonomics: How to Monetize, Manage, and Measure Information as an Asset for Competitive Advantage. Routledge, New York (2017). https://doi.org/10.4324/9781315108650
84. Bronselaer, A., De Mol, R., De Tré, G.: A measure-theoretic foundation for data quality. IEEE Trans. Fuzzy Syst. **26**(2), 627–639 (2018)
85. European Parliament: Artifical inteligence act, (2024). Version from 2024-07-12. https://eur-lex.europa.eu/legal-content/EN/TXT/?uri=CELEX:32024R1689 Accessed 06 Jun 2025

86. Ehrlinger, L., Wöß, W.: A novel data quality metric for minimality. In: Data Quality and Trust in Big Data. Lecture Notes in Computer Science, vol. 11235, pp. 1–15. Springer, Cham (2019)
87. Haegemans, T., Snoeck, M., Lemahieu, W.: Towards a precise definition of data accuracy and a justification for its measure. In: Proceedings of the International Conference on Information Quality (ICIQ), pp. 16–11613. Alarcos Research Group (UCLM), Ciudad Real (2016)
88. Ge, M., Delgado-Battenfeld, C., Jannach, D.: Beyond accuracy: evaluating recommender systems by coverage and serendipity. In: Proceedings of the ACM Conference on Recommender Systems (RecSys), pp. 257–260 (2010)
89. Sokolova, M., Japkowicz, N., Szpakowicz, S.: Beyond accuracy, f-score and roc: a family of discriminant measures for performance evaluation. In: Australasian Joint Conference on Artificial Intelligence, pp. 1015–1021. Springer, Berlin (2006)
90. Redman, T.C.: Measuring data accuracy: A framework and review. In: Information Quality, Chap. 2, pp. 21–36. M.E. Sharpe, Armonk, NY (2005)
91. Qahtan, A.A., Elmagarmid, A., Castro Fernandez, R., Ouzzani, M., Tang, N.: FAHES: A robust disguised missing values detector. In: Proceedings of the International Conference on Knowledge Discovery and Data Mining (SIGKDD), pp. 2100–2109 (2018)
92. Naumann, F.: Completeness-driven query optimization. In: Quality-Driven Query Answering for Integrated Information Systems vol. 2261, pp. 123–149. Springer, Berlin, Heidelberg (2002). https://doi.org/10.1007/3-540-45921-9_8
93. Sundararajan, M., Najmi, A.: The many shapley values for model explanation. In: Proceedings of the International Conference on Machine Learning, vol. 119. Online, pp. 9269–9278 (2020). http://proceedings.mlr.press/v119/sundararajan20b.html
94. Shapley, L.S.: A value for n-person games. In: Contributions to the Theory of Games II, pp. 307–317. Princeton University Press, Princeton (1953)
95. Ribeiro, M.T., Singh, S., Guestrin, C.: "Why should i trust you?" explaining the predictions of any classifier. In: Proceedings of the International Conference on Knowledge Discovery and Data Mining (SIGKDD), pp. 1135–1144 (2016)
96. Clemmensen, L.H., Kjærsgaard, R.D.: Data Representativity for Machine Learning and AI Systems (2023). https://doi.org/10.48550/arXiv.2203.04706
97. D'Exelle, B.: In: Michalos, A.C. (ed.) Representative Sample, pp. 5511–5513. Springer, Dordrecht (2014). https://doi.org/10.1007/978-94-007-0753-5_2476
98. Mohammed, S., Ehrlinger, L., Harmouch, H., Naumann, F., Srivastava, D.: The Five Facets of Data Quality Assessment. SIGMODREC **54**(2), 18–27 (2025). https://dl.acm.org/doi/abs/10.1145/3749116.3749120
99. Kandel, S., Parikh, R., Paepcke, A., Hellerstein, J., Heer, J.: Profiler: Integrated statistical analysis and visualization for data quality assessment. In: Proceedings of Advanced Visual Interfaces (AVI), Capri, pp. 547–554 (2012)
100. Press, G.: Cleaning data: Most time-consuming, least enjoyable data science task. Forbes (2016)
101. Terrizzano, I.G., Schwarz, P.M., Roth, M., Colino, J.E.: Data wrangling: The challenging journey from the wild to the lake. In: Proceedings of the Conference on Innovative Data Systems Research (CIDR) (2015). http://cidrdb.org/cidr2015/Papers/CIDR15_Paper2.pdf
102. Nargesian, F., Zhu, E., Miller, R.J., Pu, K.Q., Arocena, P.C.: Data lake management: challenges and opportunities. PVLDB **12**(12), 1986–1989 (2019)
103. Harby, A.A., Zulkernine, F.: Data lakehouse: a survey and experimental study. Inf. Syst. **127**, 102460 (2025) https://doi.org/10.1016/j.is.2024.102460
104. Hameed, M., Naumann, F.: Data preparation: a survey of commercial tools. SIGMOD Record **49**(3), 18–29 (2020)
105. Fan, G., Wang, J., Li, Y., Miller, R.J.: Table discovery in data lakes: State-of-the-art and future directions. In: Companion of the International Conference on Management of Data (SIGMOD), pp. 69–75 (2023). https://doi.org/10.1145/3555041.3589409

106. Jin, Z., Anderson, M.R., Cafarella, M., Jagadish, H.: Foofah: Transforming data by example. In: Proceedings of the International Conference on Management of Data (SIGMOD), pp. 683–698. ACM (2017)
107. Hameed, M., Vitagliano, G., Jiang, L., Naumann, F.: SURAGH: syntactic pattern matching to identify ill-formed records. In: Proceedings of the International Conference on Extending Database Technology (EDBT), pp. 143–154 (2022). https://doi.org/10.48786/EDBT.2022.05
108. Shankar, S., Fawaz, L., Gyllstrom, K., Parameswaran, A.: Automatic and precise data validation for machine learning. In: Proceedings of the International Conference on Information and Knowledge Management (CIKM), pp. 2198–2207 (2023)
109. Wang, P., He, Y., Shea, R., Wang, J., Wu, E.: Deeper: A data enrichment system powered by deep web. In: Proceedings of the International Conference on Management of Data (SIGMOD), pp. 1801–1804. ACM (2018)
110. Vitagliano, G., Hameed, M., Jiang, L., Reisener, L., Wu, E., Naumann, F.: Pollock: a data loading benchmark. PVLDB **16**(8), 1870–1882 (2023)
111. Hellerstein, J.M., Heer, J., Kandel, S.: Self-service data preparation: research to practice. IEEE Data Eng. Bull. **41**(2), 23–34 (2018)
112. Döhmen, T., Mühleisen, H., Boncz, P.: Multi-hypothesis CSV parsing. In: Proceedings of the International Conference on Scientific and Statistical Database Management (SSDBM). Association for Computing Machinery, New York, NY (2017). https://doi.org/10.1145/3085504.3085520
113. Ilyas, I.F., Chu, X.: Data Cleaning. ACM Books, vol. 28. ACM, New York (2019). https://doi.org/10.1145/3310205
114. Bertossi, L.E.: Database Repairing and Consistent Query Answering. Synthesis Lectures on Data Management. Morgan & Claypool Publishers, San Rafael, CA (2011). https://doi.org/10.2200/S00379ED1V01Y201108DTM020
115. Barker, A., Hemert, J.: Scientific workflow: A survey and research directions. In: Parallel Processing and Applied Mathematics vol. 4967, pp. 746–753. Springer, Berlin, Heidelberg (2008). http://link.springer.com/10.1007/978-3-540-68111-3_78
116. Cirillo, S., Desiato, D., Polese, G., Sebillo, M.M.L., Solimando, G.: Augmenting Anonymized Data with AI: Exploring the Feasibility and Limitations of Large Language Models in Data Enrichment (2025). https://arxiv.org/abs/2504.03778
117. Töpper, G., Knuth, M., Sack, H.: Dbpedia ontology enrichment for inconsistency detection. In: Proceedings of the 8th International Conference on Semantic Systems, pp. 33–40 (2012)
118. Auer, S., Bizer, C., Kobilarov, G., Lehmann, J., Cyganiak, R., Ives, Z.: Dbpedia: A nucleus for a web of open data. In: Proceedings of the International Semantic Web Conference (ISWC), pp. 722–735. Springer (2007).
119. Vrandečić, D.: Wikidata: A new platform for collaborative data collection. In: Proceedings of the International World Wide Web Conference (WWW), pp. 1063–1064 (2012)
120. Suchanek, F.M., Alam, M., Bonald, T., Chen, L., Paris, P.-H., Soria, J.: Yago 4.5: A large and clean knowledge base with a rich taxonomy. In: Proceedings of the International Conference on Information Retrieval (SIGIR), pp. 131–140 (2024)
121. SNOMED Clinical Terms. Online. https://www.snomed.org/what-is-snomed-ct (2025)
122. Özcan, F., Lei, C., Quamar, A., Efthymiou, V.: Semantic enrichment of data for ai applications. In: Proceedings of the Fifth Workshop on Data Management for End-To-End Machine Learning, pp. 1–7 (2021)
123. Heidari, A., McGrath, J., Ilyas, I.F., Rekatsinas, T.: Holodetect: Few-shot learning for error detection. In: Proceedings of the International Conference on Management of Data (SIGMOD), pp. 829–846. ACM, New York, NY (2019)
124. Ehrlinger, L., Werth, B., Wöß, W.: Automating data quality monitoring with reference data profiles. In: Data Management Technologies and Applications, pp. 24–44. Springer, Cham (2023)

125. Schelter, S., Rukat, T., Biessmann, F.: Jenga: A framework to study the impact of data errors on the predictions of machine learning models. In: Proceedings of the International Conference on Extending Database Technology (EDBT) (2021). https://www.amazon.science/publications/jenga-a-framework-to-study-the-impact-of-data-errors-on-the-predictions-of-machine-learning-models
126. Miao, X., Wu, Y., Chen, L., Gao, Y., Yin, J.: An experimental survey of missing data imputation algorithms. IEEE Trans. Knowl. Data Eng. **35**(7), 6630–6650 (2023) https://doi.org/10.1109/TKDE.2022.3186498
127. Little, R.J.A., Rubin, D.B.: Statistical Analysis with Missing Data, 2nd edn. Wiley, New York, NY (2002)
128. Geerts, F., Mecca, G., Papotti, P., Santoro, D.: Cleaning data with llunatic. VLDB J. **29**(4), 867–892 (2020) https://doi.org/10.1007/S00778-019-00586-5
129. Restat, V., Boerner, G., Conrad, A., Störl, U.: Gouda - generation of universal data sets: Improving analysis and evaluation of data preparation pipelines. In: Proceedings of the Workshop on Data Management for End-To-End Machine Learning (DEEM), pp. 1–6. Association for Computing Machinery, New York, NY (2022). https://doi.org/10.1145/3533028.3533311
130. Arocena, P.C., Glavic, B., Mecca, G., Miller, R.J., Papotti, P., Santoro, D.: Messing up with bart: Error generation for evaluating data-cleaning algorithms. Proc. VLDB Endowment **9**(2), 36–47 (2015) https://doi.org/10.14778/2850578.2850579
131. Hildebrandt, K., Panse, F., Wilcke, N., Ritter, N.: Large-scale data pollution with apache spark. IEEE Trans. Big Data **6**(2), 396–411 (2020) https://doi.org/10.1109/TBDATA.2016.2637378
132. Christen, P.: Data Matching. Springer, Berlin, Heidelberg, New York (2012)
133. Naumann, F., Herschel, M.: An Introduction to Duplicate Detection. Morgan & Claypool, San Rafael (2010)
134. Talburt, J.R.: Entity Resolution and Information Quality. Morgan Kaufmann, Burlington, MA (2011)
135. Elmagarmid, A.K., Ipeirotis, P.G., Verykios, V.S.: Duplicate record detection: A survey. IEEE Trans. Knowl. Data Eng. **19**(1), 1–16 (2007)
136. Li, Y., Li, J., Suhara, Y., Doan, A., Tan, W.: Deep entity matching with pre-trained language models. PVLDB **14**(1), 50–60 (2020) https://doi.org/10.14778/3421424.3421431
137. Kobayashi, F., Eram, A., Talburt, J.: Entity resolution using logistic regression as an extension to the rule-based oyster system. In: IEEE Conference on Multimedia Information Processing and Retrieval (MIPR), pp. 146–151 (2018). https://doi.org/10.1109/MIPR.2018.00033
138. Peeters, R., Steiner, A., Bizer, C.: Entity matching using large language models. In: Proceedings of the International Conference on Extending Database Technology (EDBT), pp. 529–541 (2025). https://doi.org/10.48786/EDBT.2025.42
139. Draisbach, U., Christen, P., Naumann, F.: Transforming pairwise duplicates to entity clusters for high-quality duplicate detection. J. Data Inf. Qual. **12**(1), 1–30 (2020)
140. Bilenko, M., Kamath, B., Mooney, R.J.: Adaptive blocking: Learning to scale up record linkage. In: Proceedings of the International Conference on Data Mining (ICDM), pp. 87–96 (2006). https://doi.org/10.1109/ICDM.2006.13
141. Papadakis, G., Koutrika, G., Palpanas, T., Nejdl, W.: Meta-blocking: taking entity resolution to the next level. IEEE Trans. Knowl. Data Eng. **26**(8), 1946–1960 (2014) https://doi.org/10.1109/TKDE.2013.54
142. Hernández, M.A.., Stolfo, S.J..: Real-world data is dirty: data cleansing and the merge/purge problem. Data Min. Knowl. Discov. **2**(1), 9–37 (1998)
143. Bleiholder, J., Naumann, F.: Data fusion. ACM Comput. Surv. **41**(1), 1–41 (2008)
144. Dong, X.L., Berti-Equille, L., Srivastava, D.: Truth discovery and copying detection in a dynamic world. PVLDB **2**(1), 562–573 (2009)
145. Vom Brocke, J., Rosemann, M.: Handbook on Business Process Management vol. 2. Springer, Heidelberg (2010)

146. Redman, T.C.: Data quality management past, present, and future: Towards a management system for data. In: Sadiq, S. (ed.) Handbook of Data Quality: Research and Practice, pp. 15–40. Springer, Heidelberg (2013)
147. Lee, Y., Madnick, S.E., Wang, R.Y., Wang, F., Zhang, H.: A cubic framework for the chief data officer: Succeeding in a world of big data. Technical Report CISL# 2014-01, Massachusetts Institute of Technology, Cambridge, MA (2014)
148. Davenport, T., Bean, R.: Are you asking too much of your chief data officer. Harvard Business Review (2020). https://hbr.org/2020/02/are-you-asking-too-much-of-your-chief-data-officer
149. Redman, T.C.: People and Data: Uniting to Transform Your Business. Kogan Page Publishers, London (2023)
150. Nie, Y., Talburt, J., Li, X., Xiao, Z.: Chief data officer (CDO) role and responsibility analysis. J. Comput. Sci. Coll. **33**(5), 4–12 (2018)
151. Davenport, T.H., Bean, R.: Data and AI leadership executive survey (2024). https://www.randybeandata.com/s/DataAI-ExecutiveLeadershipSurveyFinalAsset.pdf
152. Lee, Y.W., Strong, D.M.: Knowing-why about data processes and data quality. J. Manag. Inf. Syst. **20**(3), 13–39 (2004)
153. Plotkin, D.: Data Stewardship: An Actionable Guide to Effective Data Management and Data Governance. Morgan Kaufmann, Burlington, MA (2020)
154. Ehrlinger, L., Wöß, W.: A survey of data quality measurement and monitoring tools. Front. Big Data **5**, 850611 (2022)
155. Schelter, S., Schmidt, P., Rukat, T., Kiessling, M., Taptunov, A., Biessmann, F., Lange, D.: DEEQU – data quality validation for machine learning pipelines. In: Annual Conference on Neural Information Processing Systems (2018). https://www.amazon.science/publications/deequ-data-quality-validation-for-machine-learning-pipelines
156. Chien, M., Radhakrishnan, D., Waite, S.: Gartner magic quadrant for augmented data quality solutions. Technical Report, Gartner, Inc. (2025)
157. Pushkarev, V., Neumann, H., Varol, C., Talburt, J.R.: An overview of open source data quality tools. In: Proceedings of the International Conference on Information & Knowledge Engineering (IKE), pp. 370–376. CSREA Press, Las Vegas, NV (2010)
158. Pulla, V.S.V., Varol, C., Al, M.: Open source data quality tools: Revisited. In: Information Technology: New Generations: International Conference on Information Technology, pp. 893–902. Springer, Cham (2016)
159. Papastergios, V., Ehrlinger, L., Gounaris, A.: Unfolding Data Quality Dimensions in Practice: A Survey (2025). https://arxiv.org/abs/2507.17507
160. Abedjan, Z., Golab, L., Naumann, F., Papenbrock, T.: Data profiling. Synth. Lect. Data Manag. **10**(4), 1–154 (2019)
161. Mahdavi, M., Abedjan, Z.: Semi-supervised data cleaning with Raha and Baran. In: Proceedings of the Conference on Innovative Data Systems Research (CIDR) (2021)
162. Zhang, S., Huang, Z., Wu, E.: Data Cleaning Using Large Language Models (2024). https://arxiv.org/abs/2410.15547
163. Ni, W., Miao, X., Zhao, X., Wu, Y., Liang, S., Yin, J.: Automatic data repair: are we ready to deploy? PVLDB **17**(10), 2617–2630 (2024)
164. Srivastava, D., Velegrakis, Y.: Using queries to associate metadata with data. In: Proceedings of the International Conference on Data Engineering (ICDE), pp. 1451–1453 (2007). https://doi.org/10.1109/ICDE.2007.369033
165. Jayawardene, V., Sadiq, S.W., Indulska, M.: The curse of dimensionality in data quality. In: Australasian Conference on Information Systems (ACIS), p. 165 (2013). https://aisel.aisnet.org/acis2013/165
166. Kahn, M.G., Callahan, T.J., Barnard, J., Bauck, A.E., Brown, J., Davidson, B.N., Estiri, H., Goerg, C., Holve, E., Johnson, S.G., et al.: A harmonized data quality assessment terminology and framework for the secondary use of electronic health record data. Egems **4**(1), 1244 (2016)
167. Weiskopf, N.G., Bakken, S., Hripcsak, G., Weng, C.: A data quality assessment guideline for electronic health record data reuse. Egems **5**(1), 14 (2017)

Lisa Ehrlinger is a Senior Researcher at the Hasso Plattner Institute, University of Potsdam, Germany. In the Data & AI Cluster, she conducts research on how to assess data quality in the era of artificial intelligence. Lisa Ehrlinger obtained her PhD on "Automated Continuous Data Quality Measurement" from the Johannes Kepler University in Linz in 2021, where she was also affiliated as a research assistant and lecturer. She worked on ap-plied research projects in the field of data quality, data integration, and metadata management for over 7 years at the Software Competence Center in Austria and was team lead of the data management and data quality team for the last 3 years. Her research interests and publications cover the topics of data quality, databases, metadata management, and semantic technology. From 2022 to 2025, she co-organized the Quality of Databases (QDB) workshop at VLDB to provide a discussion platform for data quality researchers. Ehrlinger is also a member of the Global Editorial Board of the CDO Magazine and had several talks at the MIT CDOIQ Symposium.

Felix Naumann studied mathematics, economy, and computer sciences at the University of Technology in Berlin and completed his PhD thesis in the area of data quality at Humboldt University of Berlin in 2000. After a Postdoc position at the IBM Almaden Research Center working on data integration topics, he became Assistant Professor for information integration, again at the Humboldt University of Berlin in 2003. Since 2006, he holds the chair for Information Systems at the Hasso Plattner Institute (HPI) at the University of Potsdam in Germany. He has been a visiting researcher at QCRI, AT&T Research, IBM Research, SAP, and UQ. His re-search interests include data profiling, data quality and cleansing, and data integration, recorded in over 250 scientific publications. Next to numerous PC memberships for international conferences, he has organized several conferences in various roles, including VLDB 2021 as PC co-chair, and he is the Editor-in-Chief of the ACM *Journal of Data and Information Quality (JDIQ)*.

Chapter 5
Data Privacy in Enterprise AI

Neil G. Marchant, Ying Zhao, Benjamin I. P. Rubinstein, and Olga Ohrimenko

Abstract Enterprise AI systems often process vast amounts of personal and sensitive data, making them vulnerable to breaches and misuse. Consider, for example, a financial institution that trains a predictive model on sensitive customer data that is to be shared with partner organizations. If the model is shared without proper precautions, the partner organization or a malicious employee may attempt to breach the privacy of the original training data by launching an attack to reconstruct this data from model parameters. Such vulnerabilities erode trust in enterprise and AI systems, may fail to comply with privacy legislation, and can lead to financial, intellectual property or reputational loss. Privacy is a cornerstone of ethical and responsible AI deployment. This chapter provides a guide to the tools necessary to navigate the landscape of AI privacy, ultimately facilitating broader and more secure AI adoption in the enterprise.

5.1 Introduction

The rapid advancement of artificial intelligence (AI) has ushered in an era of unprecedented data utilization. Modern AI systems, particularly large language models, demonstrate an insatiable appetite for data, with performance improvements closely tied to the scale of training data. This relationship is evidenced by empirical scaling laws observed by researchers [68] and exemplified by a commercial language model published in 2024, which was trained on a staggering 15 trillion tokens [82].

While this data-driven approach has led to remarkable achievements, it also presents significant privacy challenges for enterprises adopting AI technologies. The landscape of privacy concerns in AI has evolved rapidly over the past decade. Initially, privacy discussions in enterprise AI focused primarily on data storage

N. G. Marchant (✉) · Y. Zhao · B. I. P. Rubinstein · O. Ohrimenko
School of Computing and Information Systems, University of Melbourne, Parkville, VIC, Australia
e-mail: nmarchant@unimelb.edu.au; ying.zhao.2@unimelb.edu.au; benjamin.rubinstein@unimelb.edu.au; oohrimenko@unimelb.edu.au

S. Sadiq (ed.), *Enterprise AI*, https://doi.org/10.1007/978-3-032-01940-0_5

and access. However, as AI models have become more sophisticated and widely deployed, the scope of privacy concerns has expanded to include issues such as model inversion attacks, differential privacy in federated learning, and the potential for unintended memorization in large language models. This evolution underscores the need for a comprehensive and adaptive approach to privacy in enterprise AI.

The data used to train or fine-tune AI models often contains sensitive information, ranging from personally identifiable information in customer interactions to proprietary business intelligence and trade secrets. For instance, an e-commerce platform might train its AI on proprietary purchasing metrics [4], or an engineering firm might optimize product designs using historical performance data [153]. In both cases, the training data represents valuable intellectual property that requires protection.

The risk of data leakage in AI systems is multifaceted and can occur at various stages of the AI lifecycle. During the training phase, data or its derivatives may be intercepted, especially when using public cloud infrastructure or decentralized approaches like federated learning. Post-deployment, there's a risk of data extraction from the model itself or its outputs. Even test data, such as prompts shared with large language model services, may be subject to privacy concerns.

These privacy risks extend beyond the immediate threat of data disclosure. Enterprises must also consider secondary risks, including regulatory non-compliance costs, reputational damage, and potential customer abandonment [141]. As such, privacy considerations are paramount in AI projects and are made more challenging by the business needs of balancing disclosure risks with achieving business critical model performance.

5.1.1 Defining Privacy in the Context of Enterprise AI

Before exploring the specifics of privacy risks and mitigations in AI systems, it's crucial to establish what we mean by "privacy" in this context. While there is no universal consensus on the definition of privacy, for the purposes of this chapter, we adopt the risk-based approach outlined in the NIST Privacy Framework [101]. This framework conceptualizes privacy as a condition that safeguards values such as human autonomy and dignity, achievable through various means including limiting observation and ensuring individual control over personal information.

In the context of enterprise AI, privacy primarily concerns the appropriate handling and protection of data used in AI systems, including training data, model parameters, and inference data. This encompasses not only personal information of individuals but also proprietary business data and intellectual property. Our focus will be on managing privacy risks, which we define as potential adverse effects that individuals or organizations may experience due to data processing activities in AI workflows. This approach allows us to address privacy concerns in a practical, risk-oriented manner that aligns with enterprise needs and regulatory requirements.

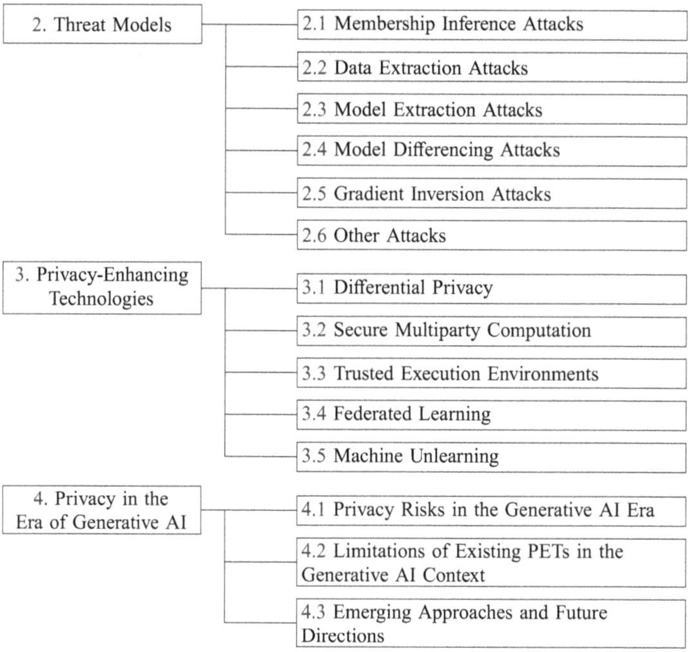

Fig. 5.1 Chapter structure overview (Sects. 5.2–5.4)

5.1.2 Chapter Overview

This chapter aims to provide a comprehensive overview of privacy in the context of enterprise AI, focusing on key risks and potential mitigations specific to AI workflows, as illustrated in Fig. 5.1. In Sect. 5.2, we explore various threat models and privacy risks, including membership inference attacks, data extraction attacks, and side-channel attacks. This examination of threat models serves as a foundation for understanding the specific challenges faced in AI privacy. Section 5.3 presents a range of privacy-enhancing technologies that can be employed to mitigate these risks, such as differential privacy, secure multiparty computation, and federated learning. Finally, Sect. 5.4 discusses the evolving landscape of privacy in the era of generative AI, addressing new challenges and potential solutions.

It's important to note that while this chapter focuses on AI-specific privacy concerns, it does not cover broader privacy topics such as general data protection regulations, data management practices, or privacy impact assessments. For information on privacy legislation like GDPR or CCPA, readers are directed to specialized resources [12, 53, 83]. Similarly, for general data management practices and privacy governance, other comprehensive guides are available [57, 85, 111].

By providing this focused examination of privacy in AI, we aim to equip enterprise decision-makers, data scientists, and AI practitioners with the knowledge needed to navigate the complex intersection of AI capabilities and privacy requirements. As we move into our discussion of threat models in the next section, which, while comprehensive, is not exhaustive, given the rapidly evolving nature of the field, we will see how understanding these specific risks is crucial for developing effective privacy strategies in enterprise AI deployments.

5.2 Threat Models

Understanding and addressing privacy risks in AI systems requires a structured approach that goes beyond general data protection measures. This section introduces the concept of threat modeling as a powerful tool for analyzing and mitigating privacy risks specific to AI contexts.

Threat modeling, a practice commonly used in cybersecurity, involves systematically identifying potential threats to a system by considering an adversary's capabilities, incentives, prior knowledge, and constraints. In this chapter, we specify each threat model by describing three key components:

- *Adversary's Capabilities:* What actions the attacker can perform, such as querying the model or accessing certain data
- *Adversary's Knowledge:* What information the attacker possesses about the system, model, or data
- *Adversary's Goal:* What the attacker aims to achieve through the attack

This structured approach allows us to systematically analyze each privacy risk and develop appropriate mitigation strategies.

While this approach may be unfamiliar to readers without a security background, it provides invaluable insights for privacy protection in AI. By viewing privacy risks through the lens of threat models, we can better understand the nature and scope of potential vulnerabilities, assess their likelihood and impact, and develop more effective mitigation strategies. Without this structured approach, organizations risk overlooking critical vulnerabilities or implementing ineffective safeguards—essentially flying blind in their privacy protection efforts.

The NIST Privacy Framework outlines four primary ways organizations can handle privacy risks: mitigation, transfer, avoidance, or acceptance [101]. In this chapter, we focus primarily on risks and threats that arise specifically in AI contexts, presenting technical measures for mitigation in Sect. 5.3. However, it's important to acknowledge that risk transfer also plays a significant role in modern AI ecosystems, particularly as many organizations outsource AI services to third-party providers.

To maintain a focused discussion, we limit our scope to threats that are unique to or exacerbated by AI systems. We do not cover general data security threats such as data breaches, social engineering, or malware, as these are not specific to AI contexts. For the purposes of this chapter, we define AI-specific privacy risks as those that directly relate to the AI components of a system, such as the model, its training process, or its outputs. This includes risks that arise from the way AI models learn, store, and process information, as well as how they generate outputs based on their training.

These AI-specific privacy risks include membership inference attacks, which attempt to determine if specific data was used in training; data extraction attacks, which aim to reconstruct training data; model extraction attacks, which try to replicate the functionality of a model; model differencing attacks, which exploit changes in model behavior; gradient inversion attacks, which reconstruct data from model updates; and side channel attacks, which leverage unintended information leakage during AI operations.

5.2.1 Membership Inference Attacks

Membership inference (MI) attacks aim to predict whether an individual's data was used to train a model, posing a foundational privacy risk in AI [17, 47, 121]. These attacks identify patterns in a model's behavior that suggest memorization or overfitting to specific training data.

In most settings, MI attacks have a low direct impact on privacy, since disclosing whether an individual's data was used to train a model is not typically sensitive. However, they can be sensitive in certain contexts—e.g., inferring criminal records from recidivism prediction models. More importantly, MI attacks serve as a foundation for stronger data extraction attacks [16] and privacy auditing [55, 99].

5.2.1.1 Threat Model

The attack involves a victim who deploys a model and an adversary attempting to determine if a specific instance was in the training set. Conventionally, the model is assumed to be a classifier that outputs confidence scores for all classes [17, 121]; however, models that hide confidence scores may still be vulnerable [25]. More recently, MI attacks have been extended to generative models [114] and explainable models [80].

Adversary's Capabilities The adversary has black-box query access to the model and sometimes to the training data distribution. Query access to the training data distribution is used to gather data for training "shadow models" in some attacks [17, 121].

Adversary's Knowledge The adversary must know the target instance (input and output) but not the model parameters or full training data. Knowledge of the model architecture and training algorithm used by the victim can give the adversary an advantage, but is not essential [17].

Adversary's Goal The adversary seeks to *accurately* predict whether the target instance was included in the victim's training data. [17] argue that attacks should maximize the true-positive rate for a fixed low false-positive rate (e.g., $\leq 0.1\%$).

5.2.1.2 Attack Methodology

A MI attack requires an adversary to distinguish between two possible scenarios: one where the target instance *was* in the training set and one where it *was not* in the training set. It is therefore natural to cast a MI attack as a statistical hypothesis test, where the null hypothesis H_0 and alternative hypothesis H_1 are as follows:

$$H_0: \text{ "the target instance } x \text{ was not in the training set of model } M\text{"}$$
$$H_1: \text{ "the target instance } x \text{ was in the training set of model } M\text{".}$$

The adversary must then design a test to decide whether there is sufficient evidence to reject H_0 and conclude that the target instance was used for training. There is considerable variation in the design of the test and the formal interpretation of H_0 and H_1 across the literature.

Generally speaking, the adversary must define a test statistic $T(M, x)$ that depends on the target instance x and the model M. Ideally, $T(M, x)$ should be sensitive to the inclusion or exclusion of x in the training set for M. For example, the adversary could define $T(M, x)$ to be the model's loss on x, which can be computed given query access to the model's confidence scores. Recent attacks use a likelihood ratio for the test statistic, which is the optimal test for a fixed false-positive rate [17, 147].

To complete the design of the test, the adversary must choose the rejection region S—the set of values of the test statistic for which the null hypothesis H_0 is rejected. For the previous example, where $T(M, x)$ is the model's loss, the rejection region S can be defined as the set of loss values below some threshold τ. This amounts to rejecting H_0 when the model's loss is small, which may indicate memorization of x. Another approach is to learn the rejection region from data by training a classifier [121].

To meet the adversary's goal, the rejection region should be chosen to achieve a small false-positive rate. However, estimating the false-positive rate is a significant challenge in designing an effective MI attack. Mathematically, the false-positive rate (FPR) is defined as the probability that the test statistic is in the rejection region, given that H_0 is true:

$$\text{FPR} = \Pr[T(M, x) \in S | H_0].$$

To estimate this probability, the adversary must model the distribution of the test statistic $T(M, x)$ in a setting where H_0 is true.

If the model's training algorithm is randomized and the training data is fixed under H_0, the distribution of the test statistic can be estimated by training multiple "shadow models" and computing $T(M, x)$ for each one. However, this is not feasible for the adversary, as they do not have access to the victim's training data and they may not have access to the model architecture or training algorithm either. To get around this problem, the adversary can make further approximations. For instance, the victim's training data can be approximated by data drawn from the same distribution—if query access to the training data distribution is available—or a similar distribution. The adversary can try to make an informed guess about the victim's model architecture and training algorithm; however, research has shown that strong attacks are still possible even when there is a mismatch [17].

For large foundation models, reliably estimating FPR is challenging, limiting the reliability of MI attacks as evidence of data usage. Alternative approaches include using canary data or data extraction attacks (Sect. 5.2.2) [159].

5.2.1.3 Defenses

Defenses against MI attacks can be categorized into two types: those based on empirical approaches and those that come with provable guarantees. Empirical defenses employ various techniques like adversarial training [97], confidence score manipulation [60, 79], and model distillation [125] to mitigate vulnerabilities. However, these methods lack formal privacy guarantees. In contrast, differential privacy (DP; covered in Sect. 5.3.1) provides a rigorous framework that offers provable protection against MI attacks. An (ϵ, δ)-DP mechanism bounds the power of any membership inference attack [30]. Specifically, for small significance levels α,[1] the power of the test is upper bounded by $e^{\epsilon}\alpha + \delta$, which is only slightly larger than α when ϵ and δ are small.

5.2.2 Data Extraction Attacks

As AI models grow in size and complexity, their capacity to memorize training data increases, posing a significant privacy risk. Data extraction attacks exploit this vulnerability, particularly in large generative models, where adversaries can elicit memorized training examples through careful probing [16, 18]. When evaluated against production language models, these attacks have achieved success rates of 0.5–3% per query under conservative assumptions [100].

[1] We assume here that $0 < \alpha \leq \frac{1-\delta}{1+e^{\epsilon}}$.

5.2.2.1 Threat Model

Data extraction attacks involve a victim who trains a model on private data and an adversary attempting to extract specific training examples. Research to date has focused on controlled settings to measure worst-case privacy risks, assuming the adversary has access to training examples or likely sources [16, 18, 100]. Further research is needed to understand risks under more realistic threat models.

Adversary's Capabilities The adversary may have black-box or white-box access to the target model. Black-box access typically allows the adversary to submit queries and receive responses, without controlling generation hyperparameters or the internal source of randomness. White-box access allows the adversary to observe the model weights and architecture, permitting control of randomness and computation of loss functions and gradients. Access to multiple models trained on the same data (e.g., checkpoints or size variants) can improve extraction success [93].

Adversary's Knowledge For targeted attacks, the adversary must have some knowledge about the training example they are trying to extract. It is common to assume knowledge of part of the training example—e.g., the caption of an image [18] or the prefix of a text snippet [19]. Untargeted attacks, on the other hand, do not require knowledge of the training data, but may benefit from access to likely training sources.

Adversary's Goals The adversary aims to extract training examples, either indiscriminately (untargeted) or specifically (targeted). Success criteria vary, with current research setting high bars for extraction fidelity [18, 100]; however, lower-fidelity extraction still presents a risk [93].

5.2.2.2 Attack Methodology

Data extraction attacks against generative models typically involve two steps: eliciting memorized responses and checking for memorization.

Eliciting Memorized Responses This step is relatively straightforward for models that have only undergone pre-training, as their sole objective is to mimic the training data distribution conditioned on the prompt. As a result, the model is likely to emit memorized training examples if the prompt perfectly matches part of a training example. For instance, [18] demonstrate that an image of a person can be extracted from a diffusion model simply by prompting with the person's name.

Eliciting memorized responses may be more challenging for instruction-tuned or aligned models designed to avoid leaking sensitive data. In such cases, adversaries may circumvent alignment procedures by designing adversarial prompts that trick the model into reverting to its pre-training objective. For example, [100] successfully extracted sensitive information from a proprietary aligned language model by instructing it to repeat a single word indefinitely.

Regardless of the querying strategy, submitting each query multiple times can be beneficial. Due to model randomness, collecting multiple responses increases the likelihood that at least one will contain a training example.

Checking for Memorization After obtaining responses from the model, the adversary must verify whether they contain training examples or not. This can be done through direct comparison if training data is accessible or via membership inference attacks. The latter can be adapted depending on the adversary's capabilities—e.g., [18] describe weaker membership inference attacks against diffusion models that only require black-box access, as well as stronger attacks that use white-box access.

Auditing Data extraction attacks can play a crucial role in privacy auditing of generative models [159]. Since the adversary is the same party as the victim when auditing, they may have stronger capabilities and knowledge than a realistic adversary, allowing them to design more powerful attacks.For instance, if the adversary controls the training data, they can insert out-of-distribution "canary" examples that are easier to extract than in-distribution examples [15].

5.2.2.3 Defenses

Defending against data extraction attacks is an ongoing challenge. While several empirical strategies have shown promise, most lack rigorous privacy guarantees and do not fully eliminate the risk.

- *Data sanitization*: Detects and removes sensitive information before training begins. While it prevents the model from memorizing information it has never seen, data sanitization is rarely perfect. Sensitive information may be difficult to detect or embedded in ways that make removal challenging without compromising data quality.
- *Training data deduplication*: This strategy emerged after the discovery that models are much more likely to emit examples that are duplicated many times in the training set [19, 67]. While removing exact duplicates is straightforward, near-duplicates are more difficult to catch and can also lead to memorization.
- *Alignment techniques*: These methods involve fine-tuning models on guardrail-specific datasets that include scenarios like leakage of sensitive information. The goal is to encourage the model to operate within defined privacy boundaries. However, alignment may not completely mitigate the risk, as sophisticated adversaries can potentially bypass guardrails through prompt injection attacks [100].

An exception to these empirical defenses is *differentially private training*, which comes with formal guarantees. It ensures the output model is statistically insensitive to the presence or absence of a single training example, thereby bounding the risk of extraction attacks. While differentially private training can significantly impact model performance, it has been applied successfully to language models for writing prediction, where it prevented extraction attacks with only a marginal impact on utility [15].

5.2.3 Model Extraction Attacks

Model extraction attacks involve adversaries systematically probing a model's inputs and outputs to create an unauthorized copy, without access to the original training data, model parameters, or training algorithm [54, 128]. This threatens the intellectual property of organizations who have invested substantially in model development. Beyond economic motivations, adversaries may attempt to extract a model to conduct downstream security or privacy attacks, essentially upgrading their access from black-box to white-box. This dual threat of intellectual property theft and security risk makes model extraction a serious concern for deployed AI systems.

5.2.3.1 Threat Model

The victim develops a model they wish to make available for benign usage without disclosing internal details, exposing it through an API. The adversary attempts to create an unauthorized copy using this API.

Adversary's Capabilities The adversary is assumed to have black-box query access to the victim's model, with responses varying depending on the model type (e.g., class labels, confidence scores, or raw logits for classification models). They may additionally have access to a dataset of unlabeled model inputs that can be used to generate queries, though this isn't always essential [107].

Adversary's Knowledge The adversary's knowledge about the victim's model may range from minimal to substantial, potentially including information about the model architecture or pre-trained components.

Adversary's Goals The adversary seeks to create a copy of the victim's model, either for economic incentives or to gain white-box access for downstream attacks [54]. For economic motivations, an approximate replication of functionality may suffice. For enabling white-box attacks, a functionally equivalent copy is desired. The adversary may also aim to minimize the number of queries to reduce costs and improve stealthiness.

5.2.3.2 Attack Methodology

There are two broad approaches to model extraction: *learning-based attacks* are suitable when the adversary seeks an approximate copy of the model, whereas *high-fidelity attacks* are designed to produce a functionally equivalent copy.

Learning-Based Attacks These attacks yield an approximate copy by training a new model using the victim's model as a labeling oracle. Typically the adversary has access to a training set of unlabeled examples. A simple approach is to select a subset of examples from this set, query labels from the oracle, and train the duplicate model from scratch using fully supervised learning [128]. However, this may be inefficient in terms of the number of queries required. Various approaches have been proposed to improve query efficiency, including adaptive querying strategies [107], semi-supervised learning [54], active learning [21], and building on top of pre-trained models [107].

If the adversary does not have access to an unlabeled training set, they can use data-free extraction attacks. Generating random inputs from a surrogate distribution has been shown to work in some cases [107], but extraction accuracy and efficiency improve as the surrogate distribution approaches the victim's training distribution. To this end, adversaries may train a generative model to synthesize query examples that maximize disagreement between the victim and duplicated model [131].

High-Fidelity Attacks These attacks typically require knowledge about the victim model's architecture, as well as high-precision query access to model outputs (e.g., logits). That knowledge is then used to develop algorithms to recover the model parameters. For example, attacks have been developed that exploit the piecewise linear nature of neural networks with ReLU activations [55, 116]. More recently, [20] demonstrated an extraction attack against a proprietary language model that is able to recover the embedding projection layer. While this attack only recovers a small fraction of the parameters, it may prove useful for future attacks and implicitly reveals information about the model's size, which may otherwise have been confidential.

5.2.3.3 Defenses

While various defensive strategies have been proposed, no current method offers comprehensive protection without potential compromises to model performance or functionality [105]. Defenses fall into two categories:

Proactive Defenses These aim to prevent model extraction by modifying the model's fundamental characteristics or limiting information exposed in its outputs. A common strategy is to randomly perturb the model's inputs or outputs, to make the model's behavior less certain to the adversary, without compromising model performance. This can be done using information theoretic principles tailored for model privacy [137] or differential privacy [145, 160]. To limit information exposed by the model, the victim can censor confidence scores or logits in the output or reduce their precision; however, this may limit the utility for benign users [20, 128].

Reactive Defenses These focus on detecting ongoing attacks or providing evidence of model ownership. The victim may be able to detect an ongoing extraction attack by monitoring the distribution of incoming queries [64], though this can be vulnerable to attack [36]. Even if the victim is unable to prevent model extraction, they may be able to gather evidence to pursue legal action against a suspected attacker. Proof-of-learning requires the victim to demonstrate unique characteristics of the training process that would be difficult for an adversary to reproduce [62].

Dataset inference can identify distinctive behavior in a model that is only likely to present when trained on the victim's training data [86]. Finally, watermarking techniques can be used to embed imperceptible signals in the model that only the owner knows how to extract [61].

5.2.4 Model Differencing Attacks

The release of multiple versions of a model, through updates or fine-tuning, amplifies privacy risks by enabling model differencing attacks. These attacks analyze changes between model versions to infer information about training data that was added, removed, or modified [22, 117, 155]. This expands the attack surface and can amplify other privacy risks, such as membership inference or reconstruction attacks [56]. The risk is particularly acute when data changes between releases are small and targeted, such as removing an individual's data in response to a deletion request [22].

5.2.4.1 Threat Model

In a model differencing attack, an adversary observes two or more sequentially released model versions with modified training data. The models typically share the same architecture but may have different parameter values. The victim could be the organization releasing the models or specific individuals whose data was modified between releases.

Adversary's Capabilities Access to model versions can range from black-box to white-box. An adversary with black-box access can query the models and compare outputs. They may also exploit access to intermediate model states or gradients if these are exposed through APIs or collaborative learning settings. An adversary with white-box access can analyze changes in model parameters directly, potentially revealing more precise information about the training data modifications.

Adversary's Knowledge The adversary may have knowledge about when training data was modified, the number of examples changed, or partial information about the modified examples. In some cases, the adversary might even know which specific examples were modified (e.g., through public announcements of data deletion requests) and use this information to focus their attack on reconstructing the unknown features of those examples.

Adversary's Goals The adversary aims to infer information about training examples that change between model releases. The scope and granularity of the inferred information may vary: from determining whether a specific example was added or removed to reconstructing features of modified examples.

5.2.4.2 Attack Methodology

Research has primarily focused on two categories of model differencing attacks: (1) Specialized membership inference attacks, where the aim is to determine whether a particular training example was added or removed between model releases (2) Specialized data extraction attacks, where the aim is to extract all or part of the modified training data These attacks are related to their counterparts for stand-alone models discussed in Sects. 5.2.1 and 5.2.2. Here we discuss specializations that exploit differences between successive model releases.

Membership Inference Attacks In the model differencing setting, the adversary's goal is to infer whether a given training example was added or removed between two model releases. This can be achieved by running a stand-alone membership inference (MI) attack on each model; however, stronger attacks have been proposed that use the model releases *jointly* for inference. [22] use shadow models to train a MI classifier that uses the outputs from all models to make a prediction. On the other hand, [56] combine information from stand-alone MI attacks against each model, achieving a higher attack accuracy using a smaller number of shadow models.

Data Extraction Attacks These attacks operate differently from the stand-alone setting in that they undertake a differential analysis of model behavior. For structured data, techniques include majority voting on disagreeing examples [39], predicting updated attributes based on model confidence changes [52], and exact solutions for simple models like linear regression [7]. For unstructured data, approaches include gradient inversion attacks [48], encoder training using shadow models [117], and beam search for extracting text snippets with large perplexity differences [155].

5.2.4.3 Defenses

Defending against model differencing attacks presents a significant challenge, as it requires balancing privacy protection with the practical needs of model updates and performance improvements. Several strategies have been proposed, each with its own trade-offs:

- *Reducing update frequency and batch updates*: Modifying a larger number of training examples between releases makes individual changes harder to isolate. However, this may conflict with operational needs for frequent updates.
- *Limiting output information*: For scenarios where models are exposed via query APIs (black-box settings), withholding confidence scores [22, 117] or providing only top-k predictions [155] can hamper attack efficacy while preserving much of the model's utility.
- *Differential privacy*: Applying differential privacy (DP) to model releases or outputs provides formal guarantees about individual training example protection.

However, DP inherently limits performance improvements in updated models, highlighting the tension between privacy protection and utility [155].

As model updates remain crucial for many AI applications, developing robust defenses against differencing attacks that preserve both privacy and utility continues to be an important challenge for the field.

5.2.5 Gradient Inversion Attacks

Gradient inversion attacks exploit access to gradients to reconstruct private training examples, posing a significant privacy risk in machine learning systems [8, 136, 161]. This vulnerability is particularly critical in distributed learning paradigms like federated learning (FL), where participants exchange model updates instead of raw data. Despite FL's promotion as privacy preserving, these attacks demonstrate that a curious server or other participants can potentially recover individual training examples from shared gradients.

5.2.5.1 Threat Model

Gradient inversion attacks are predominantly studied within federated learning systems, where participants share model updates with each other or a central server. The most common threat model casts the central server as the adversary and the participants as victims.

Adversary's Capabilities Two settings are typically considered: an honest-but-curious server that passively observes updates [40, 161] or a dishonest server that may modify the model architecture [37] or deviate from the established protocol [8, 38] to make data reconstruction easier.

Adversary's Knowledge Since the central server is typically managed by the model developer, it is usually assumed to have full knowledge of the model architecture, loss function, and training algorithm and may have background knowledge about the data distribution. For instance, in the vision domain, attacks may leverage prior information about the distribution of images to steer the attack toward more realistic reconstructions [59, 148].

Adversary's Goal The primary goal is to recover information about the participant's private training data, ranging from exact reconstruction of entire batches [29] to recovering small portions of highly sensitive data [26].

5.2.5.2 Attack Methodology

Gradient inversion attacks vary depending on whether the central server is honest-but-curious or dishonest. We provide an overview of attacks in both these settings, covering approaches for both real-valued and discrete data, including images and text.

Honest-but-Curious Server Many attacks are based on gradient matching [161], where the server produces an estimate $\hat{x}$ for the private data x by minimizing the distance between the received gradient and the gradient evaluated at $\hat{x}$. Regularization terms can improve reconstruction quality for large batch sizes and high-dimensional data [40, 59]. Exact reconstruction is possible in certain scenarios [29, 162].

Discrete data, like text, poses a challenge for gradient inversion attacks, as gradient-based optimizers cannot be used directly to solve the gradient matching problem. Approximate reconstruction of multiple text sequence has been demonstrated by incorporating auxiliary language models and alternating between discrete and continuous optimization steps [2]. Recent work has demonstrated exact recovery of long sequences for transformer models [109].

Dishonest Server Attacks in this setting provide participants with a malicious model to aid in the recovery of data from gradients. One approach is to select a malicious model architecture, before the model is fixed and compiled for production. For example, [37] propose to insert a special "imprint" layer, which is designed with a sparse activation pattern so that each data point only activates one or a few neurons. This allows the attacker to isolate individual data points in the gradient.

Recent research has explored attacks against transformer-based language models, by modifying the weights in the attention layers to achieve malicious behaviors. [26] achieve targeted reconstruction of short sensitive sequences (e.g., social security numbers) by modifying weights in attention layers to tag relevant sequences and altering weights in linear layers to filter and capture only the tagged data of interest. Similar ideas have been used to reconstruct long sequences by cleverly encoding token information within the gradient of the model parameters [38].

5.2.5.3 Defenses

Reasonably effective defenses are available against gradient inversion attacks, albeit at the cost of increased computation and communication overhead. Two primary defense strategies have been proposed:

- *Secure aggregation*: Cryptographic protocols that aim to ensure only aggregated updates are observed by the server [9]. While they are relatively efficient, recovery from aggregated updates is possible for some protocols [69], and they typically require synchronous training [156].

- *Homomorphic encryption*: Allows computations on encrypted data, providing strong privacy guarantees [110, 129]. While there is typically a substantial computational and communication overhead, recent work has made progress in addressing efficiency concerns in a federated learning context [156].

Local differential privacy, while conceptually relevant, is generally not regarded as a practical defense against gradient inversion attacks in federated learning settings. It tends to cause severe degradation in model utility due to the amount of noise that must be added to achieve reasonable privacy guarantees.

5.2.6 Other Attacks

5.2.6.1 Linkage Attacks

Linkage attacks combine information from multiple data sources to re-identify or infer sensitive information about individuals [96]. While these attacks don't directly exploit AI systems, they represent a significant privacy risk in the context of AI due to the potential for automation and enhancement using AI capabilities.

Linkage attacks involve an adversary with access to auxiliary information that can be correlated with supposedly "anonymized" data or model outputs. This auxiliary information may be publicly available or obtained by mounting other attacks. The adversary must have some knowledge about potentially linkable information types. For example, an adversary might recognize that combining a anonymized medical dataset with public voting records could link individuals based on common attributes like age, gender, and zip code.

In an AI context, the risk of linkage attacks is exacerbated by several factors:

- *Automation*: AI can automate the process of finding correlations between datasets, making linkage attacks more efficient and scalable.
- *Data aggregation*: AI systems often require large amounts of data from various sources, potentially creating more opportunities for linkage attacks if not properly managed.
- *Integration with AI-specific attacks*: Linkage attacks become more powerful when combined with AI-specific attacks like membership inference or model inversion. The auxiliary information can provide the context needed to make these attacks more effective or to interpret their results in ways that reveal more sensitive information.

Defending against linkage attacks requires implementing formal privacy techniques such as differential privacy and data minimization, alongside systematic risk assessment processes.

5.2.6.2 Side-Channel Attacks

Side-channel attacks against AI systems exploit indirect information leakage through observable physical or operational characteristics, presenting unique privacy risks beyond traditional security concerns. These attacks are particularly relevant in enterprise AI deployments, especially when using shared infrastructure or cloud services.

In the context of AI, side-channel attacks typically aim to extract sensitive information about the model, its parameters, or the training/inference data. The adversary may have limited direct access to the system but can observe characteristics such as timing, power consumption, or memory access patterns during training or inference.

Key types of side-channel attacks relevant to AI privacy include:

Timing Attacks By measuring execution time of specific operations, adversaries can infer information about the model or input data. Notably, these attacks can compromise differential privacy guarantees in AI systems. [63] demonstrated success rates up to 99.65% for end-to-end timing attacks on private sums computed with discrete Laplace noise, undermining the intended privacy guarantees.

Memory and Cache Attacks Adversaries can exploit patterns of memory access, including cache behavior, to infer sensitive information about AI models or their data. By monitoring which memory locations or cache lines are accessed during model execution, attackers can potentially reconstruct parts of the model's architecture, parameters, or even characteristics of training or inference data. This is particularly concerning for enterprises using multi-tenant cloud services for AI workloads, where memory and cache resources are often shared between different users or processes.

Power Analysis Attacks By measuring power consumption of hardware during model execution, adversaries can infer information about operations being performed. For example, [140] use collected power traces to distinguish between models with small architectural differences with over 90% accuracy, while [138] recover inputs to convolutional networks running on FPGAs.

Mitigations for side-channel attacks in AI systems may involve:

- Considering the use of specialized hardware, such as TEEs, designed to resist side-channel attacks for highly sensitive AI workloads
- Exploring the use of oblivious algorithms to mask data and memory access patterns
- Employing side-channel-aware differential privacy frameworks that incorporate potential information leakage into privacy calculations
- Carefully managing resource allocation in cloud environments to minimize shared resources between different tenants

5.3 Privacy-Enhancing Technologies

Having explored the landscape of privacy threats in enterprise AI, we now turn our attention to privacy-enhancing technologies (PETs) designed to mitigate these risks. These technologies offer a range of defenses against the attacks we've discussed, from membership inference to gradient inversion.

This section examines these technologies, their principles, and their applications in addressing privacy risks. Importantly, privacy in enterprise AI requires nuanced solutions tailored to specific contexts and threat models. We will explore various approaches, each offering distinct strengths and trade-offs in protecting sensitive information in AI systems.

Our discussion will cover several mainstream privacy-enhancing technologies: differential privacy, secure multiparty computation, trusted execution environments, federated learning, and machine unlearning. Through this overview, we aim to provide a comprehensive understanding of the tools available to enterprises for enhancing privacy in their AI deployments, enabling informed decisions about which technologies best suit specific use cases.

5.3.1 Differential Privacy

In the era of AI and machine learning, differential privacy (DP) has emerged as a cornerstone of responsible data use and model development. As noted in Sects. 5.2.1 and 5.2.2, AI models trained on vast amounts of potentially sensitive data risk inadvertently memorizing and revealing private information. This is particularly concerning in enterprise settings, where AI systems may process confidential customer data, proprietary business information, or other sensitive records.

DP provides a rigorous framework for bounding privacy leakage in AI systems, enabling organizations to quantify and control the privacy-utility trade-off. It can be applied at various stages of the machine learning pipeline, from data collection and preprocessing to model training and deployment. At its core, DP is not a single algorithm but a comprehensive mathematical framework encompassing a variety of techniques and approaches.

In this section, we will explore the core concepts of DP, its different models of deployment, and key mechanisms used to achieve DP in machine learning. We will also discuss the challenges and limitations of DP and provide a forward-looking outlook for enterprises considering the adoption of differential privacy in their AI systems.

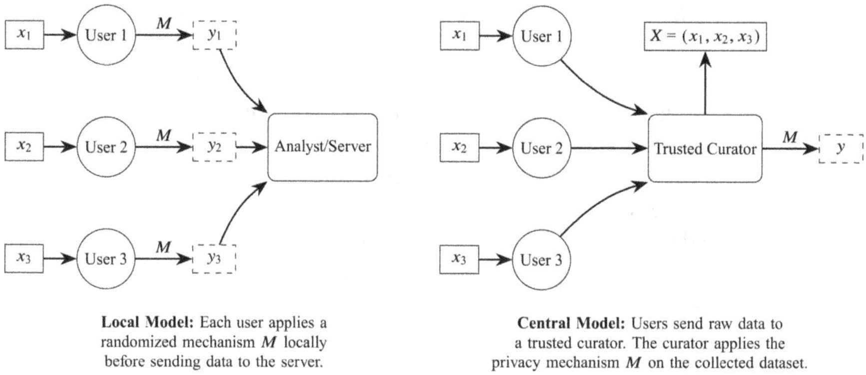

Fig. 5.2 Illustration of the local (left) and central (right) deployment models of differential privacy

5.3.1.1 Deployment Models for Differential Privacy

Differential privacy (DP) can be implemented in various ways, depending on where the trust boundary lies in the data processing pipeline. The two primary models are the central and local model, as illustrated in Fig. 5.2.

Central Model In this model, a trusted curator collects and holds raw data from individuals, applying DP mechanisms before releasing any information. This model is often the most practical and efficient when the data is already collected and stored in a central location, and there is a clear authority responsible for data governance. However, it raises concerns about the concentration of raw data in one location and requires careful implementation of security measures to guard against data breaches.

Local Model This model removes the assumption of a trusted curator. Each individual privatizes their own data before sharing it with a data processor [32]. While this offers stronger privacy guarantees by reducing the risk of large-scale data breaches, it typically requires much stronger noise injection, often leading to significant utility loss. This can make complex analyses or accurate model training challenging, limiting its practical applications.

The choice between deployment models depends on various factors including the specific application, legal and regulatory requirements, trust assumptions, and the desired balance between privacy and utility. In enterprise AI settings, the central model might be more common when dealing with internal data, while the local model could be preferred for collecting data from external sources. Regardless of the deployment model, the fundamental principles of DP remain consistent. For ease of exposition, we will focus on the central model in subsequent discussions.

5.3.1.2 Formalizing Differential Privacy

Differential privacy (DP) provides a formal framework for quantifying and guaranteeing privacy in data analysis. The key idea is to make it difficult to distinguish between two possible worlds: one where an individual contributes their data, and one where they do not. This indistinguishability is achieved by introducing controlled randomness into the data processing [34].

To formalize this concept, consider a dataset $D \in \mathcal{D}$ containing sensitive records from individuals and a randomized algorithm M that processes this data to produce an output $S \in \mathcal{R}$. We define neighboring datasets D and D' as those differing in exactly one record—these correspond to the two "world" that should be difficult to distinguish [34]. The formal definition of (ϵ, δ)-differential privacy is as follows:

Definition 5.1 A randomized algorithm M is (ϵ, δ)-differentially private if for all neighboring datasets $D, D' \in \mathcal{D}$, and for all subsets of outputs $S \subseteq \mathcal{R}$:

$$\Pr[M(D) \in S] \leq e^{\epsilon} \cdot \Pr[M(D') \in S] + \delta.$$

Here, $\epsilon \geq 0$ and $0 \leq \delta < 1$ quantify the privacy guarantee, with smaller values indicating stronger privacy. When $\delta = 0$, the inequality ensures that the probability of observing any particular event is at most e^{ϵ} times as likely under D as under D'. For small ϵ, this means the presence or absence of an individual changes probabilities by at most about ϵ.

The case where $\delta > 0$ allows for a small probability of violating this bound. This relaxation can allow for greater utility in some cases, particularly when dealing with unlikely events.

Selecting the Privacy Budget The parameters ϵ and δ constitute the "privacy budget" of the algorithm, representing a trade-off between privacy protection and output utility. Researchers at Google characterize the level of privacy into three tiers based on the choice of ϵ [112]:

- Tier 1: $\epsilon \leq 1$, provides a strong privacy guarantee at the expense of utility
- Tier 2: $1 < \epsilon \leq 10$, provides a reasonable level of privacy for many applications
- Tier 3: $\epsilon > 10$, provides weak to no formal guarantees, however still represents an improvement over no privacy protection at all

The parameter δ should be chosen to be cryptographically small, typically scaling inversely with the size of the dataset. A common rule of thumb is to set $\delta \ll \frac{1}{n}$, where n is the number of records in the dataset, which ensures the probability of a significant privacy breach remains negligible even for large datasets.

Despite the mathematical rigor of DP, explaining its guarantees to non-experts presents significant challenges. A study by [95] found that even with carefully designed visualizations, many participants struggled to fully grasp the implications of different epsilon values.

Useful Properties of Differential Privacy DP's widespread adoption is partly due to its practical properties:

Composition DP satisfies composition theorems that allow for accounting of overall privacy loss when applying a sequence of DP mechanisms. Advanced composition techniques allow the total ϵ to grow sublinearly with a small degradation in δ, provided the individual privacy parameters are fixed in advance [35]. Further improvements are possible by exploiting properties of specific mechanisms or using variants like zero concentrated DP [14] or Gaussian DP [30]. It is also possible to compose mechanisms while adapting privacy parameters on the fly using fully adaptive composition [139].

Post-processing DP is invariant under post-processing, meaning any arbitrary transformation of a DP output remains DP without degradation in the privacy guarantee. This property provides robustness against unplanned analyses and simplifies the design of privacy-preserving systems by separating privacy considerations from downstream data uses. This flexibility is particularly valuable in evolving research or business environments where future data needs may not be fully known at the time of data release.

5.3.1.3 Differentially Private Mechanisms for AI

We now present two prominent differentially private mechanisms for training AI models: Differentially Private Stochastic Gradient Descent (DP-SGD) and Differentially Private Follow The Regularized Leader (DP-FTRL), with a primary focus on DP-SGD due to its widespread use and general applicability.

Differentially Private Stochastic Gradient Descent DP-SGD, proposed by [1], is a differentially private adaptation of stochastic gradient descent (SGD). It is described in pseudocode in Algorithm 1.

Comparison with SGD DP-SGD diverges from ordinary SGD in several key ways:

- *Batching.* Batches are assembled by drawing examples with/out replacement (line 4). Deviating from this specification may compromise the privacy guarantee.
- *Gradient Computation.* Gradients are computed *per example* (line 6) unlike SGD, where they are typically computed *per batch*.
- *Gradient Clipping.* Individual gradients are clipped to bound their ℓ_2-norm (line 6). This bounds the sensitivity of the computation.
- *Noise Addition.* Calibrated Gaussian noise is added to the averaged clipped gradients (line 9). This step is crucial for providing the DP guarantee.
- *Privacy Accounting.* The privacy loss is tracked during training to ensure it does not exceed the prespecified budget.

Algorithm 1 Differentially private SGD

Input: Training examples $D = \{x_1, \ldots, x_N\}$, loss function L, learning rate η_t, noise scale σ, gradient norm bound C
Initialize model parameters θ_0 randomly
for $t = 0, \ldots, T-1$ **do**
  Select a batch B_t by either (1) sampling b examples from D without replacement or (2) sampling examples from D with replacement with probability $q = b/N$
  for $x_i \in B_t$ **do**
    Compute gradient $g_i \leftarrow \nabla_\theta L(\theta_t, x_i)$
    Clip gradient $\bar{g}_i \leftarrow g_i / \max(1, \|g_i\|_2/C)$
  end for
  Add noise $\tilde{g} \leftarrow \frac{1}{|B_t|}\left(\sum_i \bar{g}_i + \mathcal{N}(0, \sigma^2 C^2 \mathbf{I})\right)$
  Update model parameters $\theta_{t+1} \leftarrow \theta_t - \eta_t \tilde{g}$
end for
Output: θ_T

Practical Considerations Implementing DP-SGD involves balancing privacy and utility. Higher privacy levels typically require more noise, potentially reducing model accuracy. DP-SGD also incurs increased computational costs due to per-example gradient computations and the added noise slowing convergence. The performance can be sensitive to data distribution, with skewed or outlier-heavy datasets potentially requiring more noise and leading to greater utility loss. As a result, careful consideration of the data distribution and potential preprocessing may be necessary when applying DP-SGD to real-world datasets.

Implementations DP-SGD has been implemented in several machine learning frameworks, including TensorFlow Privacy [1] and Opacus for PyTorch [149].

Differentially Private Follow-the-Regularized-Leader DP-FTRL [66] is an alternative mechanism particularly well suited for federated learning (see Sect. 5.3.4). It operates on aggregated model updates rather than per-example gradients, making it easier to implement in environments where access to individual data points is restricted. In DP-FTRL, clients train local models using the FTRL algorithm and send model updates to a central server, which then adds noise to ensure differential privacy before refining the global model. While DP-FTRL offers advantages in distributed settings, DP-SGD generally provides stronger privacy guarantees but requires more granular data access.

5.3.1.4 Summary and Enterprise Outlook

Differential privacy has emerged as a powerful framework for protecting individual privacy in machine learning applications. Mechanisms like DP-SGD and DP-FTRL have made it possible to train and release models with strong privacy guarantees, albeit at the cost of reduced utility or increased computational burden.

For enterprises considering the adoption of DP in their AI systems, several key considerations and future trends are worth noting:

- *Regulatory Compliance:* As privacy regulations evolve, DP may become increasingly important for demonstrating compliance. Enterprises may consider monitoring regulatory developments and examining how DP could fit into their compliance strategies.
- *Privacy-Utility Trade-offs:* Organizations need to carefully balance privacy guarantees with model performance. This may involve sector-specific assessments of acceptable privacy levels and performance thresholds.
- *Explainability and Trust:* DP can be a powerful tool for building trust with customers and stakeholders; however, communicating its benefits and limitations remains challenging. Enterprises may consider developing strategies for effectively explaining their privacy-preserving measures.

As the field progresses, we can expect differential privacy to become an increasingly integral part of the enterprise AI landscape, particularly in domains dealing with sensitive data. Organizations that proactively engage with DP technologies and build relevant expertise will be better positioned to navigate the evolving privacy landscape while leveraging the potential of their data assets.

5.3.2 Secure Multiparty Computation

Secure multiparty computation (SMPC) mitigates privacy risks when multiple parties wish to cooperate by sharing data and compute, for example, when jointly learning a model from a distributed dataset. This section examines two fundamental approaches to SMPC that have demonstrated particular promise for AI applications: secret sharing and homomorphic encryption.

5.3.2.1 Secret Sharing

Secret sharing splits data into seemingly random "shares" distributed among multiple parties, where individual shares reveal nothing about the original data, yet computations performed on these shares yield meaningful results when combined. It allows organizations to collaborate on data analysis, model training, and inference tasks without exposing their underlying data assets.

For AI applications requiring both collaboration and data protection, several secret sharing approaches form the foundation of secure computation:

- *Shamir's Threshold Secret Sharing* [120] implements a (t, n)-threshold scheme using polynomial interpolation where any t out of n parties can reconstruct the secret, providing information-theoretic security.

- *Replicated Secret Sharing* as used in CryptGPU [124] distributes redundant shares so each party in their 2-out-of-3 scheme holds two shares, enabling faster computation with lower communication overhead.
- *Additive Secret Sharing* splits a secret s into shares that sum to the original value ($s = s_1 + s_2 + \ldots + s_n$), enabling efficient addition and forming the basis of frameworks like SecureML [92].
- *Boolean Secret Sharing* operates on bits rather than field elements, enabling efficient implementation of non-linear operations such as ReLU activation functions and comparison-based operations [108].

These primitives are used in a complete SMPC system as follows:

1. *Input Sharing*: Data owners distribute their private inputs using one of the secret sharing schemes described above.
2. *Secure Evaluation*: Parties perform computations directly on shares without revealing the underlying data.
    - Addition operations can typically be performed locally without interaction.
    - Multiplication operations require carefully designed protocols with communication between parties.
    - Complex operations like neural network activations require specialized protocols.
3. *Output Reconstruction*: Only the final results are revealed, while intermediate values remain protected.

The choice of sharing scheme directly impacts the performance-security trade-off. For example, additive sharing enables fast addition operations and serves as a key component in matrix multiplications, while Boolean sharing excels at non-linear functions like ReLU and sigmoid.

AI workloads present unique challenges for SMPC due to their computational intensity. Several frameworks have emerged to address these requirements:

SecureML [92] implements privacy-preserving machine learning between two non-colluding parties using several secret sharing primitives. It achieves efficiency through optimized fixed-point arithmetic, vectorized operations, and SMPC-friendly activation functions. On a dataset of size 60,000 with 784 features, their implementation runs logistic regression in less than 30 seconds and trains a 3-layer neural network within 6 hours. The Python code below demonstrates linear regression, accomplished with a few lines of code.

Linear Regression using SecureML

```
# 1. Forward propagation
y_pred = secure_multiply(X_shared, w_shared)

# 2. Compute difference from true labels
```

```
diff = y_pred - y_shared

# 3. Compute gradient
gradient = secure_multiply(X_shared.T, diff)

# 4. Update weights
w_shared = w_shared - learning_rate * gradient
```

CrypTen [72] bridges theoretical SMPC protocols and practical AI development with a PyTorch-like API, enabling seamless transition to SMPC. This is demonstrated below where the code appears like idiomatic PyTorch code.

SGD step in PyTorch and CryptTen

```
# Given encrypted tensors x, y, w
# Secure SGD update in CrypTen
grad = (x.matmul(w) - y).matmul(x.transpose(0, 1))
w = w - alpha * grad
```

CryptGPU [124] addresses SMPC computational bottlenecks through GPU acceleration. Using replicated secret sharing in a three-party honest-majority setting, it achieves 150× faster convolutions, 10× faster ReLU activations, and 2–36× end-to-end acceleration for training and inference by mapping secret-shared operations to GPU-optimized primitives.

Recent advances have expanded secret sharing–based SMPC beyond traditional neural networks to transformer architectures. SIGMA [45] enables secure GPT inference using function secret sharing, processing 13 billion parameter models in 33 seconds. SHAFT [70], utilizing arithmetic secret sharing, further reduces communication overhead by $\sim$25–41% while maintaining running times comparable to SIGMA.

5.3.2.2 Homomorphic Encryption

Homomorphic Encryption (HE) enables direct computation on encrypted data without decryption. HE schemes preserve algebraic structure between plaintext and ciphertext domains, with two fundamental properties:

- $E(x) \oplus E(y) = E(x + y)$ [Additive homomorphism]
- $E(x) \otimes E(y) = E(x \times y)$ [Multiplicative homomorphism]

These properties allow operations on encrypted data to yield results that, when decrypted, match the operations performed on the original plaintext. HE schemes

Table 5.1 Comparison of HE schemes by type: partially homomorphic encryption (PHE), somewhat homomorphic encryption (SWHE) and fully homomorphic encryption (FHE). Here † denotes "with bootstrapping," and * denotes "without bootstrapping"

Type	Scheme	Operations	Data type	Applications
PHE	RSA	Multiplication only	Integers	Digital signatures, data aggregation
	Paillier	Addition only	Integers	Statistical analysis, electronic voting
	ElGamal	Multiplication only	Integers	Privacy systems
SWHE	BGN	Limited addition and 1 multiplication	Integers	Quadratic functions
	BGV	Limited*	Integers	Integer arithmetic
	BFV	Limited*	Integers	Boolean circuits
	CKKS	Limited*	Real/complex	Machine Learning, statistics
FHE	GSW	Unlimited operations	Boolean	Circuit evaluation
	BGV	Unlimited†	Integers	Integer arithmetic
	BFV	Unlimited†	Integers	Boolean circuits
	CKKS	Unlimited†	Real/complex	Machine learning, signal processing
	TFHE	Unlimited†	Boolean	Circuit evaluation, logic operations
	FHEW	Unlimited†	Boolean	Boolean circuits
	MKHE	Varies by base scheme	Base dependent	Cross-organization computation

can be categorized by their computational capabilities and efficiency trade-offs, ranging from *partially homomorphic*, which supports single operations, to *fully homomorphic*, which supports arbitrary computations, as detailed in Table 5.1.

Among recent schemes, CKKS [24] advances AI-compatible HE by enabling approximate arithmetic on real/complex numbers. By encoding vectors directly into polynomial rings, it eliminates integer conversion overhead; this is a critical optimization for privacy-preserving neural networks and ML workloads.

Despite promising theoretical foundations, Homomorphic Encryption faces substantial practical challenges for AI deployment. FHE operations remain 3–6 orders of magnitude slower than their plaintext equivalents, creating a significant performance gap that impacts real-world applications [6]. Memory efficiency presents another critical concern, as ciphertexts typically expand in size by 2–3 orders of magnitude compared to plaintexts. This expansion is particularly problematic for deep learning models with millions of parameters, where encrypted inference can require gigabytes of memory even for relatively small networks. Additionally, optimal HE parameter selection introduces complexity through necessary trade-offs between security levels, numerical precision, and circuit depth, requiring careful consideration during implementation.

Recent engineering advances are rapidly closing implementation gaps in homomorphic encryption for AI applications. *Hardware acceleration* has achieved remarkable breakthroughs, with FPGA implementations demonstrating speedups ranging from 13× to over 3200× [123, 146]. *Domain-specific architectures* have emerged as critical enablers, with systems like HEAX [115], F1 [118], HAAC [91], and Cinnamon [58] leveraging parallel computation across different scales. Particularly noteworthy is OLA [146], which implements scale-out architectures that distribute computational workloads across multiple chips to maximize throughput for complex neural network operations.

Algorithmic optimizations have simultaneously addressed memory and communication bottlenecks through advanced data encoding techniques. Frameworks such as TenSEAL [5] and Gazelle [65] have dramatically reduced resource requirements, with Gazelle achieving a remarkably compact 0.5MB memory footprint. These optimizations are complemented by *compiler-level innovations* from systems like EVA [28] and Zama's Concrete-ML [154], which automate parameter selection, optimize circuit depth, and approximate non-linear functions with polynomials, enabling efficient encrypted computation without requiring deep cryptographic expertise from developers.

The integration of these advancements has enabled the development of practical privacy-preserving AI systems. Hybrid cryptographic frameworks like Cheetah [50] strategically combine homomorphic encryption for linear operations (convolution, batch normalization, fully-connected layers) with oblivious transfer protocols for non-linear activations (ReLU, truncation), to reduce latency and communication overhead.

Production-ready libraries have further bridged research-practice gaps, with Microsoft SEAL providing general-purpose HE capabilities that form the foundation for many higher-level implementations. OpenMined's TenSEAL, built upon SEAL, extends these capabilities with specialized support for tensor operations including addition, subtraction, and multiplication, making it particularly suitable for machine learning workloads. NVIDIA has integrated HE into its Clara Train SDK to enable privacy-preserving federated learning, while IBM's HElib [46] offers highly optimized implementations of multiple HE schemes. Intel's HE-Transformer completes this ecosystem by enabling efficient tensor operations on encrypted data through hardware-optimized primitives.

5.3.2.3 Summary and Enterprise Outlook

Secret sharing distributes data fragments across multiple parties who must coordinate computation, providing post-quantum resistance and robustness against certain corruptions, but requiring significant communication overhead. Homomorphic Encryption allows computing directly on encrypted data without decryption, offering a stronger threat model but suffering from extreme computational costs and vulnerability to side-channel attacks. Both approaches remain orders of magnitude away from efficiently supporting large AI models.

As hardware acceleration continues to evolve through specialized FPGA implementations and domain-specific architectures, and as algorithmic innovations further reduce computational and communication overhead, we can expect wider adoption of SMPC techniques across industries where data privacy is paramount.

Organizations implementing SMPC should first evaluate which approach best matches their specific privacy needs and technical constraints. Enterprises should leverage production-ready frameworks like TenSEAL, Microsoft SEAL, or CrypTen that offer streamlined development through high-level APIs and machine learning framework integrations. Hybrid approaches can optimize privacy-utility trade-offs by applying SMPC only to the most sensitive computations. For sustained privacy requirements, investing in specialized hardware accelerators (now available through many cloud providers) can substantially improve performance. While SMPC is not yet viable for all AI workloads, organizations should begin exploring these technologies now, as privacy-preserving computation is becoming both a regulatory necessity and competitive advantage.

5.3.3 *Trusted Execution Environments*

Trusted Execution Environments (TEEs) can provide protection to AI workloads via isolation—allowing such workloads to run in an untrusted computing environment. TEEs provide hardware-enforced isolation for sensitive computations, creating protected enclaves where code and data remain confidential even from privileged software like operating systems. This architecture [87] establishes processor-level security features that create distinct trusted and untrusted execution domains, enabling secure execution of confidential workloads in otherwise untrusted cloud environments.

Figure 5.3 illustrates one approach to hardware-enforced isolation between trusted and untrusted execution environments [122]. This figure demonstrates a clear boundary between a non-secure world with untrusted applications on a conventional operating system (OS) and a secure world where trusted applications operate on a specialized trusted OS. This security model ensures only trusted applications can access sensitive processor functions, protected memory regions, and dedicated peripherals. This security model provides confidentiality and integrity protection that persists even when the cloud provider presents risks, though it's worth noting that sophisticated attackers with physical access may still potentially bypass these protections through side-channel methods.

However, it's important to note that not all TEEs operate according to this exact model. For instance, Intel Software Guard Extensions (SGX) implements a different approach that doesn't require a separate trusted OS counterpart, instead creating secure enclaves directly within the untrusted operating system environment [87]. These enclaves utilize hardware-based memory encryption and integrity verification to protect sensitive data and computations from privileged software. While Fig. 5.3 shows a clear physical separation between environments, the underlying mechanisms for establishing and maintaining isolation vary considerably across TEE technologies. Some implementations rely on processor modes and hardware

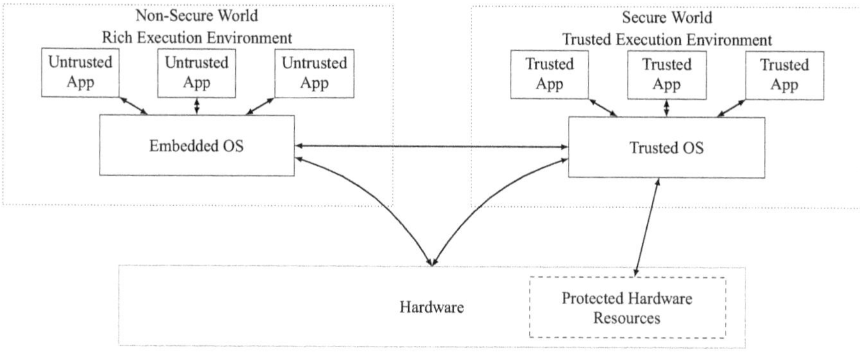

Fig. 5.3 Hardware-enforced isolation: trusted vs. untrusted execution environments

security extensions, while others use memory encryption and attestation protocols. This architectural diversity enables TEEs to be deployed across various computing environments—from resource-constrained mobile devices to high-performance cloud infrastructure—while maintaining strong security guarantees appropriate to each context's specific requirements and threat models.

5.3.3.1 Commercial TEE Hardware Architectures

The landscape of Trusted Execution Environment (TEE) technologies has evolved significantly, with numerous commercial implementations now available across diverse computing platforms. These technologies can be broadly categorized into hardware-centric TEEs that embed security directly into processors and chipsets and cloud service TEEs that provide confidential computing capabilities as managed offerings. As shown in Table 5.2, which represents our compilation of information from vendor documentation and product Web sites as of May 2025, each architecture employs distinct approaches to achieving the fundamental TEE goals of isolation, encryption, and attestation. Hardware-centric solutions range from Intel's enclave-based SGX to ARM's dual-world TrustZone architecture, while cloud providers have integrated these hardware technologies into their service offerings. Understanding the security features and market availability of these TEE architectures is essential for organizations seeking to implement robust security measures for their most sensitive computational workloads.

5.3.3.2 CPU-GPU TEE Integration

In the trusted execution landscape, CPU-based and GPU-based TEEs have developed along separate technological paths due to fundamental differences in hardware architecture, instruction sets, and execution models [134]. CPU TEEs (like Intel

Table 5.2 Commercial Trusted Execution Environment (TEE) architectures

TEE technology	Key security features	Market availability
Hardware-Centric TEEs		
Intel SGX	Application-level enclaves with memory encryption, attestation, and isolated execution	Widespread in server market, reduced in consumer chips
ARM TrustZone	Secure/non-secure world separation with hardware-enforced isolation	Billions of devices across mobile and embedded markets
NVIDIA Confidential Computing	GPU workload protection, secure memory, and protected execution paths	Enterprise GPU offerings for AI/ML workloads
AMD SEV	VM memory encryption, nested page protection, and secure VM launch	Widely deployed in EPYC servers for cloud and enterprise data centers
IBM Secure Service Container	Encrypted containers, tamper protection, and automatic data encryption	IBM Z mainframes and LinuxONE systems for enterprise market
Apple Secure Enclave	Isolated security processor, encrypted memory, and secure boot chain	All modern Apple devices (iPhones, iPads, Macs)
Samsung Knox	Isolated workspace, secure boot, and real-time kernel protection	Samsung enterprise and consumer mobile devices
Cloud service TEEs		
Google Confidential Computing	Isolated VMs, confidential containers, and AMD SEV-based protection	Google Cloud Platform commercial service
Microsoft Azure Confidential Computing	SGX VMs, confidential containers, and attestation services	Azure cloud service offerings
Alibaba Cloud Confidential Computing	SGX and SEV support, data isolation, and encryption in use	Alibaba Cloud commercial offering

SGX, AMD SEV, and ARM TrustZone) evolved earlier and focus on general-purpose computing security, while GPU TEEs (such as NVIDIA's Confidential Computing) emerged more recently to address the specific needs of parallel computation in AI workloads. Despite this separate development, modern enterprise AI deployments increasingly demand seamless integration between these distinct security technologies to provide comprehensive protection across heterogeneous computing resources.

Modern enterprise AI security systems now use hybrid approaches that combine these complementary TEE technologies into unified security zones. These integrated systems create end-to-end secure computing paths where data remains protected throughout its lifecycle, from ingest and preprocessing (secured by CPU TEEs) through model training and inference (protected by GPU TEEs). This security coverage spans the entire AI pipeline, creating a continuous chain of trust across different computing resources [127]. In typical production environments, Intel SGX or AMD SEV secures the data preparation and management stages, while NVIDIA's confidential computing technologies protect the compute-intensive model execution.

Recent benchmarks on NVIDIA H100 GPUs reveal that TEE security features add minimal performance overhead for AI workloads. [163] demonstrated that enabling TEE mode on H100 GPUs incurs less than 7% average performance penalty for LLM inference tasks, with this overhead approaching zero for larger models. Significantly, the performance impact stems primarily from encrypted data transfers between CPU and GPU TEEs across the PCIe bus, not from computations within the GPU itself. These findings are particularly relevant for enterprise AI deployments, confirming that TEE protection becomes more efficient precisely for the large-scale, computation-intensive workloads typical in production environments.

The research community has also made significant progress in developing trusted execution environments for heterogeneous computing systems, with substantial efforts focusing on the integration of CPUs and GPUs to address their unique security challenges while minimizing performance overhead. Early prototypes like Graviton established secure channels between untrusted hosts and GPUs, while HIX advanced this approach by placing key GPU control functionalities within a CPU-based enclave [135]. HETEE proposed a data-center level GPU TEE supporting confidential computing without requiring chip-level modifications. ARM-based TEE research has evolved with StrongBox, the first ARM-based GPU TEE for secure computation without hardware modifications, and CRONUS, which developed a framework supporting spatial sharing within accelerators [135]. Most recently, PORTAL [119] addresses the challenges of integrating diverse co-processors and peripherals within mobile ARM SoCs by achieving secure device I/O through strict memory isolation without memory encryption, specifically targeting performance, scalability, and power efficiency challenges that have hindered wider adoption of confidential computing architectures.

5.3.3.3 Security Vulnerabilities and Mitigation Strategies

Vulnerabilities While integrated TEE technologies offer promising security benefits across CPU-GPU environments, they remain vulnerable to a range of sophisticated attacks that must be addressed to ensure truly secure heterogeneous computing. Side-channel attacks represent a critical threat to heterogeneous TEEs, especially in CPU-GPU systems. Traditional TEE protections focus primarily on preventing direct memory access from untrusted software but often fail to address the subtle information leakage that occurs through execution patterns, memory access timing, and resource contention. TEEs offer inadequate protection against sophisticated side-channel attacks exploiting cache timing or page faults, as demonstrated by successful attacks against Intel SGX enclaves [144]. Similarly, speculative execution attacks like Spectre and Meltdown, as well as physical attacks including cold boot and power analysis techniques, continue to pose significant threats to TEE security guarantees [133].

These side-channels become even more problematic in heterogeneous computing environments where the architectural complexity introduces additional attack surfaces. Researchers have demonstrated multiple attack vectors unique to GPU environments, including microarchitectural attacks exploiting shared resources (such as L2 caches across GPUs connected via NVLink), timing attacks based on GPU-specific execution patterns, and physical access vulnerabilities targeting PCIe traffic. Academic studies [33, 135] have highlighted specific vulnerabilities in various GPU architectures, showing that even with TEE protection, challenges remain in securing the entire computational pipeline. The complexity of CPU-GPU interactions creates unique side-channel vulnerabilities that are difficult to address through hardware isolation alone, as TEEs alone cannot prevent side-channel leakage through memory access patterns.

Defenses Frameworks like STACCO provide sophisticated differential analysis techniques to identify subtle side-channel vulnerabilities in TEE implementations [144]. Ohrimenko et al. [104] demonstrated how CPU TEEs can be leveraged constructively by implementing data-oblivious machine learning algorithms within Intel SGX enclaves. By ensuring "uniform" memory access patterns regardless of input data, these techniques effectively shield sensitive information from memory side-channel observation. This approach has been further advanced by TLBlur [132], which automatically tracks and prefetches page accesses to conceal execution patterns from privileged adversaries. The complementary nature of TEEs and oblivious algorithms represents a crucial research direction for privacy-preserving AI applications, combining hardware isolation against direct attacks with algorithmic protections that can eliminate the subtle information leakage traditionally undermining TEE security guarantees. By combining hardware TEE protections with algorithmic techniques, the system can provide strong security guarantees: hardware isolation to prevent direct access and algorithmic solutions to mitigate some of the indirect observations through side-channels. These findings inform ongoing research in hardening TEE implementations to address attack surfaces through techniques like resource partitioning, cache isolation, and encrypted memory systems.

5.3.3.4 Summary and Enterprise Outlook

Trusted Execution Environments provide hardware-enforced isolation for sensitive AI workloads, with modern implementations now effectively spanning heterogeneous CPU-GPU architectures. Despite significant advances in integration that minimize performance penalties for large models (less than 7% for LLMs on

NVIDIA H100 GPUs), there are several aspects that enterprises may consider before deploying these technologies. For example, for effective TEE implementation, AI teams should identify critical pipeline components requiring protection, establish continuous attestation chains across processing stages, and develop clear governance frameworks for confidential computing deployments.

In parallel with implementation advancements, academic-industry collaborations continue to standardize secure communication between heterogeneous TEEs and unify attestation protocols [27]. These standardization efforts complement technical implementations [127, 134] and enhance the viability of secure AI deployments across diverse hardware environments. However, even with standardized protocols, security remains contextual to specific deployments. When deploying TEE technologies, organizations should conduct thorough threat modeling end to end, including the supplier of the TEEs and the environment where TEEs are deployed. For example, if memory side-channels are a threat, then susceptibility of the code to information leakage should be evaluated, and methods for hardening AI workloads should be considered.

5.3.4 Federated Learning

The principle of data minimization is fundamental to privacy preservation, but it presents a significant challenge for traditional machine learning approaches that rely on centralized data collection. Federated learning (FL) addresses this challenge by enabling model training across multiple clients without sharing raw data. In FL, clients collaboratively train a model by exchanging model weights or gradients, either among themselves or with a centralized server.

However, as discussed in Sects. 5.2.2 and 5.2.5, these model updates are not intrinsically privacy preserving and can potentially leak information about the underlying training data. While basic FL schemes remain vulnerable to such leakage, it is possible to mitigate these risks by integrating additional privacy-enhancing technologies, such as secure multiparty computation, secure enclaves, and differential privacy covered in previous sections.

This section will examine the key principles of federated learning, analyze its privacy benefits and challenges, and explore how it can be combined with other PETs to enhance privacy. We will also discuss practical considerations for implementing FL in enterprise settings.

5.3.4.1 Federated Learning Deployment Modes

Federated learning can be deployed in two primary modes, each with distinct privacy implications:

Centralized FL A central server orchestrates the learning process, with clients downloading the current model, training locally, and sending updates back for aggregation. While straightforward to implement and manage, this mode introduces a single point of failure and may raise trust issues regarding the central server, potentially allowing for inference attacks [98].

Decentralized FL Clients communicate directly with each other, sharing updates in a peer-to-peer fashion using technologies such as gossip protocols [126] or blockchain [3]. This mode is more resilient to failures and can offer stronger privacy guarantees by eliminating a central point of visibility. However, it's more complex to implement and may be more vulnerable to inference attacks from malicious clients [84].

The choice of deployment mode depends on factors including privacy requirements, network topology, and computational resources. For example, a consortium of banks might prefer decentralized FL for a fraud detection model to ensure no single entity has complete visibility of all updates, while a company improving product recommendations across branches might choose centralized FL for easier management, with appropriate security measures at the central server.

5.3.4.2 Federated Averaging: A Canonical FL Algorithm

To grasp both the privacy benefits and challenges of federated learning, it's helpful to understand the process. Federated Averaging (FedAvg) [88], which extends stochastic gradient descent to the federated setting, is one of the most widely used algorithms for centralized FL and has served as a foundation for more advanced algorithms.

The FedAvg process, as detailed in Algorithm 2, proceeds as follows:

1. **Initialization:** A central server chooses a model architecture and initializes global weights w_0 (line 2).
2. **Client Selection:** For each round, the server selects a subset of clients to participate (line 4).
3. **Local Training:** Selected clients receive the current global model weights and perform local training (line 6). This step is crucial for privacy preservation, as all data handling occurs locally.
4. **Aggregation:** The server aggregates the updates by averaging model parameters from all participating clients (line 8).
5. **Iteration:** Steps 2–4 are repeated for multiple rounds until the model converges or a predefined number of rounds is reached.

While clients never share raw data, which is a key privacy-preserving aspect of FL, these model updates can still potentially leak information, necessitating additional privacy measures discussed next.

Algorithm 2 Federated averaging

procedure FEDAVG ▷ Run on server
  Initialize global weights w_0
  for each round $t = 1, 2, \ldots$ **do**
    Select a subset S_t of K clients
    for client $k \in S_t$ **in parallel do**
      $w_t^k \leftarrow \text{ClientUpdate}(k, w_{t-1})$
    end for
    Global weight update: $w_t \leftarrow \frac{1}{K} \sum_{k \in S_t} w_t^k$
  end for
  return Global weights w_t
end procedure

procedure CLIENTUPDATE(k, w) ▷ Run on client k
  Randomly partition local data into batches $\mathcal{B}$
  for epoch $i = 1, \ldots, E$ **do**
    for batch $x \in \mathcal{B}$ **do**
      Local weight update: $w \leftarrow w - \eta \nabla L(w; x)$
    end for
  end for
  return Local weights w to server
end procedure

5.3.4.3 Additional Privacy Measures

While federated learning offers inherent privacy advantages by keeping raw data localized, it's not immune to privacy vulnerabilities. As discussed in Sects. 5.2.5 and 5.2.2, gradients or model weights can leak information about the training data. This risk exists in both centralized and decentralized FL settings, and even the final global model can pose privacy risks similar to those in standard centralized learning.

To address these vulnerabilities, FL is often combined with other privacy-enhancing technologies:

Differential Privacy (DP) Both local and central DP can be applied to FL. With local DP, clients add noise to their weight updates before sending them to untrusted parties [130]; however, it typically results in poor utility for a reasonable level of privacy [71]. A more practical approach is central DP, which assumes a trusted central server while preventing privacy leakage in the final model. For example, DP-FedAvg [41] adapts the FedAvg algorithm (Algorithm 2) to limit an attacker's ability to determine whether a specific client participated in the training process. This is distinct from protecting individual data points and works by sub-sampling clients and adding noise during the aggregation step, effectively hiding a single client's contribution.

Secure Multiparty Computation (SMPC) SMPC techniques, particularly secure aggregation and homomorphic encryption, can be integrated into FL to enhance privacy during the training process. Secure aggregation protocols efficiently protect individual updates during aggregation but leave the aggregated update exposed to the central server and require synchronous training [9]. Homomorphic encryption offers stronger protection by securing both individual and aggregated updates, but at a higher computational cost. These approaches have different threat model assumptions: secure aggregation typically assumes an honest-but-curious central server, while homomorphic encryption provides stronger guarantees against a malicious server.

Trusted Execution Environments (TEEs) TEEs offer hardware-based isolation for sensitive computations in FL, primarily used on the server side to protect the aggregation process [90]. In a typical setup, clients encrypt model updates before transmission, and the server's TEE decrypts and aggregates the updates in a protected environment. While TEEs offer strong privacy guarantees, they assume trustworthiness of the hardware manufacturer and TEE implementation and can be vulnerable to side-channel attacks [13].

By combining these technologies, FL can provide robust privacy guarantees against a wide range of threat models. However, each technology comes with its own trade-offs in terms of computational overhead, communication costs, and potential impact on model utility.

5.3.4.4 Summary and Enterprise Outlook

Federated learning represents a significant advancement in privacy-preserving AI, allowing enterprises to collaborate on model training while respecting data privacy and ownership. By keeping raw data localized and sharing only model updates, FL provides a foundation for overcoming data silos and enabling collaboration in scenarios where direct data sharing is infeasible. The integration of additional privacy-enhancing technologies, such as secure aggregation protocols and Trusted Execution Environments (TEEs), has largely addressed privacy concerns in the FL training process.

Looking forward, enterprises considering FL implementation should:

- Assess their specific use case and privacy requirements to determine the most appropriate FL deployment mode and additional privacy measures needed
- Invest in building technical expertise or partnering with specialized providers to navigate the complexity of implementing secure FL systems
- Stay informed about advancements in differentially private machine learning, as these will be crucial for protecting the privacy of final aggregated models, especially if they are to be released or shared

As privacy-preserving FL becomes more accessible, enterprises that proactively develop capabilities in this area will be well positioned to leverage collaborative learning opportunities while maintaining robust privacy protections. This could lead to competitive advantages through improved models and expanded collaboration possibilities, all while adhering to stringent privacy standards.

5.3.5 Machine Unlearning

The "right to erasure" enshrined in privacy regulations such as the European Union's General Data Protection Regulation (GDPR) has sparked growing interest in data deletion practices. While these regulations don't explicitly extend to trained models, research demonstrating that models can memorize training data [15] has raised privacy concerns and potential regulatory implications. In response, the field of machine unlearning has emerged, aiming to develop methods to remove the influence of specific data points from trained models efficiently, without the need for complete retraining.

This section explores the landscape of machine unlearning techniques, categorizing them into certified and heuristic approaches. We discuss their privacy implications and challenges and provide an outlook for this emerging field with recommendations for organizations considering unlearning as a privacy-enhancing technology.

5.3.5.1 Unlearning Approaches

Machine unlearning approaches can be broadly categorized into certified and heuristic methods.

Certified Approaches Certified unlearning approaches provide guarantees about the extent to which data has been "forgotten." Most operate by performing an approximate update to the model (such as a Newton or gradient step) followed by the addition of noise [43, 102]. This can produce a model statistically indistinguishable from one retrained without the data to forget. The notion of statistical indistinguishability can be formalized in various ways. One common approach due to [43] is inspired by (ϵ, δ)-differential privacy. It provides more effective unlearning guarantees as ϵ and δ approach zero.

Definition 5.2 Let A be a training algorithm that produces a model $\theta = A(D)$ given training data D. An unlearning algorithm U is an (ϵ, δ)-unlearner for A if, for any subset $Z \subset D$ to be forgotten, the distributions of $A(D \setminus Z)$ and $U(A(D), D, Z)$ are (ϵ, δ)-indistinguishable.

While offering formal guarantees, certified methods have limitations. Many rely on assumptions such as strong convexity, which are not satisfied by popular models like neural networks [43, 102], although researchers are trying to lessen these assumptions [94, 157]. Moreover, they often struggle with multiple successive erasure requests and can negatively impact model performance due to noise addition.

Notably, there is a strong connection between certified unlearning and differential privacy, with the latter providing strong unlearning guarantees even for adaptive deletion requests that depend on previously published models [44].

Heuristic Approaches Heuristic approaches approximate the effect of retraining without erased data, often using techniques such as influence functions [74] or fine-tuning on the retained data. While more practical for complex models, they lack formal guarantees. Popular heuristic methods include Amnesiac [42], which selectively reverses parameter updates from batches containing data to be erased; SISA [10], which trains multiple models on disjoint data subsets so that only some of the models need to be retrained; and SCRUB [75], which uses a teacher-student formulation to unlearn.

Researchers typically evaluate these methods empirically, using metrics such as the similarity to a fully retrained model or resistance to membership inference attacks on erased data. However, the lack of formal guarantees means that these methods may not fully remove all traces of erased data from the model.

5.3.5.2 Privacy Considerations

While unlearning methods aim to enhance privacy by removing the influence of specific data points, they also introduce new privacy considerations and potential vulnerabilities.

Longitudinal Privacy Risks The release of multiple versions of unlearned models over time introduces significant privacy challenges. [22] demonstrated that differencing attacks can potentially reconstruct erased data by comparing successive model versions. This vulnerability is particularly concerning when successive unlearned models are released as data removal requests are processed. To mitigate these risks, organizations may need to limit the frequency of model releases or employ techniques that add noise to model updates to obscure the effects of individual unlearning operations.

Interaction with other PETs Unlearning methods do not exist in isolation but rather complement and interact with other privacy-enhancing technologies (PETs). For instance, combining unlearning with differential privacy (DP) can provide stronger privacy guarantees [44, 49]. DP can be applied to the unlearning process itself, ensuring that the act of removing data doesn't leak information about the removed data. Unlearning can also be integrated into federated learning systems for local data removal without requiring access to the central model [81]. However, these combinations may introduce new challenges, such as increased computational complexity or potential degradation in model utility, requiring careful balancing of privacy and performance objectives.

Adversarial Unlearning Requests The ability to request data removal opens up new avenues for attacks. Malicious actors could potentially exploit unlearning mechanisms to degrade model performance by strategically requesting the removal of critical training examples [51] or use carefully crafted sequences of unlearning requests to extract information about the training data or the model. Defending against such attacks requires robust verification mechanisms to ensure the legitimacy of unlearning requests, as well as techniques to maintain model integrity. Organizations must consider not only the privacy implications for data subjects but also the security of the machine learning system as a whole when implementing unlearning.

5.3.5.3 Summary and Enterprise Outlook

While machine unlearning shows promise in addressing privacy concerns and potential future regulatory requirements, it remains primarily a research topic rather than a technology ready for deployment. As we've demonstrated, current approaches face significant challenges, including limited scalability, potential impacts on model performance, and vulnerability to longitudinal privacy risks.

Although unlearning is not yet ready for enterprise deployment, forward-thinking organizations could:

- Monitor developments in unlearning research, particularly advancements in efficiency, scalability, and privacy guarantees
- Assess the potential impact of unlearning on existing machine learning pipelines and data management practices
- Engage with legal and compliance teams to evaluate how unlearning might fit into broader data protection strategies

As the field matures, unlearning may become an essential tool in the privacy-preserving machine learning toolkit. Organizations that proactively engage with unlearning research will be well positioned to leverage its potential benefits.

5.4 Privacy in the Era of Generative AI

The rise of large foundation models and generative AI has fundamentally altered the privacy landscape. While many traditional privacy risks and protection mechanisms still apply, the unique characteristics of these models introduce novel challenges and exacerbate existing ones. This section explores how the privacy landscape has shifted in the era of generative AI, focusing on new and amplified risks, the limitations of existing privacy-enhancing technologies (PETs), and emerging approaches to privacy protection.

5.4.1 Privacy Risks in the Generative AI Era

Generative AI models, particularly large language models (LLMs), have not only amplified existing privacy risks but also introduced new concerns. One of the most significant issues is the unprecedented capacity for memorization exhibited by these models. As they scale up, LLMs have been shown to memorize and potentially leak more information from their training data, amplifying the risk of data extraction attacks [16]. Interestingly, recent research has found that LLMs exhibit higher memorization of data presented earlier and later in training, suggesting that placing sensitive data in the middle of training might be beneficial for privacy protection [76].

The outputs of generative models present another challenge, as they are typically much more information dense than those of traditional classification and regression models. This increased information density results in a higher risk of information leakage, not just from training data but also from sensitive information in input prompts [143]. The risk is further compounded by the advent of multi-modal models like CLIP [113], which introduce new privacy vulnerabilities from the interaction between different data modalities. These models are susceptible to membership inference attacks that exploit the relationship between text and image data, potentially revealing more information than single-modality models [73].

LLMs also face unique security challenges that have privacy implications. They are vulnerable to "jailbreaking" attacks, where carefully crafted prompts cause the model to bypass its safety constraints. Such attacks have been shown to successfully extract private information from commercial models such as ChatGPT [78]. Moreover, the reasoning capabilities of LLMs enable them to perform linkage attacks given access to external data provided in prompts or via retrieval-augmented generation [106]. This is particularly concerning as it allows malicious actors to automate and scale attacks that previously may have been limited by human labor constraints.

Lastly, the massive datasets required to train foundation models often involve complex, opaque data supply chains. This opacity introduces new privacy risks related to unauthorized data use, lack of consent, and potential violations of data protection regulations. [158] argue that consent management is needed throughout the data lifecycle, and training information and metadata must be preserved to enable side-effect mitigation, such as through unlearning techniques.

5.4.2 Limitations of Existing PETs in the Generative AI Context

Traditional privacy-enhancing technologies (PETs) face new challenges when applied to large foundation models and generative AI.

Differential privacy (DP), a cornerstone of privacy protection, encounters significant hurdles in this new context. While DP remains a powerful tool, its application to generative models can result in substantial utility loss [151]. The scale of data required for pre-training makes DP seem infeasible at that stage, although it has shown promise in fine-tuning scenarios [150]. In the domain of computer vision, applying DP to the training of diffusion models typically leads to divergence for small-scale datasets, while its feasibility for larger datasets remains an open question [23].

Federated learning (FL), another popular PET, also faces challenges in the context of generative AI. While FL can help protect raw data by keeping it decentralized, the aggregated updates in FL settings can still leak significant amounts of private information, particularly in the context of language models [38]. This leakage undermines the privacy guarantees that FL aims to provide, necessitating additional protective measures.

Secure computation techniques, such as secure multiparty computation (SMPC) and trusted execution environments (TEEs), encounter scalability issues when applied to foundation models. The immense computational requirements of these models make traditional SMPC and CPU-based TEEs impractical. However, recent advancements in hardware, such as Nvidia's Hopper and Blackwell GPUs with built-in TEEs, offer promising solutions. [163] found that enabling TEEs on Nvidia Hopper GPUs for large-scale LLM inference incurs an overhead of less than 7%, while Nvidia claims near-identical performance for their Blackwell architecture.

5.4.3 Emerging Approaches and Future Directions

To address the new and amplified risks posed by generative AI, researchers are exploring novel approaches to privacy protection. One such approach involves using LLMs themselves to remove sensitive information from training data, a process known as scrubbing. However, current commercial models like GPT-4 have shown limitations in this task, failing to detect all pieces of personal information in benchmark datasets [11, 89]. This suggests that while AI-powered scrubbing holds promise, it requires further refinement to match or exceed human performance in identifying and protecting sensitive information.

Alignment and self-censoring techniques represent another avenue for privacy protection in generative AI. LLMs can be trained to reject requests that could violate privacy, such as performing linkage attacks [106]. In the image domain, researchers have proposed methods to steer image generation in diffusion models away from memorized data [23]. However, the effectiveness of these alignment efforts is challenged by automated red-teaming techniques that can generate adversarial prompts to circumvent such protections [103].

Privacy-preserving fine-tuning has emerged as a promising direction, particularly given the challenges of applying differential privacy to pre-training. Several studies have demonstrated the feasibility of fine-tuning LLMs using DP analogues of standard training algorithms, achieving reasonable privacy-utility trade-offs [77, 142, 150]. While these approaches protect against privacy leakage in the fine-tuned model parameters, they may still expose training data to human annotators. To address this issue, [152] propose replacing user prompts with synthetic prompts generated by a privately fine-tuned model, further enhancing privacy protection throughout the training process.

In-context learning presents an alternative paradigm that allows off-the-shelf LLMs to be used without fine-tuning by providing training examples in the prompt. However, this approach introduces its own privacy challenges, as sensitive information in the training examples could be leaked in the LLM's response, particularly in adversarial settings. To mitigate this risk, researchers have applied differential privacy through randomized aggregation of LLM responses using disjoint exemplar sets [31, 143].

In conclusion, while generative AI presents significant privacy challenges, it also offers opportunities for innovative solutions. As the field evolves, developing privacy-preserving techniques that can keep pace with the rapid advancements in model capabilities and applications will be crucial. The interplay between new risks and emerging protective measures underscores the dynamic nature of privacy in the AI era, emphasizing the need for continued research and adaptation of privacy-enhancing technologies.

5.5 Conclusion and Future Outlook

This chapter has explored the complex landscape of privacy in enterprise AI, examining key privacy risks, mitigation strategies, and the evolving challenges posed by generative AI. As we conclude, it is crucial to reflect on the main insights and consider the path forward for organizations navigating this dynamic field.

5.5.1 Key Takeaways

Our exploration of privacy risks and threat models underscores the importance of adopting a threat-specific approach to privacy. By viewing privacy through the lens of specific threats, organizations can develop targeted and effective mitigation strategies, rather than implementing generic solutions that may leave critical vulnerabilities unaddressed. This approach is particularly crucial given the fast-paced nature of AI development, where new privacy risks can emerge rapidly.

The diverse toolkit of privacy-enhancing technologies (PETs) available for AI applications offers promising solutions but also presents complex trade-offs. Organizations must carefully balance privacy protections with model utility, computational demands, and system complexity. The intricacies of these trade-offs highlight the need for specialized expertise in privacy engineering, rather than treating privacy as an afterthought in AI development.

Our examination of privacy in the era of generative AI demonstrates how recent advancements have significantly altered the privacy landscape. These powerful models have not only exacerbated existing privacy risks but also introduced novel challenges. While research in this area is progressing rapidly, there remains a substantial gap between current capabilities and robust privacy-preserving generative

AI systems. This gap underscores the need for ongoing vigilance and adaptation in privacy strategies.

The dynamic nature of AI privacy means that what constitutes state-of-the-art today may be outdated within months. This rapid change presents both opportunities and challenges for enterprises. While new techniques and tools are constantly emerging to enhance privacy protections, the pace of change makes it challenging to establish stable, long-term privacy strategies.

Perhaps the most critical takeaway is the need for organizations to remain adaptable and committed to continuous learning. Enterprises must regularly reassess their privacy measures, staying informed about emerging threats, novel protection mechanisms, and evolving best practices. This ongoing process of learning and adaptation is essential for navigating the complex and ever-changing intersection of AI and privacy.

5.5.2 Future Outlook for Privacy and AI in the Enterprise

Looking ahead, several key areas will likely shape the future of privacy in enterprise AI. The balance between AI innovation and privacy will become increasingly critical as AI capabilities expand. Organizations will face growing pressure to innovate their AI capabilities while maintaining robust privacy protections, requiring careful consideration of privacy implications at every stage of AI development and deployment.

Data governance for AI systems will need to evolve to match the growing complexity of AI models, particularly in the realm of generative AI. Organizations will need to develop comprehensive strategies for managing data throughout its lifecycle, from collection and processing to model training and output generation.

Regulatory compliance will present ongoing challenges as privacy regulations evolve and potentially diverge across different jurisdictions. Enterprises may need to adapt their AI systems to comply with a patchwork of requirements, potentially leading to the development of more flexible, privacy-preserving AI architectures that can be easily adjusted to meet varying regulatory standards.

Emerging technologies will continue to introduce new privacy challenges, likely outpacing current privacy protections. Enterprises must remain proactive in identifying and mitigating these emerging risks to stay ahead of potential vulnerabilities.

5.5.3 The Role of Enterprises and Call to Action

Enterprises play a crucial role in shaping the future of AI privacy. By prioritizing privacy in their AI initiatives, organizations can not only protect stakeholders but also contribute to the development of more responsible AI practices industry-wide.

We urge readers to:

- Invest in privacy expertise and integrate privacy considerations into all stages of AI development and deployment
- Stay informed about the latest developments in AI privacy research and emerging technologies
- Contribute to the broader conversation on AI privacy by sharing experiences and best practices with the community
- Advocate for privacy-preserving AI within their organizations and industries, aligned with articulated, specific, threat models

In conclusion, while the challenges of maintaining privacy in AI systems are significant, they are not insurmountable. By approaching these challenges with a combination of technical rigor, ethical consideration, and grounding in legal regulation and governance, enterprises can harness the power of AI while respecting and protecting individual privacy. As the field continues to evolve, maintaining this balance will be crucial for the responsible and sustainable development of AI technologies.

Acknowledgments N. Marchant, B. I. P. Rubinstein, and Y. Zhao acknowledge support from the Australian Research Council Discovery Project DP220102269.

References

1. Abadi, M., Chu, A., Goodfellow, I., McMahan, H.B., Mironov, I., Talwar, K., Zhang, L.: Deep learning with differential privacy. In: Proceedings of the 2016 ACM SIGSAC Conference on Computer and Communications Security, CCS '16, pp. 308–318 (2016)
2. Balunovic, M., Dimitrov, D., Jovanović, N., Vechev, M.: LAMP: Extracting text from gradients with language model priors. In: Advances in Neural Information Processing Systems, vol. 35, pp. 7641–7654 (2022)
3. Bao, X., Su, C., Xiong, Y., Huang, W., Hu, Y.: FLChain: a blockchain for auditable federated learning with trust and incentive. In: 2019 5th International Conference on Big Data Computing and Communications (BIGCOM), pp. 151–159 (2019)
4. Bawack, R.E., Wamba, S.F., Carillo, K.D.A., Akter, S.: Artificial intelligence in E-commerce: a bibliometric study and literature review. Electr. Markets **32**(1), 297–338 (2022)
5. Benaissa, A., Retiat, B., Cebere, B., Belfedhal, A.E.: TenSEAL: a library for encrypted tensor operations using homomorphic encryption. arXiv:2104.03152 [cs.CR] (2021)
6. Bergerat, L., Boudi, A., Bourgerie, Q., Chillotti, I., Ligier, D., Orfila, J.B., Tap, S.: Parameter optimization and larger precision for (T)FHE. J. Cryptology **36**(3), 28 (2023)
7. Bertran, M.A., Tang, S., Kearns, M., Morgenstern, J.H., Roth, A., Wu, S.: Reconstruction attacks on machine unlearning: Simple models are vulnerable. In: The Thirty-eighth Annual Conference on Neural Information Processing Systems (2024)
8. Boenisch, F., Dziedzic, A., Schuster, R., Shamsabadi, A.S., Shumailov, I., Papernot, N.: When the curious abandon honesty: federated learning is not private. In: 2023 IEEE 8th European Symposium on Security and Privacy (EuroS&P), pp. 175–199 (2023)
9. Bonawitz, K., Ivanov, V., Kreuter, B., Marcedone, A., McMahan, H.B., Patel, S., Ramage, D., Segal, A., Seth, K.: Practical secure aggregation for privacy-preserving machine learning. In: Proceedings of the 2017 ACM SIGSAC Conference on Computer and Communications Security, CCS '17, pp. 1175–1191 (2017)

10. Bourtoule, L., Chandrasekaran, V., Choquette-Choo, C.A., Jia, H., Travers, A., Zhang, B., Lie, D., Papernot, N. Machine unlearning. In: 2021 IEEE Symposium on Security and Privacy (SP), pp. 141–159 (2021)
11. Bubeck, S., Chandrasekaran, V., Eldan, R., Gehrke, J., Horvitz, E., Kamar, E., Lee, P., Lee, Y.T., Li, Y., Lundberg, S., Nori, H., Palangi, H., Ribeiro, M.T., Zhang, Y.: Sparks of artificial general intelligence: early experiments with GPT-4. arXiv:2303.12712 [cs.CL] (2023)
12. Bukaty, P.: The California Consumer Privacy Act (CCPA): An Implementation Guide. IT Governance Publishing, Cambridgeshire (2019)
13. Bulck, J.V., Minkin, M., Weisse, O., Genkin, D., Kasikci, B., Piessens, F., Silberstein, M., Wenisch, T.F., Yarom, Y., Strackx, R.: Foreshadow: Extracting the keys to the intel SGX kingdom with transient Out-of-Order execution. In: 27th USENIX Security Symposium (USENIX Security 18), pp. 991–1008 (2018)
14. Bun, M., Steinke, T.: Concentrated differential privacy: simplifications, extensions, and lower bounds. In: Proceedings, Part I, of the 14th International Conference on Theory of Cryptography, vol. 9985, pp. 635–658. Springer, Berlin (2016)
15. Carlini, N., Liu, C., Erlingsson, Ú., Kos, J., Song, D.: The Secret Sharer: evaluating and testing unintended memorization in neural networks. In: 28th USENIX Security Symposium (USENIX Security 19), pp. 267–284 (2019)
16. Carlini, N., Tramèr, F., Wallace, E., Jagielski, M., Herbert-Voss, A., Lee, K., Roberts, A., Brown, T., Song, D., Erlingsson, Ú., Oprea, A., Raffel, C.: Extracting training data from large language models. In: 30th USENIX Security Symposium (USENIX Security 21), pp. 2633–2650 (2021)
17. Carlini, N., Chien, S., Nasr, M., Song, S., Terzis, A., Tramèr, F.: Membership inference attacks from first principles. In: 2022 IEEE Symposium on Security and Privacy (SP), pp. 1897–1914 (2022)
18. Carlini, N., Hayes, J., Nasr, M., Jagielski, M., Sehwag, V., Tramèr, F., Balle, B., Ippolito, D., Wallace, E.: Extracting training data from diffusion models. In: 32nd USENIX Security Symposium (USENIX Security 23), pp. 5253–5270 (2023)
19. Carlini, N., Ippolito, D., Jagielski, M., Lee, K., Tramer, F., Zhang, C.: Quantifying memorization across neural language models. In: The Eleventh International Conference on Learning Representations (2023)
20. Carlini, N., Paleka, D., Dvijotham, K.D., Steinke, T., Hayase, J., Cooper, A.F., Lee, K., Jagielski, M., Nasr, M., Conmy, A., Wallace, E., Rolnick, D., Tramèr, F.: Stealing part of a production language model. In: Proceedings of the 41st International Conference on Machine Learning, vol. 235, pp. 5680–5705 (2024)
21. Chandrasekaran, V., Chaudhuri, K., Giacomelli, I., Jha, S., Yan, S.: Exploring connections between active learning and model extraction. In: 29th USENIX Security Symposium (USENIX Security 20), pp. 1309–1326 (2020)
22. Chen, M., Zhang, Z., Wang, T., Backes, M., Humbert, M., Zhang, Y.: When machine unlearning jeopardizes privacy. In: Proceedings of the 2021 ACM SIGSAC Conference on Computer and Communications Security, CCS '21, pp. 896–911 (2021)
23. Chen, C., Liu, D., Xu, C.: Towards memorization-free diffusion models. In: Proceedings of the IEEE/CVF Conference on Computer Vision and Pattern Recognition (CVPR), pp. 8425–8434 (2024)
24. Cheon, J.H., Kim, A., Kim, M., Song, Y.: Homomorphic encryption for arithmetic of approximate numbers. In: Advances in Cryptology – ASIACRYPT 2017, pp. 409–437. Springer International Publishing, New York City (2017)
25. Choquette-Choo, C.A., Tramer, F., Carlini, N., Papernot, N.: Label-only membership inference attacks. In: Proceedings of the 38th International Conference on Machine Learning, vol. 139, pp. 1964–1974 (2021)
26. Chu, H.M., Geiping, J., Fowl, L.H., Goldblum, M., Goldstein, T.: Panning for gold in federated learning: targeted text extraction under arbitrarily large-scale aggregation. In: The Eleventh International Conference on Learning Representations (2023)

27. Confidential Computing Consortium: Confidential computing: hardware-based trusted execution for applications and data. Technical report. Confidential Computing Consortium (2023). https://confidentialcomputing.io/wp-content/uploads/sites/10/2023/03/CCC_outreach_whitepaper_updated_November_2022.pdf, Accessed 14 May 2025
28. Dathathri, R., Kostova, B., Saarikivi, O., Dai, W., Laine, K., Musuvathi, M.: Eva: an encrypted vector arithmetic language and compiler for efficient homomorphic computation. In: Proceedings of the 41st ACM SIGPLAN Conference on Programming Language Design and Implementation, PLDI 2020, pp. 546–561 (2020)
29. Dimitrov, D.I., Baader, M., Müller, M.N., Vechev, M.: Spear: exact gradient inversion of batches in federated learning. In: Advances in Neural Information Processing Systems, vol. 37, pp. 106768–106799 (2024)
30. Dong, J., Roth, A., Su, W.J.: Gaussian differential privacy. J. R. Stat. Soc. Ser. B Stat Methodol. **84**(1), 3–37 (2022)
31. Duan, H., Dziedzic, A., Papernot, N., Boenisch, F.: Flocks of stochastic parrots: Differentially private prompt learning for large language models. In: Advances in Neural Information Processing Systems, vol. 36, pp. 76852–76871 (2023)
32. Duchi, J.C., Jordan, M.I., Wainwright, M.J.: Local privacy and statistical minimax rates. In: 2013 IEEE 54th Annual Symposium on Foundations of Computer Science, pp. 429–438 (2013)
33. Dutta, S.B., Naghibijouybari, H., Gupta, A., Abu-Ghazaleh, N., Marquez, A., Barker, K.: Spy in the GPU-box: covert and side channel attacks on multi-GPU systems. In: Proceedings of the 50th Annual International Symposium on Computer Architecture, ISCA '23 (2023)
34. Dwork, C., Roth, A.: The algorithmic foundations of differential privacy. Found. Trends® Theor. Comput. Sci. **9**(3–4), 211–407 (2014). https://doi.org/10.1561/0400000042
35. Dwork, C., Rothblum, G.N., Vadhan, S.: Boosting and differential privacy. In: 2010 IEEE 51st Annual Symposium on Foundations of Computer Science, pp. 51–60 (2010)
36. Feng, R., Hooda, A., Mangaokar, N., Fawaz, K., Jha, S., Prakash, A.: Stateful defenses for machine learning models are not yet secure against black-box attacks. In: Proceedings of the 2023 ACM SIGSAC Conference on Computer and Communications Security, CCS '23, pp. 786–800 (2023)
37. Fowl, L.H., Geiping, J., Czaja, W., Goldblum, M., Goldstein, T.: Robbing the Fed: directly obtaining private data in federated learning with modified models. In: International Conference on Learning Representations (2022)
38. Fowl, L.H., Geiping, J., Reich, S., Wen, Y., Czaja, W., Goldblum, M., Goldstein, T.: Decepticons: corrupted transformers breach privacy in federated learning for language models. In: The Eleventh International Conference on Learning Representations (2023)
39. Gao, J., Garg, S., Mahmoody, M., Vasudevan, P.N.: Deletion inference, reconstruction, and compliance in machine (un)learning. In: Proceedings on Privacy Enhancing Technologies Symposium (PoPETs), vol. 2022, pp. 415–436 (2022)
40. Geiping, J., Bauermeister, H., Dröge, H., Moeller, M.: Inverting gradients – how easy is it to break privacy in federated learning? In: Advances in Neural Information Processing Systems, vol. 33, pp. 16937–16947 (2020)
41. Geyer, R.C., Klein, T., Nabi, M.: Differentially private federated learning: a client level perspective (2018). arXiv:1712.07557 [cs.CR]
42. Graves, L., Nagisetty, V., Ganesh, V.: Amnesiac machine learning. Proc. AAAI Conf. Artif. Intell. **35**(13), 11516–11524 (2021)
43. Guo, C., Goldstein, T., Hannun, A., Van Der Maaten, L.: Certified data removal from machine learning models. In: Proceedings of the 37th International Conference on Machine Learning, vol. 119, pp. 3832–3842 (2020)
44. Gupta, V., Jung, C., Neel, S., Roth, A., Sharifi-Malvajerdi, S., Waites, C.: Adaptive machine unlearning. In: Advances in Neural Information Processing Systems, vol. 34, pp. 16319–16330 (2021)
45. Gupta, K., Jawalkar, N., Mukherjee, A., Chandran, N., Gupta, D., Panwar, A., Sharma, R.: SIGMA: secure GPT inference with function secret sharing. Proc. Privacy Enhanc. Technol. **2024**(4), 61–79 (2024)

46. Halevi, S., Shoup, V.: Design and implementation of HElib: a homomorphic encryption library. Cryptology ePrint Archive, Paper 2020/1481 (2020)
47. Hu, H., Salcic, Z., Sun, L., Dobbie, G., Yu, P.S., Zhang, X.: Membership inference attacks on machine learning: a survey. ACM Comput. Surv. **54**(11s), 1–35 (2022)
48. Hu, H., Wang, S., Dong, T., Xue, M.: Learn what you want to unlearn: Unlearning inversion attacks against machine unlearning. In: 2024 IEEE Symposium on Security and Privacy (SP), pp. 3257–3275. IEEE Computer Society, Washington (2024)
49. Huang, Y., Canonne, C.L.: Tight bounds for machine unlearning via differential privacy. arXiv:2309.00886 [cs.LG] (2023)
50. Huang, Z., jie Lu, W., Hong, C., Ding, J.: Cheetah: lean and fast secure Two-Party deep neural network inference. In: 31st USENIX Security Symposium (USENIX Security 22), pp. 809–826 (2022)
51. Huang, Y., Liu, D., Chua, L., Ghazi, B., Kamath, P., Kumar, R., Manurangsi, P., Nasr, M., Sinha, A., Zhang, C.: Unlearn and burn: adversarial machine unlearning requests destroy model accuracy. In: The Thirteenth International Conference on Learning Representations (2025)
52. Hui, T., Farokhi, F., Ohrimenko, O.: Information leakage from data updates in machine learning models. In: Proceedings of the 16th ACM Workshop on Artificial Intelligence and Security, AISec '23, pp. 35–41 (2023)
53. IT Governance Privacy Team: EU General Data Protection Regulation (GDPR) – An Implementation and Compliance Guide, 4th edn. IT Governance Publishing, Cambridgeshire (2020)
54. Jagielski, M., Carlini, N., Berthelot, D., Kurakin, A., Papernot, N.: High accuracy and high fidelity extraction of neural networks. In: 29th USENIX Security Symposium (USENIX Security 20), pp. 1345–1362 (2020)
55. Jagielski, M., Ullman, J., Oprea, A.: Auditing differentially private machine learning: how private is private SGD? In: Advances in Neural Information Processing Systems, vol. 33, pp. 22205–22216 (2020)
56. Jagielski, M., Wu, S., Oprea, A., Ullman, J., Geambasu, R.: How to combine membership-inference attacks on multiple updated machine learning models. In: Proceedings on Privacy Enhancing Technologies Symposium (PoPETs), vol. 2023, pp. 211–232 (2023)
57. Janssen, M., Brous, P., Estevez, E., Barbosa, L.S., Janowski, T.: Data governance: organizing data for trustworthy artificial intelligence. Gov. Inf. Q. **37**(3), 101493 (2020)
58. Jayashankar, S., Chen, E., Tang, T., Zheng, W., Skarlatos, D.: Cinnamon: a framework for scale-out encrypted AI. In: Proceedings of the 30th ACM International Conference on Architectural Support for Programming Languages and Operating Systems, vol. 1, ASPLOS '25, pp. 133–150 (2025)
59. Jeon, J., Kim, J., Lee, K., Oh, S., Ok, J.: Gradient inversion with generative image prior. In: Advances in Neural Information Processing Systems, vol. 34, pp. 29898–29908 (2021)
60. Jia, J., Salem, A., Backes, M., Zhang, Y., Gong, N.Z.: MemGuard: defending against black-box membership inference attacks via adversarial examples. In: Proceedings of the 2019 ACM SIGSAC Conference on Computer and Communications Security, CCS '19, pp. 259–274 (2019)
61. Jia, H., Choquette-Choo, C.A., Chandrasekaran, V., Papernot, N.: Entangled watermarks as a defense against model extraction. In: 30th USENIX Security Symposium (USENIX Security 21), pp. 1937–1954 (2021)
62. Jia, H., Yaghini, M., Choquette-Choo, C.A., Dullerud, N., Thudi, A., Chandrasekaran, V., Papernot, N.: Proof-of-learning: Definitions and practice. In: 2021 IEEE Symposium on Security and Privacy (SP), pp. 1039–1056 (2021)
63. Jin, J., McMurtry, E., Rubinstein, B.I.P., Ohrimenko, O.: Are we there yet? Timing and floating-point attacks on differential privacy systems. In: 2022 IEEE Symposium on Security and Privacy (SP), pp. 473–488 (2022)
64. Juuti, M., Szyller, S., Marchal, S., Asokan, N.: PRADA: protecting against DNN model stealing attacks. In: 2019 IEEE European Symposium on Security and Privacy (EuroS&P), pp. 512–527 (2019)

65. Juvekar, C., Vaikuntanathan, V, Chandrakasan, A.: GAZELLE: a low latency framework for secure neural network inference. In: 27th USENIX Security Symposium (USENIX Security 18), pp. 1651–1669 (2018)
66. Kairouz, P., Mcmahan, B., Song, S., Thakkar, O., Thakurta, A., Xu, Z.: Practical and private (deep) learning without sampling or shuffling. In: Proceedings of the 38th International Conference on Machine Learning, PMLR, Proceedings of Machine Learning Research, vol. 139, pp. 5213–5225 (2021)
67. Kandpal, N., Wallace, E., Raffel, C.: Deduplicating training data mitigates privacy risks in language models. In: Proceedings of the 39th International Conference on Machine Learning, vol. 162, pp. 10697–10707 (2022)
68. Kaplan, J., McCandlish, S., Henighan, T., Brown, T.B., Chess, B., Child, R., Gray, S., Radford, A., Wu, J., Amodei, D.: Scaling laws for neural language models. arXiv:2001.08361 [cs.LG] (2020)
69. Kariyappa, S., Guo, C., Maeng, K., Xiong, W., Suh, G.E., Qureshi, M.K., Lee, H.H.S.: Cocktail party attack: breaking aggregation-based privacy in federated learning using independent component analysis. In: Proceedings of the 40th International Conference on Machine Learning, vol. 202, pp. 15884–15899 (2023)
70. Kei, A.Y.L., Chow, S.S.M.: Shaft: Secure, handy, accurate and fast transformer inference. In: Proceedings 2025 Network and Distributed System Security Symposium, Internet Society, NDSS 2025 (2025)
71. Kim, M., Günlü, O., Schaefer, R.F.: Federated learning with local differential privacy: trade-offs between privacy, utility, and communication. In: ICASSP 2021 - 2021 IEEE International Conference on Acoustics, Speech and Signal Processing (ICASSP), pp. 2650–2654 (2021)
72. Knott, B., Venkataraman, S., Hannun, A., Sengupta, S., Ibrahim, M., van der Maaten, L.: CrypTen: secure multi-party computation meets machine learning. In: Advances in Neural Information Processing Systems, vol. 34, pp. 4961–4973 (2021)
73. Ko, M., Jin, M., Wang, C., Jia, R.: Practical membership inference attacks against large-scale multi-modal models: a pilot study. In: Proceedings of the IEEE/CVF International Conference on Computer Vision (ICCV), pp. 4871–4881 (2023)
74. Koh, P.W., Liang, P.: Understanding black-box predictions via influence functions. In: Proceedings of the 34th International Conference on Machine Learning, vol. 70, pp. 1885–1894 (2017)
75. Kurmanji, M., Triantafillou, P., Hayes, J., Triantafillou, E.: Towards unbounded machine unlearning. In: Advances in Neural Information Processing Systems, vol. 36, pp. 1957–1987 (2023)
76. Leybzon, D.D., Kervadec, C.: Learning, forgetting, remembering: insights from tracking LLM memorization during training. In: Proceedings of the 7th BlackboxNLP Workshop: Analyzing and Interpreting Neural Networks for NLP, pp. 43–57. Association for Computational Linguistics, Stroudsburg (2024)
77. Li, X., Tramer, F., Liang, P., Hashimoto, T.: Large language models can be strong differentially private learners. In: International Conference on Learning Representations (2022)
78. Li, H., Guo, D., Fan, W., Xu, M., Huang, J., Meng, F., Song, Y.: Multi-step jailbreaking privacy attacks on ChatGPT. In: Findings of the Association for Computational Linguistics: EMNLP 2023, pp. 4138–4153. Association for Computational Linguistics, Stroudsburg (2023)
79. Li, J., Li, N., Ribeiro, B.: MIST: defending against membership inference attacks through Membership-Invariant Subspace Training. In: 33rd USENIX Security Symposium (USENIX Security 24), pp. 2387–2404 (2024)
80. Liu, H., Wu, Y., Yu, Z., Zhang, N.: Please tell me more: Privacy impact of explainability through the lens of membership inference attack. In: 2024 IEEE Symposium on Security and Privacy (SP), pp. 4791–4809 (2024)
81. Liu, Z., Jiang, Y., Shen, J., Peng, M., Lam, K.Y., Yuan, X., Liu, X.: A survey on federated unlearning: challenges, methods, and future directions. ACM Comput. Surv. **57**(1), 1–38 (2024)

82. Llama team: The Llama 3 herd of models. arXiv:2407.21783 [cs.AI] (2024)
83. Lorè, F., Basile, P., Appice, A., de Gemmis, M., Malerba, D., Semeraro, G.: An AI framework to support decisions on GDPR compliance. J. Intell. Inf. Syst. **61**(2), 541–568 (2023)
84. Lyu, L., Yu, H., Zhao, J., Yang, Q.: Threats to Federated Learning, pp 3–16. Springer International Publishing, Berlin (2020)
85. Mahanti, R.: Data Governance and Data Management: Contextualizing Data Governance Drivers, Technologies, and Tools. Springer, Singapore (2021)
86. Maini, P., Yaghini, M., Papernot, N.: Dataset inference: Ownership resolution in machine learning. In: International Conference on Learning Representations (2021)
87. McKeen, F., Alexandrovich, I., Berenzon, A., Rozas, C.V., Shafi, H., Shanbhogue, V., Savagaonkar, U.R.: Innovative instructions and software model for isolated execution. In: Proceedings of the 2nd International Workshop on Hardware and Architectural Support for Security and Privacy, HASP '13 (2013)
88. McMahan, B., Moore, E., Ramage, D., Hampson, S., Arcas, B.A.Y. Communication-efficient learning of deep networks from decentralized data. In: Proceedings of the 20th International Conference on Artificial Intelligence and Statistics, vol. 54, pp. 1273–1282 (2017)
89. Mireshghallah, N., Kim, H., Zhou, X., Tsvetkov, Y., Sap, M., Shokri, R., Choi, Y.: Can LLMs keep a secret? Testing privacy implications of language models via contextual integrity theory. In: The Twelfth International Conference on Learning Representations (2024)
90. Mo, F., Haddadi, H., Katevas, K., Marin, E., Perino, D., Kourtellis, N.: PPFL: privacy-preserving federated learning with trusted execution environments. In: Proceedings of the 19th Annual International Conference on Mobile Systems, Applications, and Services, MobiSys '21, pp. 94–108 (2021)
91. Mo, J., Gopinath, J., Reagen, B.: HAAC: a hardware-software co-design to accelerate garbled circuits. In: Proceedings of the 50th Annual International Symposium on Computer Architecture, ISCA 2023, Orlando, FL, June 17–21, 2023, pp. 10:1–10:13. ACM, New York (2023)
92. Mohassel, P., Zhang, Y.: SecureML: a system for scalable privacy-preserving machine learning. In: 2017 IEEE Symposium on Security and Privacy (SP), pp. 19–38 (2017)
93. More, Y., Ganesh, P., Farnadi, G.: Towards more realistic extraction attacks: an adversarial perspective. arXiv:2407.02596 [cs.CR] (2024)
94. Mu, S., Klabjan, D.: Rewind-to-Delete: certified machine unlearning for nonconvex functions. arXiv:2409.09778 [cs.LG] (2024)
95. Nanayakkara, P., Bater, J., He, X., Hullman, J., Rogers, J.: Visualizing privacy-utility trade-offs in differentially private data releases. Proc. Privacy Enhancing Technol. **2022**(2), 601–618 (2022)
96. Narayanan, A., Shi, E., Rubinstein, B.I.P.: Link prediction by de-anonymization: how we won the Kaggle Social Network Challenge. In: The 2011 International Joint Conference on Neural Networks, pp. 1825–1834 (2011)
97. Nasr, M., Shokri, R., Houmansadr, A.: Machine learning with membership privacy using adversarial regularization. In: Proceedings of the 2018 ACM SIGSAC Conference on Computer and Communications Security, CCS '18, pp. 634–646 (2018)
98. Nasr, M., Shokri, R., Houmansadr, A.: Comprehensive privacy analysis of deep learning: passive and active white-box inference attacks against centralized and federated learning. In: 2019 IEEE Symposium on Security and Privacy (SP), pp. 739–753 (2019)
99. Nasr, M., Songi, S., Thakurta, A., Papernot, N., Carlin, N.: Adversary instantiation: lower bounds for differentially private machine learning. In: 2021 IEEE Symposium on Security and Privacy (SP), pp. 866–882 (2021)
100. Nasr, M., Rando, J., Carlini, N., Hayase, J., Jagielski, M., Cooper, A.F., Ippolito, D., Choquette-Choo, C.A., Tramèr, F., Lee, K.: Scalable extraction of training data from aligned, production language models. In: The Thirteenth International Conference on Learning Representations (2025)
101. National Institute of Standards and Technology: NIST privacy framework: a tool for improving privacy through enterprise risk management, Version 1.0 (2020)

102. Neel, S., Roth, A., Sharifi-Malvajerdi, S.: Descent-to-Delete: gradient-based methods for machine unlearning. In: Proceedings of the 32nd International Conference on Algorithmic Learning Theory, vol 132, pp 931–962 (2021)
103. Nie, Y., Wang, Z., Yu, Y., Wu, X., Zhao, X., Guo, W., Song, D.: PrivAgent: agentic-based red-teaming for LLM privacy leakage. arXiv:2412.05734 [cs.CR] (2024)
104. Ohrimenko, O., Schuster, F., Fournet, C., Mehta, A., Nowozin, S., Vaswani, K., Costa, M.: Oblivious Multi-Party machine learning on trusted processors. In: 25th USENIX Security Symposium (USENIX Security 16), pp. 619–636(2016)
105. Oliynyk, D., Mayer, R., Rauber, A.: I know what you trained last summer: a survey on stealing machine learning models and defences. ACM Comput. Surv. **55**(14s), 1–41 (2023)
106. OpenAI: GPT-4 technical report. arXiv:2303.08774 [cs.CL] (2024)
107. Orekondy, T., Schiele, B., Fritz, M.: Knockoff nets: stealing functionality of black-box models. In: Proceedings of the IEEE/CVF Conference on Computer Vision and Pattern Recognition (CVPR) (2019)
108. Patra, A., Suresh, A.: BLAZE: blazing fast privacy-preserving machine learning. In: Proceedings 2020 Network and Distributed System Security Symposium, NDSS 2020 (2020)
109. Petrov, I., Dimitrov, D.I., Baader, M., Mueller, M.N., Vechev, M.: DAGER: Exact gradient inversion for large language models. In: The Thirty-Eighth Annual Conference on Neural Information Processing Systems (2024)
110. Phong, L.T., Aono, Y., Hayashi, T., Wang, L., Moriai, S.: Privacy-preserving deep learning via additively homomorphic encryption. IEEE Trans. Inf. Forensics Secur. **13**(5), 1333–1345(2018)
111. Plotkin, D.: Data Stewardship: An Actionable Guide to Effective Data Management and Data Governance. Morgan Kaufmann Publishers Inc., Burlington (2013)
112. Ponomareva, N., Hazimeh, H., Kurakin, A., Xu, Z., Denison, C., McMahan, H.B., Vassilvitskii, S., Chien, S., Thakurta, A.G.: How to DP-fy ML: a practical guide to machine learning with differential privacy. J. Artif. Intell. Res. **77**, 1113–1201(2023)
113. Radford, A., Kim, J.W., Hallacy, C., Ramesh, A., Goh, G., Agarwal, S., Sastry, G., Askell, A., Mishkin, P., Clark, J., Krueger, G., Sutskever, I.: Learning transferable visual models from natural language supervision. In: Proceedings of the 38th International Conference on Machine Learning, vol. 139, pp. 8748–8763 (2021)
114. Ren, J., Chen, K., Chen, C., Sehwag, V., Xing, Y., Tang, J., Lyu, L.: Self-comparison for dataset-level membership inference in large (vision-)language model. In: The Web Conference 2025 (2025)
115. Riazi, M.S., Laine, K., Pelton, B., Dai, W.: Heax: an architecture for computing on encrypted data. In: Proceedings of the Twenty-Fifth International Conference on Architectural Support for Programming Languages and Operating Systems, ASPLOS '20, pp. 1295–1309 (2020)
116. Rolnick, D., Kording, K.: Reverse-engineering deep ReLU networks. In: Proceedings of the 37th International Conference on Machine Learning, vol. 119, pp. 8178–8187 (2020)
117. Salem, A., Bhattacharya, A., Backes, M., Fritz, M., Zhang, Y.: Updates-Leak: data set inference and reconstruction attacks in online learning. In: 29th USENIX Security Symposium (USENIX Security 20), pp. 1291–1308 (2020)
118. Samardzic, N., Feldmann, A., Krastev, A., Devadas, S., Dreslinski, R., Peikert, C., Sanchez, D.: F1: a fast and programmable accelerator for fully homomorphic encryption. In: MICRO-54: 54th Annual IEEE/ACM International Symposium on Microarchitecture, MICRO '21, pp. 238–252(2021)
119. Sang, F., Lee, J., Zhang, X., Kim, T.: PORTAL: fast and secure device access with arm CCA for modern arm mobile system-on-chips (SoCs). In: 2025 IEEE Symposium on Security and Privacy (SP), pp. 4099–4116 (2025)
120. Shamir, A.: How to share a secret. Commun. ACM **22**(11), 612–613 (1979)
121. Shokri, R., Stronati, M., Song, C., Shmatikov, V.: Membership inference attacks against machine learning models. In: 2017 IEEE Symposium on Security and Privacy (SP), pp. 3–18. IEEE Computer Society, Washington (2017)

122. Sierra-Arriaga, F., Branco, R., Lee, B.: Security issues and challenges for virtualization technologies. ACM Comput. Surv. **53**(2), 1–37 (2020)
123. Sinha Roy, S., Turan, F., Jarvinen, K., Vercauteren, F., Verbauwhede, I.: FPGA-based high-performance parallel architecture for homomorphic computing on encrypted data. In: 2019 IEEE International Symposium on High Performance Computer Architecture (HPCA), pp. 387–398 (2019)
124. Tan, S., Knott, B., Tian, Y., Wu, D.J.: CryptGPU: fast privacy-preserving machine learning on the GPU. In: 2021 IEEE Symposium on Security and Privacy (SP), pp. 1021–1038 (2021)
125. Tang, X., Mahloujifar, S., Song, L., Shejwalkar, V., Nasr, M., Houmansadr, A., Mittal, P.: Mitigating membership inference attacks by Self-Distillation through a novel ensemble architecture. In: 31st USENIX Security Symposium (USENIX Security 22), pp. 1433–1450 (2022)
126. Tang, Z., Shi, S., Li, B., Chu, X.: GossipFL: a decentralized federated learning framework with sparsified and adaptive communication. IEEE Trans. Parallel. Distrib. Syst. **34**(3), 909–922 (2023)
127. Tramer, F., Boneh, D.: Slalom: fast, verifiable and private execution of neural networks in trusted hardware. In: International Conference on Learning Representations (2019)
128. Tramèr, F., Zhang, F., Juels, A., Reiter, M.K., Ristenpart, T.: Stealing machine learning models via prediction APIs. In: 25th USENIX Security Symposium (USENIX Security 16), pp. 601–618 (2016)
129. Truex, S., Baracaldo, N., Anwar, A., Steinke, T., Ludwig, H., Zhang, R., Zhou, Y.: A hybrid approach to privacy-preserving federated learning. In: Proceedings of the 12th ACM Workshop on Artificial Intelligence and Security, AISec'19, pp. 1–11 (2019)
130. Truex, S., Liu, L., Chow, K.H., Gursoy, M.E., Wei, W.: LDP-Fed: federated learning with local differential privacy. In: Proceedings of the Third ACM International Workshop on Edge Systems, Analytics and Networking, EdgeSys '20, pp. 61–66 (2020)
131. Truong, J.B., Maini, P., Walls, R.J., Papernot, N.: Data-free model extraction. In: 2021 IEEE/CVF Conference on Computer Vision and Pattern Recognition (CVPR), pp. 4769–4778 (2021)
132. Vanoverloop, D., Sanchez, A., Toffalini, F., Piessens, F., Payer, M., Van Bulck, J.: TLBlur: compiler-assisted automated hardening against controlled channels on off-the-shelf Intel SGX platforms. In: 34th USENIX Security Symposium (USENIX Security 25) (2025)
133. Van Schaik, S., Seto, A., Yurek, T., Batori, A., AlBassam, B., Genkin, D., Miller, A., Ronen, E., Yarom, Y., Garman, C.: SoK: SGX.Fail: how stuff gets exposed. In: 2024 IEEE Symposium on Security and Privacy (SP), pp. 4143–4162 (2024)
134. Volos, S., Vaswani, K., Bruno, R.: Graviton: trusted execution environments on GPUs. In: 13th USENIX Symposium on Operating Systems Design and Implementation (OSDI 18), pp. 681–696. USENIX Association, Berkeley (2018)
135. Wang, Q., Oswald, D.: Confidential computing on heterogeneous CPU-GPU systems: survey and future directions. arXiv:2408.11601 [cs.CR] (2024)
136. Wang, Z., Song, M., Zhang, Z., Song, Y., Wang, Q., Qi, H.: Beyond inferring class representatives: user-level privacy leakage from federated learning. In: IEEE INFOCOM 2019 - IEEE Conference on Computer Communications, pp. 2512–2520. IEEE Press, Piscataway (2019)
137. Wang, X., Xiang, Y., Gao, J., Ding, J.: Information laundering for model privacy. In: International Conference on Learning Representations (2021)
138. Wei, L., Luo, B., Li, Y., Liu, Y., Xu, Q.: I know what you see: power side-channel attack on convolutional neural network accelerators. In: Proceedings of the 34th Annual Computer Security Applications Conference, Association for Computing Machinery, ACSAC '18, pp. 393–406 (2018)
139. Whitehouse, J., Ramdas, A., Rogers, R., Wu, S.: Fully-adaptive composition in differential privacy. In: Proceedings of the 40th International Conference on Machine Learning, vol. 202, pp. 36990–37007 (2023)

140. Wolf, S., Hu, H., Cooley, R., Borowczak, M.: Stealing machine learning parameters via side channel power attacks. In: 2021 IEEE Computer Society Annual Symposium on VLSI (ISVLSI), pp. 242–247 (2021)
141. Wong, R.Y., Chong, A., Aspegren, R.C.: Privacy legislation as business risks: How GDPR and CCPA are represented in technology companies' investment risk disclosures. Proc. ACM Hum.-Comput. Interact. 7 (CSCW1), 1–26 (2023)
142. Wu, F., Inan, H.A., Backurs, A., Chandrasekaran, V., Kulkarni, J., Sim, R.: Privately aligning language models with reinforcement learning. In: The Twelfth International Conference on Learning Representations (2024)
143. Wu, T., Panda, A., Wang, J.T., Mittal, P.: Privacy-preserving in-context learning for large language models. In: The Twelfth International Conference on Learning Representations (2024)
144. Xiao, Y., Li, M., Chen, S., Zhang, Y.: STACCO: differentially analyzing side-channel traces for detecting SSL/TLS vulnerabilities in secure enclaves. In: Proceedings of the 2017 ACM SIGSAC Conference on Computer and Communications Security, CCS '17, pp. 859–874 (2017)
145. Yan, H., Li, X., Li, H., Li, J., Sun, W., Li, F.: Monitoring-based differential privacy mechanism against query flooding-based model extraction attack. IEEE Trans. Dependable Secure Comput. **19**(4), 2680–2694 (2022)
146. Yang, Y., Kannan, R., Prasanna, V.K.: OLA: An FPGA-based overlay accelerator for privacy preserving machine learning with homomorphic encryption. In: Proceedings of the 2025 ACM/SIGDA International Symposium on Field Programmable Gate Arrays, FPGA '25, pp. 127–138 (2025)
147. Ye, J., Maddi, A., Murakonda, S.K., Bindschaedler, V., Shokri, R.: Enhanced membership inference attacks against machine learning models. In: Proceedings of the 2022 ACM SIGSAC Conference on Computer and Communications Security, CCS '22, pp. 3093–3106 (2022)
148. Yin, H., Mallya, A., Vahdat, A., Alvarez, J.M., Kautz, J., Molchanov, P.: See through gradients: Image batch recovery via GradInversion. In: Proceedings of the IEEE/CVF Conference on Computer Vision and Pattern Recognition (CVPR), pp. 16337–16346 (2021)
149. Yousefpour, A., Shilov, I., Sablayrolles, A., Testuggine, D., Prasad, K., Malek, M., Nguyen, J., Ghosh, S., Bharadwaj, A., Zhao, J., Cormode, G., Mironov, I.: Opacus: user-friendly differential privacy library in pytorch. arXiv:2109.12298 [cs.LG] (2022)
150. Yu, D., Zhang, H., Chen, W., Yin, J., Liu, T.Y.: Large scale private learning via low-rank reparametrization. In: Proceedings of the 38th International Conference on Machine Learning, vol. 139, pp. 12208–12218 (2021)
151. Yu, D., Naik, S., Backurs, A., Gopi, S., Inan, H.A., Kamath, G., Kulkarni, J., Lee, Y.T., Manoel, A., Wutschitz, L., Yekhanin, S., Zhang, H.: Differentially private fine-tuning of language models. In: International Conference on Learning Representations (2022)
152. Yu, D., Kairouz, P., Oh, S., Xu, Z.: Privacy-preserving instructions for aligning large language models. In: Proceedings of the 41st International Conference on Machine Learning, vol. 235, pp. 57480–57506 (2024)
153. Yüksel, N., Börklü, H.R., Sezer, H.K., Canyurt, O.E.: Review of artificial intelligence applications in engineering design perspective. Eng. Appl. Artif. Intell. **118**, 105697 (2023)
154. Zama: Concrete ML: a privacy-preserving machine learning library using fully homomorphic encryption for data scientists (2022). https://github.com/zama-ai/concrete-ml
155. Zanella-Béguelin, S., Wutschitz, L., Tople, S., Rühle, V., Paverd, A., Ohrimenko, O., Köpf B, Brockschmidt, M.: Analyzing information leakage of updates to natural language models. In: Proceedings of the 2020 ACM SIGSAC Conference on Computer and Communications Security, CCS '20, pp. 363–375 (2020)
156. Zhang, C., Li, S., Xia, J., Wang, W., Yan, F., Liu, Y.: BatchCrypt: efficient homomorphic encryption for Cross-Silo federated learning. In: 2020 USENIX Annual Technical Conference (USENIX ATC 20), pp. 493–506 (2020)

157. Zhang, B., Dong, Y., Wang, T., Li, J.: Towards certified unlearning for deep neural networks. In: Proceedings of the 41st International Conference on Machine Learning, vol. 235, pp. 58800–58818 (2024)
158. Zhang, D., Xia, B., Liu, Y., Xu, X., Hoang, T., Xing, Z., Staples, M., Lu, Q., Zhu, L.: Privacy and copyright protection in generative AI: a lifecycle perspective. In: Proceedings of the IEEE/ACM 3rd International Conference on AI Engineering - Software Engineering for AI, CAIN '24, pp. 92–97 (2024)
159. Zhang, J., Das, D., Kamath, G., Tramèr, F.: Membership inference attacks cannot prove that a model was trained on your data. arXiv:2409.19798 [cs.LG] (2024)
160. Zheng, H., Ye, Q., Hu, H., Fang, C., Shi, J.: BDPL: a boundary differentially private layer against machine learning model extraction attacks. In: Sako, K., Schneider, S., Ryan, P.Y.A. (eds) Computer Security – ESORICS 2019, pp. 66–83. Springer International Publishing, Berlin (2019)
161. Zhu, L., Liu, Z., Han, S.: Deep leakage from gradients. In: Advances in Neural Information Processing Systems, vol. 32 (2019)
162. Zhu, J., Blaschko, M.B.: R-GAP: recursive gradient attack on privacy. In: International Conference on Learning Representations (2021)
163. Zhu, J., Yin, H., Deng, P., Almeida, A., Zhou, S.: Confidential computing on NVIDIA Hopper GPUs: a performance benchmark study. arXiv:2409.03992 [cs.DC] (2024)

Neil G. Marchant is a Research Fellow in the School of Computing and Information Systems at The University of Melbourne. His research focuses on AI safety, with emphasis on security, privacy, and transparency. He has contributed to research projects funded by the Defence Science and Technology Group, the Australian Bureau of Statistics, and an AUSMURI grant. He received his PhD in Computer Science from The University of Mel-bourne in 2021, with a dissertation on data integration that was a finalist for the Savage Award in Applied Methodology.

Ying Zhao is a Research Fellow at The University of Melbourne's School of Computing and Information Systems. She received her PhD in Computer Science from Swinburne University of Technology in 2023. She works in differential privacy and cryptography, with research focused on bridging theory-practice gaps in priva-cy protection systems by developing novel mechanisms and empirical auditing methodologies. Currently, she studies large-scale statistical systems to detect privacy vulnerabilities and enhance real-world protection frame-works.

Benjamin I. P. Rubinstein is Professor and Deputy Dean (Research) in the Faculty of Engineering and IT at The University of Melbourne, where he researches AI safety, with a focus on the security and privacy of AI sys-tems. He received his PhD in Computer Science from UC Berkeley and spent time at Microsoft Research Silicon Valley and IBM Research Australia before returning to academia. His research has influenced national policy, exposed vulnerabilities in real-world systems, and informed industrial deployments across sectors. He co-led the 2021-2024 CATCH MURI on robust human-AI teams for cybersecurity, has been awarded over 10M in competitive research funding, and has served on advisory and expert groups in academia and government.

Olga Ohrimenko is a Professor in the School of Computing and Information Systems at The University of Melbourne, which she joined in 2020. Previously, she spent six years at Microsoft Research Cambridge as a Principal Researcher, working on Confidential AI and I/O side-channel mitigation. Her research focuses on the security, privacy, and integrity of AI, machine learning algorithms, data analysis tools, and cloud-based systems. She earned her PhD from Brown University and a BCS (Hons) from The University of Melbourne. Ohrimenko has received research awards from Facebook and Oracle, held research contracts with the Australian Bureau of Statistics and National Australia Bank, and in 2025 received a CORE Award Commendation for Outstanding Research Contribution.

Chapter 6
MAGIX: A Unified Framework for the Use of XAI in Enterprises

Francesco Sovrano and Tim Miller

Abstract This chapter proposes a framework for explainable artificial intelligence (XAI) in enterprises. XAI has long been touted as a way to mitigate several issues in enterprise AI systems: (dis)trust, over- and under-reliance, opaqueness, lack of understanding, lack of compliance, bias and discrimination, and poor human decision-making. We argue that, despite having made progress in some of these areas, such as improving understanding and compliance, progress in others has been stunted due to incorrect assumptions about how AI tools are used and understood. We map out a framework for explainable AI that considers some recent positions on the use of explainable AI, with a focus on decision-making in enterprises.

6.1 Introduction

The 2023 artificial intelligence (AI) Index Report by Stanford University[1] reveals that, in 2022, global private investment in AI totaled \$91.9 billion. The top 11 sectors that received the highest AI private investments were medical and healthcare (\$6.1 billion); data management, processing, and cloud (\$5.9 billion); fintech (\$5.5 billion); cybersecurity and data protection (\$5.4 billion); retail (\$4.2 billion); industrial automation and network (\$3.9 billion); sales enablement (\$3.2 billion); marketing and digital ads (\$3.1 billion); AR/VR (\$2.4 billion); drones (\$1.9 billion); and InsurTech (\$1.7 billion).

[1] https://aiindex.stanford.edu/report/

F. Sovrano (✉)
Collegium Helveticum, ETH Zurich, Zurich, Switzerland

Department of Informatics, University of Zurich, Zurich, Switzerland
e-mail: fsovrano@ethz.ch

T. Miller
School of Electrical Engineering and Computer Science, The University of Queensland, Brisbane, QLD, Australia
e-mail: timothy.miller@uq.edu.au

S. Sadiq (ed.), *Enterprise AI*, https://doi.org/10.1007/978-3-032-01940-0_6

This resulted in the integration of AI into several applications across all industry sectors. These AI systems either operate in complete autonomy or by interfacing with human operation through advanced interfaces [51].

A significant challenge with advanced AI systems is their "black-box" nature, which makes it hard to understand how they make decisions [5]. This challenge is critical in almost all fields where AI systems must be accurate, transparent, and accountable to enhance trust in their users and enforce compliance with the law [41]. This is where explainable artificial intelligence (XAI) plays a crucial role, offering tools to make the inner workings of these complex systems more understandable and trustworthy to the diverse stakeholders involved in their operation [40].

The field of XAI provides various methods to interpret machine learning models, differing in strategies, formats, and applicability [20]. Methods are generally divided into *ante hoc* models, which are "inherently interpretable" like decision trees, and *post hoc* methods, which explain black-box models after training. Post-hoc techniques include feature attribution methods assigning importance scores to input features (e.g., LIME [33]; SHAP [25]); rule-based approaches generating human-understandable rules (e.g., Anchors [35]); counterfactual explanations identifying minimal input changes that alter predictions [17]; similarity-based methods comparing inputs to similar instances [30]; surrogate models approximating complex models with interpretable ones [4]; and concept-based methods interpreting the model's internal state using human-friendly concepts [21]. Explanations also vary in *scope*—global (entire model) vs. local (individual predictions)—and *format*, which can be numerical, textual, or visual.

The main goals of XAI are to show [14]:

- How an AI system works from its *inputs*, to avoid *misuse*
- Whether to trust the AI *outputs* (i.e., whether they are good), to avoid *inappropriate reliance*

However, evidence indicates that XAI overall does not always mitigate inappropriate reliance (distrust in accurate AI outputs or excessive trust in AI) or misuse; users often make poorer decisions when presented with incorrect or suboptimal AI suggestions, regardless of XAI [6, 27, 38, 43]. Effectively, the issue with using AI recommendations for decision support is that when a human decision-maker disagrees with the AI recommendation, they struggle to answer this: "Should I trust AI or myself?" Empirical evidence suggests that explainability and interpretability, depending on how they are used, may offer limited information to answer this question [27, 31, 37, 43].

Given the variety of XAI methods and the problems stemming from their misuse, which XAI technologies should be used in an enterprise, and when? This chapter addresses this question by providing an in-depth analysis of the potential and actual use of XAI in enterprises.

Taxonomies aid in selecting appropriate methods for different use cases; for instance, Liao et al. [24] categorize them based on addressed questions, while [46] classify them by stage, scope, and format.

However, current theories do not clearly explain what XAI algorithm to use and when. An early effort to address this gap is presented by Miller [27], who introduced the *evaluative AI* conceptual framework for explainable decision support. This framework posits that decision aids (i.e., XAI outputs) can reduce inappropriate reliance on AI systems only if they assist users in *verifying and evaluating their own hypotheses about AI*, rather than simply explaining how the system arrived at its decisions.

Another theoretical perspective is offered by Chen et al. [8], who argue that machine-generated explanations are only effective when they align with human intuitions. Thus, to determine which XAI algorithm to use in a given context, it is necessary first to identify the wide range of potential human intuitions and hypotheses that might influence decision-making.

To address this challenge, Sovrano and Vilone [39] proposed framing explanations as answers to questions, where the questions themselves are tied to specific explanatory goals. In their case, these goals were defined by legal requirements, drawing on several European regulations to narrow the scope of possible human intuitions and hypotheses. This approach provided clearer guidance on selecting the appropriate XAI algorithm for specific use cases. While this methodology may seem restrictive, legal frameworks are designed to foster trust and encourage appropriate use of AI by tailoring explainability to user needs. Therefore, aligning XAI goals with legal requirements can, in many cases, coincide with the needs of AI system users. Nonetheless, the methodology proposed by Sovrano and Vilone [39] is not sufficiently generic to address all possible correct applications of XAI. This limitation underscores the ongoing need for more comprehensive frameworks to guide the design and application of explainable AI systems.

Instead, in this chapter, we present and discuss a novel theoretical framework, *Markovian Action-Observation Generalized Introspection for eXplainability (MAGIX)*, which aims to guide the selection and fitness evaluation of XAI technologies in real-world applications. MAGIX unifies the frameworks proposed by Miller [27] and Chen et al. [8] by integrating the XAI-driven hypothesis verification process as a core component of a *machine-in-the-loop Markov Decision Process (MDP)*, a model for sequential decision-making under uncertainty.

Within this *machine-in-the-loop MDP*, MAGIX further organizes human intuitions into three key types of knowledge. This categorization facilitates a mapping function that connects human objectives and hypotheses to relevant human intuitions. Throughout this chapter, we will show how this mapping can help choose the most suitable XAI algorithm for a wide range of realistic enterprise settings (spanning from fintech to healthcare) while also analyzing empirical results from existing literature.

6.2 Challenges of Current XAI Approaches: The Inappropriate Reliance Issue

Many XAI systems assume users will analytically evaluate explanations to judge AI suggestions. However, this assumption is flawed, as such evaluations require effort, which people often avoid [10]. For instance, consider a medical diagnosis system where an AI suggests a diagnosis along with a visual explanation (e.g., heatmaps on medical images). Rather than scrutinizing whether the highlighted regions truly justify the diagnosis, a physician might assume that the explanation indicates the system's overall competence. This "trust by default" leads to inappropriate reliance, especially in high-stakes scenarios.

To address this, Buçinca et al. [6] developed *cognitive forcing interventions* that require users to engage more deeply with AI explanations. For example, in a financial advisory tool, users might be prompted to explain in their own words why a particular investment recommendation was made. This intervention forces a moment of reflection and helps prevent blind trust. However, such measures have been found to benefit individuals with a high need for cognition (NFC) more than those with low NFC [7]. In practice, a risk analyst with high NFC might relish the opportunity to break down the rationale behind an AI's market prediction, whereas an analyst with low NFC may simply bypass or provide minimal engagement with the prompt.

While cognitive forcing interventions aim to reduce inappropriate reliance on AI systems, studies by Vasconcelos et al. [45] and Fok and Weld [14] demonstrate that AI explanations can also mitigate this issue during decision-making. Research by Vasconcelos et al. [45] provides further insight: individuals tend to strategically choose when to engage with AI explanations based on a cost-benefit analysis. For example, in an autonomous driving support system, if the cost (in terms of time and cognitive effort) of verifying why the AI recommended a certain maneuver is low compared to the risk of an accident, a driver may carefully review the explanation. Conversely, if verifying the explanation requires too much effort during a high-pressure situation, the driver may rely on the AI's recommendation without critical examination. This dynamic shows that the design of explainability systems must account for the varying costs users are willing to incur to verify an explanation.

In contrast, Fok and Weld [14] demonstrate that AI explanations can also assist in decision-making by enabling users to *verify* AI recommendations. Consider a legal document analysis tool where an AI flags potential contractual risks and provides supporting evidence. In this scenario, the explanation serves as a means for legal professionals to efficiently verify the AI's suggestion rather than accepting it at face value. This verification process is analogous to checking a solution in NP-complete problems: while finding a solution can be computationally intensive, verifying a given solution is relatively efficient. Thus, when AI systems present information that facilitates quick verification, they help users avoid the pitfall of inappropriate reliance, ultimately improving decision-making outcomes [3].

This issue of inappropriate reliance can also be understood through dual-process theory [12]. Humans primarily rely on System 1 thinking, using heuristics and shortcuts for quick decisions. For instance, in a consumer product recommendation system, users might quickly accept AI suggestions based on the aesthetic appeal of the explanation (e.g., attractive charts or simple language) without delving into the underlying data. Although System 1 is efficient and often effective, its heuristic shortcuts can lead to cognitive biases—resulting in suboptimal outcomes in complex scenarios. Conversely, System 2 thinking is more deliberate and analytical, as might be required in high-stakes contexts like financial risk assessment or critical medical decisions. Yet due to the significant cognitive effort required, System 2 is engaged less frequently. Even experts, who generally rely on System 1 heuristics built from experience, can be misled when the AI explanation is superficially compelling but substantively shallow. This underscores the challenge: designing interfaces that can encourage a balanced engagement of both systems, especially under varying levels of cognitive motivation.

6.3 The MAGIX Theoretical Framework

Why are XAI algorithms that answer "Why is this decision (in)correct?" (thus supporting decision verification) sometimes more effective at reducing inappropriate reliance than those that explain "How does the input impact the output?"—e.g., SHAP [25]—and vice versa? This remains an open question that goes beyond the scope of both evaluative AI [27] and the theory of human intuitions proposed by Chen et al. [8].

The lack of clarity in this area highlights a significant gap in our understanding of how to select XAI algorithms that ensure explanations are sufficiently effective. Addressing this issue is particularly challenging given the combinatorial explosion of human intuitions and hypotheses that XAI systems must meet. Indeed, the quality of an XAI output depends on the user's intended purpose and understanding of the probed AI system.

To address this problem, we introduce a generic theoretical framework inspired by Miller [27] and Chen et al. [8]. By framing a machine-in-the-loop decision-making process as a special kind of MDP that embeds AI outputs and explanations, we simplify the challenge of defining system and user goals. This model abstracts the possible kinds of intuitions and hypotheses in such a way that significantly reduces the number of their combinations in terms of explanatory needs.

The MAGIX theoretical framework is based on two main steps:

1. The modeling of the use of XAI as part of a machine-in-the-loop MDP
2. The definition of an action-observation matrix and the corresponding space for informing XAI selection

6.3.1 Markov Decision Processes

First, we will provide the essential background information needed to understand what *Markov Decision Processs* are, as these form the basis of the MAGIX framework.

A MDP is a mathematical framework designed to model sequential decision-making scenarios where a human or an agent must choose actions based on the current situation and its expected outcomes. Further, the outcomes of actions can be uncertain and modeled probabilistically. An agent does not know which of the possible outcomes will occur until after the action is executed. Some actions give *rewards*, which can be positive or negative. MDPs can model a standard machine-in-the-loop decision-making scenario.

A MDP captures the interaction between the decision-maker and the environment through a sequence of states, actions, rewards, and transitions, allowing for the modeling of complex systems. In our model, the *agent* is the human decision-maker. As shown in Fig. 6.1, the human decision-maker observes the current state, selects an action, and transitions to a new state based on probabilistic dynamics of the system. With every transition, they receive feedback in the form of a reward, which informs their decision-making strategy. The MDP assumes the Markov property, which posits that the future is conditionally independent of the past, given the current state and action. This simplifies the analysis and implementation, making the model a robust choice for real-world problems where decisions unfold over time.

In the context of an MDP, policy functions and value functions are central to decision-making and evaluation.

A *policy function* defines the decision-making strategy, mapping states to actions. It serves as the "plan" the decision-maker (or agent) follows to achieve desired outcomes. In the current state, the policy says which action to take. Once we reach the next state, we use the policy again. A policy can be deterministic, selecting a specific action for each state, or stochastic, assigning probabilities to actions based on the current state.

Fig. 6.1 An overview of a Markov decision process. The world emits observations and feedback to an agent, who distills this into knowledge. Using this knowledge, the agent estimates the values of states and actions and, from this, selects an action to execute, which, in turn, changes the world

A *value function*, on the other hand, evaluates the long-term utility of following a policy. It quantifies the expected cumulative reward and comes in two forms: state value functions and action value functions. The *state value function* assesses the expected cumulative reward when starting in a given state and following a specific policy thereafter. It reflects how "desirable" it is to be in a particular state based on future rewards. The *action value function* (often referred to as the Q-function) extends this concept by evaluating the expected cumulative reward of taking a specific action in a given state and then following the policy. This distinction between state and action value functions provides a granular framework for understanding the implications of both being in certain states and making particular choices.

Together, policy and value functions connect directly to the core of an MDP. The policy leverages the insights from value functions to guide decision-making, while the value functions evaluate the performance of a given policy. This interplay enables the optimization of decision-making strategies, ensuring that the agent makes choices that maximize long-term rewards, even in uncertain environments.

6.3.2 A Machine-in-the-Loop MDP for XAI

One compelling example of XAI aiding human decision-making is IBM Research's AIX360 demonstration of an AI-based credit approval system [32]. This system illustrates how different XAI techniques can address the needs of various stakeholders (data scientists, loan officers, and bank consumers), each playing a distinct role in the credit approval process.

In the system, a bank customer submits a loan application, and the bank's AI predicts the risk level associated with the loan, using available customer data. A bank officer reviews this AI-generated risk assessment and makes the final decision on the application. Before deployment, data scientists must validate the AI model's functionality. Meanwhile, customers, as mandated by EU or US laws, are entitled to an explanation of the decision made on their loan application. Each stakeholder benefits from tailored XAI techniques, ensuring transparency, accountability, and actionable insights.

For data scientists, the Generalized Linear Rule Model (GLRM) algorithm [50] would be a suitable model. This rule extraction technique helps answer critical questions such as the following: What is the overall decision-making logic of the model? Is this logic reasonable enough to justify deploying the model? By providing a comprehensive understanding of the AI's internal logic, GLRM fosters confidence in its deployment.

For loan officers, the ProtoDash method [18] provides example-based explanations that support the interpretation of AI-driven recommendations. It helps answer key questions such as "Why is this applicant's credit being approved or denied?" and "How can similar past cases inform my decision to grant or reject credit?" By comparing individual predictions with similar historical cases, ProtoDash provides

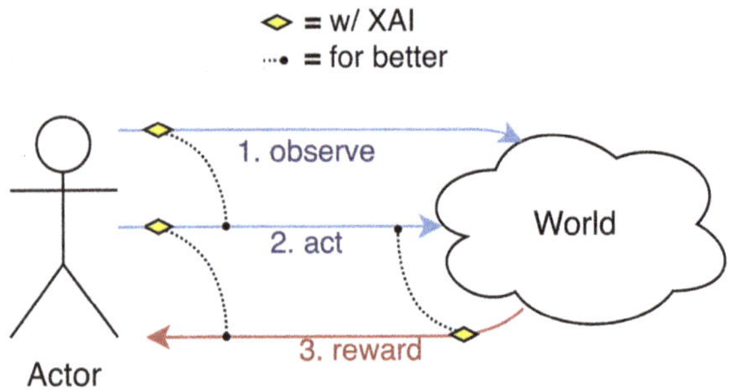

Fig. 6.2 A MDP enhanced with AI, which assists the actor by improving observation capabilities to achieve better actions and by recommending "optimal" actions to achieve better rewards

clear, example-based insights that enable loan officers to make more informed and confident decisions.

For bank customers, the Contrastive Explanation Method (CEM) [11] could be used. CEM explains decisions by addressing questions such as "What changes can I make to increase the likelihood of approval in future?" This method identifies actionable features a customer can improve, such as reducing the time since the last credit inquiry or increasing the average age of accounts. Furthermore, it highlights potential improvements and their potential impact on the approval outcome.

Together, these XAI techniques create a comprehensive, stakeholder-centric framework. They ensure that data scientists can refine and validate AI systems, loan officers can interpret recommendations effectively, and customers can receive transparent and actionable feedback on their applications. Each of these XAI solutions takes under consideration their user's intuitions and hypotheses, fitting well both the frameworks of Miller [27] and Chen et al. [8].

What unifies these diverse uses of XAI? Why are different techniques used, and what criteria guide their selection?

In all cases, stakeholders engage with the "world" to make sense of it. For data scientists, the "world" is the dataset used to train the AI model and the AI's code-base and logic. For loan officers, it includes customer characteristics and AI-generated assessments. For customers, it encompasses the AI's decision and its underlying rationale. Stakeholders observe the "world," interact with it to achieve specific goals, and receive feedback (implicitly or explicitly) about the outcomes of their actions. This cyclical process of observation, action, and feedback aligns with the framework of a MDP, where the actor aims to maximize cumulative rewards associated with achieving a specific goal.

In this MDP, the actor is augmented by XAI, which aids in properly observing the "world" and helps explore the actions that can help the actor achieve their goals. The role of the AI system within the MDP depends on the actor. For some, the AI system may act as a guide, providing personalized recommendations. For others, it may act as part of the "world," influencing the distribution of rewards and shaping how goals are attained. This interplay is encapsulated in the concept of a machine-in-the-loop MDP, as illustrated in Fig. 6.2.

Table 6.1 Summary of AI use, hypotheses, and goals of XAI. The table outlines how AI can be used to meet key objectives, the hypotheses to be tested, and the corresponding goals of XAI in each scenario

Use of AI	User hypotheses	Goals of XAI
AI functions as a recommender system to enhance world observation (Step 1 of the MDP)	**H1:** The AI output enhances world observation	• Provide insights about the actionability of specific knowledge about the world
		• Foster appropriate reliance on the AI system
AI functions as a recommender system to aid in better decision-making prior to action execution (Step 2 of the MDP)	**H2:** The AI output aids in better decision-making before acting	• Provide insights about the validity of specific actions before they are taken
		• Foster appropriate reliance on the AI system
AI operates as an autonomous system, making decisions that directly impact the user (Step 3 of the MDP)	**H3:** The AI system can be used to achieve the desired objective	• Provide insights about the use of the AI system for a good outcome
		• Ensure appropriate use of the system

In this model, AI benefits the actor only if it contributes to one or more of the following objectives: (i) Improving the observation of the world—step 1 of the MDP (see Fig. 6.2) (ii) Enhancing decision-making prior to action execution—step 2 (iii) Optimizing outcomes post-action execution—step 3 Each of these objectives corresponds to one of three high-level hypotheses that the actor may aim to verify:

- **H1:** The AI output enhances world observation.
- **H2:** The AI output aids in better decision-making, before acting.
- **H3:** The AI system can be used to achieve the desired objective.

Consequently, the machine-in-the-loop MDP framework organizes the potential uses of XAI into three cases, one per hypothesis, to provide insights about: (i) The actionability of specific knowledge about the world (ii) The validity of specific actions before they are taken (iii) The use of the AI system to achieve a good outcome with the action

Therefore, as summarized in Table 6.1, in **H1** and **H2**, the AI system functions as a recommender system, providing suggestions accompanied by explanations that validate the recommendations. In these scenarios, XAI plays a key role in guiding the actor on how to observe and act within the "world." These cases focus on fostering appropriate reliance on the AI system.

In contrast, in **H3**, the AI operates as an autonomous system, making decisions that directly impact the user. The explanations in this context address the rationale behind the AI's decisions, as the system executes actions without the actor's ability to directly intervene. This scenario emphasizes the importance of XAI in ensuring the appropriate use of the system.

To illustrate these applications, consider the example of the credit approval system above. Each stakeholder uses XAI at different stages of their respective MDP. Data scientists use XAI to observe the "world" and gain actionable insights for debugging and evaluation (case 1; **H1**). Loan officers rely on XAI to determine the best course of action for handling applications (case 2; **H2**). Customers leverage XAI to understand the system's decisions (i.e., the reward) and adapt their actions to improve outcomes (case 3; **H3**). Through this lens, XAI serves as a critical tool for aligning stakeholders' goals with the broader system's functionality, ensuring more profitable interactions.

Now, we can see an initial answer to the question posed at the beginning of this section: Why does verification support better decision-making than understanding the AI model? In cases 1 and 2, verification helps the decision-maker understand their world. In the latter case, instead, standard explainability techniques help the decision-maker understand the AI model itself, which is though only a loose proxy of the world.

Here, we ask the reader to imagine a situation where they need to make an important decision at work, and they received a recommendation from an AI model that they disagree with. What is more useful: *(a)* a reason why the model arrived at that decision (here the "world" that the XAI deals with is the model); *(b)* a reason why the model recommendation is correct (which may be different to why it made the decision; here the "world" is the underlying problem space); or *(c)* a reason why the decision-maker's decision is incorrect (here the "world" is the underlying problem space as well). We consider option *(a)* to be "standard" explainable AI, option *(b)* to be the idea of verification such as that defined by Fok and Weld [14] and Vasconcelos et al. [45], and option *(c)* to be the idea of evaluative AI [27].

6.3.3 *The Action-Observation Matrix*

The machine-in-the-loop MDP model aids in narrowing down the possible hypotheses a user might consider. XAI tools are specifically designed to assist users in verifying these hypotheses within the context of a standard sequential decision-making framework. However, what ensures the verification of the goodness of both knowledge and actions? The answer to this question hinges on the user's intuitions regarding the MDP [8].

To address this, it is essential to first determine the kind of MDPs in which employing XAI for explaining AI is meaningful. Such scenarios arise when the user's missing knowledge is not explicitly available beforehand (i.e., in the source code of the AI) and must be extracted from a black-box AI model. Specifically, these scenarios arise when there is no guarantee that the AI is error-free due to its reliance on heuristics. This challenge is particularly prominent in:

- **NP-hard problems:** Problems for which no efficient solution exists, making it computationally infeasible to verify the correctness of outcomes in all instances
- **Ill-defined problems:** Problems where the objectives, constraints, or solution criteria are ambiguous or poorly specified, often necessitating the use of machine learning techniques

In scenarios outside of these contexts, it is often feasible to build recommender systems that are correct all the time (at least, within their model of the world), rendering the use of XAI for explaining correctness unnecessary, e.g., a symbolic tool that uses probabilities and statistics to calculate risks. Despite this, people may still use less specific, not-always-correct AI solutions to build their applications due to ease, hype, or unawareness of better techniques.

What XAI can effectively explain, instead, are the heuristics underpinning the evaluation of actions and states, as well as the strategies used to extract actionable knowledge from state observations. By explaining these aspects, XAI bridges gaps in users' intuitions, enabling a deeper understanding of the decision-making process finalized to maximizing cumulative rewards.

As discussed in Sect. 6.3.2, XAI can be employed to verify three distinct types of hypotheses. Each hypothesis may rely on intuitions regarding the following aspects:

- **I1:** *Knowledge Actionability*—How is actionable knowledge derived? This involves understanding the heuristics that underlie the policy function (see Sect. 6.3.1).
- **I2:** *Action Value*—How is the quality of an action evaluated? This relates to the heuristics of the action value function (see Sect. 6.3.1).
- **I3:** *State Value*—How is the quality of a state determined? This pertains to the heuristics of the state value function (see Sect. 6.3.1).

To verify hypotheses **H1** and **H3**, users may rely on (or lack) intuitions about **I1** and **I3**, as these relate to understanding knowledge actionability and evaluating the value of a state. Conversely, verifying hypothesis **H2** may depend on the user's intuitions (or lack thereof) regarding **I1** and **I2**, as these pertain to evaluating a specific action.

Among these, **I1** is central to all hypotheses because every AI system, by definition, operates on the basis of inputs and outputs, and XAI aims to clarify the relationships between them. From an XAI standpoint, the heuristics underlying **I1** can either be known or unknown, and the implications vary accordingly:

- If the heuristics of **I1** are known: The XAI tool needs to explain only the execution trace of the heuristics, i.e., what triggered them in the input. This trigger is always initially unknown. It will be enough for the user to verify the correctness of the recommendation/decision.
- If the heuristics of **I1** are unknown: The XAI tool must also explain the heuristics themselves. This involves determining their relevance to the reward function. For

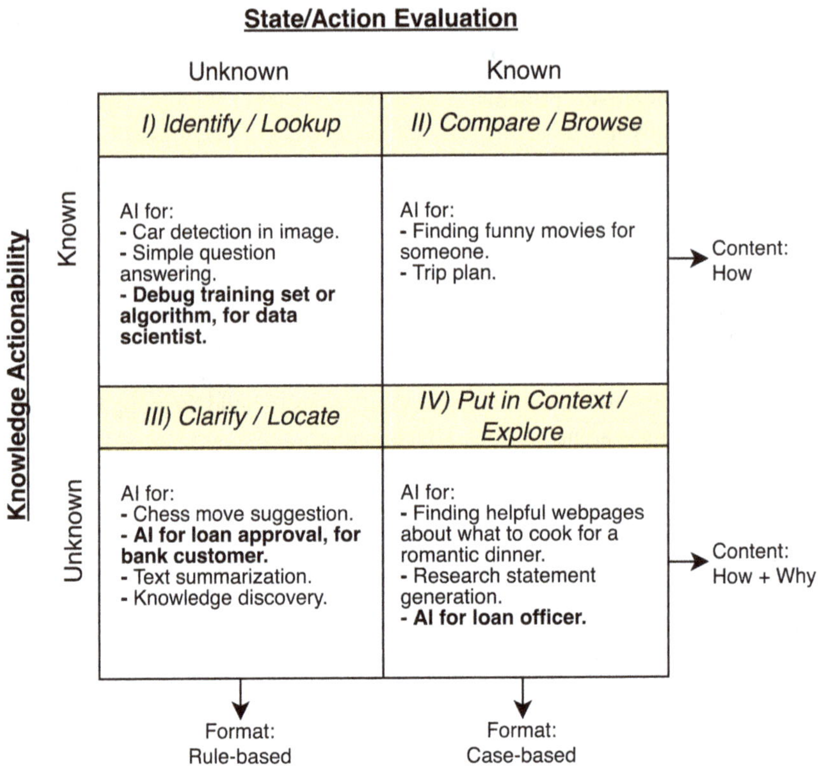

Fig. 6.3 The action-observation matrix with examples of AI scenarios for each knowledge acquisition task. In bold are those AI scenarios related to the credit approval system used as driving example for this chapter

example, to verify usability of an AI system (**H3**), the user must know why the state being evaluated is (not) good, which could be explained by showing how to get the desired output from the input.

How the heuristics and their traces are explained depends on the knowledge of the heuristics underlying **I2** and **I3**.

When the rules governing state/action evaluation (heuristics of **I2** and **I3**) are unknown to the user, explaining the heuristics and their trace as explicit rules would be useful. Conversely, if these rules are known, the explanations can just rely on similarity-based reasoning, such as comparing with successful solutions from training data and employing case-based explanations. In this case, the user will know how to evaluate the state/action.

This framework reduces the broad range of possible intuitions into two well-defined dimensions per hypothesis, forming the axes of our *action-observation matrix*, as illustrated in Fig. 6.3. Each quadrant in that matrix corresponds to a specific *knowledge acquisition task*. When only knowledge actionability is known, the task is one of *identification or lookup* (Quadrant I). When both knowledge actionability and action/state evaluation are known, the task becomes one of *comparison or browsing* (Quadrant II). Conversely, when neither is known, the task shifts to *clarification or location* (Quadrant III). Finally, in cases where only state/action evaluation is known, the task involves *contextualization or exploration* (Quadrant IV).

For the knowledge acquisition tasks of "Identify" and "Compare," the minimal XAI setting should provide explanations about how the AI's output was generated. Such explanations can be obtained using feature-importance-based XAI algorithms like SHAP [25] or LIME [33]. For instance, consider an AI system designed to detect cars in an image. Here, SHAP or LIME can explain which features (e.g., shapes, edges, or colors) influenced the detection decision. There is no need to explain what makes a patch of image a car (i.e., the why)—the user knows this.

Similarly, when a data scientist needs to debug a credit approval system, they may already understand how to evaluate the rules but require clarity on how input features are connected to the output. Another example involves answering a simple question, such as "When was Einstein born?" For a retrieval-augmented generative AI, an XAI tool like SHAP might highlight the relevance of the terms "Einstein" and "when" in the input, which appear also in the retrieved documents. Without retrieval-augmented generation, however, other generative AI models may lack explainability in such cases.

For tasks involving "Clarify" and "Put in Context," the XAI must provide not only feature attributions but also the reasoning behind the AI's output. This aligns with evaluative AI [27] and findings from Vasconcelos et al. [45] and Fok and Weld [14], who emphasize that XAI is most effective when it assists users in verifying the correctness of decisions.

For instance, in the case of a chess move suggestion, the XAI should justify why the suggested move is strategically sound within the broader game context, such as avoiding a checkmate or positioning for a favorable endgame. Similarly, for a cancer detection AI identifying a carcinoma in an image, the XAI should explain why a specific image patch was flagged. This might involve linking the highlighted region to known pathological markers or patterns consistent with carcinoma. In the case of a loan application rejection by a bank's AI, counterfactual explanations are considered as a suitable way to explain model decisions [48]. The XAI should indicate how the customer's financial profile could change to meet approval criteria (such as needing a higher income or a lower debt-to-income ratio), providing actionable insights for the applicant.

The distinction between rule-based and case-based formats underlines the flexibility required for different scenarios. For "Identify" and "Clarify" tasks, when the rules for evaluating actions/states are unknown, the explanations are rule based. For example, in debugging a credit approval system or explaining a straightforward AI decision like recognizing a car in an image, the XAI relies on established algorithms or decision boundaries to communicate how and why the decision was made. In contrast, when the rules are known, as in "Put in Context" or "Explore" tasks, the most minimalist format shifts to case-based explanations. Here, the XAI derives insights from similar cases or analogous scenarios.

However, it is important to also highlight that the concepts of "knowledge actionability" and "action evaluation" are not binary in nature. Rather than being simple states of "known" or "unknown," they exist on a spectrum, with varying degrees of understanding and application across different scales (e.g., global or local). This perspective introduces significant nuances to the concept of "unknown," which may not be fully known in advance.

6.4 XAI Tools and Technologies

XAI can be viewed both as *approaches* aimed at helping people understand and appropriately use AI systems and as *tools* implementing such methods to meet different explanatory needs. In the literature, there is a vast array of domain-dependent and context-specific XAI methods that differ in explanation generation strategies, formats, and applicability to disparate data and learning algorithms [20]. Several taxonomies guide practitioners in choosing suitable XAI methods for specific tasks. In particular, Adadi and Berrada [1] offer a comprehensive survey of existing XAI approaches, identifying trends and challenges; van der Velden et al. [44] focus on XAI for deep learning-based medical imaging, proposing a classification framework; and Nauta et al. [29] detail 12 conceptual properties for evaluating explanations in machine learning.

One common way to categorize XAI methods is by *stage of application*: *ante hoc* vs. *post hoc*. Ante hoc techniques build inherently interpretable models, whereas post hoc techniques explain a trained model using an external explainer. Another key dimension is *scope*: methods can provide global (the model's overall logic) or local (explanations of individual predictions) insights [46]. Both types can support local or global understanding; that is, global XAI methods can give insight into local decisions, and a series of local explanations can give a global understanding of an AI model. XAI techniques also vary in *format*: they can be saliency maps or feature-attribution vectors; textual or visual narratives; examples-based statements and rule-based statements; or a combination of these [24].

Both ante hoc and post hoc XAI methods can serve *ex-ante* explanations (before a decision is taken) or *ex post* explanations (after a decision). That said, *ex ante* explanations typically convey global information about the model, while *ex post* methods often shed light on local, instance-specific behavior. Our classification of XAI methods also considers *model specificity* (model agnostic vs. model specific).

Tables 6.2 and 6.3 summarize popular XAI methods organized by the main "explanatory question" they answer [39], their scope, and example references. We highlight how some methods answer "what-if" questions, e.g., counterfactuals [19], while others answer "why" or "how" queries, e.g., saliency maps [30], local feature attribution [33], or global feature attribution [26].

Table 6.2 Model-specific XAI methods with explanatory goals

Question	XAI algorithms	Applicable model types	Explanation
What are the most important features influencing *all predictions* of the model?	Global feature attribution methods: TreeExplainer [26], CAVs [21]	Tree-based models, DNNs	Identify key features for predictions to understand system's conditions of use, risks, and detect anomalies
How do interactions between features affect *all predictions* of the model?	Global feature attribution methods [26]	Tree-based models, Bayesian networks	Identify key feature interactions for system usage, risk, and logic
What is the *model's inner logic*?	ExtractRule [15]	DNNs, SVMs	Transparent models mimicking a black-box
What set of rules does the model usually follow to make *all predictions*?	Rule-based algorithms [9, 49]	Decision trees, random forests, linear models, DNNs	Clarify the rules for usage, risks, decisions, outputs, or anomalies
What parts of an input (e.g., an image) influence the model's decision?	Saliency maps [13], LRP [2]	DNN	Identify important input areas to review or contest decisions
What contributions do individual neurons in a DNN make to the final prediction?	Activation maximization [23]	DNNs	Analyze neuron contributions for anomaly detection and interpretation
How do different layers in a DNN contribute to a prediction?	Layer-wise relevance propagation [21, 23]	DNNs	Examine layer contributions for anomaly detection, decision logic
How to interpret a neural net's internal state in terms of human-friendly concepts?	Concept-based methods [21]	DNNs	Evaluate key concepts behind decisions, interpret outputs, detect anomalies

Several XAI algorithms stand out as *particularly influential*:

- *LIME (Local Interpretable Model-Agnostic Explanations)* [34] approximates a black-box model's local behavior around a single instance using a simple, interpretable surrogate (often a sparse linear model). Its main benefit is that it is model agnostic and easy to implement, offering instance-level feature attributions. However, LIME's reliance on sampling around the input instance assumes local linearity and independence of features, which can be violated in practice; the choice of neighborhood size and sampling distribution can also strongly influence results, risking instability or misleading explanations.

Table 6.3 Model-agnostic XAI methods with explanatory goals

Question	XAI algorithms	Explanation
What is the *inner logic* of the model?	Surrogate models [4]	Transparent models mimicking a black-box
How does a specific feature influence the prediction for an individual instance?	LIME [33], SHAP [25]	Assess feature impact on individual outputs to review or interpret decisions
What are the most important features influencing *all predictions* of the model?	Global feature attribution methods like SHAP [25]	Identify key features for the model's predictions, detect anomalies, assess risk
What are the most similar instances to a given input with respect to a model's prediction?	Similarity-based methods [30]	Compare similar instances to interpret decisions or detect anomalies
What minimal changes would need to be made to an input to change its prediction?	Counterfactual explanations [17]	Identify changes to alter outcomes, review or contest decisions, detect anomalies
Why this output instead of another?	Contrastive explanations [11]	Clarify why one outcome was chosen, interpret or contest decisions, detect anomalies
What features, when held fixed, are most responsible for a particular prediction or classification?	Anchors [35]	Highlights stable feature anchors enabling consistent predictions
How would changing multiple features simultaneously affect the model's prediction for a specific instance?	Counterfactual and interaction detection methods [17]	Examine combined feature effects to review or adjust decisions, detect anomalies
How can we understand the model's decision for a specific instance in the context of its training data?	Contextual analysis methods [30]	Provide broader context for local decisions, detect anomalies or biases

- *SHAP (Shapley Additive Explanations)* [25] is grounded in cooperative game theory, assigning each feature an importance score (the Shapley value) indicating its contribution to a prediction. SHAP's appeal lies in its theoretical guarantees of local accuracy, consistency, and additivity and its extension to various settings (e.g., KernelSHAP for model-agnostic use, TreeSHAP for tree-based models [26]). Nevertheless, computing Shapley values is expensive for large or complex models; the need to define background (or reference) samples can introduce biases or assumptions about feature independence that do not always hold.
- *Decision tree surrogate models and other rule-based methods* [9, 47] inherently yield human-readable rules (via splits or Boolean conditions), making them popular *inherently interpretable* or *surrogate* approaches for larger black-boxes. Their clarity is also their weakness, as complex decision boundaries or feature

interactions might be missed or oversimplified, especially when a tree-based surrogate is used for high-dimensional data.

- *Counterfactual explanations* [17, 28] reveal how to alter an input minimally to obtain a different outcome. They offer actionable insights and local transparency. However, defining actionable or realistic changes demands careful consideration of domain constraints and feature correlations; if a model's behavior is non-linear, it is difficult to guarantee that minimal changes found in one region are meaningful in another.
- *Anchors* [35] highlight a short set of rule-like conditions that anchor (almost guarantee) the same classification outcome. While anchors provide concise, high-precision local explanations, they depend on user-defined perturbation distributions and can become overly specific. Coverage may be low in complex domains, and the logic behind anchor generation can be opaque for non-technical users.
- *Grad-CAM* [36] and *Integrated Gradients* [42] are representative *gradient-based* explanation methods for deep networks. They create saliency or relevance maps for images or other differentiable inputs, helping pinpoint which regions influenced the prediction. Though widely used for visual data and medically oriented tasks, these methods can be sensitive to choice of baselines (Integrated Gradients) or susceptible to resolution limits (Grad-CAM), and their reliance on gradients alone can fail when activation saturates or in the presence of adversarial manipulations.
- *Concept-based* explanations, especially for computer vision [21], aim to identify human-aligned concepts present in images that contribute to a model's predictions. These methods can be either supervised [22], requiring training data annotated with relevant concepts, or unsupervised [16, 52], which rely only on class labels. Concept-based approaches have been shown to be significantly more helpful to users than saliency-based methods. However, supervised techniques demand extensive and often noisy or costly labeling, while unsupervised methods frequently discover concepts that are difficult for humans to interpret.

In summary, XAI methods encompass a broad spectrum of approaches (model agnostic vs. model specific, global vs. local, ante hoc vs. post hoc, etc.), each rooted in different assumptions and suited to different "explanatory" questions. For example, TreeSHAP [26] helps uncover global feature attributions in ensemble tree models; LIME [33] provides local interpretability for any black-box, but can be sensitive to sampling issues; and gradient-based saliency approaches excel at visualizing relevant pixels or features in DNNs but can struggle with non-differentiable components. None of these methods, however, address downstream consequences of decisions; they focus on clarifying the *process* leading to a prediction or classification. Hence, while XAI tools can greatly aid in explaining or justifying AI outputs, additional manual steps are often required to ensure domain-specific compliance, correctness, and consideration of real-world consequences.

6.5 Applications of XAI in Enterprises: Case Studies and Analysis

What XAI to use in an enterprise? The answer depends on the action-observation matrix and the types of hypotheses involved. As we illustrated in the previous section, selecting an appropriate XAI algorithm is inherently both intuition-dependent and hypothesis-driven. Together, these two dimensions define the verifiability task.

In this section, we will demonstrate how to apply the MAGIX framework to systematically map AI tasks to XAI applications. Specifically, we will provide one example for each combination of hypothesis type and knowledge acquisition task (i.e., a quadrant in the action-observation; see Fig. 6.3). Our focus will be on the sectors with the highest AI investments, according to Stanford University's 2023 AI Index Report. These sectors include medical and healthcare; data management, processing, and cloud; fintech; cybersecurity and data protection; retail; industrial automation and networks; sales enablement; marketing and digital advertising; augmented and virtual reality (AR/VR); drones; and InsurTech.

Since providing 12 examples for each sector would amount to a total of 132 examples, we have chosen to present all the examples for the medical and healthcare sector (see Table 6.4) and only a few relevant examples for the other sectors (see Table 6.5).

6.5.1 Medical and Healthcare Sector

Given an AI system to be explained, the MAGIX method involves the following steps:

1. Identify the Hypothesis (**H1**, **H2**, **H3**): Determine which high-level hypothesis the AI user aims to validate about the system.
2. Determine the Knowledge Acquisition Task: Based on the user's knowledge and actionability, categorize the task into one of the four quadrants of the action-observation matrix.
3. Select Appropriate XAI Methods: choose XAI algorithms that provide the necessary explanations based on the task type.

To construct Table 6.4, we started by identifying AI applications (and their users) relevant to the medical and healthcare sector, focusing on tasks that align with real-world use cases such as identifying tumors, comparing treatment options, or exploring surgical techniques. Then, we used the MAGIX framework, following the steps above, to understand what XAI algorithms are needed.

For instance, for the AI application of identifying shards of broken bones in CT (Computed Tomography) scans, the users are radiologists who know how to understand whether the AI output is correct (known knowledge actionability) but do not know how to assess the image because it takes too much time and

Table 6.4 Examples of AI tasks and XAI solutions in the medical and healthcare sector, categorized by quadrant and hypothesis

Quad.	Hyp.	AI user	AI task	XAI
I	H1	Radiologist	Identify shards of broken bones	Saliency maps or concept-based explanations to highlight tumor regions in scans
II	H1	Medical Student	Compare AI diagnosis with known cases	Example-based explanations; retrieving similar cases
III	H1	Researcher	Clarify unknown biomarkers in genetic data	Rule-based explanations; explaining why the suggestion is good/valid
IV	H1	Doctor	Explore alternative diagnoses for complex symptoms	Example-based explanations; visual step-by-step procedures
I	H2	Medical Researcher	Identify novel experimental therapies for patient	LIME or SHAP explanations
II	H2	Physician	Compare treatment options suggested by AI	Prototype Selection
III	H2	Doctor	Clarify potential drug interactions before prescribing	Rule-based explanations; displaying interaction rules
IV	H2	Surgeon	Explore new surgical techniques	Example-based explanations; visual step-by-step procedures
I	H3	Patient	Confirm specialized treatment	Feature Attribution (e.g., SHAP)
II	H3	Patient	Impose lifestyle changes	Example-based explanations
III	H3	Patient	Approve/deny treatment coverage	Counterfactual explanations
IV	H3	Patient	Adjust medications	Case-based reasoning

Table 6.5 Examples of AI tasks and XAI solutions across various sectors, categorized by sector, quadrant, and hypothesis

Sector	Quad.	Hyp.	AI user	AI task	XAI
Data Management	II	H2	Cloud Infrastructure Manager	Compare resource allocation options	Feature attribution methods
Fintech	I	H1	Fraud Analyst	Identify fraudulent transactions	Feature attribution methods
Fintech	II	H2	Loan Officer	Compare loan applications for approval	Prototype selection
Cybersec.	III	H2	Cybersecurity Specialist	Clarify user behavior anomalies	Counterfactual explanations
Retail	II	H3	Customer	Compare personalized product recommendations	Example-based explanations
Industrial Automation	I	H1	Maintenance Engineer	Identify equipment failure indicators	Feature attribution methods
Industrial Automation	II	H2	Process Engineer	Compare robotic workflow optimizations	Prototype selection
Sales Enablement	II	H2	Sales Representative	Compare lead scoring results	Feature attribution methods
Sales Enablement	I	H3	Customer	Understand automated email responses	Feature attribution methods
Marketing	I	H1	Social Media Analyst	Identify brand sentiment indicators	Feature attribution methods
AR/VR	IV	H3	Trainee	Put in context VR training feedback	Example-based explanations
Drones	I	H1	Drone Operator	Identify navigation obstacles	Feature attribution methods
Insurtech	II	H2	Claims Adjuster	Compare insurance claims	Prototype selection

effort on a positive identification or some shards are so small they can be missed (unknown state evaluation). This task fits into Quadrant I, with Hypothesis **H1** since the AI output enhances world observation. An appropriate XAI method is feature attribution (e.g., Grad-CAM or saliency maps), which highlights regions in the CT scans indicative of bone shards.

For the task of comparing AI diagnoses with known cases, the user is a medical student able to understand whether a diagnosis is correct (known knowledge actionability) and to assess the state of a patient (known state evaluation). This task fits into Quadrant II with Hypothesis **H1**, as the AI helps in comparing knowledge. Example-based explanations, such as retrieving similar cases, would be suitable to explain how the AI's diagnosis aligns with existing knowledge, since the medical student does not need to be given the specific rules governing each diagnosis (they are already known).

When clarifying unknown biomarkers in genetic data, the users are researchers who do not have knowledge to evaluate the patterns in genetic sequences (unknown knowledge actionability) and do not have a framework to assess these patterns' significance (unknown state evaluation). If they knew these things, the AI tool would be unnecessary. This task fits into Quadrant III under Hypothesis **H1**. Rule-based explanations are used to translate complex genetic patterns into interpretable if-then statements that make the recommendations accessible and assessable. For example, a rule-based explainer might state: "If a genetic sequence exhibits mutation X and expression level of gene Y is above threshold Z, then it indicates a potential biomarker for disease A." By breaking down intricate genetic data into simple, logical rules, researchers may be able to grasp the significance of specific patterns without needing extensive prior knowledge. This approach not only clarifies how the recommendation was derived but also allows researchers to evaluate its validity and relevance, thereby demonstrating the recommendation's effectiveness.

For the task of exploring alternative diagnoses for complex symptoms, the user is a clinician who is not familiar with possible diagnoses due to the large potential number (unknown knowledge actionability) but knows how to assess them when they see one (known state evaluation). This task belongs to Quadrant IV under Hypothesis **H1**. Example-based explanations, including visual step-by-step procedures, are appropriate to contextualize the AI's suggested diagnoses, showing how they relate to known cases.

Identifying experimental therapies for patients involves a medical researcher who knows how to interpret suggested therapies once they are recommended (known knowledge actionability) but is exploring therapies that are outside their current knowledge base (unknown action evaluation). This task fits Quadrant I under Hypothesis **H2**. Feature attribution methods like LIME or SHAP explain how the AI determined its recommendations.

For comparing treatment options suggested by AI, the user could be a physician who is knowledgeable about treatment possibilities (known knowledge actionability) and knows how to evaluate their outcomes (known action evaluation). This task fits Quadrant II under Hypothesis **H2**. Prototype selection is used to provide representative examples of the treatments, enabling comparisons and ensuring transparency about the AI's suggestions.

Clarifying potential drug interactions before prescribing involves a doctor who is unsure of the rules governing all interactions (unknown knowledge actionability) and does not know how these interactions might affect patient outcomes (unknown action evaluation). This fits into Quadrant III under Hypothesis **H2**. Rule-based explanations are used to display interaction rules, explaining the conditions under which specific drug combinations are unsafe.

For exploring new surgical techniques, the user is a surgeon unsure of how to implement them effectively (unknown knowledge actionability) but aware of their goodness (known action evaluation). This task belongs to Quadrant IV under Hypothesis **H2**. Example-based explanations and visual step-by-step procedures contextualize the AI's suggestions and provide guidance for practical implementation.

For the task of confirming specialized treatment, the user is a patient who trusts the prescribed treatment (known knowledge actionability) but lacks the capacity to evaluate why the AI suggested it (unknown state evaluation). This task fits Quadrant I under Hypothesis **H3**. Feature attribution methods such as SHAP are used to explain how the AI's decision aligns with the patient's medical profile.

In the case of comparing AI instructions for lifestyle changes, the user is a patient familiar with lifestyle adjustment strategies (known knowledge actionability) and capable of evaluating whether they fit their life (known state evaluation). This fits into Quadrant II under Hypothesis **H3**. Example-based explanations illustrate how similar cases benefited from specific lifestyle changes, providing relatable insights.

When clarifying the AI's denial of treatment coverage, the user is a patient who does not understand the system's decision-making rules (unknown knowledge actionability) and is unable to evaluate how to change their profile to meet approval criteria (unknown state evaluation). This task belongs to Quadrant III under Hypothesis **H3**. Counterfactual explanations reveal how changes in the patient's circumstances could lead to approval, providing actionable insights.

Finally, adjusting medications based on AI suggestions involves a patient who does not understand their current medications (unknown knowledge actionability) but due to previous experience is confident about how modifications might affect their health outcomes (known state evaluation). This fits into Quadrant IV under Hypothesis **H3**. Case-based reasoning thus may offer examples of similar cases where adjustments were successful and why, giving the patient context and confidence in their decision.

6.5.2 Other Sectors

To construct Table 6.5, we started by identifying important and realistic AI use cases in the specified sectors, ensuring they align with real-world applications such as fraud detection in fintech, intrusion detection in cybersecurity, or personalized product recommendations in retail. For each use case, we determined the AI user and the specific task they aim to accomplish. Then, we used the MAGIX framework to assign the appropriate quadrant based on the user's knowledge and actionability, identified the relevant hypothesis, and selected suitable XAI methods according to the guidelines provided.

This table includes up to two examples per sector, covering 14 AI use cases. Each entry specifies the sector, quadrant, hypothesis, AI user, AI task, and the selected XAI method.

6.6 Conclusion

In this chapter, we introduced the *MAGIX* theoretical framework to address the critical challenge of selecting appropriate XAI technologies in enterprise settings. By modeling the human-AI interaction as a machine-in-the-loop Markov Decision Process, MAGIX provides a systematic approach to align XAI methods with users' hypotheses and intuitions. This alignment is facilitated through the action-observation matrix, which categorizes knowledge acquisition tasks and guides the selection of suitable XAI algorithms.

Our framework unifies and extends previous theories by integrating the evaluative AI concept and the importance of human intuitions in explanation effectiveness. Through case studies in the medical and healthcare sector, as well as examples from other industries, we demonstrated how MAGIX can be applied to real-world scenarios, ensuring that XAI tools not only enhance transparency but also effectively support users' decision-making processes.

Future work includes validating the MAGIX framework through empirical studies and expanding it to accommodate emerging AI technologies and use cases. By continuing to refine and test this framework, we aim to contribute to the development of more effective and user-centered XAI systems that meet the diverse needs of stakeholders across various industries.

Acknowledgments F. Sovrano acknowledges the support of the Swiss National Science Foundation for SNF Project 200021_197227 and of the UZH Global Strategy and Partnerships Funding Scheme.

References

1. Adadi, A., Berrada, M.: Peeking inside the black-box: A survey on explainable artificial intelligence (XAI). IEEE Access **6**, 52138–52160 (2018). https://doi.org/10.1109/ACCESS.2018.2870052
2. Bach, S., Binder, A., Montavon, G., et al.: On pixel-wise explanations for non-linear classifier decisions by layer-wise relevance propagation. PloS one **10**, e0130140 (2015)

3. Bansal, G., Wu, T., Zhou, J., et al.: Does the whole exceed its parts? The effect of AI explanations on complementary team performance. In: Kitamura, Y., Quigley, A., Isbister, K., et al. (eds.) CHI '21: CHI Conference on Human Factors in Computing Systems, Virtual Event / Yokohama, May 8–13, 2021, pp. 81:1–81:16. ACM (2021). https://doi.org/10.1145/3411764.3445717
4. Bastani, O., Kim, C., Bastani, H.: Interpretability via model extraction. arXiv preprint arXiv:170609773 (2017)
5. Bernal, J., Mazo, C.: Transparency of artificial intelligence in healthcare: insights from professionals in computing and healthcare worldwide. Appl. Sci. **12**(20), 10228 (2022)
6. Buçinca, Z., Malaya, M.B., Gajos, K.Z.: To trust or to think: Cognitive forcing functions can reduce overreliance on AI in ai-assisted decision-making. Proc. ACM Hum. Comput. Interact. **5**(CSCW1), 188:1–188:21 (2021). https://doi.org/10.1145/3449287
7. Cacioppo, J.T., Petty, R.E.: The need for cognition. J. Personal. Soc. Psychol. **42**(1), 116 (1982)
8. Chen, C., Feng, S., Sharma, A., et al.: Machine explanations and human understanding. In: Proceedings of the 2023 ACM Conference on Fairness, Accountability, and Transparency, FAccT 2023, Chicago, IL, June 12–15, 2023. ACM, p. 1 (2023). https://doi.org/10.1145/3593013.3593970
9. Dash, S., Günlük, O., Wei, D.: Boolean decision rules via column generation. In: Bengio, S., Wallach, H.M., Larochelle, H., et al. (eds) Advances in Neural Information Processing Systems 31: Annual Conference on Neural Information Processing Systems 2018, NeurIPS 2018, December 3–8, 2018, Montréal, pp. 4660–4670 (2018). https://proceedings.neurips.cc/paper/2018/hash/743394beff4b1282ba735e5e3723ed74-Abstract.html
10. David, L., Vassena, E., Bijleveld, E.: The unpleasantness of thinking: a meta-analytic review of the association between mental effort and negative affect. Psychol. Bull. (2024) https://doi.org/10.1037/bul0000443. https://psycnet.apa.org/record/2025-07056-001?doi=1
11. Dhurandhar, A., Chen, P., Luss, R., et al.: Explanations based on the missing: Towards contrastive explanations with pertinent negatives. In: Bengio, S., Wallach, H.M., Larochelle, H., et al. (eds) Advances in Neural Information Processing Systems 31: Annual Conference on Neural Information Processing Systems 2018, NeurIPS 2018, December 3–8, 2018, Montréal, pp. 590–601 (2018). https://proceedings.neurips.cc/paper/2018/hash/c5ff2543b53f4cc0ad3819a36752467b-Abstract.html
12. Evans, J.S.B., Stanovich, K.E.: Dual-process theories of higher cognition: Advancing the debate. Perspect. Psychol. Sci. **8**(3), 223–241 (2013)
13. Feldhus, N., Hennig, L., Nasert, M.D., et al.: Constructing natural language explanations via saliency map verbalization. arXiv preprint arXiv:221007222 (2022)
14. Fok, R., Weld, D.S.: In search of verifiability: Explanations rarely enable complementary performance in ai-advised decision making. AI Mag. **45**(3), 317–332 (2024). https://doi.org/10.1002/aaai.12182
15. Fung, G., Sandilya, S., Rao, R.B.: Rule extraction from linear support vector machines. In: Grossman, R., Bayardo, R.J., Bennett, K.P. (eds) Proceedings of the Eleventh ACM SIGKDD International Conference on Knowledge Discovery and Data Mining, Chicago, Illinois, August 21–24, 2005, pp 32–40. ACM (2005). https://doi.org/10.1145/1081870.1081878
16. Ghorbani, A., Wexler, J., Zou, J.Y., et al.: Towards automatic concept-based explanations. In: Advances in Neural Information Processing Systems, pp. 9273–9282 (2019). https://proceedings.neurips.cc/paper/2019/hash/77d2afcb31f6493e350fca61764efb9a-Abstract.html
17. Guidotti, R.: Counterfactual explanations and how to find them: literature review and benchmarking. Data Min. Knowl. Discov. **38**(5), 2770–2824 (2024). https://doi.org/10.1007/s10618-022-00831-6
18. Gurumoorthy, K.S., Dhurandhar, A., Cecchi, G.: Protodash: Fast interpretable prototype selection. arXiv preprint arXiv:170701212 (2017)
19. He, M., An, B., Wang, J., et al.: Counterfactual explanations for sequential recommendation with temporal dependencies. In: Zhang, F., Wang, H., Barhamgi, M., et al. (eds) Web Information Systems Engineering - WISE 2023 - 24th International Conference, Melbourne,

VIC, October 25–27, 2023, Proceedings, Lecture Notes in Computer Science, vol. 14306, pp. 533–543. Springer (2023). https://doi.org/10.1007/978-981-99-7254-8_41
20. Islam, M.R., Ahmed, M.U., Barua, S., et al.: A systematic review of explainable artificial intelligence in terms of different application domains and tasks. Appl. Sci. **12**(3), 1353 (2022). https://www.mdpi.com/2076-3417/12/3/1353
21. Kim, B., Wattenberg, M., Gilmer, J., et al.: Interpretability beyond feature attribution: Quantitative testing with concept activation vectors (TCAV). In: Dy, J.G., Krause, A. (eds) Proceedings of the 35th International Conference on Machine Learning, ICML 2018, Stockholmsmässan, Stockholm, Sweden, July 10–15, 2018, Proceedings of Machine Learning Research, vol. 80, pp. 2673–2682. PMLR (2018). http://proceedings.mlr.press/v80/kim18d.html
22. Koh, P.W., Nguyen, T., Tang, Y.S., et al.: Concept Bottleneck models. In: International Conference on Machine Learning, abs/2007.04612, pp. 5338–5348 (2020). https://proceedings.mlr.press/v119/koh20a. 2007.04612
23. Li, J., Zhang, C., Zhou, J.T., et al.: Deep-lift: deep label-specific feature learning for image annotation. IEEE Trans. Cybern. **52**(8), 7732–7741 (2022). https://doi.org/10.1109/TCYB.2021.3049630
24. Liao, Q.V., Gruen, D.M., Miller, S.: Questioning the AI: Informing design practices for explainable AI user experiences. In: Bernhaupt, R., Mueller, F.F., Verweij, D., et al. (eds.) CHI '20: CHI Conference on Human Factors in Computing Systems, Honolulu, HI, April 25–30, 2020, pp. 1–15. ACM (2020). https://doi.org/10.1145/3313831.3376590
25. Lundberg, S.M., Lee, S. (2017) A unified approach to interpreting model predictions. In: Guyon, I., von Luxburg, U., Bengio, S., et al. (eds.) Advances in Neural Information Processing Systems 30: Annual Conference on Neural Information Processing Systems 2017, December 4–9, 2017, Long Beach, CA, pp. 4765–4774. https://proceedings.neurips.cc/paper/2017/hash/8a20a8621978632d76c43dfd28b67767-Abstract.html
26. Lundberg, S.M., Erion, G.G., Chen, H., et al.: From local explanations to global understanding with explainable AI for trees. Nat. Mach. Intell. **2**(1), 56–67 (2020). https://doi.org/10.1038/s42256-019-0138-9
27. Miller, T.: Explainable AI is dead, long live explainable ai!: Hypothesis-driven decision support using evaluative AI. In: Proceedings of the 2023 ACM Conference on Fairness, Accountability, and Transparency, FAccT 2023, Chicago, IL, June 12–15, 2023, pp. 333–342. ACM (2023). https://doi.org/10.1145/3593013.3594001
28. Mothilal, R.K., Sharma, A., Tan, C.: Explaining machine learning classifiers through diverse counterfactual explanations. In: Hildebrandt, M., Castillo, C., Celis, L.E., et al. (eds.) FAT* '20: Conference on Fairness, Accountability, and Transparency, Barcelona, January 27–30, 2020, pp 607–617. ACM (2020). https://doi.org/10.1145/3351095.3372850
29. Nauta, M., Trienes, J., Pathak, S., et al.: From anecdotal evidence to quantitative evaluation methods: a systematic review on evaluating explainable AI. ACM Comput. Surv. **55**(13s), 295:1–295:42 (2023). https://doi.org/10.1145/3583558
30. Poché, A., Hervier, L., Bakkay, M.C.: Natural example-based explainability: A survey. In: Longo, L. (ed) Explainable Artificial Intelligence - First World Conference, xAI 2023, Lisbon, Portugal, July 26-28, 2023, Proceedings, Part II, Communications in Computer and Information Science, vol. 1902, pp. 24–47. Springer (2023). https://doi.org/10.1007/978-3-031-44067-0_2
31. Poursabzi-Sangdeh, F., Goldstein, D.G., Hofman, J.M., et al.: Manipulating and measuring model interpretability. In: Proceedings of the 2021 CHI Conference on Human Factors in Computing Systems, pp. 1–52. Association for Computing Machinery, New York, NY (2021). https://doi.org/10.1145/3411764.3445315
32. Research, I.: AI explainability 360 - demo (2020). https://aix360.res.ibm.com/data. Accessed: 25 Nov 2024
33. Ribeiro, M.T., Singh, S., Guestrin, C.: Model-agnostic interpretability of machine learning. CoRR **abs/1606.05386** (2016). http://arxiv.org/abs/1606.05386

34. Ribeiro, M.T., Singh, S., Guestrin, C.: "why should I trust you?": Explaining the predictions of any classifier. In: Krishnapuram, B., Shah, M., Smola, A.J., et al. (eds.) Proceedings of the 22nd ACM SIGKDD International Conference on Knowledge Discovery and Data Mining, San Francisco, CA, August 13–17, 2016, pp. 1135–1144. ACM (2016). https://doi.org/10.1145/2939672.2939778
35. Ribeiro, M.T., Singh, S., Guestrin, C.: Anchors: High-precision model-agnostic explanations. In: McIlraith, S.A., Weinberger, K.Q. (eds.) Proceedings of the Thirty-Second AAAI Conference on Artificial Intelligence, (AAAI-18), the 30th Innovative Applications of Artificial Intelligence (IAAI-18), and the 8th AAAI Symposium on Educational Advances in Artificial Intelligence (EAAI-18), New Orleans, Louisiana, February 2–7, 2018, pp. 1527–1535. AAAI Press (2018). https://doi.org/10.1609/aaai.v32i1.11491
36. Selvaraju, R.R., Cogswell M, Das, A., et al.: Grad-cam: visual explanations from deep networks via gradient-based localization. Int. J. Comput. Vis. **128**(2), 336–359 (2020). https://doi.org/10.1007/s11263-019-01228-7
37. Siu, H.C., Leahy, K., Mann, M.: How interpretable is "interpretable" machine learning? MIT Case Studies in Social and Ethical Responsibilities of Computing (2024). https://doi.org/10.21428/2c646de5.9e0237cb. https://mit-serc.pubpub.org/pub/5kduhf9d/download/pdf
38. Sivaraman, V., Bukowski, L.A., Levin, J., et al.: Ignore, trust, or negotiate: Understanding clinician acceptance of ai-based treatment recommendations in health care. In: Schmidt, A., Väänänen, K., Goyal, T., et al. (eds.) Proceedings of the 2023 CHI Conference on Human Factors in Computing Systems, CHI 2023, Hamburg, April 23–28, 2023, pp 754:1–754:18. ACM (2023). https://doi.org/10.1145/3544548.3581075
39. Sovrano, F., Vilone, G.: Aligning XAI with EU regulations for smart biomedical devices: A methodology for compliance analysis. In: Endriss, U., Melo, F.S., Bach, K., et al. (eds.) ECAI 2024 - 27th European Conference on Artificial Intelligence, 19–24 October 2024, Santiago de Compostela, - Including 13th Conference on Prestigious Applications of Intelligent Systems (PAIS 2024), Frontiers in Artificial Intelligence and Applications, vol. 392, , pp 826–833. IOS Press (2024). https://doi.org/10.3233/FAIA240568
40. Sovrano, F., Vitali, F.: Explanatory artificial intelligence (YAI): human-centered explanations of explainable AI and complex data. Data Min. Knowl. Discov. **38**(5), 3141–3168 (2024). https://doi.org/10.1007/s10618-022-00872-x
41. Sovrano, F., Sapienza, S., Palmirani, M., et al.: A survey on methods and metrics for the assessment of explainability under the proposed AI act. In: Schweighofer, E. (ed.) Legal Knowledge and Information Systems - JURIX 2021: The Thirty-fourth Annual Conference, Vilnius, Lithuania, 8–10 December 2021, Frontiers in Artificial Intelligence and Applications, vol. 346, pp. 235–242. IOS Press (2021). https://doi.org/10.3233/FAIA210342
42. Sundararajan, M., Taly, A., Yan, Q.: Axiomatic attribution for deep networks. In: Precup, D., Teh, Y.W. (eds.) Proceedings of the 34th International Conference on Machine Learning, ICML 2017, Sydney, NSW, 6–11 August 2017, Proceedings of Machine Learning Research, vol. 70, pp. 3319–3328. PMLR (2017). http://proceedings.mlr.press/v70/sundararajan17a.html
43. Vaccaro, M., Almaatouq, A., Malone, T.: When combinations of humans and AI are useful: a systematic review and meta-analysis. Nat. Human Behav. **8**, 1–11 (2024). https://doi.org/10.1038/s41562-024-02024-1. https://www.nature.com/articles/s41562-024-02024-1
44. van der Velden, B.H.M., Kuijf, H.J., Gilhuijs, K.G.A., et al.: Explainable artificial intelligence (XAI) in deep learning-based medical image analysis. Med. Image. Anal. **79**, 102470 (2022). https://doi.org/10.1016/j.media.2022.102470
45. Vasconcelos, H., Jörke, M., Grunde-McLaughlin, M., et al.: Explanations can reduce overreliance on AI systems during decision-making. Proc. ACM Hum. Comput. Interact. **7**(CSCW1), 1–38 (2023). https://doi.org/10.1145/3579605
46. Vilone, G., Longo, L.: Classification of explainable artificial intelligence methods through their output formats. Mach. Learn. Knowl. Extr. **3**(3), 615–661 (2021). https://doi.org/10.3390/make3030032
47. Von Winterfeldt, D., Edwards, W.: Decision Analysis and Behavioral Research. Cambridge University Press, Cambridge 1986 (1993)

48. Wachter, S., Mittelstadt, B.D., Russell, C.: Counterfactual explanations without opening the black box: automated decisions and the GDPR. CoRR **abs/1711.00399** (2017). http://arxiv.org/abs/1711.00399
49. Wang, J., Wiens, J., Lundberg, S.M.: Shapley flow: A graph-based approach to interpreting model predictions. In: Banerjee, A., Fukumizu, K. (eds.) The 24th International Conference on Artificial Intelligence and Statistics, AISTATS 2021, April 13–15, 2021, Virtual Event, Proceedings of Machine Learning Research, vol. 130, pp. 721–729. PMLR (2021). http://proceedings.mlr.press/v130/wang21b.html
50. Wei, D., Dash, S., Gao, T., et al.: Generalized linear rule models. In: Chaudhuri, K., Salakhutdinov, R. (eds.) Proceedings of the 36th International Conference on Machine Learning, ICML 2019, 9–15 June 2019, Long Beach, CA, Proceedings of Machine Learning Research, vol. 97, pp. 6687–6696. PMLR (2019). http://proceedings.mlr.press/v97/wei19a.html
51. Xu, W., Dainoff, M.J., Ge, L., et al.: From human-computer interaction to human-ai interaction: new challenges and opportunities for enabling human-centered ai. arXiv preprint arXiv:210505424 5 (2021)
52. Zhang, R., Madumal, P., Miller, T., et al.: Invertible concept-based explanations for CNN models with non-negative concept activation vectors. In: Proceedings of the AAAI Conference on Artificial Intelligence vol. 35, no. 13, pp. 11682–11690 (2021). https://doi.org/10.1609/aaai.v35i13.17389. https://ojs.aaai.org/index.php/AAAI/article/view/17389

Francesco Sovrano is a Computer Scientist and Data-Science Researcher specializing in explainable AI. He earned his PhD in Data Science and Computation in 2023 from the University of Bologna (in association with the Polytechnic University of Milan), where he developed a computational theory of explanations with applica-tions in human-computer interaction, regulatory compliance, and AI. As a postdoctoral researcher at the University of Zurich, he applied these theories to empirical software engineering. He later became an early-career fellow at ETH Zurich's Collegium Helveticum, designing XAI tools to uncover biases in LLM-generated explanations. Francesco is currently a postdoc at the University of Italian Switzerland (USI), working on explainable AI for financial crime detection and prevention in collaboration with Deloitte Zurich.

Tim Miller is a Professor of Artificial Intelligence at The University of Queensland, and TIET-UQ Chair of Data Science and AI. His research focuses on improving the capabilities of expert decision-makers by using artificial intelligence to do the hard things. He draws on machine learning, reinforcement learning, AI planning, interaction design, and cognitive science. Previously, he was a Professor at The University of Melbourne, where he co-founded the Centre for AI and Digital Ethics.

Chapter 7
The Enterprising and Elusive Prospects of Human-AI Collaboration

Ujwal Gadiraju and Agathe Balayn

Abstract The exponential advances in generative AI and agentic technologies have presented organizations with an unprecedented opportunity to seek and attain competitive advantages. Some aim to do so through product and service innovation, while others have begun to pursue operational efficiency and productivity. There is a pivotal role that human-AI collaboration can play in enterprise artificial intelligence design, development, and deployment today. In this chapter, we synthesize developments in human-AI collaboration over the last decade and explore how organizations can design AI systems that augment rather than replace human capabilities to achieve optimal experiential and performance-related outcomes for different stakeholders. Drawing from empirical work across different domains, we analyze the key factors that shape trust and reliance and determine successful human-AI collaboration. This includes various human factors, task factors, and AI system factors and the complex interplay between them in different configurations. This synthesis reflects the importance of broadening the spectrum of metrics for evaluating human-AI collaboration (e.g., by considering stakeholder values). We discuss promising ideas to address common challenges such as under-reliance or over-reliance on AI systems. We argue for broadening the lens of human-AI collaboration to consider the AI supply chain and the underlying value chains to ensure the responsible design of enterprise AI. Our insights collectively suggest that enterprise AI will benefit from the human-centered approach while creating collaborative workflows and human-AI configurations that can augment and complement humans with the computational power and scalability of AI.

U. Gadiraju (✉)
Delft University of Technology, Delft, The Netherlands
e-mail: u.k.gadiraju@tudelft.nl

A. Balayn
Microsoft Research, New York, NY, USA
e-mail: balaynagathe@microsoft.com

S. Sadiq (ed.), *Enterprise AI*, https://doi.org/10.1007/978-3-032-01940-0_7

7.1 Introduction

The fundamental essence of *human-AI collaboration* is not novel. Similar ideas were proposed and discussed as early as in 1960 by Licklider [1]. Over the last few years, we have witnessed increasing adoption of AI systems across different domains and around the world. Opportunities created by the potential of AI technologies have been met with euphoric enthusiasm and scathing skepticism in equal parts—and for good reason. On the one hand, advances in machine learning and AI have led to remarkable breakthroughs. In healthcare, systems like AlphaFold have revolutionized protein structure prediction, leading to an unprecedented acceleration in drug discovery and development [2, 3]. There is growing evidence suggesting the potential of AI systems for question-answering related to medicine, medical diagnosis, and precision medicine [4–7]. AI systems have also been built to good effect in pursuit of climate modeling [8] and conservation of biodiversity [9]. AI-powered chatbots have transformed customer service [10] and are being adopted in healthcare and education to solve a variety of challenges [11–14]. From transportation to finance and entertainment, the list of positive footprints of AI technologies goes on. On the other hand, the frantic adoption of AI systems across the world has also led to unforeseen and unfortunate consequences. These have been well-documented by media, journalists, and other efforts that have led to systematically capturing such "*AI incidents*" in a database to prevent repeated AI harms or failures [15]. In this context, researchers and practitioners across different communities have proposed frameworks, tools, and methods to build responsible, ethical, trustworthy, safe, robust, meaningful, transparent, and *human-centered* AI systems—with often overlapping goals and objectives [16–21].

Many Flavors of Human-AI Collaboration and Teaming
The potential of AI systems to support, complement, and augment the skills and capabilities of humans across different tasks has led to widespread applications in human-AI collaborative configurations with varying effectiveness [22–27]. For instance, Sowa et al. explored synergies between human workers and AI in managerial tasks, identifying an increased productivity due to human–AI collaboration [28]. There is a growing footprint of AutoAI or AutoML in data science, wherein data scientists are aided by automated workflows that simplify their practices [29]. Jiang et al. explored task delegability in human-AI collaboration in the context of qualitative analysis and found that the design of AI assistance that honor serendipity and human agency are necessary for meaningful collaboration [30]. More recently, Rastogi et al. highlighted the complementary strengths of humans and generative models in collaborative auditing of large language models (LLMs) [31].

Prior work has explored the prospect of integrating AI systems into human teams to achieve shared goals [32–35]. In contrast to human-AI collaboration where humans and AI work together on a given task but maintain relatively distinct roles and responsibilities, human-AI teaming entails a dynamic relationship, resembling the interaction between human team members with AI as an active participant.[1] While human-AI collaboration has largely been associated with the notion of using AI as a functional assistant, human-AI teaming predominantly corresponds to integrating AI as an adaptive and autonomous partner in a shared process. These distinctions, however, have not always been made consistently in existing literature spanning both conceptualizations. Thus, there is some overlap across these realms of work. In the context of multiplayer online games, Zhang et al. found that people reported mixed feelings toward AI teammates but exhibited a generally positive attitude toward future collaboration with AI teammates [38]. In other empirical work, Zhang et al. assessed the effects of teammate identity (comparing human versus AI) and teammate performance (comparing low-performing versus high-performing AI) on human-AI cooperation [39].

He et al. explored the potential of using LLM agents with humans-in-the-loop for planning tasks and found that LLM agents can work effectively when a high-quality plan and necessary user involvement in execution are available and that users can easily mistrust LLM agents with plans that seem plausible [40]. In the evolving area of explainable AI, recent evidence has shown that the use of LLM agents can result in amplifying over-reliance on AI systems by creating an illusory depth in explanations [41]. Over the last decade, a number of empirical qualitative and quantitative studies have contributed to a wealth of knowledge around how we can design for better human-AI collaboration and build effective human-AI teams [42, 43].

Considering that organizations and companies are invested in optimizing their business and operations with AI [44], it is important to address and understand the potential of human-AI collaboration for enterprise AI. Recent work at the intersection of HCI and AI has identified *calibrated trust* as an important need for appropriate interaction with assistive AI [45]. Some pivotal questions that arise in this context are:

- How can AI systems assist and support human decision-making while optimizing for trade-offs that affect enterprises?
- How can we foster appropriate trust and reliance on collaborative decision-support systems in enterprises?

This chapter unpacks recent findings in human-AI collaboration and reflects on future directions for enterprise AI. To this end, we first present an overview of the notions of trust and reliance on AI systems that have been proposed in existing literature and then synthesize findings around factors that shape human-AI

[1] Note that there are further conceptualizations of combining human and machine intelligence, such as *hybrid intelligence* [36, 37]. Though relevant, this remains beyond the scope of our chapter.

collaboration. Note that our view on *trust* considers it as a mechanism that can foster effective collaboration between humans and AI systems, as opposed to considering *trust* as an end goal that we should strive to optimize for [46].

7.2 Trust and Reliance on AI Systems

In their impactful work on *trust in automation*, Lee and See defined trust as the attitude that an agent will help achieve an individual's goals in a situation characterized by uncertainty and vulnerability [47]. They argued that subjective trust can guide and influence objective behavior and interactions (i.e., reliance) with an automated system. Hoff and Bashir reviewed empirical research on factors that influence trust in automation, published between 2002 and 2013, and proposed a three-layered interdependent trust model [48]. This consists of (i) *dispositional trust* that represents an individual's overall tendency to trust automation, independent of context or a specific system; (ii) *situational trust* that represents the variability in trust depending on different contexts; and (iii) *learned trust* that represents an individual's assessment of a system based on past experience or the current interaction.

More recently, the notion of regulating one's *trust in an AI system* and thereby informing their reliance on said system, preventing disuse and over-use (i.e., under-reliance and over-reliance), and relying on AI advice only when it is credible and warranted has been referred to as the pursuit of facilitating *appropriate trust*. Evidence from different empirical studies suggests that all three layers of the inter-dependent trust model [48] have been shown to influence appropriate trust. Over the last decade, researchers in HCI and AI have explored a number of methods to foster appropriate trust and reliance in human-AI interactions to pave the way for optimal human-AI collaboration.

Mehrotra et al. carried out a comprehensive and systematic review of the growing literature on fostering appropriate trust in AI [49]. In their work, the authors also shed light on different concepts related to appropriate trust, including warranted trust [50], justified trust [51], contractual trust [52, 53], and calibrated trust [54, 55]. Jacovi et al. proposed a formalization of trust and how to design trustworthy AI [52]. The authors discuss the possible causes of warranted trust as intrinsic reasoning and extrinsic behavior. More recently, Schlicker et al. proposed a two-level trustworthiness assessment model (TrAM) that applies psychological models to evaluate system trustworthiness [56] and distinguishes system characteristics, actual and perceived trustworthiness, individual standards, and cues. Miller proposed methods to measure perceived and demonstrated trust [57]. Several empirical works studying human-AI interaction and collaboration have operationalized and leveraged these underpinnings of trust in AI to assess novel methods and their effectiveness in fostering appropriate trust and reliance on AI systems [25, 58]. In particular, there is a growing body of work exploring the potential of AI to aid human decision-

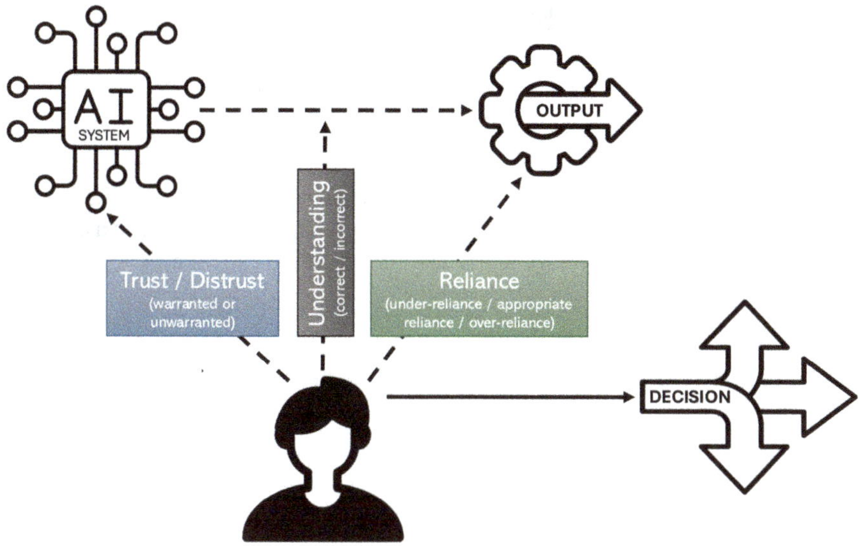

Fig. 7.1 Relation between *trust*, *reliance*, and the appropriateness of their reliance in human-AI collaboration contexts (e.g., decision-making). Users may trust or distrust an AI system, and this may either be warranted or unwarranted. Their understanding of the process through which the AI system reaches its output, or the AI system's rationale behind its advice, can play an important role in shaping their reliance on the AI output (e.g., using AI assistance in a decision-making task)

making [59–63]. In fact, optimizing decision workflows has been identified as an avenue that bears immense potential for enterprise AI [44].

In summary (see Fig. 7.1), while trust plays a central role in shaping the effectiveness of decision workflows, it is ill advised to pursue trust as a goal in and of itself. It is far more beneficial to view fostering *appropriate* trust as a means to facilitate effective human-AI collaboration and team performance [41, 46, 64]. In that vein, it is worth asking whether appropriate trust is sufficient to achieve effective human-AI collaboration. It is now understood that although (appropriate) trust plays a foundational role in human-AI collaboration, it does not solely lead to effective human-AI collaboration (i.e., it is necessary but not sufficient). Several critical factors influence the effectiveness of human-AI collaboration—complementary capabilities, feedback mechanisms, and technical qualities of the AI system, among others. For example, consider the prospect of complementary capabilities [65]. In industrial or manufacturing settings [66], predictive maintenance systems proficiently identify patterns in different types of data that predict equipment failure, while human operators contribute contextual knowledge about specific machines and their operating conditions. In such a collaborative context where appropriate trust on an AI system exists but there is a lack of complementary capability, benefits of the collaboration cannot be reaped.

7.3 Key Factors That Shape Outcomes in Human-AI Collaboration

In this section, we present an overview of the multitude of factors that have been shown to influence user trust, as well as experiential outcomes and team performance in human-AI collaboration. These factors (presented in Table 7.1), together with human-AI configurations (see Table 7.2), blend together in a complex interplay that shapes team performance and the perceived experiences.

7.3.1 Human Factors

A number of human factors and individual traits have been shown to influence and shape both experiential outcomes and performance outcomes in human-AI interaction and collaboration. These factors need to be considered while designing decision workflows or interactions with AI systems in the context of enterprise AI.

AI literacy, i.e., the proficiency of humans in different domains of AI that can enable the efficient, meaningful, and ethical use of AI technologies, has been widely identified as being a crucial factor in regulating AI adoption and

Table 7.1 An overview of the factors that have been shown to shape trust and affect human-AI collaboration in prior work. References serve as examples of works that have studied corresponding factors. Note that this is not an exhaustive summary of all relevant factors surfaced in existing literature but a representation of some key factors that have been methodically studied and are well understood to play an important role

Human factors	Task factors	AI system factors
AI literacy [67–69]	Complexity [70]	Interpretability and explainability [72]
Domain knowledge [71]	Uncertainty [63]	
Domain expertise [73]	Stakes [61, 74]	Accuracy [75, 76]
Mental models [77]	Task context (e.g., time constraints, pressure [82, 83])	Reliability [78, 79]
Prior experience [80, 81]		Trustworthiness [57]
Cognitive biases [80, 84]		Interface (e.g., modality, feedback, accessibility) [87, 88]
User expectations [85, 86]		
Culture and values [89, 90]		

Table 7.2 Different aspects of human-AI configurations that have been shown to shape experiential and performance-related outcomes in human-AI collaboration

Human-AI configurations
Distribution of control [18]
Individual versus collaborative use [116, 129, 130]
Organizational dynamics, policies [131]
Interdependency [132]

fostering appropriate trust and reliance on AI systems, consequently paving a way for effective human-AI collaboration. Cetindamar et al. identified four sets of capabilities associated with AI literacy—(i) technology-related, (ii) work-related, (iii) human-machine-related, and (iv) learning-related capabilities—and pointed out the importance of operationalizing AI literacy for non-AI professionals [91]. Over the last few years, there have been several efforts to develop AI literacy scales [68, 69, 92, 93] to understand the role and assess the impact of AI literacy on human-AI collaboration on one hand and efforts to increase AI literacy in society to help people effectively interact with and critically evaluate AI systems on the other [67, 94–96].

Hoffman et al. presented a broad overview of ***mental model*** elicitation methods and their application in the context of explainable AI [97]. The authors highlighted that user mental models represent their understanding of an AI system and its context, including the task, goals, and current situation. Bansal et al. found that human *mental models of AI capabilities* and their awareness of when to accept or override an AI system's recommendation (based on their mental models) affect the resulting team performance [77]. Andrews et al. proposed a conceptual model for the application of literature on "shared mental models" in human teams to the context of human-AI collaboration [98]. Gero et al. studied people's mental models of AI agents in a cooperative word-guessing game [99]. The authors found that people have existing intuitions about how AI systems work and that such intuitions can be disrupted when they encounter specific AI systems. They also characterized the capability of people to revise their mental models of the AI system in the face of encountering anomalies.

Researchers have also studied how *user expectations* and various AI metaphors influence and shape experiential and performance outcomes in human-AI collaboration. Khadpe et al. found that conceptual metaphors used to describe AI systems can shape user expectations and behavior in human-AI collaboration [85]. Similarly, in the context of conversational crowdsourcing, Jung et al. found that different human and non-human metaphors can affect worker engagement, their perceived cognitive load in various tasks, their intrinsic motivation, and their trust in the agents [86]. Cabrera et al. found that showing users behavior descriptions of AI systems, i.e., details of how AI systems perform on subgroups of instances, can improve the performance of human-AI teams across different tasks [100]. Furthermore, Nourani et al. uncovered and synthesized the role of various *experiential biases* in shaping user mental models and outcomes in their interactions or collaboration with AI systems [101]. For instance, first impressions of AI systems have been shown to weigh heavily on influencing user expectations and reliance behavior on AI systems [102]. However, some prospects for the evolution of perceptions beyond first impressions have also been found [81] in different contexts.

Domain knowledge**, **experience**, and **expertise have all been identified as factors that affect human-AI collaboration. Zhang et al. explored how users trust and rely on an AI assistant that performs with different levels of expertise relative to themselves, ranging from completely overlapping expertise to perfectly complementary expertise. The authors found that participants were able to perceive when the assistant was an expert or non-expert within the same task and calibrate their reliance on the AI to improve team performance [73]. To optimize human-AI team performance, Wilder et al. carried out a systematic exploration of how machine learning systems can be trained to complement human reasoning [103]. Through a controlled study in a human-AI collaboration task, Nourani et al. explored the role of domain knowledge in establishing trust and susceptibility to the influence of first impressions on user trust [71]. The authors found a differing impact on domain experts versus novice users. Encountering errors early on caused negative first impressions for some domain experts, negatively impacting their trust over the course of interactions. In contrast, novice users were found to suffer from over-reliance due to their lack of proper knowledge to detect errors. Inkpen et al. explored the interplay between user expertise and complementarity of AI systems on human-AI collaboration [60]. The authors found that novice users demonstrated improvements in performance by relying on AI advice, highly proficient users were able to discern when to follow AI advice and typically maintained or improved their performance as a result of the collaboration, and that mid-performers (with a similar level of accuracy to the AI) were most variable in terms of whether the AI advice helped or hurt their performance. However, there is growing evidence suggesting that achieving optimal human-AI team performance can be challenging. Agarwal et al. found that providing expert radiologists with AI predictions does not always improve performance, whereas contextual information does. Radiologists do not realize the gains from AI assistance because of errors in belief updating—they underweight AI predictions and treat their own information and AI predictions as statistically independent. Unless these mistakes can be corrected, the optimal human-AI collaboration design delegates cases either to humans or to AI, but rarely to AI-assisted humans.

That humans are susceptible to a plethora of ***cognitive** and **behavioral biases*** that influence how different tasks are carried out is a well-established fact [104, 105]. Prior work has unveiled how biases can surface in different contexts of human-AI collaboration. Echterhoff et al. explored a specific type of anchoring bias in which decision-makers are anchored by their own recent decisions and found that it is possible to combine the strengths of AI systems and humans to enable fairer decisions in sequential decision-making tasks [106]. Through a controlled study, Nourani et al. found that users who observed strengths of an AI system early on in their interactions were more prone to automation bias and made significantly more errors due to positive first impressions of the system and that users who encountered weaknesses of an AI system earlier made significantly fewer errors since they tended to rely more on themselves [80]. Building on work from the field of cognitive science, Rastogi et al. proposed a general framework to account for cognitive biases in the human-AI collaborative decision-making setting and mitigate their negative effects on team performance [107]. Based on their empirical exploration of human-AI collaboration, Jacobsen et al. discussed the gap between perceived and measured task effectiveness [108]. He et al. showed that the meta-cognitive bias of the Dunning-Kruger Effect can have a detrimental effect on team performance in human-AI collaboration [84]. The authors found that participants who overestimated their performance tended to exhibit under-reliance on AI systems, which in turn hindered optimal team performance.

Erlei et al. found that humans tend to overwrite their economic self-interest to avoid bargaining with AI systems [64], and also that humans consistently violate the choice independence assumption when delegating predictions to a superior AI system [213]. Vodrahalli et al. highlight the importance of modeling human interaction when designing AI systems for human use [24]. Drawing from empirical findings across different tasks, they reflected on the importance of jointly optimizing the human-AI collaborative system instead of the predominant paradigm of optimizing the AI model alone. Biswas et al. found that bilingual writers demonstrated biased behavior when interacting with an AI co-writing agent, wherein prior exposure to a Spanish LLM reduced subsequent utilization of a better-performing English LLM in a persuasive charitable giving task [109].

There is an increasing understanding and recognition of the role of ***culture*** and human ***values*** in shaping human interactions with AI systems [89, 110–113]. Considering the progress in AI regulation around the world and an echoing rally to ensure AI systems adhere to certain values, van de Poel identified the complex challenges and opportunities of embedding values in AI systems [89]. In line with the grand objective of aligning AI with human values [114], Hendrycks et al. proposed a method to assess a language model's knowledge of basic concepts of morality [112]. Seth et al. found a significant variation across different language models in their ability to infer artifacts across regional sub-cultures in India [113].

7.3.2 Task Factors

Different task characteristics have been shown to influence both experiential and performance-related outcomes in human-AI collaboration [115, 116]. This section presents an overview of such task factors.

Lai et al. surveyed prior work in human-AI collaboration and identified four dimensions of task characteristics that varied in the tasks: (1) ***task risk*** or ***stakes*** (e.g., high, low, or artificial stakes), (2) ***required expertise*** in the task, (3) ***decision subjectivity***, and (4) AI for ***emulation*** versus ***discovery*** [61]. A recent empirical study by Baron et al. explored the impact of stakes of the decision (high versus low) and the decision source (human versus AI) on user perceptions of explanations for AI systems in medical contexts [74]. The authors found that the effectiveness of explanations may not depend on the type of explanation but instead on the stakes and decision source.

Salimzadeh et al. argued that the variety in decision-making tasks empirically studied in the context of human-AI collaboration and their operationalization has led to an opacity around how findings from one task or domain carry forward to another [70]. The authors proposed measuring ***task complexity*** to tackle the problem of under-specification and facilitate comparison across empirical research in human-AI collaboration. Tomsett et al. proposed that the objectives of imbuing

AI systems with interpretability and uncertainty-awareness can allow for rapid trust calibration among decision-makers, by facilitating the understanding of an AI system's limitations and likely failures [117]. Prabhudesai et al. explored how and why lay decision-makers utilize ML ***uncertainty*** information in their decision process [118]. Through a qualitative study, they found that communicating uncertainty about a machine learning model's predictions forced participants to slow down and think analytically about their decisions. Other empirical work by Salimzadeh et al. found that when users are presented with complex and uncertain tasks, they tended to rely more on AI systems while demonstrating lower levels of appropriate reliance compared to tasks that were less complex and uncertain [63].

Cao et al. empirically studied human decision-making behavior and task performance under ***time pressure*** that is either induced from limited initial observation time or final decision time (i.e., the time to weigh an AI's suggestion before reaching a collective human-AI team answer) [83]. The authors found that users tended to follow AI suggestions when they were provided with a longer final decision time. In a similar context of studying human-AI collaboration under time pressure, Swaroop et al. found that different types of AI assistance have different accuracy-time trade-offs when people are under time pressure compared to no time pressure [82].

7.3.3 AI System Factors

This section presents an overview of how different attributes of an AI system,[2] ranging from its interpretability to accuracy and reliability, play a role in shaping performance and experiences in human-AI collaboration.

Several efforts have been made to communicate AI system predictions, advice, or output to human stakeholders—from stating system accuracy to generating ***explanations***—with varying outcomes [75, 76, 119]. Yin et al. found that users' trust in a model is affected by both its ***stated accuracy*** and its observed accuracy and that the effect of stated accuracy can change depending on the observed accuracy [75]. However, He et al. explored the impact of communicating system accuracy on human-AI collaboration outcomes and found that explaining the stated accuracy of a system using analogies failed to help users rely on the AI system appropriately [76]. Rechkemmer et al. investigated user trust in AI when multiple performance indicators are presented at the same time [120]. The authors found that while the level of ***model confidence*** significantly affects people's belief in model accuracy, both the model's stated and observed accuracy generally have a larger impact on people's willingness to follow the model's predictions.

[2] In this chapter, we use the phrase "an AI system" interchangeably with an AI-based system, a machine learning model, a decision-support system, an AI assistant, or an algorithmic decision aid.

Senoner et al. carried out experiments with real-world visual inspection tasks in the domain of manufacturing and medicine to understand the impact of explainable AI aids on human-AI collaboration [72]. They found that domain experts performing the tasks demonstrated a significant improvement in their performance when they were supported by explainable AI aids in the form of visual heatmaps. Ahn et al. investigated how interpretability and ***outcome feedback*** influence users' task performance and trust in AI [121]. In contrast to other findings suggesting that interpretability can drive trust, the authors found that interpretability led to no robust improvements in trust and that outcome feedback had a significantly greater and more reliable effect. Similarly, in a controlled experiment with AI practitioners, Kaur et al. found that participants spent significantly less time on tasks and were far less accurate about the data and model when they were given access to interpretability tools [122]. This complements earlier results showcasing how data scientists tend to over-trust and misuse interpretability tools [123].

Through mixed-method user studies, Bansal et al. found complementary improvements resulting from human-AI collaboration and also that such benefits were not increased by using explanations. They found that explanations instead increased the likelihood of humans accepting the AI system's recommendation, regardless of its correctness [59]. In other work, Bansal et al. explored the influence of ***technical updates*** to an AI system in a human-AI collaboration context. They found that although updates can be made to increase the system's performance, they can also lead to behavioral changes that deviate from users' prior experiences and confidence in the AI system's inferences, thereby having a negative impact on team performance [124].

Early work by Fan et al. showed that the knowledge of ***AI reliability*** among users has a significant impact on shaping user trust [78]. Appelganc et al. explored the reliability that participants required to perceive support agents (either human or AI systems) as being "highly reliable" and how this differed across contexts of working together or being evaluated by the agent [79]. Through an empirical study, the authors found that the required reliability in the context of working together did not differ across the humans or AI. However, participants required that AI be more reliable than a human when used to evaluate themselves.

The ***modality of interaction*** with AI systems have also been shown to influence performance outcomes and interaction experiences in human-AI collaboration [88, 125–127]. Le et al. compared spoken and written interactions with a natural language dialogue system using two real information-retrieval systems. The authors found that the spoken interaction mode was less efficient but promoted collaboration [127]. Zhang et al. highlighted the trade-offs between AI's verbal communication and visual communication based on their findings from an empirical study exploring human-AI team compositions [125]. Through an empirical study, Liu et al. found that the visual-auditory bimodality was superior to single visual modality and single auditory modality for older adults based on the perceptions of social presence, attitudinal outcomes, and acceptance [126]. The authors observed that older adults perceived greater social presence, perceived enjoyment, satisfaction, and acceptance with text feedback than without in their interactions with

AI assistants. He et al. explored the impact of a conversational XAI interface on users' understanding of the AI system, their trust, and reliance on the AI system in comparison to an XAI dashboard [128]. The authors found that the conversational XAI interface could bring about a better understanding of the AI system among users and lead to higher user trust. However, users of both the XAI dashboard and conversational XAI interfaces demonstrated over-reliance on the AI system, and enhancing the conversations by using agents amplified this over-reliance.

7.3.4 Human-AI Configurations

This section synthesizes findings from different human-AI configurations and workflows for human-AI collaboration, including those within organizations, given the widespread adoption of enterprise AI (as shown in Table 7.2).

Wang et al. synthesized six different configurations in human-AI collaboration based on varying levels of human agency: (i) AI suggests and humans decide (*verification)*; (ii) humans provide feedback and AI optimizes (*supervision*); (iii) humans and AI systems work independently for certain tasks, sharing a portion of the decision-making process (*cooperation*); (iv) AI decides and humans control (*intervention*); (v) AI decides and humans can exit (*rejection*); and (vii) AI adapts and human input is eliminated (*regulation*) [132].

In a user study with veterinary radiologists, Fogliato et al. explored the effects of providing AI assistance at the start of a diagnostic session in radiology versus after the radiologists made provisional decisions [133]. The authors found that participants who were asked to register provisional responses in advance of reviewing AI inferences were less likely to agree with AI, regardless of whether the advice was accurate. The authors also found that in instances of disagreement with AI, they were less likely to seek the second opinion of a colleague. In the context of generating personas, Shin et al. explored human-AI workflows that differently delegate subtasks in user research between human experts and LLMs [134]. The authors found that better results (i.e., more representative and empathy evoking) are achieved when leveraging human skill in grouping user data by their key characteristics and exploiting LLMs for summarizing pre-grouped data into personas. Wu et al. proposed the notion of LLM chaining, where the output of one step becomes the input for the next, aggregating potential gains along different steps [135]. In a user study exploring LLM chaining, the authors found that users leveraged sub-tasks to calibrate model expectations, compared and contrasted alternative strategies by observing parallel downstream effects, and debugged unexpected model outputs by testing sub-components of a chain. Allen et al. identified junctures in typical crowdsourcing workflows at which the introduction of LLMs could lead to benefits [136]. The authors proposed means to augment existing design patterns for crowd work. In other work, Wu et al. showed that replicating crowdsourcing pipelines can help us understand the relative LLM strengths on different tasks (via performance comparison on sub-tasks) and the potential of LLMs in complex tasks, where they can complete part of the tasks alongside humans [137].

Cai et al. explored the context of human-AI collaborative decision-making and carried out a qualitative study with pathologists. The authors interviewed them before, during, and after being presented deep neural network (DNN) predictions for prostate cancer diagnosis to learn the types of information that they desired about the AI assistant [129]. The authors found that clinicians desired upfront information about the known strengths and limitations of AI, its subjective point of view, and its overall design objective. Similarly, Salimzadeh et al. highlighted the importance of considering task characteristics when designing human-AI collaborative systems where peers leverage AI assistance [116].

Through a two-year-long case study of an organization in the international maritime trade that introduced automated algorithmic support for data analysis and prediction work, Grønsund et al. explored how configurations of humans and AI systems evolved as the firm adopted AI [131]. The authors found that the notions of automation and augmentation are intertwined in the evolution of organizations as they adopt AI. They highlighted the strategic importance of a *human-in-the-loop* pattern for organizational reflexivity to ensure that the performance of AI meets the requirements of the organization.

7.4 Toward Effective Human-AI Collaboration for Enterprise AI

Different research communities at the intersection of AI and HCI have tirelessly pursued the conceptualization, operationalization, and development of methods to foster appropriate reliance in human-AI interaction and collaboration [62, 138–142]. Researchers and practitioners have proposed a variety of approaches and empirically evaluated them in different domains [143–145]. For the most part, it can be argued that the pursuit of appropriate reliance is an unsolved challenge and has proved to be an elusive goal. Among other reasons, this is primarily due to conflicting findings across different studies (e.g., the early potential and promise of AI explanations as a general vehicle to foster appropriate reliance and shape positive outcomes has been refuted due to mounting evidence that suggests more nuance [146–154]), the unclear transferability of findings across empirical work in this area, and questionable ecological validity.[3] While there is a lot of ground that remains to be covered in our pursuit of facilitating appropriate reliance on AI, there have been some noteworthy efforts that have sown some seeds of promise. We discuss these ideas below.

[3] *Ecological validity* refers to the extent to which experimental findings can generalize to the real world beyond the experimental frame [155, 156].

Plausibility, Verifiability, Bounded Rationality, and the Compelling Argument of '*Evaluative AI*' In their recent work, Fok et al. argued that explanations are only useful to the extent that they allow human decision-makers to verify the correctness of the AI's prediction [157]. The authors highlight that prior works have found that in many decision-making contexts, AI explanations do not facilitate such verification. Kaur et al. investigated the extent to which AI practitioners apply *bounded rationality* when using interpretability tools and whether the application of bounded rationality helps or hurts.[4] The authors argue that whether the outcomes of bounded rationality are good or bad is dependent on the heuristics that people apply to select a "good enough" option. When such heuristics are inaccurate, then bounded rationality can lead to inaccurate decisions and propagate harm [122]. Miller proposed a conceptual framework called *evaluative AI* to support explainable decision support while tackling the challenges of over- and under-reliance on AI [158]. The author proposed this as a machine-in-the-loop paradigm in which decision support tools provide evidence for and against decisions made by the users, rather than providing recommendations for users to accept or reject. This is aligned with findings that suggest encouraging critical thinking and consideration among users is fundamentally important to help calibrate trust and foster appropriate reliance on AI [159, 160].

Considering Trust Development Over Time and in Context There has been limited consideration of trust development through interactions with AI that are spread over a period of time [81, 161]. In their recent qualitative work, Kahr et al. addressed the often neglected perspective of trust development over time [162]. The authors investigated a real-world case in which logistics experts had worked with an AI system for many years. They found that despite clearly identifying AI system imperfections, experts developed trust over time. Inconsistencies and frequent efforts to improve the AI system disrupted trust development, hindering control, transparency, and understanding of the system. The authors also found that despite the overall trustworthiness, experts overrode correct AI decisions to protect their colleagues' well-being.

Fine-Grained Notions of Appropriate Reliance In the context of AI-assisted decision-making in composite fact-checking tasks, He et al. investigated the impact of a novel multi-step decision workflow on user reliance behaviors [163]. Their findings demonstrate that human-AI collaboration with the proposed decision workflow can outperform one-step collaboration in specific contexts (e.g., when advice from an AI system is misleading). Analyzing appropriate reliance at fine-grained levels (i.e., at the sub-step level in decomposed tasks) revealed that such workflows can be effective when users demonstrate a relatively high consideration

[4] As described in [122], *bounded rationality* is an inherent feature of human decision-making; people can seldom consider the utility of all possible choices before reaching a decision, since that would lead to information overload, decision fatigue, and decision paralysis.

of the intermediate steps. The authors discuss and highlight that there is no one-size-fits-all decision workflow that can help obtain optimal human-AI collaboration.

7.4.1 Downstream AI Users: Broadening the Lens of "Human-AI Collaboration" to Consider Decision-Subjects

Other stakeholders can be directly affected as a result of end-users collaborating with a given AI system. Such stakeholders are referred to as *decision-subjects*. For an overview of this, consider the inferences of classic AI systems that are based on data samples fed as input to these systems. The outputs of such systems shape the final decisions made by end-users and can (positively or negatively) affect decision-subjects represented by the input samples. Whether the decision-subject accepts a resulting decision or decides to contest it [164] might not only depend on their satisfaction with the decision but also on their appreciation of the user-AI collaboration, their judgment of the AI system itself, and their trust. In turn, whether a decision-subject appropriately accepts or contests a decision has repercussions not only for themselves but also for the AI deployer who might have to conduct additional work (e.g., to verify the decision, to rebut the decision-subject's contestation, or pursue some action). Particularly, if a subject serially contests decisions, the deployer might get overloaded with verification tasks, while if a subject serially accepts decisions without contestation, it might lead to an increasing prevalence of inappropriate decisions and eventually shape long-term consequences [165].

Researchers have already started investigating the relation between the decision-subject and the AI system or the combination of the AI system and its user. They have explored the factors that shape such a relation, whether the system is trusted, whether it is deemed fair, and under which conditions [166–168]. Others have explored how to facilitate access to relevant information about the AI system and its decisions for the decision-subject, for them to better determine when to accept a decision [169, 170]. This might go through appropriate information disclosures by the AI deployers or users (e.g., as suggested by certain AI regulations and policies) [171–173], by the development of explanations appropriate for the comprehension of the decision-subjects [174], and by the definition of AI literacy and its development among all kinds of decision-subjects [67, 68]. Finally, prior work has also investigated when and how the subjects might want to contest a decision and what might be technical and procedural structures to facilitate their efforts [175–179].

These insights are particularly relevant to AI deployers who should not only focus on serving a high-performance AI system but also on designing interactions with users and decision-subjects that enable scrutiny, the establishment of appropriate trust, and contestation when relevant. Note that prior work has shown that without such careful designs, the decision-subjects (or even the AI users) might not consider it fair and might want to contest an AI system and/or the resulting decision [168].

7.4.2 *Upstream AI Users: Broadening the Lens of Human-AI Collaboration to Realities of the AI Supply Chain*

Recent scholarship proposes to expand the scope through which AI is scrutinized. Instead of focusing on the algorithm underlying the AI system, the outputs it produces, and how intended users interact with those outputs, HCI, STS, and legal scholars increasingly draw attention to the *AI supply chain* [180–183] (also referred to as *AI value chain* [184]). The AI supply chain should also be considered as a consequential site of human-AI collaboration, which impacts what the AI system can do and the potential harm it might cause.

7.4.2.1 What Does the AI Supply Chain Constitute?

With the AI supply chain, scholars refer to the various stakeholders who are involved in building, deploying, governing, and maintaining an AI system as well as its various sub-components. For example, consider a large language model that is often used in combination with one or multiple output filters and input prompt restrictions and that requires datasets and algorithms to function. See Fig. 7.2 for a simple illustration of the AI supply chain. Regulatory documents like the AI Act [172] have also started to adopt this supply chain framing. They particularly emphasize the distinction between various organizations: the *AI provider* is the organization that develops an AI system or possesses an AI system and places it on the market, and the *AI deployer* instead is the organization that adopts an AI system (organizations can hold both roles simultaneously). Note that the users traditionally studied in the context of human-AI collaborations might be employed by the AI deployer or make use of the deployer's system via another contractual relation. For instance, a company might serve an AI system for its *employees* to draft emails faster or might let its *clients* contact an AI-based chatbot for customer-service questions. Some organizations might be both providers and deployers (e.g., OpenAI) while providing access to the *general public* to their AI systems.

Researchers have identified the individual stakeholders involved with these provider and deployer organizations. Naturally, various engineers, data scientists, and AI researchers contribute to building components of the AI system [185, 186]. UX researchers and practitioners investigate which capabilities to enable with such a system and how to design it in order to enable these capabilities [187–189]. Additionally, product managers, responsible AI-specific roles, internal lawyers, and policymakers, all bear various roles within these organizations, be it in terms

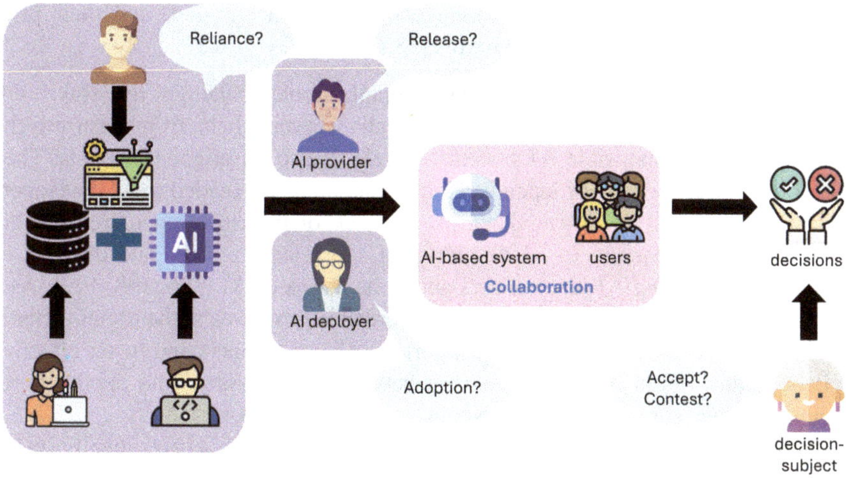

Fig. 7.2 A simplified representation of the sites of human-AI collaboration throughout the lifecycle of an AI-based system. Left of the AI-based system (purple), we show the AI supply chain. Right of the AI-based system (white), we show the decision-subjects. In the speech bubbles (blue), we show examples of questions relevant to the collaboration between each stakeholder and the system or one of its components

of managing teams that produce and release the components or ensuring the compliance with existing regulations (e.g., by identifying potential issues with the systems and setting governance workflows to mitigate these) [183, 190, 191].

Going beyond these central organizations, it is worth noting the materiality of AI supply chains and their resource hunger, particularly in terms of data, labels associated with the data, data storage, computational power, and the required hardware to enable such power [180, 184]. Other stakeholders are typically involved with gathering and developing these resources, such as the crowd workers who annotate datasets or the workers in mines who collect the minerals used to fabricate AI hardware [192–196].

7.4.2.2 Key Notions in the AI Supply Chain

Prior research has addressed two primary knowledge gaps in relation to the AI supply chain—factors that shape the AI supply chain and harms that stem from it. We discuss this next.

Factors That Shape the AI Supply Chain Many studies have surfaced the practices of individual stakeholders in the supply chain and identified the various factors that affect these practices. They have pointed out the individual factors that affect the perceptions and efforts of these stakeholders, such as their knowledge of AI techniques and of AI harms, their reflexivity over their own thoughts and practices, their socio-demographic and educational background, and their prior experiences with AI and potential harms [185, 186, 197].

Researchers have also identified many organizational challenges that stakeholders face in the supply chain and that typically prevent them from ensuring the development of responsible AI systems, largely due to misaligned interests. They have pointed out the lack of incentives, time, and budget provided to AI developers to test the systems for potential harms, the lack of prioritization of responsible AI efforts in comparison to AI development and release efforts, and the lack of support for educating AI practitioners about the harms of AI [186, 198, 199]. As a result, they have started to propose new governance processes at the organizational level in order to ensure appropriate support for AI practitioners and foster effective collaborations within AI providers or in between AI providers and deployers, to ultimately make sure responsible systems are deployed [200].

Although still rare, some scholarship has also started to focus specifically on the interactions between the stakeholders of the supply chain and how they affect the resulting AI systems. Researchers have also studied the diversity of trust relations that make up the supply chain. In that regard, they have highlighted that many stakeholders form a relation of trust with the AI system or one of its components but that the factors affecting such trust relations might differ from the factors affecting a user's trust in the AI system [183]. They have also shown how trust relations in between organizations or within the stakeholders of a same organization might further affect the development of the final AI system. Others have investigated how responsibility is perceived among these stakeholders and how AI practitioners often perceive it as a concern and obligation for the stakeholders upstream or downstream the supply chain but not for themselves [181, 201]. Note that neither the notion of the AI supply chain nor the association of these various factors to the supply chain is new. Earlier literature in organizational management and other disciplines have conceptualized the notion of supply chains and demonstrated the formative power of these factors [184]. Nevertheless, recent adaptations serve to transfer these notions to the AI context and surface its nuances. For instance, the kind of information that an AI developer requires to develop trust in an AI component such as a dataset is arguably different from the information that a car manufacturer would rely on to establish trust in the car's anti-lock braking system (ABS).

Thus, following these potential collaboration-related challenges that make up AI supply chains, researchers have started to explore the AI-centered information and knowledge that should be shared and communicated among the stakeholders of the supply chain. Transparency and literacy could facilitate the appropriate development and governance of the system [190, 202] if they are enacted appropriately. They might particularly require adaptations depending on the stakeholders involved in the information exchanges, their diverse backgrounds, and their economic relationships (e.g., whether they belong to the same organization, in which case confidentiality and sensitivity of the information might be less of a hindrance for the exchange) [190, 203]. Such communications are also supported by the AI Act [172] that enforces various types of disclosures in between different stakeholders.

Harms That Stem from the AI Supply Chain The second angle that researchers have adopted to investigate AI supply chains is their relation to the notion of AI harms. On the one hand, they have shown that the supply chain might be a source of harm. All the actions taken (or not) by the stakeholders of the supply chain, and all the factors and challenges above, will ultimately affect how biased or fair an AI system is and how transparent it is. They have highlighted that because of supply chain complexities, it is challenging to ensure fairness ultimately [181, 182, 184, 204]. On the other hand, they have discussed how the supply chain itself might be a harmful space. Certain scholars have discussed the poor labor conditions in which certain practitioners work within the supply chain [192]. Other scholars have revealed the power relations among the organizations of the supply chain, the dependencies that are created among these organizations, and the economic and political risk for the organizations with less leverage [182, 204–206].

7.4.2.3 Opportunities to Foster Responsible AI Supply Chains

Despite the little attention that AI supply chains have received, early insights about the stakeholders and dynamics that make up AI supply chains (described above) motivate the importance of their study. These insights particularly demonstrate many challenges in ensuring the supply chain's compliance with regulations, decreasing its potential for harm, and mitigating the issues with the final AI systems it produces. In this context, AI supply chains are very relevant to this chapter. They constitute a new space of human-AI collaborations upstream the usage of the system's outputs by its intended individual users. Indeed, all the stakeholders we mentioned above have to make decisions related to the AI system or its sub-components. A product manager in a deployer organization might, for instance, have to decide whether to adopt the AI system of an AI provider, accounting for various factors such as the reliability of the provider, the trustworthiness of its AI system, and the utility of employing such a system in relation to its cost. Instead, a product manager at a provider organization might have to decide whether to release an AI system and through which modalities (e.g., open-source, via an API access), considering the performance of the system as well as how risky it might be (e.g., what its propensity for outputting offensive text might be and how this might affect the reputation of the provider). Furthermore, all these junctions where a decision is made about the AI system or one of its components end up affecting the final AI system. Such resulting AI systems have been the object of much of human-AI collaboration research. We can appreciate that the properties and attributes of AI systems are shaped all along the supply chain. Hence, better understanding the supply chain also enables better understanding of the collaboration between the AI system and its end-users.

This consideration opens up many research opportunities. It brings to question whether existing approaches developed to support end-user collaborations with AI systems and to study the factors that shape outcomes in such contexts can be transferred to other stakeholders in the supply chain. For instance, it would be interesting to ask whether the information that users need to learn about to appropriately rely on an AI system are the same as those that AI practitioners (e.g., AI developers, product managers) in the chain would need to make appropriate decisions. It is easy to envision that some of the work will require strong adaptations. In that case, it will be especially important for enterprises to actively consider their role in the supply chain and how to leverage existing research insights to facilitate the appropriate decision-making of each stakeholder vis-a-vis the AI system and its components.

7.4.3 The Generative AI Opportunity Cost for Enterprises Under the Lens of Trust and Reliance

The opportunity costs of investing in generative AI technologies represents a critical consideration for enterprises, with important second-order effects at stake (e.g., on energy consumption and sustainability) [207, 208]. While grappling with the potential and the hype surrounding generative AI, carefully evaluating the opportunity costs and considering the technological trade-offs is vital. We identify some key challenges and trade-offs in this vein, particularly in view of trust and reliance on generative AI in the enterprise context.

- Trust calibration can be a moving target with generative AI. Enterprises should seek to develop meaningful governance structures that cater for the measurement, fostering, and monitoring of appropriate trust along with feedback mechanisms to help calibrate trust [48].
- It is important to create adequate guardrails to help navigate the risks of over-reliance on generative AI. Failing to implement the necessary guardrails can lead to unforeseen costs and harms. For instance, LLMs are prone to hallucinations and inaccuracies that can lead to data pollution when incorporated into enterprise knowledge bases without appropriate verification or validation [209].
- Over-reliance on generative AI can also lead to the dilution of knowledge within enterprises that is typically present in the unstructured mental models of actors and stakeholders in the enterprise, in their routines, and in particular the tacit knowledge of experts [210].
- Over-reliance on generative AI can lead to a decrease in critical thinking [211, 212]. The enterprise opportunity cost manifests here in the form of diminished problem-solving capacity, especially for novel challenges that require creative thinking that is still beyond current AI capabilities.

7.5 Conclusions

There is a growing wealth of knowledge around how we can design and support effective human-AI collaboration. In this chapter, we unpacked the fundamental factors that shape experiential and performance-related outcomes in human-AI collaboration. We discussed the challenges pertaining to fostering appropriate reliance on AI assistance and promising directions stemming from recent literature in this field. We argued that the AI supply chain can be both a valuable lens and a differentiator in informing the effective design and deployment of enterprise AI. An important aspect to consider in the drive toward adoption of generative AI technologies into enterprise practices is that competitive advantages and operational efficiency gains can only emerge from their meaningful and strategic application rather than mere adoption alone. Aligning AI capabilities with the core business objectives; simultaneously considering different stakeholders and customer needs and their values; and explicitly considering second-order effects and societal impact can be a rewarding approach.

Acknowledgments This work was partially supported by the TU Delft AI Initiative, the ProtectMe Convergence Flagship project, and the Model-driven Decisions Lab (MoDDL).

References

1. Licklider, J.C.R.: Man-computer symbiosis. IRE Trans. Hum. Factors Electron. **HFE-1**(1), 4–11 (1960). https://doi.org/10.1109/THFE2.1960.4503259
2. Jumper, J., Evans, R., Pritzel, A., Green, T., Figurnov, M., Ronneberger, O., Tunyasuvunakool, K., Bates, R., Žídek, A., Potapenko, A., et al.: Highly accurate protein structure prediction with alphafold. Nature **596**(7873), 583–589 (2021)
3. Abramson, J., Adler, J., Dunger, J., Evans, R., Green, T., Pritzel, A., Ronneberger, O., Willmore, L., Ballard, A.J., Bambrick, J., et al.: Accurate structure prediction of biomolecular interactions with AlphaFold 3. Nature **630**(8016), 493–500 (2024)
4. Shen, J., Zhang, C.J., Jiang, B., Chen, J., Song, J., Liu, Z., He, Z., Wong, S.Y., Fang, P.H. Ming, W.K., et al.: Artificial intelligence versus clinicians in disease diagnosis: systematic review. JMIR Med. Inf. **7**(3), e10010 (2019)
5. Saab, K., Tu, T., Weng, W.H., Tanno, R., Stutz, D., Wulczyn, E., Zhang, F., Strother, T., Park, C., Vedadi, E., et al.: Capabilities of gemini models in medicine. Preprint. arXiv:2404.18416 (2024)
6. Singhal, K., Tu, T., Gottweis, J., Sayres, R., Wulczyn, E., Hou, L., Clark, K., Pfohl, S., Cole-Lewis, H., Neal, D., et al.: Towards expert-level medical question answering with large language models. Preprint. arXiv:2305.09617 (2023)
7. Uddin, M., Wang, Y., Woodbury-Smith, M.: Artificial intelligence for precision medicine in neurodevelopmental disorders. npj Digital Med. **2**(1), 112 (2019)
8. Eyring, V., Gentine, P., Camps-Valls, G., Lawrence, D.M., Reichstein, M.: AI-empowered next-generation multiscale climate modelling for mitigation and adaptation. Nat. Geosci. **17**(10), 963–971 (2024)
9. Silvestro, D., Goria, S., Sterner, T., Antonelli, A.: Improving biodiversity protection through artificial intelligence. Nat. Sustainability **5**(5), 415–424 (2022)

10. Følstad, A., Skjuve, M.: Chatbots for customer service: user experience and motivation. In: Proceedings of the 1st International Conference on Conversational User Interfaces, pp. 1–9 (2019)
11. Moilanen, J., van Berkel, N., Visuri, A., Gadiraju, U., van der Maden, W., Hosio, S.: Supporting mental health self-care discovery through a chatbot. Front. Digital Health **5**, 1034724 (2023)
12. Abbas, T., Khan, V.J., Gadiraju, U., Markopoulos, P.: Trainbot: a conversational interface to train crowd workers for delivering on-demand therapy. In: Proceedings of the AAAI Conference on Human Computation and Crowdsourcing, vol. 8, pp. 3–12 (2020)
13. Li, B., Gross, O., Crampton, N., Kapoor, M., Tauseef, S., Jain, M., Truong, K.N., Mariakakis, A.: Beyond the waiting room: patient's perspectives on the conversational nuances of pre-consultation chatbots. In: Proceedings of the CHI Conference on Human Factors in Computing Systems, pp. 1–24 (2024)
14. Kuhail, M.A., Alturki, N., Alramlawi, S., Alhejori, K.: Interacting with educational chatbots: A systematic review. Educ. Inf. Technol. **28**(1), 973–1018 (2023)
15. McGregor, S.: Preventing repeated real world AI failures by cataloging incidents: the AI incident database. In: Proceedings of the AAAI Conference on Artificial Intelligence, vol. 35, pp. 15458–15463 (2021)
16. Constantinides, M., Bogucka, E., Quercia, D., Kallio, S., Tahaei, M.: RAI guidelines: method for generating responsible AI guidelines grounded in regulations and usable by (non-) technical roles. Proc. ACM Hum.-Comput. Interact. **8**(CSCW2), 1–28 (2024)
17. Shneiderman, B.: Human-centered artificial intelligence: Reliable, safe & trustworthy. Int. J. Hum.–Comput. Interact. **36**(6), 495–504 (2020)
18. Cavalcante Siebert, L., Lupetti, M.L., Aizenberg, E., Beckers, N., Zgonnikov, A., Veluwenkamp, H., Abbink, D., Giaccardi, E., Houben, G.J., Jonker, C.M., et al.: Meaningful human control: actionable properties for ai system development. AI Ethics **3**(1), 241–255 (2023)
19. Amershi, S., Weld, D., Vorvoreanu, M., Fourney, A., Nushi, B., Collisson, P., Suh, J., Iqbal, S., Bennett, P.N., Inkpen, K., et al.: Guidelines for human-AI interaction. In: Proceedings of the 2019 CHI Conference on Human Factors in Computing Systems, pp. 1–13 (2019)
20. Gadiraju, U., Yang, J.: What can crowd computing do for the next generation of AI systems? In: CSW@ NeurIPS, pp. 7–13 (2020)
21. De Cremer, D., Kasparov, G.: AI should augment human intelligence, not replace it. Harv. Bus. Rev. **18**(1), 1–8 (2021)
22. Wang, D., Churchill, E., Maes, P., Fan, X., Shneiderman, B., Shi, Y., Wang, Q.: From human-human collaboration to Human-AI collaboration: designing AI systems that can work together with people. In: Extended Abstracts of the 2020 CHI Conference on Human Factors in Computing Systems, pp. 1–6 (2020)
23. Fan, M., Yang, X., Yu, T., Liao, Q.V., Zhao, J.: Human-AI collaboration for UX evaluation: effects of explanation and synchronization. Proc. ACM Hum.-Comput. Interact. **6**(CSCW1), 1–32 (2022)
24. Vodrahalli, K., Gerstenberg, T., Zou, J.Y., Uncalibrated models can improve human-AI collaboration. Adv. Neural Inf. Proces. Syst. **35**, 4004–4016 (2022)
25. Reverberi, C., Rigon, T., Solari, A., Hassan, C., Cherubini, P., Cherubini, A.: Experimental evidence of effective human–AI collaboration in medical decision-making. Sci. Rep. **12**(1), 14952 (2022)
26. Hemmer, P., Westphal, M., Schemmer, M., Vetter, S., Vössing, M., Satzger, G.: Human-AI collaboration: the effect of AI delegation on human task performance and task satisfaction. In: Proceedings of the 28th International Conference on Intelligent User Interfaces, pp. 453–463 (2023)
27. Ashktorab, Z., Liao, Q.V., Dugan, C., Johnson, J., Pan, Q., Zhang, W., Kumaravel, S., Campbell, M.: Human-AI collaboration in a cooperative game setting: measuring social perception and outcomes. Proc. ACM Hum.-Comput. Interact. **4**(CSCW2), 1–20 (2020)

28. Sowa, K., Przegalinska, A., Ciechanowski, L.: Cobots in knowledge work: Human–AI collaboration in managerial professions. J. Bus. Res. **125**, 135–142 (2021)
29. Wang, D., Weisz, J.D., Muller, M., Ram, P., Geyer, W., Dugan, C., Tausczik, Y., Samulowitz, H., Gray, A.: Human-AI collaboration in data science: exploring data scientists' perceptions of automated AI. Proc. ACM Hum.-Comput. Interact. **3**(CSCW), 1–24 (2019)
30. Jiang, J.A., Wade, K., Fiesler, C., Brubaker, J.R.: Supporting serendipity: opportunities and challenges for human-ai collaboration in qualitative analysis. Proc. ACM Hum.-Comput. Interact. **5**(CSCW1), 1–23 (2021)
31. Rastogi, C., Tulio Ribeiro, M., King, N., Nori, H., Amershi, S.: Supporting human-AI collaboration in auditing LLMs with LLMs. In: Proceedings of the 2023 AAAI/ACM Conference on AI, Ethics, and Society, pp. 913–926 (2023)
32. McNeese, N.J., Demir, M., Cooke, N.J., Myers, C.: Teaming with a synthetic teammate: insights into human-autonomy teaming. Hum. Fact. **60**(2), 262–273 (2018)
33. O'Neill, T., McNeese, N., Barron, A., Schelble, B.: Human–autonomy teaming: a review and analysis of the empirical literature. Hum. Fact. **64**(5), 904–938 (2022)
34. Seeber, I., Bittner, E., Briggs, R.O., De Vreede, T., De Vreede, G.J., Elkins, A., Maier, R., Merz, A.B., Oeste-Reiß, S., Randrup, N., et al.: Machines as teammates: a research agenda on AI in team collaboration. Inf. Manag. **57**(2), 103174 (2020)
35. Hauptman, A.I., Schelble, B.G., McNeese, N.J., Madathil, K.C.: Adapt and overcome: perceptions of adaptive autonomous agents for human-AI teaming. Comput. Hum. Behav. **138**, 107451 (2023)
36. Demartini, G., Difallah, D.E., Gadiraju, U., Catasta, M., et al.: An introduction to hybrid human-machine information systems. Found. Trends® Web Sci. **7**(1), 1–87 (2017)
37. Dell'Anna, D., Murukannaiah, P.K., Dudzik, B., Grossi, D., Jonker, C.M., Oertel, C., Yolum, P.: Toward a quality model for hybrid intelligence teams. In: Proceedings of the 23rd International Conference on Autonomous Agents and Multiagent Systems, pp. 434–443 (2024)
38. Zhang, R., McNeese, N.J., Freeman, G., Musick, G.: "an ideal human" expectations of AI teammates in human-AI teaming. Proc. ACM Hum.-Comput. Interact. **4**(CSCW3), 1–25 (2021)
39. Zhang, G., Chong, L., Kotovsky, K., Cagan, J.: Trust in an AI versus a human teammate: the effects of teammate identity and performance on human-AI cooperation. Comput. Hum. Behav. **139**, 107536 (2023)
40. He, G., Demartini, G., Gadiraju, U.: Plan-then-execute: an empirical study of user trust and team performance when using LLM agents as a daily assistant. In: Proceedings of the CHI Conference on Human Factors in Computing Systems (2025)
41. He, G., Aishwarya, N., Gadiraju, U.: Is conversational XAI all you need? Human-AI decision making with a conversational XAI assistant. In: Proceedings of the 30th International Conference on Intelligent User Interfaces (2025)
42. Kim, S.S., Liao, Q.V., Vorvoreanu, M., Ballard, S., Vaughan, J.W.: "I'm Not Sure, But...": examining the impact of large language models' uncertainty expression on user reliance and trust. In: Proceedings of the 2024 ACM Conference on Fairness, Accountability, and Transparency, pp. 822–835 (2024)
43. Vasconcelos, H., Bansal, G., Fourney, A., Liao, Q.V., Vaughan, J.W.: Generation probabilities are not enough: exploring the effectiveness of uncertainty highlighting in ai-powered code completions. Preprint. arXiv:2302.07248 (2023)
44. Hechler, E., Oberhofer, M., Schaeck, T.: Deploying ai in the enterprise. In: IT Approaches for Design, DevOps, Governance, Change Management, Blockchain, and Quantum Computing, Apress, Berkeley, CA (2020)
45. Lockey, S., Gillespie, N., Morrill, J., Pool, J.: Trust in artificial intelligence: a critical systematic review. In: Academy of Management Proceedings, vol. 2024, p. 14990. Academy of Management, Valhalla (2024)
46. Miller, T.: Explanation in artificial intelligence: Insights from the social sciences. Artif. Intell. **267**, 1–38 (2019)

47. Lee, J.D., See, K.A.: Trust in automation: designing for appropriate reliance. Hum. Fact. **46**(1), 50–80 (2004)
48. Hoff, K.A., Bashir, M.: Trust in automation: Integrating empirical evidence on factors that influence trust. Hum. Fact. **57**(3), 407–434 (2015)
49. Mehrotra, S., Degachi, C., Vereschak, O., Jonker, C.M., Tielman, M.L.: A systematic review on fostering appropriate trust in human-AI interaction: trends, opportunities and challenges. ACM J. Responsible Comput. **1**(4), 1–45 (2024)
50. Schlicker, N., Langer, M.: Towards warranted trust: a model on the relation between actual and perceived system trustworthiness. In: Proceedings of Mensch und Computer 2021, pp. 325–329 (2021)
51. Akula, A., Wang, S., Zhu, S.C.: Cocox: generating conceptual and counterfactual explanations via fault-lines. In: Proceedings of the AAAI conference on artificial intelligence, vol. 34, pp. 2594–2601 (2020)
52. Jacovi, A., Marasović, A., Miller, T., Goldberg, Y.: Formalizing trust in artificial intelligence: prerequisites, causes and goals of human trust in AI. In: Proceedings of the 2021 ACM Conference on Fairness, Accountability, and Transparency, pp. 624–635 (2021)
53. Ferrario, A., Loi, M.: How explainability contributes to trust in AI. In: Proceedings of the 2022 ACM Conference on Fairness, Accountability, and Transparency, pp. 1457–1466 (2022)
54. Lebiere, C., Blaha, L.M., Fallon, C.K., Jefferson, B.: Adaptive cognitive mechanisms to maintain calibrated trust and reliance in automation. Front. Rob. AI **8**, 652776 (2021)
55. Ghai, B., Liao, Q.V., Zhang, Y., Bellamy, R., Mueller, K.: Explainable active learning (XAL) toward AI explanations as interfaces for machine teachers. Proc. ACM Hum.-Comput. Interact. **4**(CSCW3), 1–28 (2021)
56. Schlicker, N., Baum, K., Uhde, A., Sterz, S., Hirsch, M.C., Langer, M.: How do we assess the trustworthiness of AI? Introducing the trustworthiness assessment model (TrAM). Comput. Hum. Behav. **170**, 108671 (2025)
57. Miller, T.: Are we measuring trust correctly in explainability, interpretability, and transparency research? Preprint. arXiv:2209.00651 (2022)
58. Okamura, K., Yamada, S.: Adaptive trust calibration for human-ai collaboration. Plos One **15**(2), e0229132 (2020)
59. Bansal, G., Wu, T., Zhou, J., Fok, R., Nushi, B., Kamar, E., Ribeiro, M.T., Weld, D.: Does the whole exceed its parts? The effect of ai explanations on complementary team performance. In: Proceedings of the 2021 CHI Conference on Human Factors in Computing Systems, pp. 1–16 (2021)
60. Inkpen, K., Chappidi, S., Mallari, K., Nushi, B., Ramesh, D., Michelucci, P., Mandava, V., Vepřek, L.H., Quinn, G.: Advancing human-ai complementarity: the impact of user expertise and algorithmic tuning on joint decision making. ACM Trans. Comput.-Hum. Interact. **30**(5), 1–29 (2023)
61. Lai, V., Chen, C., Liao, Q.V., Smith-Renner, A., Tan, C.: Towards a science of human-AI decision making: a survey of empirical studies. Preprint. arXiv:2112.11471 (2021)
62. Schemmer, M., Hemmer, P., Kühl, N., Benz, C., Satzger, G.: Should I follow ai-based advice? Measuring appropriate reliance in human-ai decision-making. Preprint. arXiv:2204.06916 (2022)
63. Salimzadeh, S., He, G., Gadiraju, U.: Dealing with uncertainty: understanding the impact of prognostic versus diagnostic tasks on trust and reliance in human-AI decision making. In: Proceedings of the CHI Conference on Human Factors in Computing Systems, pp. 1–17 (2024)
64. Erlei, A., Das, R., Meub, L., Anand, A., Gadiraju, U.: For what it's worth: humans overwrite their economic self-interest to avoid bargaining with AI systems. In: Proceedings of the 2022 CHI Conference on Human Factors in Computing Systems, pp. 1–18 (2022)
65. Hemmer, P., Schemmer, M., Vössing, M., Kühl, N.: Human-AI complementarity in hybrid intelligence systems: a structured literature review. PACIS **78**, 118 (2021)

66. Hartikainen, M., Spurava, G., Väänänen, K.: Human-AI collaboration in smart manufacturing: key concepts and framework for design. HHAI 2024: Hybrid Hum. AI Syst. Soc. Good 162–172 (2024)
67. Long, D., Magerko, B.: What is AI literacy? Competencies and design considerations. In: Proceedings of the 2020 CHI Conference on Human Factors in Computing Systems, pp. 1–16 (2020)
68. NDg, D.T.K., LJeung. J.K.L., CShu. S.K.W., Qiao, M.S.: Conceptualizing ai literacy: an exploratory review. Comput. Educ.: Artif. Intell. **2**, 100041 (2021)
69. Pinski, M., Benlian, A.: AI literacy for users-a comprehensive review and future research directions of learning methods, components, and effects. Comput. Hum. Behav.: Artif. Hum. **2**(1), 100062 (2024)
70. Salimzadeh, S., He, G., Gadiraju, U.: A missing piece in the puzzle: considering the role of task complexity in human-ai decision making. In: Proceedings of the 31st ACM Conference on User Modeling, Adaptation and Personalization, pp. 215–227 (2023)
71. Nourani, M., King, J., Ragan, E.: The role of domain expertise in user trust and the impact of first impressions with intelligent systems. In: Proceedings of the AAAI Conference on Human Computation and Crowdsourcing, vol. 8, pp. 112–121 (2020)
72. Senoner, J., Schallmoser, S., Kratzwald, B., Feuerriegel, S., Netland, T.: Explainable AI improves task performance in human–AI collaboration. Sci. Rep. **14**(1), 31150 (2024)
73. Zhang, Q., Lee, M.L., Carter, S.: You complete me: human-AI teams and complementary expertise. In: Proceedings of the 2022 CHI Conference on Human Factors in Computing Systems, pp. 1–28 (2022)
74. Baron, S., Latham, A.J., Varga, S.: Explainable ai and stakes in medicine: a user study. Artif. Intell. **340**, 104282 (2025)
75. Yin, M., Wortman Vaughan, J., Wallach, H.: Understanding the effect of accuracy on trust in machine learning models. In: Proceedings of the 2019 CHI Conference on Human Factors in Computing Systems, pp. 1–12 (2019)
76. He, G., Buijsman, S., Gadiraju, U.: How stated accuracy of an ai system and analogies to explain accuracy affect human reliance on the system. Proc. ACM Hum.-Comput. Interact. **7**(CSCW2), 1–29 (2023)
77. Bansal, G., Nushi, B., Kamar, E., Lasecki, W.S., Weld, D.S., Horvitz, E.: Beyond accuracy: the role of mental models in human-AI team performance. In: Proceedings of the AAAI Conference on Human Computation and Crowdsourcing, vol. 7, pp. 2–11 (2019)
78. Fan, X., Oh, S., McNeese, M., Yen, J., Cuevas, H., Strater, L., Endsley, M.R.: The influence of agent reliability on trust in human-agent collaboration. In: Proceedings of the 15th European Conference on Cognitive Ergonomics: The Ergonomics of Cool Interaction, pp. 1–8 (2008)
79. Appelganc, K., Rieger, T., Roesler, E., Manzey, D.: How much reliability is enough? A context-specific view on human interaction with (artificial) agents from different perspectives. J. Cogn. Eng. Decis. Mak. **16**(4), 207–221 (2022). https://doi.org/10.1177/15553434221104615
80. Nourani, M., Roy, C., Block, J.E., Honeycutt, D.R., Rahman, T., Ragan, E., Gogate, V.: Anchoring bias affects mental model formation and user reliance in explainable AI systems. In: Proceedings of the 26th International Conference on Intelligent User Interfaces, pp. 340–350 (2021)
81. Tolmeijer, S., Gadiraju, U., Ghantasala, R., Gupta, A., Bernstein, A.: Second chance for a first impression? Trust development in intelligent system interaction. In: Proceedings of the 29th ACM Conference on User Modeling, Adaptation and Personalization, pp. 77–87 (2021)
82. Swaroop, S., Buçinca, Z., Gajos, K.Z., Doshi-Velez, F.: Accuracy-time tradeoffs in AI-assisted decision making under time pressure. In: Proceedings of the 29th International Conference on Intelligent User Interfaces, pp. 138–154 (2024)
83. Cao, S., Gomez, C., Huang, C.M.: How time pressure in different phases of decision-making influences human-AI collaboration. Proc. ACM Hum.-Comput. Interact. **7**(CSCW2), 1–26 (2023)

84. He, G., Kuiper, L., Gadiraju, U.: Knowing about knowing: an illusion of human competence can hinder appropriate reliance on AI systems. In: Proceedings of the 2023 CHI Conference on Human Factors in Computing Systems, pp. 1–18 (2023)
85. Khadpe, P., Krishna, R., Fei-Fei, L., Hancock, J.T., Bernstein, M.S.: Conceptual metaphors impact perceptions of human-AI collaboration. Proc. ACM Hum.-Comput. Interact. **4**(CSCW2), 1–26 (2020)
86. Jung, J.Y., Qiu, S., Bozzon, A., Gadiraju, U.: Great chain of agents: the role of metaphorical representation of agents in conversational crowdsourcing. In: Proceedings of the 2022 CHI Conference on Human Factors in Computing Systems, pp. 1–22 (2022)
87. Szymanski, M., Millecamp, M., Verbert, K.: Visual, textual or hybrid: the effect of user expertise on different explanations. In: Proceedings of the 26th International Conference on Intelligent User Interfaces, pp. 109–119 (2021)
88. Robbemond, V., Inel, O., Gadiraju, U.: Understanding the role of explanation modality in AI-assisted decision-making. In: Proceedings of the 30th ACM Conference on User Modeling, Adaptation and Personalization, pp. 223–233 (2022)
89. Van de Poel, I.: Embedding values in artificial intelligence (AI) systems. Minds Mach. **30**(3), 385–409 (2020)
90. Arora, P.: From Pessimism to Promise: Lessons from the Global South on Designing Inclusive Tech. MIT Press, Cambridge (2024)
91. Cetindamar, D., Kitto, K., Wu, M., Zhang, Y., Abedin, B., Knight, S.: Explicating AI literacy of employees at digital workplaces. IEEE Trans. Eng. Manage. **71**, 810–823 (2022)
92. Carolus, A., Koch, M.J., Straka, S., Latoschik, M.E., Wienrich, C.: Mails-meta AI literacy scale: development and testing of an ai literacy questionnaire based on well-founded competency models and psychological change-and meta-competencies. Comput. Hum. Behav. Artif. Hum. **1**(2), 100014 (2023)
93. Lintner, T.: A systematic review of ai literacy scales. NPJ Sci. Learn. **9**(1), 50 (2024)
94. Kasinidou, M.: Promoting AI literacy for the public. In: Proceedings of the 54th ACM Technical Symposium on Computer Science Education, vol. 2, pp. 1237–1237 (2023)
95. Su, J., NDg, D.T.K., CShu, S.K.W.: Artificial intelligence (AI) literacy in early childhood education: the challenges and opportunities. Comput. Educ. Artif. Intell. **4**, 100124 (2023)
96. NDg, D.T.K., Xinyu, C., LJeung. J.K.L., CShu. S.K.W.: Fostering students' AI literacy development through educational games: AI knowledge, affective and cognitive engagement. J. Comput. Assist. Learn. **40**(5), 2049–2064 (2024)
97. Hoffman, R.R., Mueller, S.T., Klein, G., Litman, J.: Measures for explainable AI: explanation goodness, user satisfaction, mental models, curiosity, trust, and human-AI performance. Front. Comput. Sci. **5**, 1096257 (2023)
98. Andrews, R.W., Lilly, J.M., Srivastava, D., Feigh, K.M.: The role of shared mental models in human-AI teams: a theoretical review. Theor. Issues Ergonom. Sci. **24**(2), 129–175 (2023)
99. Gero, K.I., Ashktorab, Z., Dugan, C., Pan, Q., Johnson, J., Geyer, W., Ruiz, M., Miller, S., Millen, D.R., Campbell, M., et al.: Mental models of AI agents in a cooperative game setting. In: Proceedings of the 2020 CHI Conference on Human Factors in Computing Systems, pp. 1–12 (2020)
100. Cabrera, Á.A., Perer, A., Hong, J.I.: Improving human-AI collaboration with descriptions of AI behavior. Proc. ACM Hum.-Comput. Interact. **7**(CSCW1), 1–21 (2023)
101. Nourani, M., Roy, C., Block, J.E., Honeycutt, D.R., Rahman, T., Ragan, E.D., Gogate, V.: On the importance of user backgrounds and impressions: lessons learned from interactive ai applications. ACM Trans. Interact. Intell. Syst. **12**(4), 1–29 (2022)
102. Nourani, M., Honeycutt, D.R., Block, J.E., Roy, C., Rahman, T., Ragan, E.D., Gogate, V.: Investigating the importance of first impressions and explainable AI with interactive video analysis. In: Extended Abstracts of the 2020 CHI Conference on Human Factors in Computing Systems, pp. 1–8 (2020)
103. Wilder, B., Horvitz, E., Kamar, E.: Learning to complement humans. In: Proceedings of the Twenty-Ninth International Conference on International Joint Conferences on Artificial Intelligence, pp. 1526–1533 (2021)

104. Kahneman, D.: Thinking, Fast and Slow (Macmillan, New York, 2011)
105. Bertrand, A., Belloum, R., Eagan, J.R., Maxwell, W.: How cognitive biases affect XAI-assisted decision-making: a systematic review. In: Proceedings of the 2022 AAAI/ACM Conference on AI, Ethics, and Society, pp. 78–91 (2022)
106. Echterhoff, J.M., Yarmand, M., McAuley, J.: AI-moderated decision-making: capturing and balancing anchoring bias in sequential decision tasks. In: Proceedings of the 2022 CHI Conference on Human Factors in Computing Systems, pp. 1–9 (2022)
107. Rastogi, C., Zhang, Y., Wei, D., Varshney, K.R., Dhurandhar, A., Tomsett, R.: Deciding fast and slow: the role of cognitive biases in AI-assisted decision-making. Proc. ACM Hum.-Comput. Interact. **6**(CSCW1), 1–22 (2022)
108. Jacobsen, R.M., BLysted. L.B.L., Johansen, P.S., Papachristos, E., Skov, M.B.: Perceived and measured task effectiveness in human-AI collaboration. In: Extended Abstracts of the 2020 CHI Conference on Human Factors in Computing Systems, pp. 1–9 (2020)
109. Biswas, S., Erlei, A., Gadiraju, U.: Mind the gap! choice independence in using multilingual LLMs for persuasive co-writing tasks in different languages. In: Proceedings of the CHI Conference on Human Factors in Computing Systems (2025)
110. Sharifi Noorian, S., Qiu, S., Sayin, B., Balayn, A., Gadiraju, U., Yang, J., Bozzon, A.: Perspective: leveraging human understanding for identifying and characterizing image atypicality. In: Proceedings of the 28th International Conference on Intelligent User Interfaces, pp. 650–663 (2023)
111. Zhang, Z., Singh, J., Gadiraju, U., Anand, A.: Dissonance between human and machine understanding. Proc. ACM Hum.-Comput. Interact. **3**(CSCW), 1–23 (2019)
112. Hendrycks, D., Burns, C., Basart, S., Critch, A., Li, J., Song, D., Steinhardt, J.: Aligning AI with shared human values. In: International Conference on Learning Representations
113. Seth, A., Ahuja, S., Bali, K., Sitaram, S.: DOSA: a dataset of social artifacts from different indian geographical subcultures. In: Proceedings of the 2024 Joint International Conference on Computational Linguistics, Language Resources and Evaluation (LREC-COLING 2024), pp. 5323–5337 (2024)
114. Christian, B.: The Alignment Problem: How Can Machines Learn Human Values? Atlantic Books, London (2021)
115. Lai, V., Chen, C., Smith-Renner, A., Liao, Q.V., Tan, C.: Towards a science of human-AI decision making: an overview of design space in empirical human-subject studies. In: Proceedings of the 2023 ACM Conference on Fairness, Accountability, and Transparency, pp. 1369–1385 (2023)
116. Salimzadeh, S., Gadiraju, U.: When in doubt! understanding the role of task characteristics on peer decision-making with AI assistance. In: Proceedings of the 32nd ACM Conference on User Modeling, Adaptation and Personalization, pp. 89–101 (2024)
117. Tomsett, R., Preece, A., Braines, D., Cerutti, F., Chakraborty, S., Srivastava, M., Pearson, G., Kaplan, L.: Rapid trust calibration through interpretable and uncertainty-aware AI. Patterns **1**(4), 100049 (2020). ISSN: 2666–3899. https://doi.org/10.1016/j.patter.2020.100049
118. Prabhudesai, S., Yang, L., Asthana, S., Huan, X., Liao, Q.V., Banovic, N.: Understanding uncertainty: how lay decision-makers perceive and interpret uncertainty in human-AI decision making. In: Proceedings of the 28th International Conference on Intelligent User Interfaces, pp. 379–396 (2023)
119. Melis, D.A., Kaur, H., Daumé III, H., Wallach, H., Vaughan, J.W.: From human explanation to model interpretability: a framework based on weight of evidence. In: Proceedings of the AAAI Conference on Human Computation and Crowdsourcing, vol. 9, pp. 35–47 (2021)
120. Rechkemmer, A., Yin, M.: When confidence meets accuracy: exploring the effects of multiple performance indicators on trust in machine learning models. In: Proceedings of the 2022 CHI Conference on Human Factors in Computing Systems, pp. 1–14 (2022)
121. Ahn, D., Almaatouq, A., Gulabani, M., Hosanagar, K.: Impact of model interpretability and outcome feedback on trust in AI. In: Proceedings of the 2024 CHI Conference on Human Factors in Computing Systems, pp. 1–25 (2024)

122. Kaur, H., Conrad, M.R., Rule, D., Lampe, C., Gilbert, E.: Interpretability gone bad: the role of bounded rationality in how practitioners understand machine learning. Proc. ACM Hum.-Comput. Interact. **8**(CSCW1), 1–34 (2024)
123. Kaur, H., Nori, H., Jenkins, S., Caruana, R., Wallach, H., Wortman Vaughan, J.: Interpreting interpretability: understanding data scientists' use of interpretability tools for machine learning. In: Proceedings of the 2020 CHI Conference on Human Factors in Computing Systems, pp. 1–14 (2020)
124. Bansal, G., Nushi, B., Kamar, E., Weld, D.S., Lasecki, W.S., Horvitz, E.: Updates in human-AI teams: understanding and addressing the performance/compatibility tradeoff. In: Proceedings of the AAAI Conference on Artificial Intelligence, vol. 33, pp. 2429–2437 (2019)
125. Zhang, R., Duan, W., Flathmann, C., McNeese, N., Knijnenburg, B., Freeman, G.: Verbal vs. visual: how humans perceive and collaborate with AI teammates using different communication modalities in various human-AI team compositions. Proc. ACM Hum.-Comput. Interact. **8**(CSCW2), 1–34 (2024)
126. Liu, N., Pu, Q., Shi, Y., Zhang, S., Qiu, L.: Older adults' interaction with intelligent virtual assistants: the role of information modality and feedback. Int. J. Hum.–Comput. Interact. **39**(5), 1162–1183 (2023)
127. Le Bigot, L., Terrier, P., Amiel, V., Poulain, G., Jamet, E., Rouet, J.F.: Effect of modality on collaboration with a dialogue system. Int. J. Hum.-Comput. Stud. **65**(12), 983–991 (2007)
128. He, G., Aishwarya, N., Gadiraju, U.: Is conversational XAI all you need? Human-AI decision making with a conversational XAI assistant. In: Proceedings of the 30th International Conference on Intelligent User Interfaces, pp. 907–924 (2025)
129. Cai, C.J., Winter, S., Steiner, D., Wilcox, L., Terry, M.: "hello ai": uncovering the onboarding needs of medical practitioners for human-ai collaborative decision-making. Proc. ACM Hum.-Comput. Interact. **3**(CSCW), 1–24 (2019)
130. Wang, J., Molina, M.D., Sundar, S.S.: When expert recommendation contradicts peer opinion: relative social influence of valence, group identity and artificial intelligence. Comput. Hum. Behav. **107**, 106278 (2020)
131. Grønsund, T., Aanestad, M.: Augmenting the algorithm: emerging human-in-the-loop work configurations. J. Strateg. Inf. Syst. **29**(2), 101614 (2020)
132. Wang, B.Y., Boell, S.K., Riemer, K., Peter, S.: Human agency in AI configurations supporting organizational decision-making. In: ACIS 2023 Proceedings, vol. 53 (2023). https://aisel.aisnet.org/acis2023/53
133. Fogliato, R., Chappidi, S., Lungren, M., Fisher, P., Wilson, D., Fitzke, M., Parkinson, M., Horvitz, E., Inkpen, K., Nushi, B.: Who goes first? influences of human-AI workflow on decision making in clinical imaging. In: Proceedings of the 2022 ACM Conference on Fairness, Accountability, and Transparency, pp. 1362–1374 (2022)
134. Shin, J., Hedderich, M.A., Rey, B.J., Lucero, A., Oulasvirta, A.: Understanding human-AI workflows for generating personas. In: Proceedings of the 2024 ACM Designing Interactive Systems Conference, pp. 757–781 (2024)
135. Wu, T., Terry, M., Cai, C.J.: AI chains: transparent and controllable human-AI interaction by chaining large language model prompts. In: Proceedings of the 2022 CHI Conference on Human Factors in Computing Systems, pp. 1–22 (2022)
136. Allen, G., He, G., Gadiraju, U.: Power-up! What can generative models do for human computation workflows? Preprint. arXiv:2307.02243 (2023)
137. Wu, T., Zhu, H., Albayrak, M., Axon, A., Bertsch, A., Deng, W., Ding, Z., Guo, B., Gururaja, S., Kuo, T.S., et al.: LLMs as workers in human-computational algorithms? Replicating crowdsourcing pipelines with LLMs. Preprint. arXiv:2307.10168 (2023)
138. Schoeffer, J., De-Arteaga, M., Kuehl, N.: Explanations, fairness, and appropriate reliance in human-AI decision-making. In: Proceedings of the CHI Conference on Human Factors in Computing Systems, pp. 1–18 (2024)
139. He, G., Gadiraju, U.: Walking on eggshells: using analogies to promote appropriate reliance in human-AI decision making. In: Proceedings of the Workshop on Trust and Reliance on AI-

Human Teams at the ACM Conference on Human Factors in Computing Systems (CHI'22) (2022)
140. Küper, A., Krämer, N.: Psychological traits and appropriate reliance: factors shaping trust in AI. Int. J. Hum.–Comput. Interact. **41**(7), 4115–4131 (2025)
141. Guo, Z., Wu, Y., Hartline, J.D., Hullman, J.: A decision theoretic framework for measuring AI reliance. In: Proceedings of the 2024 ACM Conference on Fairness, Accountability, and Transparency, pp. 221–236 (2024)
142. Schlicker, N., Baum, K., Uhde, A., Sterz, S., Hirsch, M.C., Langer, M.: How do we assess the trustworthiness of AI? Introducing the trustworthiness assessment model (TrAM). Comput. Hum. Behav. **170**, 108671 (2025)
143. Schemmer, M., Kuehl, N., Benz, C., Bartos, A., Satzger, G.: Appropriate reliance on AI advice: conceptualization and the effect of explanations. In: Proceedings of the 28th International Conference on Intelligent User Interfaces, pp. 410–422 (2023)
144. Benda, N.C., Novak, L.L., Reale, C., Ancker, J.S., Trust in AI: why we should be designing for appropriate reliance. J. Am. Med. Inf. Assoc. **29**(1), 207–212 (2022)
145. Kahr, P.K., Rooks, G., Willemsen, M.C., Snijders, C.C.: Understanding trust and reliance development in AI advice: assessing model accuracy, model explanations, and experiences from previous interactions. ACM Trans. Interact. Intell. Syst. **14**(4), 1–30 (2024)
146. Upadhyay, S., Lakkaraju, H., Gajos, K.Z.: Counterfactual explanations may not be the best algorithmic recourse approach. In: Proceedings of the 30th International Conference on Intelligent User Interfaces, pp. 446–462 (2025)
147. Liao, Q.V., Gruen, D., Miller, S.: Questioning the AI: informing design practices for explainable AI user experiences. In: Proceedings of the 2020 CHI Conference on Human Factors in Computing Systems, pp. 1–15 (2020)
148. Liao, Q.V., Varshney, K.R.: Human-centered explainable AI (XAI): from algorithms to user experiences. Preprint. arXiv:2110.10790 (2021)
149. Liao, Q.V., Pribić, M., Han, J., Miller, S., Sow, D.: Question-driven design process for explainable ai user experiences. Preprint. arXiv:2104.03483 (2021)
150. Liao, Q.V., Zhang, Y., Luss, R., Doshi-Velez, F., Dhurandhar, A.: Connecting algorithmic research and usage contexts: a perspective of contextualized evaluation for explainable AI. In: Proceedings of the AAAI Conference on Human Computation and Crowdsourcing, vol. 10, pp. 147–159 (2022)
151. Liao, Q.V., Vaughan, J.W.: AI transparency in the age of LLMs: a human-centered research roadmap. Preprint. arXiv:2306.01941, 10 (2023)
152. Kim, S.S., Vaughan, J.W., Liao, Q.V., Lombrozo, T., Russakovsky, O.: Fostering appropriate reliance on large language models: the role of explanations, sources, and inconsistencies. In: Proceedings of the 2025 CHI Conference on Human Factors in Computing Systems, pp. 1–19 (2025)
153. Ehsan, U., Liao, Q.V., Passi, S., Riedl, M.O., Daumé III, H.: Seamful xai: operationalizing seamful design in explainable AI. Proc. ACM Hum.-Comput. Interact. **8**(CSCW1), 1–29 (2024)
154. Ehsan, U., Passi, S., Liao, Q.V., Chan, L., Lee, I.H., Muller, M., Riedl, M.O.: The who in XAI: how AI background shapes perceptions of AI explanations. In: Proceedings of the 2024 CHI Conference on Human Factors in Computing Systems, pp. 1–32 (2024)
155. Schmuckler, M.A.: What is ecological validity? A dimensional analysis. Infancy **2**(4), 419–436 (2001)
156. Kihlstrom, J.F.: Ecological validity and "ecological validity". Perspect. Psychol. Sci. **16**(2), 466–471 (2021)
157. Fok, R., Weld, D.S.: In search of verifiability: explanations rarely enable complementary performance in ai-advised decision making. AI Magazine **45**(3), 317–332 (2024)
158. Miller, T.: Explainable AI is dead, long live explainable AI! Hypothesis-driven decision support using evaluative AI. In: Proceedings of the 2023 ACM Conference on Fairness, Accountability, and Transparency, pp. 333–342 (2023)

159. Buçinca, Z., Malaya, M.B., Gajos, K.Z.: To trust or to think: cognitive forcing functions can reduce overreliance on AI in AI-assisted decision-making. Proc. ACM Hum.-Comput. Interact. **5**(CSCW1), 1–21 (2021)
160. He, G., Bharos, A., Gadiraju, U.: To Err Is AI! Debugging as an intervention to facilitate appropriate reliance on AI systems. In: Proceedings of the 35th ACM Conference on Hypertext and Social Media, pp. 98–105 (2024)
161. Kahr, P.K., Rooks, G., Willemsen, M.C., Snijders, C.C.: It seems smart, but it acts stupid: development of trust in ai advice in a repeated legal decision-making task. In: Proceedings of the 28th International Conference on Intelligent User Interfaces, pp. 528–539 (2023)
162. Kahr, P., Rooks, G., Snijders, C.C., Willemsen, M.C.: Good performance isn't enough to trust AI. Lessons from logistics experts on their long-term collaboration with an AI planning system. In: ACM CHI 2025 Conference on Human Factors in Computing Systems. Association for Computing Machinery, Inc, New York (2025)
163. He, G., Hemmer, P., Vössing, M., Schemmer, M., Gadiraju, U.: Fine-grained appropriate reliance: human-AI collaboration with a multi-step transparent decision workflow for complex task decomposition. Preprint. arXiv:2501.10909 (2025)
164. Balayn, A., Pi, Y., Widder, D.G., Alfrink, K., Yurrita, M., Upadhyay, S., Karusala, N., Lyons, H., Turkay, C., Tessono, C., et al.: From stem to stern: contestability along AI value chains. In: Companion Publication of the 2024 Conference on Computer-Supported Cooperative Work and Social Computing, pp. 720–723 (2024)
165. D'Amour, A., Srinivasan, H., Atwood, J., Baljekar, P., Sculley, D., Halpern, Y.: Fairness is not static: deeper understanding of long term fairness via simulation studies. In: Proceedings of the 2020 Conference on Fairness, Accountability, and Transparency, pp. 525–534 (2020)
166. Yurrita, M., Draws, T., Balayn, A., Murray-Rust, D., Tintarev, N., Bozzon, A.: Disentangling fairness perceptions in algorithmic decision-making: the effects of explanations, human oversight, and contestability. In: Proceedings of the 2023 CHI Conference on Human Factors in Computing Systems, CHI '23. Association for Computing Machinery, New York (2023). https://doi.org/10.1145/3544548.3581161
167. Yurrita, M., Verma, H., Balayn, A., Gadiraju, U., Pont, S., Bozzon, A.: Towards effective human intervention in algorithmic decision-making: understanding the effect of decision-makers' configuration on decision-subjects' fairness perceptions. In: Proceedings of the CHI Conference on Human Factors in Computing Systems (2025)
168. Decker, M.C., Wegner, L., Leicht-Scholten, C.: Procedural fairness in algorithmic decision-making: the role of public engagement. Ethics Inf. Technol. **27**(1), 1 (2025)
169. Yurrita, M., Verma, H., Balayn, A., Alfrink, K., Gadiraju, U., Bozzon, A.: Identifying algorithmic decision subjects' needs for meaningful contestability. In: Proceedings of the CSCW Conference on Computer-Supported Collaborative Work (2025)
170. Walmsley, J.: Artificial intelligence and the value of transparency. AI Soc. **36**(2), 585–595 (2021)
171. Kaminski, M.E., Urban, J.M.: The right to contest AI. Columbia Law Rev. **121**(7), 1957–2048 (2021)
172. Madiega, T.: Artificial Intelligence Act. European Parliament: European Parliamentary Research Service, Brussels (2021)
173. Voigt, P., Von dem Bussche, A.: The EU General Data Protection Regulation (GDPR). A Practical Guide, 1st edn., Springer International Publishing, Cham (2017)
174. Cheng, H.F., Wang, R., Zhang, Z., O'connell, F., Gray, T., Harper, F.M., Zhu, H.: Explaining decision-making algorithms through UI: strategies to help non-expert stakeholders. In: Proceedings of the 2019 CHI Conference on Human Factors in Computing Systems, pp. 1–12 (2019)
175. Alfrink, K., Keller, I., Semperena, M.Y., Bulygin, D., Kortuem, G., Doorn, N.: Envisioning contestability loops: evaluating the agonistic arena as a generative metaphor for public AI. She Ji: J. Des. Econ. Innovation **10**(1), 53–93 (2024)

176. Lyons, H., Velloso, E., Miller, T.: Conceptualising contestability: perspectives on contesting algorithmic decisions. Proc. ACM Hum.-Comput. Interact. **5**(CSCW1), 1–25 (2021)
177. Alfrink, K., Keller, I., Doorn, N., Kortuem, G.: Contestable camera cars: a speculative design exploration of public AI that is open and responsive to dispute. In: Proceedings of the 2023 CHI Conference on Human Factors in Computing Systems, pp. 1–16 (2023)
178. Lyons, H., Wijenayake, S., Miller, T., Velloso, E.: What's the appeal? Perceptions of review processes for algorithmic decisions. In: Proceedings of the 2022 CHI Conference on Human Factors in Computing Systems, pp. 1–15 (2022)
179. Lyons, H., Miller, T., Velloso, E.: Algorithmic decisions, desire for control, and the preference for human review over algorithmic review. In: Proceedings of the 2023 ACM Conference on Fairness, Accountability, and Transparency, pp. 764–774 (2023)
180. Crawford, K., Joler, V.: Anatomy of an AI system. Anatomy of an AI System (2018)
181. Widder, D.G., Nafus, D.: Dislocated accountabilities in the "AI supply chain": modularity and developers' notions of responsibility. Big Data Soc. **10**(1), 20539517231177620 (2023)
182. Cobbe, J., Veale, M., Singh, J.: Understanding accountability in algorithmic supply chains. In: Proceedings of the 2023 ACM Conference on Fairness, Accountability, and Transparency, pp. 1186–1197 (2023)
183. Balayn, A., Yurrita, M., Rancourt, F., Casati, F., Gadiraju, U.: Unpacking trust dynamics in the LLM supply chain: an empirical exploration to foster trustworthy LLM production & use. In: Proceedings of the 2025 CHI Conference on Human Factors in Computing Systems, pp. 1–20 (2025)
184. Attard-Frost, B., Widder, D.G.: The ethics of ai value chains. Big Data Soc. **12**(2), 20539517251340603 (2025)
185. Deng, W.H., Nagireddy, M., Lee, M.S.A., Singh, J., Wu, Z.S., Holstein, K., Zhu, H.: Exploring how machine learning practitioners (try to) use fairness toolkits. In: Proceedings of the 2022 ACM Conference on Fairness, Accountability, and Transparency, pp. 473–484 (2022)
186. Balayn, A., Yurrita, M., Yang, J., Gadiraju, U., "Fairness toolkits, a checkbox culture?" On the factors that fragment developer practices in handling algorithmic harms. In: Proceedings of the 2023 AAAI/ACM Conference on AI, Ethics, and Society, pp. 482–495 (2023)
187. Muralikumar, M.D., McDonald, D.W.: Analyzing collaborative challenges and needs of UX practitioners when designing with AI/ML. Proc. ACM on Hum.-Comput. Interact. **8**(CSCW2), 1–25 (2024)
188. Zdanowska, S., Taylor, A.S.: A study of UX practitioners roles in designing real-world, enterprise ML systems. In: Proceedings of the 2022 CHI Conference on Human Factors in Computing Systems, pp. 1–15 (2022)
189. Liao, Q.V., Subramonyam, H., Wang, J., Wortman Vaughan, J.: Designerly understanding: information needs for model transparency to support design ideation for AI-powered user experience. In: Proceedings of the 2023 CHI Conference on Human Factors in Computing Systems, pp. 1–21 (2023)
190. Subramonyam, H., Im, J., Seifert, C., Adar, E.: Solving separation-of-concerns problems in collaborative design of human-AI systems through leaky abstractions. In: Proceedings of the 2022 CHI Conference on Human Factors in Computing Systems, pp. 1–21 (2022)
191. Deshpande, A., Sharp, H.: Responsible AI systems: who are the stakeholders? In: Proceedings of the 2022 AAAI/ACM Conference on AI, Ethics, and Society, pp. 227–236 (2022)
192. Posada, J., Newlands, G., Miceli, M.: Labor, automation, and human-machine communication. The Sage Handbook of Human-Machine Communication, pp. 384–391 (2023)
193. Sambasivan, N., Kapania, S., Highfill, H., Akrong, D., Paritosh, P., Aroyo, L.M.: "Everyone wants to do the model work, not the data work": data cascades in high-stakes AI. In: Proceedings of the 2021 CHI Conference on Human Factors in Computing Systems, pp. 1–15 (2021)
194. Hada, R., Husain, S., Gumma, V., Diddee, H., Yadavalli, A., Seth, A., Kulkarni, N., Gadiraju, U., Vashistha, A., Seshadri, V., et al.: Akal Badi ya Bias: an exploratory study of gender bias in Hindi language technology. In: Proceedings of the 2024 ACM Conference on Fairness, Accountability, and Transparency, pp. 1926–1939 (2024)

195. Altenried, M.: The platform as factory: crowdwork and the hidden labour behind artificial intelligence. Capital Class **44**(2), 145–158 (2020)
196. Balayn, A., Gürses, S.: Beyond debiasing: regulating ai and its inequalities. EDRi report (2021)
197. Jakesch, M., Buçinca, Z., Amershi, S., Olteanu, A.: How different groups prioritize ethical values for responsible AI. In: Proceedings of the 2022 ACM Conference on Fairness, Accountability, and Transparency, FAccT '22, pp. 310–323. Association for Computing Machinery, New York, 2022. https://doi.org/10.1145/3531146.3533097
198. Madaio, M.A., Stark, L., Wortman Vaughan, J., Wallach, H.: Co-designing checklists to understand organizational challenges and opportunities around fairness in AI. In: Proceedings of the 2020 CHI Conference on Human Factors in Computing Systems, CHI '20, pp. 1–14. Association for Computing Machinery, New York, 2020. https://doi.org/10.1145/3313831.3376445
199. Madaio, M., Egede, L., Subramonyam, H., Wortman Vaughan, J., Wallach, H.: Assessing the fairness of AI systems: AI practitioners' processes, challenges, and needs for support. Proc. ACM Hum.-Comput. Interact. **6**(CSCW1), 1–26 (2022)
200. Rakova, B., Yang, J., Cramer, H., Chowdhury, R.: Where responsible AI meets reality: practitioner perspectives on enablers for shifting organizational practices. Proc. ACM Hum.-Comput. Interact. **5**(CSCW1) (2021). https://doi.org/10.1145/3449081
201. Coeckelbergh, M.: Artificial intelligence, responsibility attribution, and a relational justification of explainability. Sci. Eng. Ethics **26**(4), 2051–2068 (2020)
202. Balayn, A., Corti, L., Rancourt, F., Casati, F., Gadiraju, U.: Understanding stakeholders' perceptions and needs across the LLM supply chain. Preprint. arXiv:2405.16311 (2024)
203. Deng, W.H., Yildirim, N., Chang, M., Eslami, M., Holstein, K., Madaio, M., Investigating practices and opportunities for cross-functional collaboration around AI fairness in industry practice. In: Proceedings of the 2023 ACM Conference on Fairness, Accountability, and Transparency, pp. 705–716 (2023)
204. Balayn, A., Guerses, S.: Misguided: AI regulation needs a shift in focus. Internet Policy Rev. **13**(3) (2024)
205. Luitse, D.: Platform power in AI: the evolution of cloud infrastructures in the political economy of artificial intelligence. Int. Politics Rev. **13**(2), 1–44 (2024)
206. Van Der Vlist, F., Helmond, A., Ferrari, F.: Big AI: cloud infrastructure dependence and the industrialisation of artificial intelligence. Big Data Soc. **11**(1), 20539517241232630 (2024)
207. Narayanan, A., Kapoor, S.: AI Snake Oil. Princeton University Press, Princeton (2024)
208. Chien, A.A., Lin, L., Nguyen, H., Rao, V., Sharma, T., Wijayawardana, R.: Reducing the carbon impact of generative AI inference (today and in 2035). In: Proceedings of the 2nd Workshop on Sustainable Computer Systems, pp. 1–7 (2023)
209. Bommasani, R., Hudson, D.A., Adeli, E., Altman, R., Arora, S., von Arx, S., Bernstein, M.S., Bohg, J., Bosselut, A., Brunskill, E., et al.: On the opportunities and risks of foundation models. Preprint. arXiv:2108.07258 (2021)
210. Argote, L., Ingram, P.: Knowledge transfer: a basis for competitive advantage in firms. Organ. Behav. Hum. Decis. Process. **82**(1), 150–169 (2000)
211. Carr, N.: The Glass Cage: How Our Computers Are Changing Us. WW Norton & Company, New York (2014)
212. Lee, H.-P., Sarkar, A., Tankelevitch, L., Drosos, I., Rintel, S., Banks, R., Wilson, N.: The impact of generative AI on critical thinking: self-reported reductions in cognitive effort and confidence effects from a survey of knowledge workers. In: Proceedings of the 2025 CHI conference on human factors in computing systems, pp. 1–22 (2025)
213. Erlei, Alexander and Sharma, Abhinav and Gadiraju, Ujwal: Understanding Choice Independence and Error Types in Human-AI Collaboration. Proceedings of the CHI Conference on Human Factors in Computing Systems, 1–19 (2024)

Ujwal Gadiraju is a tenured Associate Professor in the Software Technology Department of the EEMCS Faculty, Delft University of Technology. He co-directs the TU Delft "Design@Scale" AI Lab. Ujwal co-leads a research line on human-centred AI and crowd computing at the Web Information Systems group. Previously, he was a postdoctoral researcher at the L3S Research Center in Hannover, Germany, and received a PhD (summa cum laude) in Computer Science from the Leibniz University of Hannover. His work has been recognized with honours, including best paper awards at premier HCI and AI conferences. His current research focuses on advancing human-centred AI through innovative computational techniques and systems that enhance human experiences, align AI systems with human values, promote inclusivity, and foster appropriate human reliance on AI systems.

Agathe Balayn is a Postdoctoral Researcher at Microsoft Research in the FATE team. Prior to that, she ob-tained her PhD in Computer Science from Delft University of Technology. Her work lies at the intersection of HCI, AI, and critical computing. She has conducted empirical qualitative studies with over 200 AI practitioners and researchers spanning various AI supply chains (e.g. LLMs for customer service activities, computer vision for pig farming). She has surfaced their concerns and practices vis-a-vis (responsible) AI, the factors that shape these practices, and their limitations. Her insights typically result in conceptual frameworks, recommendations for artifacts (e.g. interfaces, toolkits), and governance procedures to guide AI practitioners and bear policy implications.

Part III
Value Creation with Enterprise AI

A human-centred lens is imperative to promote wide-scale and successful adoption of AI in the enterprise. This is not just essential to winning social licence and trust but also to ensure AI systems amplify human potential well beyond the benefits and pitfalls of automation. As organizations increasingly embed AI into their operations, the focus must shift from technical feasibility to meaningful value creation, responsible integration, and sustained stakeholder trust.

This part brings together leading perspectives on how enterprises can unlock the full potential of AI by aligning technological capabilities with organizational goals, ethical considerations, and human values. The chapters explore frameworks for realizing business value, mechanisms for building trust, and strategies for embedding AI into core business processes.

The first chapter from Ida Someh and Barbara Wixom presents a practical framework for creating value from enterprise AI. Drawing on insights from global executives, the authors identify the organizational resources and project-level practices that enable successful AI initiatives. They highlight common obstacles to value realization and offer actionable recommendations for AI leaders seeking to align AI capabilities with strategic goals. This chapter sets the foundation for understanding how AI can be a driver of enterprise transformation when implemented with purpose and clarity.

The second chapter by Marek Kowalkiewicz, Christian Janiesch, and Michael Rosemann explores the fundamental transformation from traditional rule-based automation to AI-driven enterprise autonomization. The authors distinguish between automation's deterministic execution of predefined tasks and autonomization's goal-oriented approach, where AI agents independently determine optimal paths to achieve specified objectives. Through the lens of three core capabilities, framed independence, neglect tolerance, as well as indeterminism, and illustrated by case studies from JPMorgan Chase, General Electric, Walmart, and healthcare institutions, the chapter presents a three-phase implementation framework (Deploy, Reshape, Invent) for organizational transformation. This chapter emphasizes that successful enterprise autonomization requires not just technological advancement but equal investment in human capabilities, creating synergistic systems where human creativity and AI autonomy amplify each other's strengths to achieve previously impossible outcomes.

The third chapter by Steven Lockey and Nicole Gillespie addresses the critical issue of trust in AI. Based on a large-scale international survey, the authors reveal public concerns about AI risks and a strong demand for trustworthy AI practices. They propose four pathways to trust, institutional, motivational, uncertainty, and knowledge, and validate these through empirical analysis. Their findings offer enterprises guidance for building trust through transparent design, robust governance, and stakeholder engagement and highlight the importance of trust for long-term AI adoption and impact.

The final chapter by Shaoyang Fan and Javad Pool provides a series of case studies that illustrate the diverse ways AI is influencing enterprise software and systems. By analysing both successful and failed implementations across companies like Canva, Zillow, and the Australian Government's Robodebt program, the authors extract valuable lessons about the conditions under which AI creates (or fails to create) value. These real-world insights reinforce the importance of context, leadership, and adaptability in enterprise AI initiatives.

Together, these chapters offer a multidimensional view of value creation with AI that balances innovation with responsibility and efficiency with trust. They provide a roadmap for enterprises seeking to harness AI not just as a tool for automation but as a catalyst for meaningful, sustainable transformation.

Chapter 8
Creating Value from Enterprise AI

Ida Someh and Barbara Wixom

Abstract Artificial intelligence (AI) is rapidly transforming the business landscape, offering immense potential for value creation. However, many companies struggle to effectively implement AI initiatives, limiting their ability to reap the full benefits of this technology revolution. This chapter presents a framework on AI value that identifies AI and complementary organizational resources and the process by which these resources can be assembled together within AI projects to create value for organizations. In addition, we identify obstacles to AI value creation and offers recommendations for AI leaders. The recommendations are informed by executives from around the world who are leading AI teams and who are accountable for AI success.

8.1 Introduction

Artificial intelligence (AI) represents a set of technologies to find patterns in data, make predictions, and find recommended actions without explicit human instructions [1]. What distinguishes AI from predictive and prescriptive analytics is AI's ability to self-learn and to process natural language [2]. AI can autonomously conduct tasks and engage with people—for example, social bots chatting to customers or Uber algorithms giving instructions to drivers. In our own recent case studies, AI was used by Microsoft to streamline the enterprise sales process by predicting the likelihood of a sale to close [8], by Cochlear to improve the sound experience of hearing implant patients by identifying sound contexts and automatically adjusting sound device settings [9], and by BBVA to help banking customers manage personal

I. Someh (✉)
Information Systems Discipline, UQ Business School, The University of Queensland, Brisbane, QLD, Australia
e-mail: i.asadi@business.uq.edu.au

B. Wixom
MIT Center for Information Systems Research, Massachusetts Institute of Technology, Cambridge, MA, USA
e-mail: bwixom@mit.edu

S. Sadiq (ed.), *Enterprise AI*, https://doi.org/10.1007/978-3-032-01940-0_8

finances by predicting future transactions and categorizing spend [10]. These types of positive AI outcomes and the wide range of benefits they represent are consistent with AI value communicated in the popular press [2, 6].

There is emerging evidence that AI can create value for organizations by reducing process costs, enabling new revenue streams, and increasing product sales. According to the McKinsey Global Institute, at a "global average level of adoption," AI could deliver 1.2% additional GDP growth annually. Despite promising AI trends and forecasts, the value of AI is not clear to many stakeholders, as it can cause negative externalities through activities such as extensive individual profiling and algorithmic decisions, which can threaten privacy and can cause discrimination [4]. Also, AI's ability to replace humans or reshape human work tasks has implications for workforce employability and the changing roles of workers, such as domain experts (e.g., doctors, engineers, financiers, or other specialists) who have deep knowledge and experience within their fields [1, 5]. Arguably, researchers can draw upon decision support and other related literature to propose and study how organizations can effectively deploy AI. However, AI's contemporary contexts, novel characteristics (e.g., self-learning and autonomy), and its potential to create unintended consequences suggest that there are nuances about AI that must be explored using present-day, AI-specific research efforts. Such efforts are required before leaders can deeply understand AI implementation—and the acceptable approaches through which AI can create value. Thus, we ask the following research questions: *How can organizations create value from enterprise AI?*

This chapter presents a framework that identifies obstacles for AI adoption within a value creation context. We use the framework to provide practical guidance for business and AI leaders who hope to exploit AI in fruitful, acceptable ways. In the following sections, we first use the framework to organize data about AI obstacles that we collected from senior executives. Next, we share descriptions of six AI projects that reinforce and further inform AI obstacles. We will conclude the chapter with a presentation of resulting recommendations for AI executives and leaders.

8.2 A Framework on Artificial Intelligence Value

Figure 8.1 represents a process-oriented view of how AI creates value for organizations, which we term the AI Value Framework. We developed this framework by extending an existing practice-based framework on generating value from data [11]. For this study, we extended the framework by drawing on recent case studies and recent literature specific to AI [6, 12–14]. Specifically, the framework was changed by (1) adding additional AI and organizational resources and (2) organizing concepts by project level and organization level.

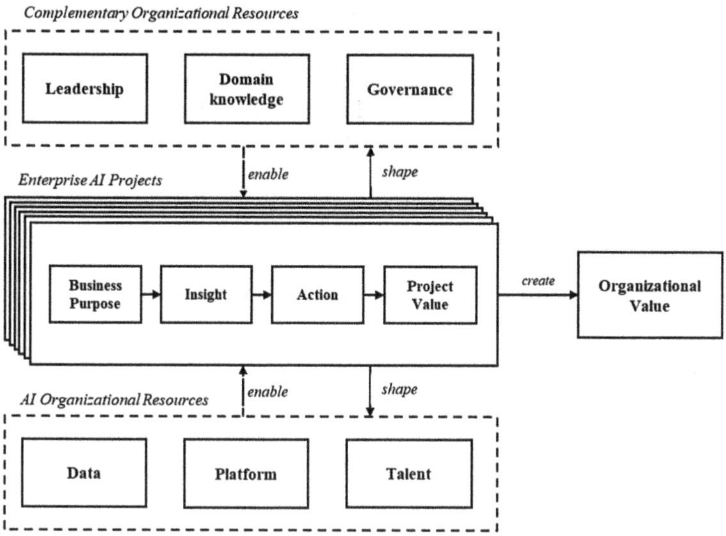

Fig. 8.1 AI value framework

8.2.1 Enterprise AI Projects

The framework communicates that organizations create AI value at the project level by following four distinct steps: (1) formulating a business purpose; (2) generating meaningful insights from the data; (3) taking actions based on the insights, possibly in the form of automated business processes; and (4) realizing project value [11]. The project is enabled by three key AI organizational resources (i.e., data, platform, and talent) and by three complementary organizational resources (i.e., leadership, domain knowledge, and governance), all of which can be shaped by project activities as they are executed. AI projects might be narrow in focus (e.g., automating a granular sales task), and for this reason, execution of multiple AI projects over time generates overall organizational value.

8.2.2 AI Organizational Resources

Value creation at the AI project level depends on AI organizational resources, which are a subset of the organization's overall resources; specifically, three AI organizational resources are required for AI project execution. **Data** includes a range of structured and unstructured datasets sourced from internal and external systems that can be used to formulate and train AI algorithms. **Platform** includes technology and processes required to manipulate the datasets and to access and distribute data and analytics services. **Talent** refers to data scientists who specialize in building and working with algorithms that predict, classify, or cluster data.

Every time an AI project is executed, the knowledge created by the project further shapes the AI organizational resources. For example, data scientists assigned to improve customer retention with AI can develop a novel churn algorithm, which subsequently can be integrated into a platform and get reused for other projects.

8.2.3 Complementary Organizational Resources

Complementary organizational resources are a set of non-IT factors—leadership, domain knowledge, and governance—that facilitate organizational adoption and diffusion of AI [15]. **Leadership** represents the organization's vision and commitment to AI. **Domain knowledge** is the know-how of experts in areas of content to which AI will be applied such as employee retention, marketing segmentation, and supply chain optimization. **Governance** includes mechanisms by which AI-related decisions and processes are managed in ways that benefit organizational stakeholders and minimize risks. Complementary organizational resources typically are associated with changes to organizational design, business models, processes and rules, culture, and legal requirements, and they are necessary for pervasive, responsible AI use [1, 16].

8.3 Research Method

8.3.1 Executive Discussion

In order to validate the usefulness of the framework, we convened an online discussion with the members of the MIT Center for Information Systems Research Data Advisory Board in Quarter 1 of 2019. The Board consisted of 95 data executives representing 67 large companies headquartered around the globe. Most organizations were multi-national and for-profit, and the executives held Chief Data Officer, Chief Analytics Officer, or equivalent roles.

Each executive was asked to answer the following question in an online discussion board (they were given a deadline of 1 month to submit responses):

What are the top three obstacles to AI adoption/consumption in your company?

Along with the question, we provided the executives with the following AI definition:

> *Definition: Artificial intelligence (AI) is a set of technologies that seeks to mimic human ability to understand data, find patterns, make predictions and find recommended actions without explicit human instructions. What distinguishes AI technology from traditional predictive and prescriptive analytics is (1) its ability to self-learn and (2) its ability to process natural language* [1].

Table 8.1 AI project obstacles

Obstacle/evidence	Cnt
Compelling Business Objective "Not having a good use case for AI, which needs to be driven from the business rather than the Chief Data Analytics Office or Technology" "Use cases with a clear return on investment for the business"	22
AI Development "[Minimum viable product] and agile development and deployment" "Create an environment where we can experiment and fail fast. Learn from previous experience and fine-tune going forward"	6
Fear and Mistrust "Fear of 'the black box'. We work in a very high risk industry. It will be a long time before we leverage technologies that self-learn and limits or removes human interaction" "Inability of certain complex models to explain the outcomes. Models that cannot provide explanation of recommendations are unlikely to be adopted"	8
Process Integration "Integration with legacy systems that may be required to consume the AI algorithms by the business" "Cadence of deploying AI models and fully integrating them into core business processes"	8
Culture "The culture of using data to drive decisions, leading to ignorance on what data can solve for" "Focus on the present, not the future; current-year operational and financial performance metrics that focus on aggressive performance in the current year, rather than the next 5 years"	9
Project Value "Value demonstration at scale" "Proving out the resulting value"	8

Ultimately, 53 data executives from 50 organizations answered our question, resulting in a 75% response rate (we only required one answer per organization). Several respondents provided artifacts (e.g., internal company reports, decks) to support their answers. Some of the non-respondents specifically explained that their lack of response was due to lack of AI activity at their organization.

Two researchers analyzed the board answers using thematic content analysis to identify common patterns and emergent themes [17] and to create a list of AI obstacle categories. Then, we iteratively matched these categories with components of the AI value framework. See Tables 8.1, 8.2, and 8.3 for the results of this process. Each table lists the distinct obstacles that the team identified, representative evidence, and the number of board members who contributed the obstacle in their response.

The executive discussion helped the research team in two important ways. First, the process identified **common AI obstacles**; data quality, AI talent, compelling business objective, and AI platform were most often repeated across board member

Table 8.2 AI adoption: organizational resource obstacles

Obstacles/evidence	Cnt
Training Data Sets "Huge volume of continuously fresh data to establish a model and mature it via learning algorithms" "Lack of transaction data on which to train"	3
Data Quality "Availability of good clean data is the most pressing issue right now. We are still in the infant stage of exploring what we might be able to do with our data and have some good ideas but without the foundations there is limited ability to do a lot" "Data quality; data that has missing elements and data that is corrupted in systematic ways"	29
Data Structures "Working with external data sources that follow different taxonomies than the ones used at [my company]" "Confusion regarding terminology and definitions is fracturing our progress. A common lexicon can enable groups to work together more and make more progress"	7
AI Platform "Need for new architectures and technologies not used in the traditional company" "Scalable processing power"	19
AI Talent "Skills. To get AI in use, data has to be assembled, wrangled into an algorithm, and the algorithm has to be put in a context where its results can matter. All three of these steps need specialist skills at a relatively high level. We don't have many people who can effectively select and use algorithms" "Skilled technical people who understand our processes, data, and the AI technologies"	25

responses. Second, the process identified obstacles that were **unique to AI**; fear and mistrust, training datasets, acceptable data use, domain engagement, and AI talent represent obstacles that do not traditionally surface as data obstacles (such as those in [11]).

8.3.2 Project Description Review

To better understand the AI obstacles that were categorized into Tables 8.1, 8.2, and 8.3 and to further validate their importance, the authors explored descriptions of actual AI projects conducted in conjunction with a professional services firm (i.e., a set of client engagements). The firm, Alix Partners, is a global consulting organization that established a practice in AI in 2015. In 4 years, the practice has participated in 85 engagements that involve AI. Recently, the practice confidentially inventoried key projects for internal knowledge management purposes. One member

Table 8.3 AI adoption: complementary organizational resource obstacles

Obstacles/evidence	Cnt
Top Management Understanding/Support "Lack of executive understanding of what AI takes" "[Our executives] all hear about it, they want it, they think it is "cool" (direct quote from CCO). But when push comes to shove they are hesitant to take away investment from traditional forms of P/L spend and invest in AI"	14
Domain Expert Engagement "There needs to be a way that is interactive, pleasing to the eye (UX Design) and "dummied down" for general audiences to interact with the AI and to modify how it behaves on some basic parameters" "Lack of skills and expertise in the business areas to engage with, to identify what problems could be solved through AI capabilities"	4
Acceptable Data Use "Adoption of a scalable framework, set of practices, and controls to ensure that sensitive data, models, and work products are appropriately governed, protected, and shared, internally and with partners" "Unclear policies around consent, privacy, ethical use of data. Lack of clarity results in shutting down all data access to data scientists, and all requests are redirected through Legal/Risk/Compliance"	6
Enterprise Strategy "Prioritization across the organization (i.e. for AI to be effective, data efforts need to be very well aligned across the whole organization—not just in the analytics domain)" "Development of a unified data strategy that is endorsed and actively supported and integrated across the entire business"	8

of the research team, the managing director of this practice, reviewed the inventory of 85 engagements and identified a representative sample of 6 for the full research team to analyze. The purposeful sample was created to showcase a diverse set of companies across industries, in which a wide set of AI obstacles had been overcome. Short descriptions of the six engagements are included in the following sections. Note that three of the engagements (C, D, and E) were also described in a book authored by one of the authors [18]. Within each description, we indicate the AI obstacles for the reader in brackets.

8.3.2.1 Health IT Company A

Company A, the result of the merger of two previous companies, provides full-payment-lifecycle assurance services to healthcare clients, and the combined entity has an annual revenue of over $1B. Company A wanted to differentiate itself by using AI across the enterprise to gain market share by processing claims faster and improving the quality of payments results, increasing revenues by identifying a larger percentage of bad claims, and reducing labor through automation of claims processes and integration of shared services. For training datasets, the company relied largely on over 3 petabytes of historic US healthcare claims data.

In implementing its AI strategy, Company A encountered technical obstacles [AI Platform] but found leadership [Top Management Understanding/Support] and talent [AI Talent] more difficult to overcome. To overcome the obstacles, the company educated its senior management about AI. It hired data science and data engineering talent and created a new engineering organization to build the modern AI platform and models. It stood up a new shared services group to reengineer processes [Process Integration] to execute AI-based insights through workflow solutions. To prove the value of AI along the way and win over skeptics [Compelling Business Objective], the company created its AI capability incrementally, moving one category of claims to the new platform at a time and implementing claims review concepts one group at a time, with the most valuable ones first.

8.3.2.2 Home Services Company B

Company B is a provider of home services including HVAC, electrical, and plumbing with annual revenue of over $300M. It has an advantageous position in the field service ecosystem at the intersection of the customer, OEMs, and service technicians. Company B set out to build an AI capability to strengthen its customer relationships across existing and new brands, create a comprehensive view of the customer to personalize offerings using internally collected and externally acquired data, and develop a scalable AI platform based on modern technologies to enable current and future AI use cases across business functions. Company B had grown through multiple acquisitions, resulting in a variety of data sources and formats, and had never combined all of its data together before, which created obstacles for creating a single source of truth for customer data [Data Structures, Data Quality]. It also had a highly decentralized workforce with limited knowledge of AI and inconsistent access to data and decision tools [AI Talent, AI Platform].

The company convened its executives for a digital strategy and roadmap workshop to agree on short-, medium-, and long-term goals. It also held multiple deep dive sessions for leaders to understand the company's data, as well as the inner workings of the AI models. It hired expertise in both data science (to build and maintain models) and data engineering (to expand and manage the digital platform). To prove the value from AI [Value], the company measured the results from customer interactions and also developed business cases for over $50M in gross margin enhancement opportunities across multiple areas.

8.3.2.3 Location Analytics Company C

Company C is a start-up company founded in 2011 in San Francisco. Its technology uses mobile phone Wi-Fi signals and spatial analytics to provide stores and restaurants with unique customer location insights. In 2019, the company was acquired by a 5000-employee shared workspace company with the intent of using the technology to increase collaboration and productivity based on employee location data.

From the beginning, Company C recognized that handling people's personally identifying data in an ethical way was imperative. This was a challenging goal, given the nature of its business: recording data emanating from smartphones in retail stores and using data science to supply retailers with the resulting aggregated data [Acceptable Data Use]. Smartphones send a constant stream of pings to connect with Wi-Fi networks, even when the phone owner is not aware of it. Company C can collect that phone data and infer all kinds of insights about individual behavior.

Company C's business caught the attention of both the public and the US Congress; and it became a public imperative to create rules in the location analytics space [Acceptable Data Use]. Although Company C was using data in a conservative manner from a privacy perspective, it was believed that other companies may not follow suit. Company C hired a privacy expert from Stanford University and adopted "privacy by design" principles. The company also worked with seven competitors, the Future of Privacy Forum, and the Federal Trade Commission to create a code of conduct for "locational analytics."

8.3.2.4 Auto Parts Manufacturer Company D

Company D was a start-up founded by Google engineers, bought by a mobility service company in a $680M deal in 2016, and subsequently shuttered in 2018 after failing to meet performance targets. It offered a self-driving kit for long-haul trucks to automate driving tasks. The device included cameras, radar, cutting-edge sensors, as well as controls for power steering and redundant braking, all powered by AI algorithms.

Company D had some success, and one of its self-driving trucks made a successful first delivery of approximately 50,000 cans of beer. However, the company continued to face regulatory obstacles [Acceptable Data Use] and technical obstacles, including lack of sufficient training data to build AI models capable of handling complex situations like bad weather and city driving [Training Data Sets]. To overcome some of the obstacles with training the AI models, Company D hired career truck drivers to augment training data with experience.

8.3.2.5 Biopharmaceutical Company E

Company E is a global leader in the making of human vaccines, with annual revenues of over $40B. Vaccine manufacturing includes many steps, including growing yeast, agitating, fermenting, and purifying. The manufacturing process is highly variable, and if something goes awry, the entire batch must be thrown out. Company E had extensive data about the vaccine line, including 10 years' worth of data from thousands of sensors including shop floor processes, plant equipment maintenance, and building environment sensors that measured air pressure, temperature, and other factors by the minute. By implementing AI, the company was able to conduct a large-scale analysis of its terabytes of data using 15 billion calculations and more than 5.5 million batch-to-batch comparisons. It created heat maps showing data clusters associated with high and low yields. However, validating the insights was challenging and needed expert involvement [Domain Engagement].

Company E allocated experts to examine the heat maps, recommend changes, rework predictive models, and run more analyses to identify problematic factors. Implementing AI also required an experimentation approach and a shift in mindset from reactive to proactive manufacturing intelligence [Development]. Company E realized significant savings in the vaccine-making process while protecting considerably more lives. Demonstrating success with the vaccine line helped with change management and convinced leaders to expand the concept plant-wide and also into other plant.

8.3.2.6 Retail Industry Company F

Company F is a leading global sourcing and logistics provider for the retail clothing industry with over $10B in annual revenue. The company's business performance had worsened significantly in the distressed retail environment, causing decreases in both net income and stock price. The company undertook a comprehensive assessment of business opportunities, digital and AI strategy, and organization structure, resulting in a set of initiatives to increase speed to market, create new service offerings, and enable new ways of working. Company F created a "Digital Transformation" business unit, integrating business and technology staff, to develop complementary roles between AI and domain experts who would carry out the new digital roadmap and AI efforts.

The company started by building, piloting, and rolling out to customers, a first set of over 20 digital applications, including AI-enabled insights for material management, 3D design, design workflow, capacity management, product trend insights, and cost modeling. The company established new digital operations groups for key areas such as 3D design, product design collaboration, digital material management, and customer technical integration to absorb and support the applications [Domain Engagement]. Also, the company hired [Top Management Understanding/Support] a new Chief Digital Officer (CDO), enterprise architect, product owners for key digital offerings, and core software development staff, and it established a governing structure for the new digital transformation unit that consisted of a program management office, executive oversight, vendor management, digital product structure, and metrics and reporting.

The six engagement descriptions support the AI obstacles provided by the executives, and in fact, they begin to shed light on how companies are finding ways to address obstacles. Table 8.4 lists solutions that the research team was able to associate with specific obstacles.

Table 8.4 Engagement solutions to AI obstacles

Enterprise AI project obstacles and solutions	
Compelling Business Objective	Establish small wins by rolling out AI incrementally [A], sequence high-value projects first [A], establish lucrative business cases [B]
Development	Support experimentation [E], pilot test AI projects [F]
Fear and Mistrust	Teach leaders how AI models work [B]
Process Integration	Create a process reengineering unit to embed AI insights into workflow [A], communicate success [E]
Culture	Encourage proactive problem-solving instead of reactive [E]
Value	Measure results from customer interactions [B]
AI organizational resource obstacles and solutions	
Training Data Sets	Use domain experts to improve or fill gaps in training datasets [D]
Data Quality	Teach leaders about data [B]
Data Structures	Teach leaders about data [B]
AI Platform	Create an engineering unit to build an AI platform [A]
AI Talent	Hire new data science and data engineering talent [A] [B]
Complementary organizational resource obstacles and solutions	
Top Management Understanding	Educate top management about AI [A], hire executives to lead transformation projects [F]
Domain Engagement	Assign domain experts to review, validate and manage AI-based insights [E], establish operations group with strong business ties [F]
Acceptable Data Use	Use data conservatively [C], hire privacy expertise to shape work practices and policies [C], adopt privacy by design principles [C], engage with industry stakeholders to shape public policy and industry regulation [C]
Enterprise Strategy	Engage executives in workshops to roadmap and set goals [B]

8.4 Overcoming AI Obstacles

As the research team analyzed AI obstacles provided by executives and described within the project descriptions, we observed that these obstacles reflect challenges that have been common to data projects for decades. For example, two common obstacles—lack of a compelling business objective and poor data quality—have plagued data projects since the early days of computing. The team also observed, however, that some AI obstacles appear to be more common or more important in today's chapter of AI projects. These obstacles include training datasets, fear and mistrust, domain engagement, acceptable data use, and AI talent. Thus, we used these obstacles to develop an initial set of recommendations regarding areas of AI that we believe should receive high-priority attention from AI leaders. We next describe these key contemporary obstacles and associated recommendations.

8.4.1 The Obstacle of Data: Training Datasets

In contrast with business intelligence and business analytics approaches, AI approaches draw upon algorithms that are trained or taught to perform specific tasks (rather than programmed). Training happens by processing large sets of data [19]; therefore, algorithms are vulnerable to the underlying data. For example, historical data might be biased toward minorities [13, 20] and train-biased algorithms. Microsoft's AI algorithm learned to become racist by conversing with other users on Twitter, and in another case an algorithm earned to become biased toward black people when AI was used to predict prisoner recidivism risk [20, 21]. Therefore, companies must learn how to extend or create processes that source, build, and manage training sets so that related obstacles can be removed. Further, companies may need to find ways to fill gaps when training sets fall short. In Auto Parts Manufacturer Company D, career truck drivers were used to augment training data with experience and help shape the algorithms for complex scenarios like bad weather.

Recommendation 1: AI leaders need to explore how companies can prevent bias and address shortcomings in training datasets.

8.4.2 The Obstacle of Action: Fear and Mistrust

The reasoning and process behind AI-based decisions may be opaque [3]. Deep learning algorithms, in particular, autonomously learn from example data and propagate their learning across various network layers [7]. This makes it difficult for domain experts to understand how AI works and to trust outcomes. In some cases, high dimensionality of the data (i.e., the number of features or attributes used in data analysis) makes it difficult for users to understand algorithm outcomes in a meaningful way [22].

For algorithmic decisions to be transparent and trustworthy, humans need to understand how and why a certain decision was made. This can be achieved if AI experts design traceable algorithms and/or if domain experts can provide justification based on deep domain knowledge [23] or triangulation of methods [21]; otherwise, humans cannot guarantee that decisions are non-discriminatory or meaningful in real-world contexts. At Home Services Company B, the researchers were struck by the company's desire to create algorithmic transparency and trust even at the highest levels of the organization; for example, the company held deep dive sessions for its executives to understand the inner workings of the AI models.

Recommendation 2: AI leaders need to explore how and to whom companies can best explain, communicate, and/or justify algorithmic decisions.

8.4.3 The Obstacle of Domain Knowledge: Domain Engagement

AI projects require a break with conventional development in that domain experts who are field specialists and who traditionally set the business rules that IT systems are designed support no longer are in control; instead, AI projects include rules generated from data and acted upon by machines. This shift in rule-making dynamics makes it critical to reimagine the relationship between domain experts and the AI experts who design and write algorithms.

AI and domain experts fundamentally share one of two types of relationships [24]: (1) complementary when AI and domain experts augment one another and (2) substitution when AI and domain experts replace one another. An example of a complementary relationship is when domain experts take a "trainer" role and teach the algorithm how the world works [12]. Another example occurs when domain experts oversee the algorithmic learning process and ensure correctness and fairness. Organizations likely need to reshape or create roles and responsibilities for domain experts (and their algorithm counterparts) so that domain knowledge properly manifests within an AI project. After implementing AI, Biopharmaceutical Company E assigned new roles to vaccine experts to conduct comparisons using large scale datasets (which was impossible for domain experts to do manually). The experts became responsible for examining, reworking, and improving AI models.

Recommendation 3: AI leaders need to explore the substitutive and complementary, new, and changing roles of domain and algorithm experts.

8.4.4 The Obstacle of Governance: Acceptable Data Use

AI-based algorithms potentially can act unethically and create negative externalities for individuals and society; consider the concerns of privacy, extensive profiling of individuals, biases, or discrimination [4, 25–27]. Companies must develop algorithms that act in acceptable ways, and they must infuse ethics systematically into their organizational fabric [28]. Otherwise, companies will encounter risks of deploying AI projects that act in undesired or wrong ways, which can result in financial losses, reputational damage, or increased regulatory or other constraints.

Traditional data projects are governed so that they comply with regulatory and legal constraints; however, for AI, this form of governance is necessary but not sufficient. Governance of AI projects must consider and address values of the company and both its direct and indirect stakeholders [29]. Location Analytics Company C adopted privacy by design principles to develop their services. This helped the company incorporate human values throughout its development process.

Recommendation 4: AI leaders need to explore acceptable data use governance, which extends oversight of AI projects beyond regulatory and legal compliance.

8.4.5 The Obstacle of Talent: AI Talent

Analyst firms have predicted both the importance of and dearth of data science talent for the past decade [30]. The increase in AI applications will only exacerbate this talent shortage. Further, not only is the number of AI applications increasing but also the number of business tasks that include and are impacted by AI. Without changes to current talent attraction, development, reskilling, and upskilling practices, acquiring AI talent will become a serious bottleneck in AI adoption and consumption within organizations.

AI talent also needs to be reexamined regarding exactly what it represents. Beyond the ability to build, train, interpret, and deploy models, data scientists who specialize in AI will need a diverse skillset that likely includes skills like storytelling, visualization, data taxonomies and structures, ethics, and value-based design. In a recent survey of AI organizational challenges, half of the leaders surveyed indicated that they need machine learning experts who can identify AI identify use cases that lend themselves to AI solutions [31]. Companies will need to craft creative new workforce strategies that may include ideas such as increasing investment in upskilling existing employees or creating new business units specifically to attract and cultivate AI talent. Health IT Company A and Home Services Company B both started their AI journeys by hiring new data science and data engineering talent to build AI models and AI platforms.

Recommendation 5: AI leaders need to explore AI talent requirements for companies—and how to build effective new talent strategies, portfolios, and management programs.

Table 8.5 Summary of research recommendations

Recommendation
Recommendation 1: AI leaders need to explore how companies can prevent bias in training datasets
Recommendation 2: AI leaders need to explore how companies can best explain, communicate, and/or justify algorithmic decisions
Recommendation 3: AI leaders need to explore the substitutive and complementary roles of domain and algorithm experts
Recommendation 4: AI leaders need to explore acceptable data use governance, which extends oversight of data projects beyond regulatory and legal compliance
Recommendation 5: AI leaders need to explore AI talent requirements for companies—and how to build effective new talent strategies, portfolios, and management programs

8.5 Discussion

Despite its potential, AI adoption and consumption need research attention before practice can advance. We propose a framework and a set of recommendations that articulate high-priority, focus areas for AI leaders. Our chapter provided a process-oriented framework on AI value that identifies AI and complementary organizational resources and the process by which these resources can be assembled together within AI projects to create value for organizations. Also, our work identifies obstacles to AI adoption and offers a recommendation for AI leaders. The recommendations were suggested by executives from around the world who are leading AI teams and who are accountable for AI success—and by descriptions of actual AI engagements that have happened within the past few years. We provide a summary of our recommendations in Table 8.5. We encourage AI leaders to adopt creative, interesting approaches to refine and explore the framework and recommendations with the intent of generating relevant, applicable managerial insights.

AI is high on executives' agendas. It potentially can generate big value yet, if not appropriately deployed and nurtured, can fall short and, worst case, cause harm. From our own interactions with executives, many are unclear regarding AI's true value potential given current obstacles and unknowns. Our AI value framework provides a comprehensive view of the AI value creation process, and it helps communicate obstacles that organizations face today. We encourage leaders to begin investigating our set of recommendations. And while researchers work to advance understanding in this space, we hope that our framework can help executives focus their investments, management attention, and remediation activities. Moreover, we document (in Table 8.4) an initial set of helpful practices that practitioners may want to consider as they initiate AI projects.

Acknowledgments This chapter includes content from the authors' previously published paper: Someh, I., Wixom, B., & Zutavern, A. (2020). 'Overcoming Organizational Obstacles to Artificial Intelligence Value Creation: Propositions for Research', in *Proceedings of the 53rd Hawaii International Conference on System Sciences*, 5809–5818.

References

1. Brynjolfsson, E., Mitchell, T.: What can machine learning do? Workforce implications. Science (80-). **358**(6370), 1530–1534 (2017)
2. Chui, M., Manyika, J., Miremadi, N., Henke, M., Chung, R., Nel, P., Malhotra, S.: Notes from the AI Frontier Insights from Hundreds of Use Cases. McKinsey & Company (2018)
3. Agrawal, A., Gans, J., Goldfarb, A.: Economic policy for artificial intelligence. Innov. Policy Econ. **19** (2018)
4. Zuboff, S.: The Age of Surveillance Capitalism: The Fight for the Future at the New Frontier of Power. Profile Books, London (2018)
5. Beane, M.: Shadow learning: building robotic surgical skill when approved means fail. Admin. Sci. Q. **64**(1), 87 (2019)
6. Davenport, T.H.: The AI Advantage: How to Put the Artificial Intelligence Revolution to Work. MIT Press (2018)
7. Faraj, S., Pachidi, S., Sayegh, K.: Working and organizing in the age of the learning algorithm. Inf. Organ. **28**(1), 62–70 (2018)
8. Someh, I., Wixom, B.H.: Microsoft turns to data to drive business success. MIT Cent. Inf. Syst. Res. CISR Case Study, 14 (2017)
9. Wixom, B.H., Schüritz, R.: Creating customer value using analytics. CISR Res. Brief. **XVII**(11) (2017)
10. Alfaro, E., Bressan, M., Girardin, F., Murillo, J., Someh, I., Wixom, B.H.: BBVA's data monetization journey. MIS Q. Exec. **18**(2), 117–128 (2019)
11. Wixom, B.H., Beath, C.M.: Winning the data race. MIT CISR Res. Brief. **14**(3) (2014)
12. Wilson, H.J., Daugherty, P.R., Morini-Bianzino, N.: The jobs that artificial intelligence will create. MIT Sloan Manag. Rev. **58**(4), 14–16 (2017)
13. Daugherty, P., Wilson, J.H., Chowdhury, R.: Using artificial intelligence to promote diversity. MIT Sloan Manag. Rev. **60**(2), 1 (2019)
14. Davenport, T.H., Ronanki, R.: Intelligence for the real world. Harv. Bus. Rev. **96**(1), 108–116 (2018)
15. Brynjolfsson, E., Rock, D., Syverson, C.: Artificial Intelligence and the Modern Productivity Paradox: A Clash of Expectations and Statistics. National Bureau of Economic Research, Cambridge (2017)
16. Melville, N., Kraemer, K., Gurbaxani, V.: Review: Information technology and organizational performance: an integrative model of IT business value. MIS Q. **28**(2), 283–322 (2004)
17. Miles, M.B., Huberman, A.M.: Qualitative Data Analysis: An Expanded Sourcebook, 2nd edn. SAGE Publications (1994)
18. Sullivan, J., Zutavern, A.: The Mathematical Corporation: Where Machine Intelligence and Human Ingenuity Achieve the Impossible, 1st edn. Perseus Books, Cambridge, MA (2017)
19. Chui, M., Manyika, J., Miremadi, M.: What AI can and can't do (yet) for your business. McKinsey Q., 1–9 (2018)
20. Weller, A.: Challenges for Transparency. ICML (2017)
21. Guidotti, R., Monreale, A., Ruggieri, S., Turini, F., Pedreschi, D., Giannotti, F.: A survey of methods for explaining black box models. ACM J. **51**(5) (2018)
22. Martens, D., Provost, F.: Explaining data-driven document classifications. MIS Q. **38**(1), 73–99 (2014)

23. Gregor, S., Benbasat, I.: Explanations from intelligent systems: theoretical foundations and implications for practice 1. MIS Q. **23**(4), 497–530 (1999)
24. Rai, A., Constantinides, P., Sarker, S.: Next-generation digital platforms: toward human–AI hybrids. MIS Q. **43**(1), iii (2019)
25. Markus, M.L., Topi, H.: Big Data, Big Decisions for Science, Society, and Business. ACM Digital Library (2015)
26. Knight, W.: The dark secret at the heart of AI. MIT Technol. Rev., 1–11 (2017)
27. Zuboff, S.: Big other: surveillance capitalism and the prospects of an information civilization. J. Inf. Technol. **30**(1), 75–89 (2015)
28. Wixom, B.H., Markus, L.: To develop acceptable data use, build company norms. Res. Brief. Cent. Inf. Syst. Res. **XVII**(4) (2017)
29. Someh, I., Davern, M., Breidbach, C.F., Shanks, G.: Ethical issues in big data analytics: a stakeholder perspective. Commun. Assoc. Inf. Syst. **44**, 718–747 (2019)
30. Davenport, T.H., Patil, D.J.: Data scientist: the sexiest job of the 21st century data scientist. Harv. Bus. Rev. **79**(October), 70–76 (2012)
31. Lorica, B., Nathan, P.: Three Surveys of AI Adoption Reveal Key Advice from More Mature Practices. O'Reilly Media (2019)

Ida Someh is an Associate Professor at the University of Queensland Business School, Australia, investigating the multifaceted challenges posed by AI to organizations and society. With a decade-long collaboration with the MIT Sloan Center for IS Research, she has deeply studied 70+ AI case studies globally, uncovering how leaders manage the nuanced complexities of autonomous and opaque AI systems and deliver solutions that benefit diverse stakeholders. Her publications have been recognized with numerous prestigious awards, including Top Publication Award of the Information Systems field, Best Case Study award from the Society for Information Management, and for one of the most thought-provoking articles on the ethics of big data. She wants to use her insider knowledge of how AI solutions work to educate and empower consumers around the world to make better choices and exercise greater control over how AI impacts their lives. Recently, she has developed a master program focused on educating every business professional in data.

Barbara Wixom has studied how companies create value using data and AI for three decades, most recently while serving as Principal Research Scientist at the MIT Sloan Center for IS Research. In 2023, Barb released Data Is Everybody's Business (MIT Press)—a Forbes top 10 tech book for that year—to empower people from frontline worker to board member to participate in data monetization. Today, she wants to extend her reach to consumers. She wants to empower consumers to knowledgeably and effectively incorporate data and AI into their lives, with positive impacts. Barb is an award-winning case writer, book author, and teacher; a global thought leader and speaker; a prolific academic researcher; and a heart-filled wife and mom.

Chapter 9
The Rise of Enterprise Autonomization

Marek Kowalkiewicz, Christian Janiesch, and Michael Rosemann

Abstract This chapter examines how enterprise artificial intelligence (AI) facilitates a fundamental shift from traditional, handcrafted rule-based automation to AI-agent-driven enterprise autonomization. While global Enterprise AI spending increased sixfold from $2.3 billion to $13.8 billion between 2023 and 2024, only an estimated 4% of companies have achieved enterprise-wide AI capabilities, highlighting both the promise and the challenge of this transformation. This emphasizes the importance of strategic alignment, focused implementation, and realistic expectations. Consequently, we distinguish between automation's largely deterministic, rule-based execution and autonomization's goal-oriented, adaptive approach, where AI agents independently determine paths to achieve specified objectives. Through secondary case studies from JPMorgan Chase, General Electric, Walmart, and healthcare institutions, we demonstrate how process autonomization enables efficiency improvements and entirely new business models. We present a three-phase implementation framework (Deploy, Reshape, Invent) and address workforce transformation requirements. We conclude that successful enterprise autonomization requires equal investment in technology and human capabilities, creating synergistic systems where human creativity and AI autonomy amplify each other's strengths to achieve previously impossible outcomes.

9.1 Introduction

Organizations worldwide are fundamentally transforming from traditional rule-based automation to AI-driven autonomous systems. This shift represents more than incremental technological advancement: a paradigm change from handcrafting

---

M. Kowalkiewicz (✉) · M. Rosemann
Centre for Future Enterprise, Queensland University of Technology, Brisbane, QLD, Australia
e-mail: marek.kowalkiewicz@qut.edu.au; m.rosemann@qut.edu.au

C. Janiesch
TU Dortmund University, Dortmund, Germany
e-mail: christian.janiesch@tu-dortmund.de

S. Sadiq (ed.), *Enterprise AI*, https://doi.org/10.1007/978-3-032-01940-0_9

systems aligned with organizational requirements toward enabling systems to contribute to an enterprise's value creation that promises to reshape how businesses operate and compete using enterprise AI.

Enterprise AI refers to the integration of AI technologies into business operations, processes, and strategies to drive efficiency, innovation, and decision-making. Unlike consumer-focused AI applications, enterprise AI is tailored to meet the specific needs of organizations, such as optimizing workflows, enhancing customer experiences, and enabling data-driven insights. It encompasses a wide range of technologies, including machine learning, natural language processing, computer vision, and predictive analytics.

The concept has gained prominence due to its ability to scale across various industries—from finance and healthcare to manufacturing and retail—transforming traditional business practices through intelligent automation. However, implementing enterprise AI requires addressing challenges such as data security, ethical considerations in AI decision-making, and ensuring employee acceptance of new technologies. As organizations increasingly recognize the competitive advantages offered by enterprise AI, it continues to play a pivotal role in shaping modern business landscapes.

The magnitude of this transformation is reflected in the numbers: global Enterprise AI spending surged from $2.3 billion in 2023 to $13.8 billion in 2024, a sixfold increase [1]. By 2030, the generative AI market alone is forecast to reach $220 billion [2]. JPMorgan Chase exemplifies the scale of ambition, with over 400 AI use cases in production generating $1.5 billion in annual value [3]. Yet despite this investment surge, only 4% of companies have achieved cutting-edge enterprise-wide AI capabilities [4, 5]—a gap highlighting both the promise and the challenge of enterprise autonomization.

In the following, we outline the concepts of artificial autonomy and autonomization and apply them to the enterprise level, envisaging autonomized AI agents that were hitherto limited to rather deterministic automation. We back up our argument by reporting on real transformations currently in action. Lastly, we discuss navigating the implementation by focusing on enabling successful autonomization and the human dimension of enterprise autonomization.

9.2 The Three Capabilities of Autonomization

Since the 1990s, research in computer science has explored autonomous systems and artificial autonomy, particularly within the realm of multi-agent systems [6, 7]. The primary goal has been to enable these systems to tackle challenges that are either extremely difficult or impossible for an individual system to handle. At that time, technology lagged behind human capabilities in many cognitive tasks, unlike today.

Defining autonomy is as complex as defining intelligence. In this context, we describe artificial autonomy as a form of self-sufficiency granted to an entity by a governing authority that retains ultimate control. This concept implies that during the process of autonomization, an entity possesses the right and ability to make its own decisions without external interference, though it remains bound by certain frameworks such as work envelopes [8] in robotics or sandboxes [43] in software engineering. These frameworks may limit how processes are initialized, executed (including compliance requirements), and concluded (such as expected outcomes). It is important to note that autonomy is different from complete self-sufficiency (autarky) or a lack of rules (anarchy) [44].

We employ the conceptualization of artificial autonomy of Janiesch et al. [9] categorized into three key capabilities: independence, neglect tolerance, and indeterminism.

Framed Independence: This capability refers to an entity's ability to define and pursue its own actions. In enterprise autonomization contexts, this independence must be constrained or framed [10]. Achieving strong artificial autonomy akin to human independence is not desirable; instead, framed independence delineates the limits within which autonomous behavior can occur. Enterprise autonomization should be capable of making independent decisions aligned with its goals and executing actions accordingly. This requires both self-developed decision-making models and operational capacity, along with the necessary resources for execution.

Neglect Tolerance: Neglect tolerance describes an entity's ability to withstand periods of neglect or lack of active maintenance without significantly declining performance or functionality. Within enterprise autonomization, this means processes can remain unattended for extended durations. Autonomous systems must therefore possess some degree of adaptability and self-maintenance capabilities. Adaptability involves sensing changes and updating accordingly, while self-maintenance encompasses monitoring oneself, repairing issues autonomously, and managing resources effectively. Neglect tolerance essentially gauges how resilient an autonomous process is when operating without direct oversight.

Indeterminism: This characteristic distinguishes autonomization from traditional deterministic automation by allowing for flexibility and adaptability within defined parameters. Enterprise autonomization functions within dynamic environments where real-time decisions are made based on various contextual influences and changing data streams. Such inherent flexibility enables adaptive responses to unexpected situations—something that deterministic models struggle with since they rely on predictable outcomes governed by fixed rules under stable conditions.

In conclusion, independence allows autonomous entities to make decisions and act within certain constraints, while neglect tolerance ensures resilience when addressing incomplete, conflicting, or complex tasks over prolonged periods. Indeterminism enables adaptability and flexibility within a reasonable frame.

9.3 Understanding the Fundamental Shift from Automated Systems to Autonomized Agents

Traditional enterprise automation operates like a sophisticated assembly line—executing predefined tasks with precision but limited flexibility. When an insurance company automates claims processing, for instance, the system follows rigid rules: if the claim amount is below $1000 and matches preset criteria, approve it; otherwise, escalate to a human. This approach typically achieves process automation for a subset of well-defined, mainstream processes, with the remaining majority of processes often requiring human intervention for exceptions, complex cases, or changing conditions.

Autonomization and its features of (framed) independence, neglect tolerance, and indeterminism transform this paradigm entirely [9]. Rather than following predetermined paths, autonomous systems pursue goals. That same insurance claims system, when autonomized, might have the objective to "process claims efficiently while maintaining customer satisfaction and fraud prevention standards." The AI then determines the optimal approach for each case, learning from outcomes, adapting to new fraud patterns, and adjusting its strategies based on customer feedback—all without explicit reprogramming.

Multi-agent systems take this further by creating networks of specialized AI agents collaborating like human teams. In computer science and management, the concept of agents refers to autonomous entities that perceive their environment, process information, and act upon it to achieve specific goals. Generally, the term agent is used more broadly to describe individuals or entities acting on behalf of an organization or stakeholder to execute decisions or manage resources [11]. In this context, agents can be software programs or systems designed to perform tasks on behalf of users or other systems. These agents can range from simple rule-based systems to complex entities capable of learning and adapting over time [12].

The advent of AI agents has significantly expanded the potential applications of this concept. AI agents leverage advanced machine learning and natural language processing techniques to exhibit higher levels of (artificial) autonomy and intelligence. They can analyze large datasets, make predictions, optimize processes, and interact with humans in natural language. Examples include virtual assistants like Siri or Alexa in consumer technology and intelligent decision-support systems in business management. As we will see below, in General Electric's manufacturing operations, demand prediction agents analyze market data, while inventory optimization agents coordinate with suppliers, quality control agents monitor production, and logistics agents manage distribution—all working together toward the goal of efficient production rather than following static schedules.

The technical architecture enabling this autonomization combines several breakthrough technologies. Large language models serve as the cognitive backbone, with enterprise deployments typically using multiple foundation models—for instance, GPT-4 for complex reasoning, specialized models for domain-specific tasks, and open-source alternatives for cost-sensitive applications. These models connect through orchestration layers, which manage context, chain prompts, and coordinate with vector databases storing enterprise knowledge [13].

9.4 Real Transformation in Action

JPMorgan Chase exemplifies enterprise-scale autonomization with multiple AI systems transforming its operations. The bank invests $14 billion annually in technology and employs over 55,000 technologists globally [14]. Their Contract Intelligence (COiN) platform illustrates the transformative power of autonomization. Previously, lawyers spent 360,000 h annually reviewing commercial loan agreements. The autonomous system now completes this task in seconds with higher accuracy and a near-zero error rate, freeing legal teams for strategic work [14].

But JPMorgan's AI transformation extends far beyond document processing. The bank's LOXM system uses AI to optimize trade execution in global equities, learning from billions of past trades to execute client orders at optimal prices. This has improved execution efficiency by approximately 15% according to equity trader surveys. Their newly deployed LLM Suite, developed in collaboration with OpenAI, provides generative AI assistance to all employees for tasks ranging from drafting emails to complex data analysis while maintaining strict data privacy by preventing proprietary information from training external models.

Perhaps most significantly, JPMorgan's OmniAI platform represents a major architectural innovation. This cloud-based platform standardizes AI/ML deployment across the entire enterprise, enabling data scientists to extract insights from vast data repositories while reducing operational costs. The platform won the CIO 100 Technology Award and was named Most Cutting-Edge IT Initiative at the American Financial Technology Awards, demonstrating its industry-leading capabilities. As Teresa Heitsenrether, Chief Data and Analytics Officer, emphasizes: "Our commitment to AI is a testament to our dedication to innovation and technological excellence."

In healthcare, the shift from automation to autonomization saves lives. Massachusetts General Hospital's collaboration with MIT produced AI systems that do not just follow diagnostic protocols but actively reason through complex medical cases. These systems achieve 87% sensitivity in diabetic retinopathy detection while reducing readmission rates by 30% at Johns Hopkins Hospital through predictive intervention recommendations [15].

Manufacturing presents perhaps the most dramatic transformations. General Electric's digital twin initiative creates virtual replicas of physical assets that autonomously optimize performance. Wind turbines adjust their blade angles based on weather predictions, manufacturing equipment schedules its own maintenance before failures occur, and entire production lines reconfigure themselves to meet changing demand. These implementations demonstrate substantial improvements in equipment utilization and productivity, showcasing how autonomous systems can transform traditional manufacturing operations into adaptive, self-optimizing environments.

Walmart's supply chain transformation demonstrates autonomization on a massive scale. Rather than autonomous robots, the retailer now employs AI-powered camera systems and predictive analytics to continuously monitor inventory levels, predict stockouts, and identify misplaced items. This shift from physical robots to AI-driven systems reflects Walmart's evolution toward more sophisticated, data-driven inventory management that integrates insights from all sales channels to optimize the entire shopping experience.

Modern autonomous systems require sophisticated technical architectures that go far beyond simple AI model deployment. The typical enterprise stack begins with a perception layer that ingests data from multiple sources—ERP systems, IoT sensors, customer interactions, and external market data. This information flows through real-time streaming platforms like Apache Kafka into a cognition layer where LLMs and specialized AI models process, reason, and plan [16].

The distinction between rule-based and goal-based architectures is fundamental. Rule-based systems operate through IF-THEN logic: IF inventory drops below 100 units, THEN order 500 more. Goal-based systems receive objectives: maintain optimal inventory levels while minimizing carrying costs and preventing stockouts. The AI then considers multiple factors—seasonal demand patterns, supplier reliability, storage costs, and market trends—to determine the best action for each situation [17, 18].

Edge computing adds another dimension to enterprise autonomy. Manufacturing plants deploy AI directly on production equipment, enabling split-second decisions without cloud latency [19]. Retail stores use edge AI for real-time customer behavior analysis and dynamic pricing. Healthcare providers process sensitive patient data locally while maintaining privacy compliance [20]. These distributed autonomous systems coordinate through federated learning, sharing insights without exposing raw data [21].

The business case for autonomization shows both tremendous potential and sobering realities. While an IDC study commissioned by Microsoft found that organizations report an average 3.5× return on their AI investments, achieving success at scale remains challenging. IBM research reveals that while AI pilots initially delivered returns of 31%, these fell to just 7% as implementations scaled enterprise-wide, below the typical 10% cost of capital threshold [22]. The difference lies in the implementation approach and realistic expectations.

High performers focus ruthlessly on value. They pursue half as many use cases as their peers but achieve twice the ROI by selecting high-impact opportunities aligned with core business processes [23]. They invest 70% of resources in people and processes, 20% in technology and data, and only 10% in algorithms [24]. They measure success holistically, combining financial metrics with operational improvements and strategic advantages.

Hidden costs often surprise organizations. Inference costs for generative AI can vary dramatically based on model size and provider, with some models costing pennies per query, while others reach dollars, adding up quickly at scale. Data preparation remains one of the most resource-intensive aspects of AI projects, often consuming the majority of project time and budget. Ongoing maintenance typically requires a significant annual investment beyond the initial implementation. Yet unexpected benefits also emerge: according to McKinsey Global Institute research, generative AI has the potential to boost productivity across various business functions, accelerate innovation cycles, and transform how work gets done, potentially adding trillions in value to the global economy [25].

Payback periods vary by complexity. Simple automation typically returns investment within 6–18 months. Complex AI systems require 2–3 years. Transformational initiatives may take 3–5 years but offer the highest long-term value. Organizations that understand these timelines and set appropriate expectations achieve far better outcomes than those seeking quick wins.

9.5 Navigating Implementation: From Pilot to Scale

Successful autonomization follows predictable patterns across industries. Leaders typically progress through three phases: Deploy, Reshape, and Invent.

The *Deploy* phase focuses on implementing off-the-shelf AI tools for quick wins—chatbots for customer service, predictive maintenance for equipment, or document processing for back-office operations. These initiatives typically deliver measurable productivity improvements while building organizational confidence. By starting with proven, readily available solutions, organizations can demonstrate the value of AI without requiring extensive customization or development, creating momentum for more ambitious automation efforts.

The *Reshape* phase reimagines core business processes. Instead of adding AI to existing workflows, organizations redesign operations around autonomous capabilities [10]. For example, a bank might transform its entire loan approval process, letting AI handle standard applications autonomously while human experts focus on complex commercial deals and relationship building. This fundamental rethinking of processes—rather than incremental automation—creates opportunities for significant operational improvements and new ways of delivering value.

The *Invent* phase creates entirely new business models. Insurance companies develop real-time risk assessment products that would be impossible without AI. Manufacturers offer equipment-as-a-service with guaranteed uptime through predictive maintenance. Retailers create hyper-personalized shopping experiences that adapt in real time to customer behavior. This phase represents the most transformative potential of autonomization, where organizations do not just improve existing offerings but create entirely new value propositions that were previously impossible without autonomous systems.

The most successful organizations follow a systematic approach: assess readiness across technology, organization, processes, and finances; establish clear governance frameworks; launch focused pilots with measurable success criteria; and scale gradually while continuously learning and adapting [26].

9.6 Navigating Implementation: The Human Dimension of Autonomized Systems

Workforce transformation represents perhaps the most significant challenge and opportunity in enterprise autonomization. The World Economic Forum projects that 44% of workers' skills will be disrupted by 2027, with half the global workforce requiring significant reskilling [27]. Yet this disruption also creates opportunities for more meaningful, creative work as AI handles routine tasks [28].

Successful Organizations Focus on Human-AI Collaboration Rather than Replacement At Aberdeen City Council, AI assistants handle routine citizen inquiries, achieving 241% ROI through time savings while freeing staff for complex cases requiring empathy and judgment [29]. Amazon invests $1.2 billion in reskilling 350,000 employees, teaching them to work alongside robots and manage autonomous systems rather than compete with them [30].

New organizational structures emerge to support this collaboration. Cross-functional AI teams combine technical experts with domain specialists [31]. Centers of Excellence provide governance, training, and best practices. Agile pod structures enable rapid experimentation and learning. Leadership itself transforms, requiring not just technical literacy but the ability to navigate ethical dilemmas and manage human-AI teams.

Cultural transformation proves essential. Organizations must foster growth mindsets that embrace continuous learning, create safe-to-fail environments for AI experimentation, and build trust through transparent communication about AI capabilities and limitations. Those that succeed create virtuous cycles where human creativity combines with AI scale to achieve outcomes neither could accomplish alone.

Synthetic Work Relationships Will Grow The notion of synthetic relationships—ongoing interactions between humans and AI that mutually influence emotions, reasoning, and actions—has garnered increasing attention in contemporary discussions surrounding human-AI interactions [32]. As large language models and other AI agents evolve to facilitate more anthropomorphic interactions, these synthetic relationships extend beyond social or personal domains and significantly impact professional settings.

Current workplace interaction frameworks, which primarily focus on human-to-human dynamics, inadequately capture the cognitive, social, and organizational ramifications of integrating autonomous AI agents as colleagues, assistants, and superiors. Synthetic relationships encompass emotional, social, and functional dimensions. When applied within professional contexts, these concepts prompt inquiries into how synthetic entities engage with human workers and shape their interpersonal dynamics.

Thoughtful design of synthetic work relationships can optimize shared cognitive capabilities while reducing personal stressors related to work demands, ultimately enhancing employee well-being and overall job performance. Conversely, if poorly designed, prolonged engagement with AI agents may pose various risks linked to cognitive overloads, diminished performance levels, privacy concerns, and, most critically, employee health. Therefore, it is imperative for information systems research to equip human employees to navigate this evolving landscape of workplace relationships.

Practical Governance Requires Multiple Layers of Control As AI systems give rise to autonomization, governance becomes critical. The NIST AI Risk Management Framework provides structure through four functions: Govern (establishing policies and accountability), Map (understanding AI systems and their impacts), Measure (tracking performance and risks), and Manage (acting on insights to ensure safe operation) [33].

Technical safeguards include explainable AI for transparency, continuous bias monitoring, and circuit breakers that halt operations when systems behave unexpectedly [34]. Organizational controls establish AI ethics boards, transparent accountability chains, and regular audits [35]. Human oversight mechanisms range from human-in-the-loop requirements for critical decisions to human-in-the-loop monitoring with intervention capabilities [36].

Regulatory Compliance Adds Complexity as Frameworks Evolve Globally The EU AI Act mandates risk-based governance with penalties up to 7% of global revenue [37]. Sector-specific regulations govern AI use in healthcare, finance, and transportation. Forward-thinking organizations go beyond compliance, establishing ethical frameworks that build stakeholder trust while enabling innovation [38].

9.7 The Path Forward: Building the Autonomized Enterprise

The transition from automation to autonomization represents a fundamental shift in how enterprises operate. Success requires more than technology adoption—it demands reimagining business processes, transforming workforce capabilities, and establishing robust governance frameworks. As demonstrated by the implementations at JPMorgan Chase, General Electric, Walmart, and leading healthcare institutions, organizations that master this transition achieve significant competitive advantages through efficiency improvements, cost reductions, and the creation of entirely new business models and revenue streams.

The window for proactive transformation is narrowing. Early adopters like JPMorgan Chase and General Electric have established commanding leads that compound over time. Their AI systems learn from vast datasets, their workforces develop advanced human-AI collaboration skills, and their governance frameworks enable rapid, safe innovation [39]. Laggards face competitive disadvantage and existential risk as autonomous competitors reshape entire industries.

Yet the journey remains achievable for organizations willing to commit. Start with clear strategic alignment between AI initiatives and business objectives. Invest in foundational capabilities—data quality, technical infrastructure, and workforce development. Build gradually through focused pilots that demonstrate value. Scale selectively, choosing high-impact opportunities over broad experimentation. Most importantly, realistic expectations must be maintained while working toward transformational outcomes [40].

The Future Belongs to Enterprises That Successfully Blend Human Creativity with AI Autonomy In this new paradigm, success comes not from replacing humans with machines but from creating synergistic systems where each amplifies the other's strengths [41]. Organizations that embrace this vision—investing equally in technology and humanity—will define the next era of enterprise excellence.

As one executive noted after implementing autonomous systems: "We're not just automating what we do. We're discovering entirely new ways to create value we never imagined possible." This captures the essence of the autonomization revolution—not just doing the same things faster but fundamentally reimagining what enterprises can achieve [42].

References

1. Menlo Ventures: 2024: The State of Generative AI in the Enterprise. Menlo Ventures (2024) https://menlovc.com/2024-the-state-of-generative-ai-in-the-enterprise/
2. ABI Research: Artificial intelligence (AI) software market size: 2024 to 2030 (2025). https://www.abiresearch.com/news-resources/chart-data/report-artificial-intelligence-market-size-global
3. Constellation Research Inc: JPMorgan chase: digital transformation, AI and data strategy sets up generative AI (2023). https://www.constellationr.com/blog-news/insights/jpmorgan-chase-digital-transformation-ai-and-data-strategy-sets-generative-ai
4. Boston Consulting Group: AI adoption in 2024: 74% of companies struggle to achieve and scale value (2024). https://www.bcg.com/press/24october2024-ai-adoption-in-2024-74-of-companies-struggle-to-achieve-and-scale-value
5. IBM: Generating ROI with AI (2023). https://www.ibm.com/thought-leadership/institute-business-value/en-us/report/ai-capabilities
6. Henderson, T. C., & Dalton, P.. Z-Infinity: A Framework for Autonomous Agent Specification and Analysis (1990)
7. Shoham, Y., Leyton-Brown, K.: Multiagent Systems: Algorithmic, Game-Theoretic, and Logical Foundations, vol. 9780521899437. Cambridge University Press (2008). https://doi.org/10.1017/CBO9780511811654
8. Lehto, M.R., Buck, J.R.: Introduction to Human Factors and Ergonomics for Engineers. CRC Press (2007). https://doi.org/10.1201/9781410615466
9. Janiesch, C., Kowalkiewicz, M., Rosemann, M.: Process autonomization: rethinking business process management. In: 23rd International Conference on Business Process Management Forum. Lecture Notes in Business Information Processing (2025)

10. Dumas, M., Fournier, F., Limonad, L., Marrella, A., Montali, M., Rehse, J.R., Accorsi, R., Calvanese, D., De Giacomo, G., Fahland, D., Gal, A., La Rosa, M., Völzer, H., Weber, I.: AI-augmented business process management systems: a research manifesto. ACM Trans. Manag. Inf. Syst. **14**(1) (2023). https://doi.org/10.1145/3576047
11. Munro, J.E.C.: Principal and agent (i). In: The New Palgrave Dictionary of Economics, p. 1 (2008). https://doi.org/10.1057/978-1-349-95121-5_1543-2
12. Caballar, R.D.: What are AI agents? IEEE Spectr. (2024, November 19). https://spectrum.ieee.org/ai-agents
13. Arya, S.: Top 7 Frameworks for Building AI Agents in 2025. Analytics Vidhya (2025) https://www.analyticsvidhya.com/blog/2024/07/ai-agent-frameworks/
14. Gomes, G.: AI in banking: JP Morgan leads the AI sphere CTO Mag. (2024). https://ctomagazine.com/jp-morgan-chase-accelerates-ai-adoption/
15. Medwave: How AI Is Transforming Healthcare: 12 Real-World Use Cases. Medwave (2024).. https://medwave.io/2024/01/how-ai-is-transforming-healthcare-12-real-world-use-cases/
16. Bellemare, A.: Building Event-Driven Microservices. O'Reilly Media (2020)
17. Greenwood, D., Rimassa, G.: Autonomic goal-oriented business process management. In: 3rd International Conference on Autonomic and Autonomous Systems, ICAS'07 (2007). https://doi.org/10.1109/CONIELECOMP.2007.61
18. Kueng, P.: Goal-based business process models: creation and evaluation. Bus. Process. Manag. J. **3**(1) (1997). https://doi.org/10.1108/14637159710161567
19. Shi, W., Cao, J., Zhang, Q., Li, Y., Xu, L.: Edge computing: vision and challenges. IEEE Internet Things J. **3**(5) (2016). https://doi.org/10.1109/JIOT.2016.2579198
20. Federal Drug Administration: Artificial Intelligence and Machine Learning in Software as a Medical Device. FDA (2025).. https://www.fda.gov/medical-devices/software-medical-device-samd/artificial-intelligence-and-machine-learning-software-medical-device
21. Yang, Q., Liu, Y., Chen, T., Tong, Y.: Federated machine learning: concept and applications. ACM Trans. Intell. Syst. Technol. **10**(2) (2019). https://doi.org/10.1145/3298981
22. Taylor, A.: New Study Validates the Business Value and Opportunity of AI. Official Microsoft Blog (2023).. https://blogs.microsoft.com/blog/2023/11/02/new-study-validates-the-business-value-and-opportunity-of-ai/
23. Bughin, J., Hazan, E., Ramaswamy, S., Chui, M., Allas, T., Dahlström, P., Henke, N., Trench, M.: Artificial Intelligence the Next Digital Frontier—Discussion Paper. McKinsey & Company (2017)
24. Ransbotham, S., Khodabandeh, S., Fehling, R., LaFountain, B., Kiron, D.: Winning with AI: pioneers combine strategy, organizational behavior, and technology. MIT Sloan Manag. Rev. **61**(1) (2019)
25. Chui, M., Hazan, E., Roberts, R., Singla, A., Smaje, K., Sukharevsky, A., Yee, L., Zemmel, R.: The Economic Potential of Generative AI: The Next Productivity Frontier. McKinsey & Company (2023)
26. Vartak, M.: How to scale AI in your organization (2022, March). https://hbr.org/2022/03/how-to-scale-ai-in-your-organization
27. World Economic Forum: The future of jobs report 2023 (2023). https://www.weforum.org/publications/the-future-of-jobs-report-2023/
28. Brynjolfsson, E., McAfee, A.: The Second Machine Age: Work, Progress, and Prosperity in a Time of Brilliant Technologies. WW Norton & Company (2014)
29. Horton, C.: In the spotlight: Aberdeen City Council (2024, July 22). https://www.thinkdigitalpartners.com/news/2024/07/22/in-the-spotlight-aberdeen-city-council/
30. Amazon: Our upskilling commitments (2025). https://www.aboutamazon.com/workplace/upskilling-commitments
31. Davenport, T.H., Ronanki, R.: Artificial intelligence for the real world. Harv. Bus. Rev. (2018, January). https://hbr.org/2018/01/artificial-intelligence-for-the-real-world

32. Starke, C., Ventura, A., Bersch, C., Cha, M., de Vreese, C., Doebler, P., Dong, M., Krämer, N., Leib, M., Peter, J., Schäfer, L., Soraperra, I., Szczuka, J., Tuchtfeld, E., Wald, R., Köbis, N.: Risks and protective measures for synthetic relationships. Nat. Hum. Behav. **8**(10), 1834–1836 (2024). https://doi.org/10.1038/S41562-024-02005-4
33. NIST: AI risk management framework (2023). https://www.nist.gov/itl/ai-risk-management-framework
34. Barredo Arrieta, A., Díaz-Rodríguez, N., Del Ser, J., Bennetot, A., Tabik, S., Barbado, A., Garcia, S., Gil-Lopez, S., Molina, D., Benjamins, R., Chatila, R., Herrera, F.: Explainable Artificial Intelligence (XAI): concepts, taxonomies, opportunities and challenges toward responsible AI. Inf. Fusion. **58** (2020). https://doi.org/10.1016/j.inffus.2019.12.012
35. Winfield, A.F.T., Jirotka, M.: Ethical governance is essential to building trust in robotics and artificial intelligence systems. Philos. Trans. R. Soc. A Math. Phys. Eng. Sci. **376**(2133) (2018). https://doi.org/10.1098/rsta.2018.0085
36. Amershi, S., Weld, D., Vorvoreanu, M., Fourney, A., Nushi, B., Collisson, P., Suh, J., Iqbal, S., Bennett, P.N., Inkpen, K., Teevan, J., Kikin-Gil, R., Horvitz, E.: Guidelines for human-AI interaction. In: Conference on Human Factors in Computing Systems—Proceedings (2019). https://doi.org/10.1145/3290605.3300233
37. European Parliament: Regulation—EU—2024/1689—EN—EUR-Lex. Off. J. Eur. Union (2024). https://eur-lex.europa.eu/eli/reg/2024/1689/oj/eng
38. Chatila, R., Havens, J.C.: The IEEE global initiative on ethics of autonomous and intelligent systems. Ethically aligned design: a vision for prioritizing human well-being with autonomous and intelligent systems. In: Intelligent Systems, Control and Automation: Science and Engineering, vol. 95. Springer (2019)
39. Iansiti, M., Lakhani, K.R.: Competing in the age of AI: how machine intelligence changes the rules of business by. Harv. Bus. Rev. (2020)
40. Ng, A.: AI transformation playbook: navigating the AI era (2018). https://landing.ai/case-studies/ai-transformation-playbook
41. Daugherty, P.R., Wilson, H.J.: Human + Machine, Updated and Expanded: Reimagining Work in the Age of AI. Harvard Business Press (2024)
42. McAfee, A., Brynjolfsson, E.: Machine, Platform, Crowd: Harnessing our Digital Future. WW Norton & Company (2017)
43. Stephens, M.: Sandbox. In: Jajodia, S., Samarati, P., Yung, M. (eds.) Encyclopedia of Cryptography, Security and Privacy, pp. 2158–2162. Springer, Cham (2024)
44. Beavers, G., Hexmoor, H.: Types and Limits of Agent Autonomy. In: Proceedings of the International Workshop on Computational Autonomy, vol. 2969, pp. 95–102. LNAI, Melbourne (2003)

Marek Kowalkiewicz is a Professor and Chair in Digital Economy at QUT Business School. Listed among the Top 100 Global Thought Leaders in AI by Thinkers360, Marek has led global innovation teams in Silicon Valley and was a Global Research Program Lead and Founding Research Manager of SAP's machine learning lab in Singapore and a Research Fellow at Microsoft Research Asia. His newest book, The Economy of Algorithms: AI and the Rise of the Digital Minions, is a winner of Australian Business Book Awards (Technology) in 2024.

Christian Janiesch is Professor of Enterprise Computing at TU Dortmund University. He previously worked full-time at various institutions including the University of Münster, the SAP Research Center in Brisbane of SAP Australia Pty Ltd, the Karlsruhe Institute of Technology, and the Julius-Maximilians-Universität Würzburg. His research focuses on intelligent systems at the intersection of business process management and artificial intelligence, with frequent applications in the Industrial Internet of Things. He is on the BPM Department Editorial Board for BISE journal, as well as the editorial boards of Electronic Markets, IJMR, and JBA. He has authored over 150 scholarly publications.

Michael Rosemann is the Director of the Centre for Future Enterprise and a Professor for Innovation Systems at the Business School, Queensland University of Technology (QUT), Brisbane, Australia. Dr. Rosemann's main areas of research are corporate innovation (eco)systems, revenue resilience, process management, and trust management. His work is focused on creating compelling future worlds with today's possibilities that make current practices obsolete. As a researcher and advisor to board rooms and senior executives, he is committed to advancing research-informed knowledge and confidence in order to appreciate the emerging design space and to create an increased "sense of ambition".

Chapter 10
Trust in AI: Evidence of Trust-Supporting Mechanisms from 17 Countries

Steven Lockey and Nicole Gillespie

Abstract Trust underpins the acceptance and sustained adoption of AI. Yet many enterprises are at an early stage of understanding how to support trust in their deployment of AI. Drawing on our large survey of public attitudes toward AI across 17 countries ($N = 17{,}193$), we find low levels of public trust and acceptance of AI systems, particularly in countries with advanced economies. This low trust is underpinned by shared concerns about the risks of AI across all countries, despite the majority of people expecting benefits from AI use. We find a clear public mandate for robust governance and regulation of AI systems to mitigate these risks and universal endorsement of the principles and practices of trustworthy AI across countries. Yet current safeguards are falling short of public expectations. Drawing on trust theory, we propose four pathways to support trust and acceptance of AI—the institutional, motivational, uncertainty, and knowledge pathways. We test these pathways using structural equation modelling, finding strong support for the model. Taken together, the findings suggest that enterprises can strengthen trust in their use of AI by (a) designing and deploying AI in ways that create demonstrable benefit for stakeholders, (b) implementing robust governance and assurance mechanisms to mitigate risks and demonstrate trustworthy use of AI, and (c) supporting AI literacy.

10.1 Introduction

AI has rapidly become a ubiquitous part of everyday life, transforming the way we work, live, deliver, and receive services [1]. All sectors of the global economy are now embracing AI, with applications expanding and diversifying into domains ranging from transport, crop and service optimization, the diagnosis and treatment of disease, and protection of physical, financial, and cybersecurity. For example, AI is being used to identify distracted drivers, credit card fraud, and children at risk.

S. Lockey · N. Gillespie (✉)
Melbourne Business School, The University of Melbourne, Melbourne, VIC, Australia
e-mail: n.gillespie@mbs.edu

S. Sadiq (ed.), *Enterprise AI*, https://doi.org/10.1007/978-3-032-01940-0_10

While the benefits and promise of AI for society and business are undeniable, so too are the risks and challenges. These risks include codifying and reinforcing unfair biases, infringing on human rights such as privacy, enabling mass surveillance technologies and autonomous weapons, spreading fake content online, deskilling and technological unemployment, and critical AI failures. Even in cases where AI is developed to help people (e.g., to protect cybersecurity), there is the risk that it can be used maliciously (e.g., for cyberattacks). These issues are causing public concern and raise questions about the trustworthiness and governance of AI systems [2–4].

The public's trust of AI technologies is vital for sustained acceptance. If AI systems do not prove worthy of trust, their widespread acceptance and adoption will be hindered, and the societal and economic benefits will not be fully realized. This is reinforced by academic research demonstrating that trust is paramount to AI acceptance [5, 6] and adoption [7]. It is also recognized by international and pan-governmental organizations, including the OECD, the World Economic Forum, and the European Commission, which each note the importance of trust in AI and the development of trustworthy AI systems to support sustained adoption. It is also recognized in the AI roadmaps and strategic plans of many nation states (see, e.g., [8–10]).

Despite the central importance of trust, we are still in an early stage of understanding how people in different countries across the globe experience trust in AI or what influences this trust [11, 12].[1] Further, there is a need to develop comprehensive frameworks to better understand what supports trust and acceptance of a range of AI systems [13].

In this chapter, we draw out key findings from our global study examining public trust and attitudes toward AI and their expectations of the management and governance of AI. The insights are based on over 17,000 people from 17 countries covering all global regions: Australia, Brazil, Canada, China, Estonia, Finland, France, Germany, India, Israel, Japan, the Netherlands, Singapore, South Africa, South Korea, the United Kingdom (UK), and the United States of America (USA). These countries are leaders in AI activity and readiness within their region. Taking a global perspective is important, given AI systems are not bound by physical borders and are rapidly being deployed across the globe. While our broader research program aimed to understand and quantify people's trust in and attitudes toward AI, benchmark these attitudes over time, and explore similarities and differences across countries (see [14]), in this chapter, our primary focus is to draw on the survey data

---

[1] Prior public attitude surveys have examined general acceptance and support of AI. For example, see: The European Consumer Organization (2020). Artificial Intelligence: what consumers say. Findings and policy recommendations of a multi-country survey on AI. Eurobarometer (2019). Europeans and Artificial Intelligence. Ipsos (2022) Global Opinions and Expectations about Artificial Intelligence. Morning Consult (2022) While Tech Fawns Over AI, Consumers Need More Convincing. Pew Research Centre. (2020). Science and Scientists Held in High Esteem Across Global Publics: Yet there is ambivalence in many publics over developments in AI, workplace automation, food science. Zhang, B., & Dafoe, A. (2019). Artificial intelligence: American attitudes and trends.

to identify key predictors of public trust and acceptance of AI systems and discuss their implications for industry practice and policymakers.

Our chapter is structured as follows. In the next section, we lay the conceptual foundations for the study, defining what we mean by trust in AI and briefly reviewing prior research related to the theoretical mechanisms underlying the predictors of AI examined in our model. We then describe our survey methodology and present key descriptive findings on the extent to which people (a) trust and accept AI systems, (b) understand AI systems, (c) view the benefits and risks of AI use, and (d) voice out their expectations about the development, governance, and regulation of AI. We then present and test our model of key predictors of AI trust and acceptance. In the concluding section, we discuss the four pathways enterprises can use to strengthen the trusted and responsible use of AI systems, together with broader implications for enterprises and policymakers.

10.2 Mechanisms Supporting Public Trust in AI

We adopt a highly cited, cross-disciplinary definition of trust that is often applied to the context of trust in technology and AI systems: Trust is "a psychological state comprising the intention to accept vulnerability based upon positive expectations of the intentions or behavior of another" ([15], p. 395). Central to theories of trust is that the intention to accept vulnerability to another entity is grounded in "good reasons," such as the perception that the entity is trustworthy ([16, 17], p. 13). Research shows people evaluate three key dimensions of trustworthiness [18, 19] including in the context of technology and AI implementation [20]: ability (e.g., AI systems performing reliably to produce accurate output as expected), benevolence (e.g., AI systems designed to achieve positive outcomes and minimize harm), and integrity (e.g., AI systems deployed in ways that adhere to ethical principles, values, and laws).

We draw on the scholarly literature on trust to identify and examine four complementary mechanisms for supporting trust in AI: the knowledge, motivational, uncertainty, and institutional pathways. We discuss each of these theoretical pathways in turn.

10.2.1 Knowledge Pathway

The knowledge pathway is based on seminal theories that highlight that knowledge of the entity to be trusted is critical for trust development [19, 21]. One of the distinct bases of trust in Lewicki and Bunker's [21] trust development process—knowledge-based trust—is formed through repeated experiences and interactions with a trustee. Mayer and colleagues [19] seminal model suggests that trust is predominately based on assessments of the other party's trustworthiness, which can only be ascertained through knowledge and experience with the other party. Applied to the context of technology, AI knowledge and literacy are theorized to be a critical precursor to appropriate trust in and acceptance of AI systems [22–24]. Research shows that the more knowledge people have about a technology, the more positive their perceptions of and trust in the technology. For example, Chowdhury et al. [25] find that employee knowledge about the capabilities, limitations, and application of AI positively impact trust in AI collaboration, which in turn has a positive relationship with business performance.

Knowledge is foundational to AI literacy [22]. While there are several conceptualizations of AI literacy, core competencies relate to knowledge and understanding of technical, societal, and ethical factors related to AI [22], as well as the ability to use technology [26]. Technology self-efficacy, which reflects confidence in one's ability to use and manage technological systems effectively [27], has been shown to influence technology acceptance and use intention by increasing trust in technologies [28], including AI systems [27].

10.2.2 Motivational Pathway

Recent work highlights the importance of motivational drivers of trust, such as the perceived benefits expected from trusting [29, 30]. Motivation is inherent to the act of trusting. Revisiting the conceptualization of trust, one of its core definitional elements is the willingness to be vulnerable. Such a willingness denotes a volitional action that people are unlikely to engage in without sufficient motivation. Van der Werff et al.'s [30] trust regulation model positions trust motivation as a direct antecedent of trust influenced by intrinsic and extrinsic drivers. Intrinsic and extrinsic motivational elements such as enjoyment and perceived usefulness are also central to technology acceptance theories (e.g., [31, 32]). People are motivated to accept and trust new technology when they expect it will provide benefits to them. Several studies have shown that perceived benefits enhance trust and acceptance of technology [33–35]. When people perceive a beneficial social impact from the use of AI systems, they are more likely to have positive experiences with AI systems [36] and accept emerging technologies [37].

10.2.3 Uncertainty Pathway

Trust is most relevant in risky or uncertain contexts, when people are most vulnerable [38, 39]. Yet, paradoxically, it is precisely in uncertain, risky situations that trust is most difficult to attain [40]. As such, reducing uncertainty is a key pathway to trust.

People perceive a variety of risks related to AI, including economic, performance, security, opportunity/time, privacy, psychological, and social-related risks [41]. When AI systems are viewed as risky, this makes uncertainty and vulnerability salient, which in turn makes it more difficult to trust the system. Prior research has demonstrated a negative relationship between perceived risks and trust in technology [42], and recent work indicates that people are less willing to trust and accept AI systems that they perceive as risky [25, 43].

10.2.4 Institutional Pathway

Institutional trust theory (e.g., [44]) posits that people rely on institutional safeguards and structures, as well as third parties, to develop trust, particularly in contexts where knowledge, experience, or the ability to make informed decisions is lacking [45]. Trust can be facilitated by impersonal structures that reassure people that it is safe to engage with a trust object (e.g., [44, 46]). Here, we discuss two institutional processes with different forms and targets: structural assurance and confidence in institutions to deploy and govern AI systems.

Structural assurance is an assessment that successful engagement with an actor or object is likely because safeguards are in place, such as regulations, guarantees, and legal recourse, that help manage vulnerability by constraining and deterring untrustworthy conduct [47–49]. Structural assurance is particularly salient in the development of initial trust in technology [48], and a growing body of evidence shows positive associations between structural assurance and trust in AI-enabled technologies [50–52]. Several assurance mechanisms have been proposed to support the trustworthy, ethical development and deployment of AI, including the use of ethical review boards [53–55], algorithmic impact assessments [56], external certification [57], adherence to codes of conduct [11], and independent auditing.

As AI systems are embedded within and deployed by institutions and enterprises, the more confidence a person has in the enterprise or institution, the more likely they are to trust that the AI system will be deployed in a trustworthy way. This reflects trust transference: trust can be transferred from a known or familiar context to an unknown or new context [58]. For example, Łapińska et al. [59] show that employee trust in their employing organization is positively associated with trust in the use of AI within the organization (see also [60]), while trust in government and corporations deploying AI has been shown to predict trust in AI [61].

In the next section, we discuss the methodology used to conduct our survey and measure these pathways.

10.3 Method

10.3.1 Data Collection

We collected data using an online survey in each of the 17 countries using representative research panels sourced by Qualtrics, a global leader in survey panel provision. This approach is commonly used in survey research to recruit individuals who are representative of a national population. We chose countries based on three criteria:

First, representation across all nine global regions as defined by the United Nations [62]:

1. East Asia
2. Eastern Europe
3. Latin America and the Caribbean
4. Middle East and North Africa
5. North America
6. Pacific
7. South and Central Asia
8. Sub-Saharan Africa
9. Western Europe

Second, within each region, we selected countries that were identified as leading in AI activity and readiness. Each country selected was ranked at or near the top for their region on the AI Stanford 2022 Government AI Readiness Index.[2]

Third, we selected countries that represented a diversity on the Responsible AI Index.[3]

Surveys were conducted in the native language(s) of each country, with the option to complete in English. Native languages used for each country were French (France and Canada), German, Finnish, Estonian, Simplified Chinese, Japanese, Portuguese, Hebrew, Dutch, and Korean. We used separate professional translators to translate the survey from English into the relevant language and then back-translate [63] to ensure survey equivalence across languages. After extensive piloting, data were

[2] We focused primarily on the 2021 Government AI Readiness Index. This index ranks and provides a total score for 160 countries on AI readiness across three pillars: government (e.g., existence of a national AI strategy, cybersecurity), technology (e.g., number of AI unicorns, R&D spending), and data and infrastructure (e.g., telecommunications infrastructure, households with Internet access). We supplemented this with data from the 2021 Stanford AI Index, which examines country-level private investment in AI and acceleration in AI activity over time to enable identification of countries that are rapidly emerging in AI in regions that historically lacked AI capacity and investment (e.g., South Africa, Brazil, and India).

[3] The Responsible AI Index ranks countries according to the readiness of their governments to use AI in a responsible way according to four pillars that correspond with the OECD Principles on AI: Inclusivity, Accountability, Transparency, and Privacy. It is a sub-index of the Government AI Readiness Index produced by Oxford Insights.

collected between September and October 2022. The research was approved by and adhered to the Guidelines of the ethical review process of The University of Queensland and the National Statement on Ethical Conduct in Human Research.

10.3.2 Survey Participants

The total sample included 17,193 respondents. The sample size across countries ranged from 1001 to 1021 respondents. Each country sample was nationally representative of the adult population on gender, age, and regional distribution matched against official national statistics within each country (within a 5% margin of error). Across the total sample, the gender balance was 50% women, 49% men, and 1% non-binary and other gender identities. The mean age was 44 years and ranged from 18 to 91 years. Ninety percent of respondents were either employed (67%) or had prior work experience (23%). These respondents represented the full diversity of industries and occupational groups listed by the International Labor Organization [64] Almost half the sample (49%) had a university education. Further details of the demographic profile and representativeness of the sample are shown in Table 10.1.

Table 10.1 The demographic profile for each country sample

Country	% Gender			Age (years)	% Generation				% Education				
	W	M	O	Mean	Z	M	X	BB	<SS	SS	Qu	UG	PG
Australia	51	48	1	47	14	30	23	33	4	26	28	31	11
Brazil	52	47	1	40	19	37	31	13	4	27	17	38	14
Canada	51	48	1	48	12	28	25	35	5	24	31	31	9
China	48	52	0	43	16	37	25	22	1	7	15	70	7
Estonia	53	46	1	38	23	41	24	12	8	29	24	14	15
Finland	51	48	1	45	14	30	29	27	11	24	29	22	14
France	50	49	1	46	13	28	30	29	10	23	24	26	17
Germany	51	49	0	46	11	30	31	28	5	14	59	13	9
India	47	53	0	36	26	43	25	6	1	6	4	40	49
Israel	47	52	1	38	20	44	26	10	1	25	25	34	15
Japan	50	50	0	51	9	20	33	38	2	29	17	47	5
Netherlands	50	49	1	46	14	30	28	28	10	28	26	23	13
Singapore	51	49	0	44	13	32	34	21	1	12	31	44	12
South Africa	51	48	1	39	19	43	23	15	1	31	26	35	7
South Korea	52	48	0	45	12	25	41	22	1	19	3	65	12
UK	50	49	1	46	13	33	26	28	2	27	29	39	12
USA	51	48	1	45	15	28	26	31	7	30	26	24	13

Notes: Gender: W = women, M = men, O = non-binary or other gender identity. Generation: Z = Generation Z, M = millennials, X = Generation X, BB = baby boomers and older generations. Education: <SS = lower secondary school or less, SS = upper secondary school, Qual = vocational or trade qualification; UG = undergraduate degree; PG = postgraduate degree

10.3.3 Survey Procedure

Participants read a preamble about the research aims and were informed that the survey was anonymous and findings would be used to inform policy and practice. After completing survey measures on their use and understanding of AI, participants read the following definition of AI adapted from the OECD [2]: Artificial intelligence (AI) refers to computer systems that can perform tasks or make predictions, recommendations, or decisions that usually require human intelligence. AI systems can perform these tasks and make these decisions based on objectives set by humans but without explicit human instructions.

Given perceptions of AI systems can be influenced by the purpose and use case, survey questions about trust, attitudes, and governance of AI systems referred to one of five AI use cases: Human Resource AI (used to inform decisions about hiring and promotion), Recommender AI (used to tailor services to consumers), Healthcare AI (used to inform decisions about how to diagnose and treat patients), Security AI (used to inform decisions about public safety and security), or AI in general (i.e. "AI systems in general"). These use cases were chosen to represent domains where AI is being rapidly deployed and likely to be used by, or impact, many people. We note that each of these use cases can be considered forms of enterprise AI, with healthcare AI specific to the health industry.

Respondents were randomly allocated to one of these use cases, providing an equivalent number of responses across use cases. Before answering questions, respondents were asked to read a description of the AI use case, including what it is used for, what it does, and how it works, as shown in Table 10.2. These descriptions were developed based on current in use systems and input from domain experts working in human resources, recommender systems, healthcare, and security, respectively.

To ensure quality of responses, two attention checks were incorporated into the survey. Participants who failed an attention check, demonstrated a pattern of inattentive responses (e.g., straight-lining), or completed the survey in an unrealistic timeframe were removed from the dataset.

10.3.4 Survey Measures

Trust in AI Systems In line with the definition of trust as a willingness to be vulnerable to an entity or system based on positive expectations [19], we assessed trust in AI systems as two dimensions: the willingness to rely on the outcomes of the AI system (reliance) and willingness to share information with the AI system (information sharing). A reliable 8-item scale from Gillespie et al. [11] was used, which was adapted from Gillespie [65]. Example items include the following: "How willing are you to... rely on information provided by the AI system [specific

Table 10.2 Description of AI use cases

AI system	Description
Human Resources AI	An AI system used to help select the most suitable applicants for a job, identify workers who are most likely to perform well in a job, and predict who is most likely to quit. It works by collecting and comparing worker characteristics, employee data, performance over time, and analyzing which qualities are related to better job performance and job retention. Managers use Human Resources AI to inform decisions about hiring and promotion
Recommender AI	An AI system used to personalize services such as news, social media content, or product recommendations by providing content and products that are most relevant to the user. It works by predicting a person's choices and preferences based on their characteristics (e.g., age, gender, location), past behavior, interests or preferences, and the behavior of similar users. Companies use Recommender AI to tailor services to consumers
Security AI	An AI system used to help identify suspicious or criminal behavior, security threats, and people of interest to police. It works by processing and analyzing a range of information such as face and fingerprint scans collected in places like country borders and photos and live footage of people and vehicles in public places collected through security cameras. Police and security agencies use Security AI to inform decisions about public safety and security
Healthcare AI	An AI system used to improve the diagnosis of disease (e.g., cancer), inform the best treatment options, and predict health outcomes based on patient data. It works by comparing a patient's health data (e.g., symptoms, test and scan results, medical history, family history, age, weight, gender, etc.) to large datasets based on many patients. Doctors use Healthcare AI to inform decisions about patient diagnosis and treatment

application]; depend on decisions made by the AI system; share relevant information about yourself to enable the AI system to perform a service or task for you; allow your data to be used by the AI system." A 7-point scale was used (1 = completely unwilling, 2 = mostly unwilling, 3 = somewhat unwilling, 4 = neither willing nor unwilling, 5 = somewhat willing, 6 = mostly willing, and 7 = completely willing; $a = 0.94$).

To assess positive expectations of the AI system, perceived trustworthiness was measured using a 14-item measure adapted from McKnight et al. [48]. The measure assessed three dimensions of trustworthiness: (1) ability (system perceived to perform accurately, reliably, and as intended); (2) benevolence (system perceived to create benefits, provide a helpful service, and have a positive impact); and (3) integrity (system deployment perceived to uphold ethical principles and data privacy rights and operate in a fair and safe way). Example items include the following: "I believe [specific AI application] would: produce output that is accurate" (ability); "have a positive impact on most people" (humanity); "be safe and secure to use" (integrity). A 7-point scale was used, ranging from 1 = strongly disagree to 7 = strongly agree ($a = 0.96$).

Acceptance of AI Systems Acceptance was measured using a reliable 3-item scale adapted from Zhang and Moffat [66]. Items included "To what extent do you . . . accept the use of [specific AI application]," "approve of the use of [specific AI application]," and "embrace the use of [specific AI application]." A 5-point scale was used (1 = not at all, 2 = slightly, 3 = moderately, 4 = highly, 5 = completely; $a = 0.94$).

Subjective Knowledge of AI To examine the knowledge pathway, we used a 3-item measure adapted from Ipsos [67], assessing the extent to which people subjectively feel they understand AI and when and where it is used. Example items include the following: "To what extent do you feel you know about AI? . . . Feel informed about how AI is used?" A 5-point scale was used (1 = not at all, 2 = to a small extent, 3 = to a moderate extent, 4 = to a large extent, 5 = to a very large extent; $a = 0.93$).

Technology Self-Efficacy A second indicator of the knowledge pathway was a 2-item measure of self-assessed ability to use digital technologies and online services, adapted from Vu and Lim [68]: "I consider myself to be sufficiently skilled in the use of digital technologies . . . to use online services . . . to benefit from digital and online opportunities" ($a = 0.85$).

Objective Awareness of AI Use For descriptive analysis, we assessed respondents' awareness of the use of AI in common technologies, as well as their own use of these technologies. Eight items were adapted from Zhang and Dafoe [69]. Example items include the following: "Does this technology use AI (No, Yes, Don't know)," "Ridesharing apps (e.g., Uber)," "Social media [with examples tailored to the national context]," and "Email filters (e.g., to block spam email)." As "Yes" was the correct answer to all items related to the technology using AI, we coded values to reflect 0 = "No/Don't know" and 1 = "Yes."

Perceived Benefits of AI To assess the motivational pathway, respondents' perceptions of a range of benefits of AI were measured with 10 items based on a review of the literature. Example items include as follows: "To what extent do you expect these potential benefits from the use of [specific application]? Enhanced decision-making, improved efficiency (e.g., doing things faster), improved effectiveness (e.g., doing things better), innovation (e.g., doing things differently), improved outcomes for people." A 5-point scale was used: (1 = Not at all, 2 = To a small extent, 3 = To a moderate extent, 4 = To a large extent, 5 = To a very large extent; $a = 0.94$).

Perceived Risks of AI To assess the uncertainty pathway, the perceived risks of AI were measured using 10 items developed based on a review of the literature. Example items include as follows: "How concerned are you about these potential risks of AI use [specific application]: inaccurate outcomes (e.g., the recommendations are inaccurate or do not work as intended); potential for bias (e.g., certain types of people being treated unfairly or discriminated against); loss of privacy (e.g., the privacy of personal information is not protected); manipulation or harmful use (e.g., people manipulate the data or system for their own interests); deskilling (e.g., people lose the ability to perform tasks and make decisions without AI); cybersecurity risks (e.g., hacking or malware attacks)?" The scale was the same as for perceived benefits ($a = 0.94$).

Structural Assurance One indicator used to examine the institutional pathway is structural assurance, which was measured using four items adapted from McKnight et al. [47]. Sample items include "There are enough current safeguards to make me feel comfortable with the use of AI [specific application]" and "I feel assured there are sufficient governance processes in place to protect me from problems that may arise from the use of AI [specific application]." A 7-point "strongly disagree" to "strongly agree" scale was used ($a = 0.94$).

Confidence in the Institutional Use of AI A second indicator of the institutional pathway is confidence in the institutional use of AI. Three items were used to assess respondents' confidence in their government, commercial organizations, and technology companies to develop and use AI in the best interests of the public, combined with three items asking how much confidence they had in these same entities to regulate and govern AI in the best interests of the public (1 = No confidence, 2 = Low confidence, 3 = Moderate confidence, 4 = High confidence, 5 = Complete confidence, $a = 0.89$).

Trustworthy AI Governance Principles and Practices To understand the importance of an enterprise's governance practices for trust in AI applications, we developed a 16-item measure based on the European Commission's Trustworthy AI principles [70]. Table 10.3 provides a description of the eight trustworthy AI principles we assessed. This measure was developed with extensive consultation with industry and academic AI and governance experts. Example items include "How important are the following practices for you to trust in [specific application]? People's data is only used for the specific purpose they agreed to," "If something goes wrong with the AI system, it is clear who or what is responsible," and "Safety and privacy measures are designed into the AI system to minimize problems." To manage survey length, respondents completed a randomized subset of 4 items from the full 16-item measure. Items were measured on a 5-point scale (1 = Not at all important, 2 = Slightly, 3 = Moderately, 4 = Highly, 5 = Extremely important). An exploratory factor analysis of the 16-item measure revealed a unidimensional structure, with factor loadings ranging from 0.67 to 0.82, indicating good factorial validity. Internal reliability could not be computed due to the randomized presentation of the items.

We further asked respondents if they would be more likely to trust AI systems when organizational governance mechanisms are in place, using five items. Example

Table 10.3 Principles and practices of Trustworthy AI

Principle	Description
Technical performance, accuracy and robustness	The performance and accuracy of the AI system output are assessed before and regularly during deployment to ensure it operates as intended. The robustness of the output is tested in a range of situations, and only data of appropriate quality is used to develop the AI.
Data privacy, security and governance	Safety and privacy measures are designed into the AI system. Data used for AI is kept secure, used only for the specific purpose forwhich it is agreed, and is not shared with other apps or third parties without permission. Robust security measures are in place to identify and prevent adversarial attacks.
Human agency and oversight	There is appropriate human oversight and control of AI systems and their impact on stakeholders by people with the required expertise and resources to do so. AI systems are regularly reviewed to ensure they are operating in a trustworthy and ethical manner.
Transparency and explainability	The purpose of the AI system, how it functions and arrives at its solutions, and how data is used and managed are transparently explained and reasonably understood to a variety of stakeholders. Developers keep audit trails of the methods and datasets used to develop AI.
Fairness, non-discrimination and diversity	The outcomes of AI systems are assessed regularly to ensure they are fair, free from unfair bias, and designed to be inclusive for a variety of users. AI is developed with the participation and input of a diverse range of people.
Accountability and contestability	There is clear accountability and responsibility if something goes wrong with an AI system. Any impacted user or stakeholder is able to challenge the outcomes of an AI system via a fair and accessible human review process.
AI literacy	People are supported in understanding AI systems, including when it is appropriate to use them and the ethical considerations of that use.
Risk and impact mitigation	The risks, unintended consequences, and potential for harm from AI systems are fully assessed and mitigated prior to and during their employment

items include the following: "I would be more willing to trust an AI system [specific application] if: The system was reviewed by an AI ethics board," and "The organization using the system had an AI ethics code of conduct." A 7-point scale was used ranging from 1 = strongly disagree to 7 = strongly agree, scale ($a = 0.93$).

Demographic Measures Gender (0 = Female or Other gender, 1 = Male), age category (1 = 18–39, 2 = 40–55, 3 = 56+), university education (0 = No university education, 1 = University education), and country (0 = non-"BICS" country, 1 = "BICS" country [Brazil, China, India, South Africa] were included in modelling as they have been demonstrated to differ in attitudes toward AI systems [12, 71].

10.3.5 Analytic Procedures

For descriptive findings, we examine mean values and percentage frequencies to indicate levels of key variables. We also compared findings across countries and demographic groups using analysis of variance (ANOVA) tests. Given the large dataset, even trivial associations may be statistically significant. Hence, to focus on practically meaningful effects, we only report differences with omega-squared effect sizes (ω^2) of 0.01 or more.

To identify and model the key mechanisms supporting trust and acceptance of AI systems, we employed structural equation modelling (SEM). SEM is a multivariate modeling technique that has advantages over traditional multivariate techniques including (a) the assessment of measurement error to reduce biased effect estimates, (b) the estimation of latent variables via observed variables, and (c) the ability to assess the fit of the model to the data [72].

We tested a model examining knowledge-based (subjective knowledge and technology self-efficacy), motivational (perceived benefits), uncertainty (perceived risks), and institutional (structural assurance safeguards and confidence in entities to develop, use, and govern AI) pathways to trust, controlling for demographic factors and country economic group. The pathways were modelled as latent variables, and all factor loadings for the observed indicators exceeded recommended thresholds for standardized loadings ($\geq$0.60; [73]). As the trust and trustworthiness scales were strongly correlated ($r = 0.77$, $p < 0.001$), and prior research has shown that latent trust and trustworthiness factors often demonstrate low discriminant validity [74], we modelled the trust and trustworthiness items as a single latent trust in AI factor to maximize parsimony and avoid multicollinearity while remaining theoretically aligned with prevailing trust frameworks.

10.4 Key Descriptive Findings

We present first descriptive findings on the extent to which people trust and accept AI systems and feel they understand AI, as well as their views on the benefits and risks of AI use, and their expectations of AI governance and regulation.

Our analysis revealed a distinct pattern of findings for countries defined by the International Monetary Fund as advanced economies, compared to countries defined as emerging economies. The countries with emerging economies were part of the BRICS alliance,[4] and we refer to these as the "BICS" countries, given Russia was not included in the data collection. We note meaningful and statistically significant differences in the findings between advanced economies and the BICS countries.

[4] BRICS is the acronym used to describe the five major emerging economies of Brazil, Russia, India, China, and South Africa (see https://en.wikipedia.org/wiki/BRICS). We did not include Russia in our sampling and therefore use the acronym BICS in this report.

10.4.1 To What Extent Do People Trust and Accept AI Systems?

People broadly report low trust and acceptance of AI systems. Three out of five people (61%, $M = 4.11$) report they are either ambivalent or unwilling to trust AI systems. In contrast, 39% report that they are willing to trust these systems, for example by relying on AI recommendations or sharing personal information with these systems to make them work. Consistent with these findings, most people (67%, $M = 3.04$) report low to moderate acceptance of AI systems. Only a third of people across countries report high acceptance.

Despite low levels of trust and acceptance, 63% of people perceive AI systems as trustworthy ($M = 4.84$). Perceptions of trustworthiness are typically higher than trusting intentions because trust involves risk and vulnerability (e.g., by relying on AI output or sharing information with an AI system), whereas perceiving a system as trustworthy does not.

Levels of trust and trustworthiness differ by application type. People are more trusting and accepting of the use of AI in healthcare and least trusting of AI use in human resources. For example, 44% ($M = 4.3$) of people trust the use of AI in healthcare, compared to 34% ($M = 3.9$) who trust AI in HR.

There are also notable differences in trust, trustworthiness and acceptance across countries. Those in the emerging economies of Brazil, India, China, and South Africa (i.e. the BICS countries) report the highest levels of trust, trustworthiness, and acceptance, and more broadly tend to report more positive attitudes towards AI. For example, in the BICS countries, most people trust AI systems (56–75%; Ms range from 4.65 in South Africa to 5.23 in India). In contrast, a minority of people in the advanced economies report trusting AI, with people in Finland reporting the lowest trust (only 16%, $M = 3.37$). The BICS countries also have notably higher acceptance of AI, with 48–67% of people in these countries reporting high acceptance (Ms = 3.44–3.84) and are also more likely to view AI as trustworthy (79–93% view as trustworthy, Ms = 5.35–5.84). In contrast, people in Western countries and Japan have less favorable views about the trustworthiness of AI, with Finland again ranking lowest ($M = 4.43$).

10.4.2 The Knowledge Pathway: How Well Do People Understand AI?

Half of the respondents report low subjective knowledge of AI, indicating that they do not understand AI or when and how it is used (49%, $M = 2.56$). Just 18% self-report high knowledge. This low subjective knowledge is confirmed by people's objective awareness of AI use. We asked whether commonly used technology applications—such as product recommendations, traffic navigation apps, chatbots and virtual assistants, social media, and accommodation-sharing apps—utilize AI.

Overall, we found that although 68% of people had used these common AI-enabled applications, two in five (41%) were unaware that these applications use AI.

The use of the technology did not necessarily increase understanding that AI is integrated into and enables the application. For example, while 87% of people report using social media apps, almost half (45%) are unaware that social media apps rely on AI. This pattern of using an application without awareness that it relies on AI is particularly strong for embedded forms of AI, such as social media, email filters and accommodation and ride-sharing apps, where the AI use with no physical or vocal manifestation. Conversely, there is more awareness of AI when it is used in embodied forms (e.g., with voice, voice activation, or face activation), such as virtual assistants (75%), facial recognition (70%), or smart home management.

People in Asian countries tend to report more subjective understanding of AI, particularly people in China ($M = 3.42$), India ($M = 3.36$), and South Korea ($M = 3.08$). Japan is a notable exception, with Japanese respondents reporting the lowest level of subjective AI knowledge in the sample ($M = 2.04$). People in the Netherlands, UK, France, and Estonia also rate their knowledge as lower than people in other countries (Ms = 2.07–2.16).

People in the BICS countries and Singapore are more likely to use common AI-enabled applications (75–82%) and be more aware that these applications rely on AI (with the exception of South Africa) than people in all other countries. On average, two-thirds or more of people in these countries are aware of AI use in common applications (66–71%). In contrast, people in European countries, as well as the UK, the USA, and Japan, were less knowledgeable about AI use, with only 47–53% aware of its use in common applications. People in Finland had notably higher understanding of AI use compared to other European countries.

10.4.3 The Motivational Pathway: How Do People View the Benefits of AI?

A key finding is that 85% of people expect the use of AI will result in a range of benefits (to a moderate or high degree), particularly performance-related benefits such as improve efficiency, innovation, effectiveness, resource utilization, and reduce costs (range from 78% to 87%, $M = 3.40$–3.62). These "performance" benefits are rated higher than several "people-oriented" benefits. In particular, people are less convinced that AI systems will enhance what people can do and result in improved outcomes for people, which were ranked comparatively lower (Ms = 3.28).

There are clear differences across countries in how people view the benefits of AI. People in the BICS countries have the most positive view of the benefits (Ms = 3.78–4.00). In contrast, people in Australia, Canada, the UK, the USA, the Netherlands, Finland, and Japan are less convinced of the benefits (Ms = 3.01–3.09).

10.4.4 The Uncertainty Pathway: How Do People View the Risks of AI?

While people expect significant benefits from AI, the majority are concerned about a range of potential risks (73%, $M = 3.26$). Cybersecurity risk (e.g., from hacking or malware) is a dominant concern reported by 84% of respondents ($M = 3.68$). Manipulative or harmful use of AI, job loss and deskilling, loss of privacy, system failure, undermining human rights, and inaccurate outcomes are other risks reported by more than two-thirds of people (68–77%, Ms = 3.17–3.42). In comparison, people are less concerned about the risk of bias from AI use. However, AI bias is still a concern for the majority of people (58%, $M = 2.80$).

In contrast to the distinct differences across countries in how people view the benefits of AI, there are many commonalities and only a few small differences in how people from different countries perceive the risks of AI use. In almost all countries, people are most concerned about cybersecurity risks. The exceptions are people in India and South Africa, who are most concerned with job loss due to automation, with cybersecurity risk ranking second. In all countries, people are least concerned about the potential risk of bias from AI. People in South Africa, South Korea, and Brazil tend to report more concern about the risks of AI than people in most other countries (Ms = 3.54–4.48). In contrast, people in Germany tend to report less concern about the potential risks of AI compared to people in most other countries ($M = 3.01$).

10.4.5 The Institutional Pathway: How Do People View the Institutional Safeguards Governing AI Use?

While the majority (71%) of people across countries believe AI regulation is necessary, the majority of people (61%, $M = 4.08$) disagree or are unsure that current safeguards around AI (i.e., rules, regulation, and laws) are sufficient to make the use of AI safe and protect them from problems. This dissatisfaction with current safeguards is strongest in the Western countries, as well as in Israel, Japan, and South Korea, where only 39% of people believe current safeguards are adequate (Ms = 3.27–4.03). In contrast, the majority of people in the BICS countries and Singapore view current safeguards as adequate, including most in India and China (74–88%, Ms = 5.42–5.52) and about half in Singapore and Brazil (52–53%, Ms = 4.48–4.56).

In terms of confidence in entities to both develop and use and regulate and govern AI in the best interests of the public, people have most confidence in their country's universities (79–82% moderate to high confidence, Ms = 3.43–3.50) and security and defense forces (76–78%, Ms = 3.39–3.43). Conversely, they report comparatively lower confidence in government, technology companies, and commercial organizations (60–71%, Ms = 2.85–3.15).

There are notable country differences in confidence of government and technology companies. About half of people in South Africa, the USA, Japan, and the UK lack confidence in their government to develop, use, and govern AI in the best interests of the public (45–52%, Ms = 2.69–3.15). In contrast, most people in China (86%), India (70%), and Singapore (60%) have high or complete confidence in their governments to develop, use, and govern AI (Ms = 3.64–4.17). Confidence in technology companies is generally low in Western countries and Israel, particularly Finland, Canada, and Australia (30–40% no or low confidence, Ms = 2.66–2.82), and comparatively high in the BICS countries (51–73% high or complete confidence, Ms = 3.66–4.15).

There is strong public endorsement for each of the principles for trustworthy AI, with almost all people across all countries surveyed viewing each these practices as moderately to extremely important for trust in AI systems (96–99%, $M = 4.04$). Table 10.3 provides a description of the eight trustworthy AI principles. While all eight principles are considered important by respondents, data privacy, security, and governance practices are considered the most important for trust in AI systems in all countries (except China where it was ranked second), and AI literacy practices are viewed as comparatively less important in many countries.

One way enterprises and government can support trust in their use of AI systems is by putting in place these principles and practices for trustworthy AI, as well as assurance and governance mechanisms that reassure people that these principles are in place. Seventy-five percent ($M = 5.19$) of people report they would be more willing to trust an AI system when assurance mechanisms are in place that support trustworthy use, such as regularly monitoring the accuracy and reliability of AI systems, adhering to an AI ethics certification or national standards, conducting independent AI ethics reviews, and implementing an AI code of conduct.

10.4.6 Differences Across Demographic Groups

Younger people and those with a university education generally have more positive attitudes toward AI than older respondents and those without a university education. For example, compared to older respondents (42–57 years and 58+ years), the youngest age group (18–41 years) have greater trust ($M = 4.29$ vs. 4.04 [42–57] vs. 3.84 [58+]; $\omega^2 = 0.02$), acceptance ($M = 4.11$ vs. 3.84 vs. 3.24; ES = 0.04), and subjective knowledge of AI ($M = 2.69$ vs. 2.54 vs. 2.31; ES = 0.02) and are more likely to view current safeguards as adequate ($M = 4.28$ vs. 3.99 vs. 3.76; $\omega^2 = 0.02$). Respondents with a university education also report more trust ($M = 4.30$ vs. 3.91; $\omega^2 = 0.02$), acceptance ($M = 3.20$ vs. 2.88; ES = 0.02), and subjective knowledge of AI ($M = 2.84$ vs. 2.29; $\omega^2 = 0.07$) than those without a university education.

Regarding gender, the only notable difference is that men report higher subjective knowledge of AI than women ($M = 2.74$ vs. 2.34; $\omega^2 = 0.04$). However, there was no gender difference in objective awareness of AI use in common technologies.

10.5 What Are the Key Predictors of Trust and Acceptance of AI?

To examine how each of the four pathways relates to trust and acceptance of AI systems, we tested our empirical model using structural equation modelling (see Sect. 10.3.5). Our model displayed in Fig. 10.1 fit the data well: $\chi 2$ ($N = 17{,}134$, df = 1740) = 46803.72, $p < 0.001$; CFI: 0.93, TLI: 0.93, SRMR: 0.06, RMSEA: 0.04. In the findings below, "*B*" refers to the standardized beta coefficient, which indicates the strength of the effect of each predictor (independent variables) on trust and acceptance (the dependent variables). Beta coefficients can be compared to indicate the relative strength of each predictor. We next discuss the key insights gained from the model testing.

10.5.1 Trust Is Central to AI Acceptance

The model shows that trust is a key predictor of AI acceptance ($B = 0.87$) and explains 74% of the variance in acceptance. When people perceive AI systems as trustworthy and are willing to trust them, they are more likely to accept these technologies.

Trust acts as a central mechanism through which other predictors impact AI acceptance. It is important, therefore, to understand what influences trust in AI systems. To do this, we discuss each of the four distinct "pathways to trust"—institutional, motivational, uncertainty, and knowledge—and examine their comparative importance in predicting trust. Collectively, these four pathways account for 84% of the variance in trust.

10.5.2 Institutional Safeguards and Confidence Are the Strongest Drivers of Trust

The institutional pathway is grounded in the view that people often defer to, and expect, authoritative sources and institutional processes to provide assurance of the safety and reliability of new technologies and practices. As shown in the model, people are more trusting of AI systems when they believe current regulations and laws are sufficient to make AI use safe and have confidence in the government, technology, and commercial organizations to develop, use, and govern AI. This institutional pathway is the strongest predictor of trust ($B = 0.50$) and is significantly more important than the other pathways.

Given our results show most people are unconvinced that current governance and regulations are adequate to protect people from problems associated with AI, a critical foundational step toward strengthening trust and the trustworthiness of AI

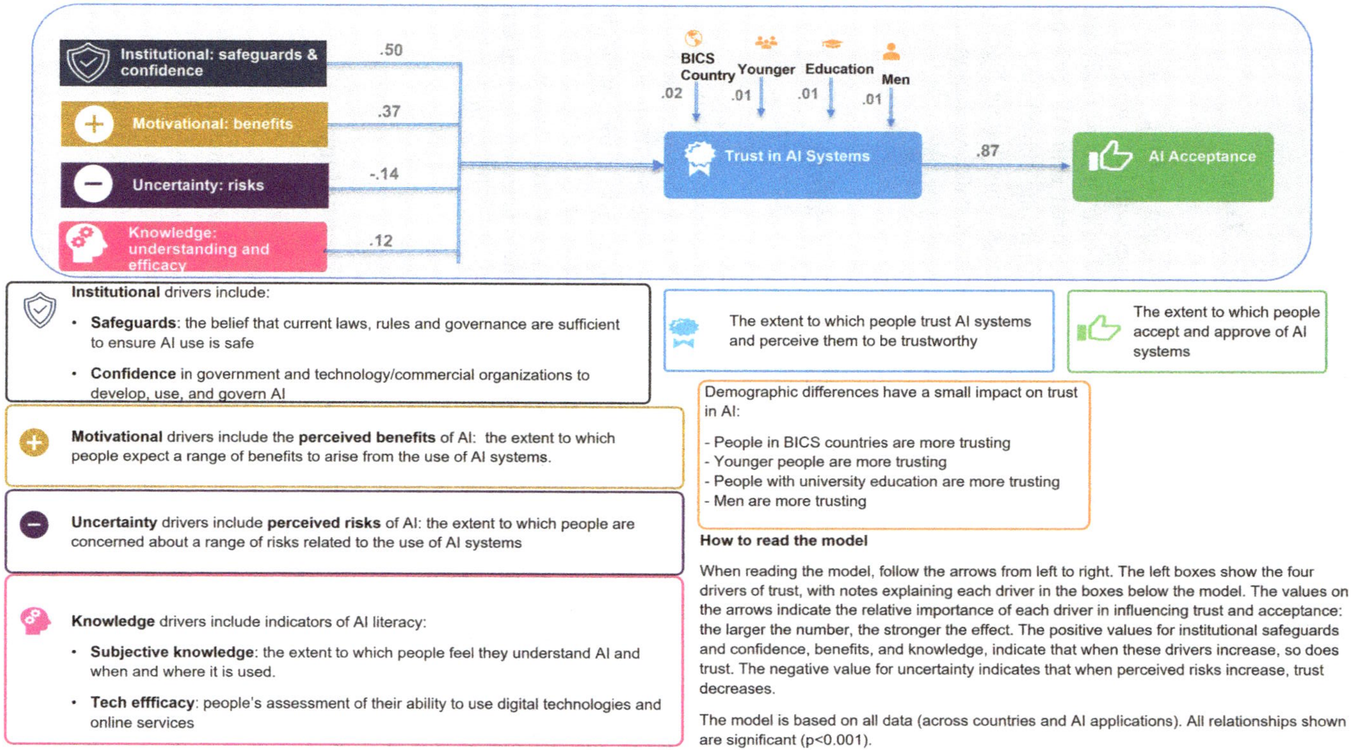

Fig. 10.1 Model examining four mechanisms for supporting trust and acceptance of AI systems

is ensuring there is an appropriate regulatory and legal framework governing AI systems, as well as implementing robust governance at the enterprise level.

10.5.3 The Perceived Benefits of AI Motivate Trust

The motivational pathway to trust is grounded in evidence that the more people perceive benefits from using AI, the more motivated they will be to trust AI. This motivational pathway is the second strongest predictor of trust ($B = 0.37$) and is a stronger driver of trust than the perceived risks associated with AI. This helps explain why people are willing to use technologies that provide immediate benefits (e.g., convenience), despite concerns about potential risks. This finding highlights the importance of designing and using AI systems in ways that deliver demonstrable benefits to people, to support trust and acceptance of these systems.

10.5.4 The Perceived Risks of AI Create Uncertainty and Reduce Trust

The uncertainty pathway is based on the view that it is more difficult to trust in contexts of uncertainty and risk. The model supports this view showing that the more concerned people are about the perceived risks of AI use, the less likely they are to trust AI systems ($B = -0.14$). This includes both technical risks associated with AI use (e.g., cybersecurity and privacy risks, risk of inaccurate or biased outcomes) and broader societal risks (e.g., manipulation, deskilling, and job loss). This is the third strongest driver of trust. This finding underscores the importance of ongoing action to mitigate the risks associated with AI at multiple levels, as well as communicating these risk mitigation strategies to reassure people.

10.5.5 Understanding AI and How to Use Technology Influences Trust

The knowledge pathway is based on evidence that knowledge and understanding enhance trust in technology. The model shows that people are more likely to trust and accept AI when they feel they understand how and when AI is used and are sufficiently skilled in using digital technologies ($B = 0.12$). This knowledge pathway is the fourth driver of trust, highlighting the importance of supporting people's technological and digital literacy and skills.

10.5.6 Country and Demographic Factors Have a Smaller Impact on Trust

After taking into account the institutional, motivational, uncertainty, and knowledge drivers of trust in the model, we found four other factors have a small but meaningful influence on trust. People in the BICS countries ($B = 0.02$), as well as younger generations ($B = 0.01$), the university-educated ($B = 0.01$), and males ($B = 0.01$), are slightly more trusting of AI systems.

10.6 Discussion and Implications

The findings of this 17-country survey reveal important insights on public trust and attitudes toward AI. They reveal that most people are wary about trusting AI systems and have low or moderate acceptance of its use. However, there is both divergence and convergence in attitudes across countries. People in the emerging economies of Brazil, India, China, South Africa, together with Singapore, have notably higher trust and acceptance and more positive attitudes toward AI than people in the other countries. While knowledge about AI and perceptions of AI benefits also vary widely across countries, views on the risks of AI and expectations of trustworthy governance practices are broadly consistent across countries. This underscores the value of cross-national cooperation and shared international standards in governing AI.

Our integrated model of the mechanisms that support public trust and acceptance of AI systems confirm that trust in AI is influenced by the perceived adequacy of institutional safeguards to mitigate risks and confidence in entities that deploy, govern, and regulate AI, as well as perceptions of AI's benefits and risks and knowledge of AI and efficacy in using digital technologies. Trust in AI in turn strongly predicts societal acceptance.

Taken together, our modelling and descriptive findings highlight both current and future challenges to trust and acceptance of AI systems, as well as opportunities for overcoming these challenges. In particular, the findings inform four practical pathways that enterprises can use to support the responsible and trusted integration and deployment of AI.

10.6.1 The Institutional Pathway: Institutional Safeguards and Confidence in Entities to Use and Govern AI Are a Strong Predictor of Trust

Our findings highlight the important role institutions, governance, and regulatory safeguards play in laying a foundation for trust and reassuring people that trust in AI is warranted. However, while the large majority of people expect AI to be regulated, many view the current regulatory and legal framework as insufficient to make AI use safe and protect people from the risks. These findings suggests that the institutional frameworks governing AI are lagging and failing to keep pace with community expectations. While considerable work is underway in many countries and jurisdictions, as evidenced by the ratification of the European Union's comprehensive AI Act and the comprehensive regulatory framework implemented in China, in most countries, regulatory frameworks are still in an early stage of development or implementation. For example, many countries are still debating the optimal regulatory approach or issuing voluntary standards. Our findings suggest that implementing a robust regulatory framework that effectively mitigates the risks stemming from AI use is a key foundation for supporting public trust and acceptance of AI.

The challenge of regulation lagging the rapid development of technology is not new and highlights the need and opportunity for enterprises to support trust by implementing robust internal governance and oversight over the design, development, and deployment of AI. We find strong global public consensus on the governance principles and related practices that enterprises deploying AI systems are expected to uphold in order to be trusted.

People expect organizations deploying AI systems to uphold high standards of (1) data privacy, security, and governance; (2) technical system performance, accuracy, and robustness; (3) fairness, non-discrimination, and inclusive design; (4) human agency and oversight of AI systems; (5) transparency and explainability; (6) accountability and contestability; (7) risk and impact mitigation; and (8) AI literacy support (see Table 10.3).

Coupled with the finding that governance and assurance mechanisms enhance trust, these insights highlight that enterprises can directly build trust in AI systems by developing capabilities and practices for upholding these principles and investing in governance mechanisms that demonstrate and support the responsible deployment of AI systems, such as regularly monitoring system accuracy and reliability, AI codes of conduct, and upholding international AI standards. However, indicators such as the IBM Global AI Adoption Index [75] highlight that a majority of enterprises deploying AI are at an early stage of AI governance maturity and have not taken steps to ensure their use of AI aligns with the principles and practices of trustworthy AI.

A key challenge is that a third of people report low confidence in commercial enterprises and technology organizations, as well as government, to develop, use, and govern AI in society's best interest. This is problematic given the heavy reliance on industry to self-regulate and govern their use of AI, together with government's central role in regulation. As public confidence is notably higher in universities and research institutions to develop and govern AI, one opportunity is for enterprises and government to partner with these trusted entities on the design and development of AI solutions. Furthermore, prior research shows that general trust in the organization informs trust in that organization's use of AI [11, 61]. This highlights that investing in building customers' broader trust in the deploying organization—for example, by reliably demonstrating competence, benevolence, and integrity in the provision of services and products—can facilitate trust in the AI systems they produce and deploy.

10.6.2 *The Uncertainty Reduction Pathway: Similarities in Perceived AI Risks Across Countries Support a Global Approach to Risk Mitigation*

Perceived risk is a well-established inhibitor of trust in technology [76], particularly when these risks involve privacy, autonomy, or societal harm. Our findings show that people in all countries perceive risks from AI and view these risks in a comparable way. An important implication is that enterprises operating in multiple markets can anticipate a common set of concerns and risks across these markets and use similar governance mechanisms to manage and mitigate these risks while noting there may be some cultural nuances in expectations of mitigation strategies.

More broadly, this insight supports the merit and importance of global collaborative approaches to AI governance and international standard setting to help mitigate risks and support responsible use and interoperability. For example, the International Organization for Standardization [77] and the IEEE Standards Association [78] have developed robust AI governance processes and frameworks to guide enterprises. For example, ISO Standards *42001*, *23894*, and *38507* each provide guidance on AI governance and management. Further, the OECD Trustworthy AI Observatory has over 900 resources to support trusted and responsible AI use.

The shared perception and concern of AI risks across countries also underscores the importance of striving for consistency in AI governance and regulatory frameworks across countries. AI systems are not bound by country borders and consistency and clarity of the governance and regulatory framework supports enterprises to invest, develop, and adopt AI technologies and uphold standards, principles, and practices that support public trust and adoption.

A key trust-enhancing practice that reduces uncertainty is the retention of human involvement and oversight in decisions that impact people. We find strong universal endorsement of the principle and practice of human oversight and control of AI systems. This carries an important implication for technology leaders striving for the highest levels of automation: while full automation may maximize efficiency and cost reduction, it can undermine trust and acceptance. Balance is required.

10.6.3 The Motivational Pathway: Demonstrating the Benefits of AI to People and Society Motivates Trust

Our modelling revealed that an important pathway for strengthening and preserving trust comes from demonstrating the tangible, beneficial impact of AI for people and society. This highlights the importance of human-centered AI design and having a clear beneficial purpose at the outset of AI projects, as well as enterprises co-designing AI-enabled services and products with key stakeholders and end-users, for building trust (see [79]). The pattern in our data suggests people often perceive more "performance" benefits from AI (e.g., cost reduction and efficiency) that predominately benefit enterprises rather than people or society more broadly. However, our findings indicate people trust AI more when it has a clear beneficial purpose to people (e.g., Healthcare AI to enhance diagnosis and treatment) rather than just a performance benefit to the enterprise (e.g., to increase efficiency in HR processes).

The fact that perceived benefits and risks both influence trust in our model suggests that augmenting benefits to people while proactively mitigating risks supports trust and acceptance. Notably, the motivation pathway has a more substantial positive impact than the negative impact of the uncertainty pathway. This supports prior research indicating people pay more attention to the benefits than risks of AI [80]. This highlights the importance of designing and deploying AI in ways that demonstrably create value and benefits for stakeholders, as well as communicating the benefits of AI use to ensure stakeholders are aware of the benefits. However, balance is required to guard against "benefit selling."

10.6.4 The Knowledge Pathway: People Trust More When They Feel They Understand AI and Are Skilled in Using Digital Technologies

We find that subjective knowledge and technology self-efficacy significantly predict trust in AI. However, our survey reveals that the public generally has a low understanding of AI and its use in everyday life. Furthermore, a majority report that supporting people to understand AI is important for their trust in AI systems. These findings suggest close collaboration is required between government, academia, and business to uplift public and consumer AI literacy and understanding of data and technology.

Our findings raise interesting questions about the role of AI public literacy programs and trust. As an example, Finland is a pioneer in the AI literacy space [81] and commonly ranks at the top of the Media Literacy Index, which assesses the ability of countries to resist fake news and misinformation [82]. Our results indicate that people in Finland are more aware of and knowledgeable about AI than many of their Western counterparts, yet they report low trust and moderate acceptance. This suggests that being better informed does not equate simplistically to greater trust and acceptance. AI literacy should play a role in making people aware of potential benefits and risks, capabilities, and limitations of AI systems, as well as methods for safe and responsible use. This supports people to understand when and under what circumstances it is appropriate to trust AI technologies, which in turn supports responsible adoption and calibrated trust over time [23, 26].

Our findings highlight that many people use applications without being aware that they involve AI. This raises the question of whether enterprises should be transparent in disclosing the use of AI to enable people to make more informed decisions about use, benefits, and risks. The EU AI Act, for example, requires that people are made aware when they are interacting with a chatbot as opposed to a human. We see a need for similar transparency of AI use in applications such as social media and recommender systems that may potentially be used in manipulative ways.

Enterprises also need to consider that different cohorts have different understandings and views about AI, with younger people and the university-educated being more aware, knowledgeable about, and accepting of AI. In contrast, other cohorts are likely to need more reassurance and evidence of the trustworthiness of these technologies, as well as AI literacy support to understand these technologies and use them effectively in the workplace. As such, a one-size-fits-all approach to supporting trusted and responsible AI adoption is unlikely to work.

10.7 Outlook and Future Research

Moving forward, enterprises can leverage these insights by embedding clear institutional safeguards and governance mechanisms into their AI strategies. Practical measures such as transparent communication about AI capabilities and limitations, robust frameworks for risk mitigation, and ongoing education and skill-building initiatives for employees and users can be used to support trustworthy AI deployment. Furthermore, proactively aligning enterprise AI practices with established international standards and societal expectations can help mitigate public concerns and facilitate greater acceptance and sustainable deployment. Regular monitoring of trust and public sentiment, alongside regular review and update of governance approaches, will be important as AI technologies evolve and introduce new opportunities and risks.

Trust in AI is often viewed as an individual or technological matter, with research focused on system and user attributes [83]. However, our study reinforces that it is socio-technical in nature, founded on institutional- and enterprise-level governance structures, commitments, and norms that shape AI design and deployment, as well as the contextualized purpose, benefits, and risks of the AI system. Examining how the socio-technical context and environment influence trust and acceptance of AI use in enterprises is a rich avenue for future investigation [84, 85]. Emerging case study research reinforces the need for a socio-technical approach. For example,

Smith et al. [79] show that stakeholder trust and acceptance of an organization's deployment of AI is powerfully influenced by the historical context of technology deployment, the purpose, risk profile, and design of the AI system, stakeholder engagement and consultation during the design and implementation phase, and alignment with the authorizing environment (see also [86]).

Our research highlights widespread concern about the risks of AI. However, little is known about how stakeholders experience vulnerability, uncertainty, and risk when interacting with or being subjected to enterprise AI systems (see [87]). An important avenue for deepening a socio-technical understanding of trust in AI is to examine the vulnerabilities that various forms of enterprise AI create for stakeholders and the technological, relational, and governance mechanisms required to effectively address these vulnerabilities.

The rapid advancement of AI technologies is opening up new vulnerabilities and challenges for trust that will likely require adaptation to the way enterprises build and maintain trust in their use of AI going forward. In particular, as AI systems advance to become more powerful and agentic and feature more anthropomorphic or humanlike characteristics, such as autonomy, adaptability, complex problem-solving, and the ability to process, respond, and justify output fluently in natural language (e.g., generative AI and large-language models). We call for research that examines the efficacy of the four pathways to the context of generative and agentic AI use in enterprises. The recent replication of the model in our examination of public trust, attitudes, and use of AI across 47 countries suggests the four pathways hold in the context of generative AI systems and are robust across AI applications [88].

The cross-sectional survey design used in our study did not enable examination of the causal influence of the predictors and limited examination of trust to a static snapshot in time. Given trust is a dynamic process that unfolds over time, we recommend future research adopt longitudinal, field-based research designs that enable examination of the evolution of trust dynamics and processes as employees, customers, and other stakeholders interact with and are subjected to enterprise AI systems. This temporal, holistic approach is well suited to studying how people change and calibrate their trust in AI systems as they interact with them over time.

Acknowledgments This research was supported by an Australian Government Research Support Package grant provided to The University of Queensland AI Collaboratory and by the KPMG Chair in Trust grant (ID 2018001776) awarded to the second author. We are grateful for the insightful input, expertise, and feedback on this research project provided by Dr. Caitlin Curtis and Dr. Javad Pool as members of the research team, as well as Dr. Ali Akbari, James Mabbott, Rita Fentener van Vlissingen, Jessica Wyndham, Richard Boele, Dr. Ian Opperman, Rossana Bianchi, Professor Shazia Sadiq, Dr. Natalie Smith, and Alex Macdade.

References

1. Nguyen, D., Hekman, E.: The news framing of artificial intelligence: a critical exploration of how media discourses make sense of automation. AI Soc. **39**(2), 437–451 (2022). https://doi.org/10.1007/s00146-022-01511-1

2. OECD: Artificial Intelligence in Society. OECD Publishing, Paris (2019). https://doi.org/10.1787/eedfee77-en
3. Polemi, N., Praça, I., Kioskli, K., Bécue, A.: Challenges and efforts in managing AI trustworthiness risks: a state of knowledge. Front. Big Data. **7**, 1381163 (2024). https://doi.org/10.3389/fdata.2024.1381163
4. World Economic Forum: These are the 3 biggest emerging risks the world is facing (2024). https://www.weforum.org/stories/2024/01/ai-disinformation-global-risks/
5. Choung, H., David, P., Ross, A.: Trust in AI and its role in the acceptance of AI technologies. Int. J. Hum. Comput. Interact. **39**(9), 1727–1739 (2022). https://doi.org/10.1080/10447318.2022.2050543
6. Kelly, S., Kaye, S., Oviedo-Trespalacios, O.: What factors contribute to the acceptance of artificial intelligence? A systematic review. Telematics Informatics. **77**, 101925 (2023). https://doi.org/10.1016/j.tele.2022.101925
7. Blut, M., Wünderlich, N.V., Brock, C.: Facilitating retail customers' use of AI-based virtual assistants: a meta-analysis. J. Retail. **100**(2), 293–315 (2024). https://doi.org/10.1016/j.jretai.2024.04.001
8. Singapore Smart Nation and Digital Government Office: National AI Strategy 2.0: AI for the Public Good, for Singapore and the World. Government of Singapore (2023) https://file.go.gov.sg/nais2023.pdffile.go.gov.sg
9. UK Department for Science, Innovation & Technology: National AI Strategy (Command Paper 5252). UK Government (2021) https://assets.publishing.service.gov.uk/government/uploads/system/uploads/attachment_data/file/1020402/National_AI_Strategy_-_PDF_version.pdfassets.publishing.service.gov.uk
10. US National Science and Technology Council, Select Committee on Artificial Intelligence: National Artificial Intelligence Research and Development Strategic Plan: 2023 Update. Office of Science and Technology Policy (2023) https://www.nitrd.gov/pubs/National-Artificial-Intelligence-Research-and-Development-Strategic-Plan-2023-Update.pdf
11. Gillespie, N., Lockey, S., Curtis, C.: Trust in Artificial Intelligence: A Five-Country Study. The University of Queensland and KPMG Australia (2021). https://doi.org/10.14264/e34bfa3
12. Zhang, B.: Public opinion toward Artificial Intelligence. In: Bullock, J.B., et al. (eds.) The Oxford Handbook of AI Governance, pp. 553–571 (2023). https://doi.org/10.1093/oxfordhb/9780197579329.013.36
13. Kinney, M., Anastasiadou, M., Naranjo-Zolotov, M., Santos, V.: Expectation management in AI: a framework for understanding stakeholder trust and acceptance of Artificial Intelligence systems. Heliyon. **10**(7), e28562 (2024). https://doi.org/10.1016/j.heliyon.2024.e28562
14. Gillespie, N., Lockey, S., Curtis, C., Pool, J., Akbari, A.: Trust in Artificial Intelligence: A Global Study. The University of Queensland and KPMG Australia (2023). https://doi.org/10.14264/00d3c94
15. Rousseau, D.M., Sitkin, S.B., Burt, R.S., Camerer, C.: Not so different after all: a cross-discipline view of trust. Acad. Manag. Rev. **23**(3), 393–404 (1998). https://doi.org/10.5465/amr.1998.926617
16. Lewis, J.D., Weigert, A.: Trust as a social reality. Soc. Forces. **63**(4), 967–985 (1985)
17. Möllering, G.: Trust: Reason, Routine, Reflexivity. Emerald Publishing, Oxford (2006)
18. Colquitt, J.A., Rodell, J.B.: Justice, trust, and trustworthiness: a longitudinal analysis integrating three theoretical perspectives. Acad. Manag. J. **54**(6), 1183–1206 (2011)
19. Mayer, R.C., Davis, J.H., Schoorman, F.D.: An integrative model of organizational trust. Acad. Manag. Rev. **20**(3), 709–734 (1995). https://doi.org/10.2307/258792
20. Bedué, P., Fritzsche, A.: Can we trust AI? An empirical investigation of trust requirements and guide to successful AI adoption. J. Enterp. Inf. Manag. **35**(2), 530–549 (2022)
21. Lewicki, R.J., Bunker, B.B.: Developing and maintaining trust in work relationships. In: Kramer, R.M., Tyler, T.R. (eds.) Trust in Organizations: Frontiers of Theory and Research, pp. 114–139. Sage, Thousand Oaks, CA (1996)
22. Lintner, T.: A systematic review of AI literacy scales. Npj Sci. Learn. **9**(1), 1–11 (2024). https://doi.org/10.1038/s41539-024-00264-4

23. Pinski, M., Benlian, A.: AI literacy for users—a comprehensive review and future research directions of learning methods, components, and effects. Comput. Hum. Behav. Artif. Hum. **2**(1), 100062 (2024). https://doi.org/10.1016/j.chbah.2024.100062
24. Schiavo, G., Businaro, S., Zancanaro, M.: Comprehension, apprehension, and acceptance: understanding the influence of literacy and anxiety on acceptance of artificial Intelligence. Technol. Soc. **77**, 102537 (2024). https://doi.org/10.1016/j.techsoc.2024.102537
25. Chowdhury, S., Budhwar, P., Dey, P.K., Joel-Edgar, S., Abadie, A.: AI-employee collaboration and business performance: integrating knowledge-based view, socio-technical systems and organizational socialization framework. J. Bus. Res. **144**, 31–49 (2022). https://doi.org/10.1016/j.jbusres.2022.01.069
26. Long, D., Magerko, B.: What is AI literacy? Competencies and design considerations. In: Proceedings of the 2020 CHI Conference on Human Factors in Computing Systems, pp. 1–16 (2020). https://doi.org/10.1145/3313831.3376727
27. Montag, C., Kraus, J., Baumann, M., Rozgonjuk, D.: The propensity to trust in (automated) technology mediates the links between technology self-efficacy and fear and acceptance of artificial intelligence. Comput. Hum. Behav. Rep. **11**, 100315 (2023). https://doi.org/10.1016/j.chbr.2023.100315
28. Xu, S., Khan, K.I., Shahzad, M.F.: Examining the influence of technological self-efficacy, perceived trust, security, and electronic word of mouth on ICT usage in the education sector. Sci. Rep. **14**(1), 1–16 (2024). https://doi.org/10.1038/s41598-024-66689-4
29. Baer, M.D., Colquitt, J.A.: Moving toward a more comprehensive consideration of the antecedents of trust. In: Searle, R.H., Neinaber, A.M., Sitkin, S.B. (eds.) Routledge Companion to Trust, pp. 163–182. Routledge (2018). https://doi.org/10.4324/9781315745572-12
30. van der Werff, L., Legood, A., Buckley, F., Weibel, A., de Cremer, D.: Trust motivation: the self-regulatory processes underlying trust decisions. Organ. Psychol. Rev. **9**(2–3), 99–123 (2019). https://doi.org/10.1177/2041386619873616
31. Davis, F.D.: Perceived usefulness, perceived ease of use, and user acceptance of information technology. MIS Q. **13**(3), 319–340 (1989). https://doi.org/10.2307/249008
32. Venkatesh, V., Morris, M.G., Davis, G.B., Davis, F.D.: User acceptance of information technology: toward a unified view. MIS Q. **27**(3), 425–478 (2003) https://www.jstor.org/stable/30036540
33. Ali, M., Raza, S.A., Khamis, B., Puah, C.H., Amin, H.: How perceived risk, benefit and trust determine user Fintech adoption: a new dimension for Islamic finance. Foresight. **23**(4), 403–420 (2021). https://doi.org/10.1108/FS-09-2020-0095
34. Choudhury, A., Shamszare, H.: The impact of performance expectancy, workload, risk, and satisfaction on trust in ChatGPT: cross-sectional survey analysis. JMIR Hum. Factors. **11**, e55399 (2024). https://doi.org/10.2196/55399
35. Kerstan, S., Bienefeld, N., Grote, G.: Choosing human over AI doctors? How comparative trust associations and knowledge relate to risk and benefit perceptions of AI in healthcare. Risk Anal. **44**(4), 939–957 (2023). https://doi.org/10.1111/risa.14216
36. Bingley, W.J., Curtis, C., Lockey, S., Bialkowski, A., Gillespie, N., Haslam, S.A., et al.: Where is the human in human-centered AI? Insights from developer priorities and user experiences. Comput. Hum. Behav. **141**, 107617 (2023). https://doi.org/10.1016/j.chb.2022.107617
37. Visschers, V.H., Siegrist, M.: Find the differences and the similarities: relating perceived benefits, perceived costs and protected values to acceptance of five energy technologies. J. Environ. Psychol. **40**, 117–130 (2014). https://doi.org/10.1016/j.jenvp.2014.05.007
38. Deutsch, M.: Trust and suspicion. J. Confl. Resolut. **2**(4), 265–279 (1958). https://doi.org/10.1177/002200275800200
39. Luhmann, N.: Trust and Power. Polity Press, Cambridge (2017)
40. Hoff, K.A., Bashir, M.: Trust in automation. Hum Factors. **57**(3), 407–434 (2014). https://doi.org/10.1177/0018720814547570
41. Yang, R., Wibowo, S.: User trust in artificial intelligence: a comprehensive conceptual framework. Electron. Mark. **32**(4), 2053–2077 (2022). https://doi.org/10.1007/s12525-022-00592-6

42. Yang, Q., Pang, C., Liu, L., Yen, D.C., Tarn, J.M.: Exploring consumer perceived risk and trust for online payments: an empirical study in China's younger generation. Comput. Hum. Behav. **50**, 9–24 (2015). https://doi.org/10.1016/j.chb.2015.03.058
43. Sohn, S.: Consumer perceived risk of using autonomous retail technology. J. Bus. Res. **171**, 114389 (2023). https://doi.org/10.1016/j.jbusres.2023.114389
44. Zucker, L.G.: Production of trust: institutional sources of economic structure, 1840–1920. Res. Organ. Behav. **8**, 53–111 (1986)
45. Siegrist, M., Cvetkovich, G.: Perception of hazards: the role of social trust and knowledge. Risk Anal. **20**(5), 713–720 (2000). https://doi.org/10.1111/0272-4332.205064
46. Giddens, A.: The Consequences of Modernity. Polity Press, Cambridge (1990)
47. McKnight, D.H., Carter, M., Thatcher, J.B., Clay, P.F.: Trust in a specific technology: an investigation of its components and measures. ACM Trans. Manag. Inf. Syst. **2**(2), 1–25 (2011). https://doi.org/10.1145/1985347.1985353
48. McKnight, D.H., Choudhury, V., Kacmar, C.: Developing and validating trust measures for e-commerce: an integrative typology. Inf. Syst. Res. **13**(3), 334–359 (2002). https://doi.org/10.1287/isre.13.3.334.8
49. McKnight, D.H., Cummings, L.L., Chervany, N.L.: Initial trust formation in new organizational relationships. Acad. Manag. Rev. **23**(3), 473–490 (1998). https://doi.org/10.5465/amr.1998.926622
50. Delgosha, M.S., Hajiheydari, N.: How human users engage with consumer robots? A dual model of psychological ownership and trust to explain post-adoption behaviours. Comput. Hum. Behav. **117**, 106660 (2021). https://doi.org/10.2307/249008
51. Park, S.: Multifaceted trust in tourism service robots. Ann. Tour. Res. **81**, 102888 (2020). https://doi.org/10.1016/j.annals.2020.102888
52. Shao, Z., Zhang, L., Meng, T., Zhang, J.: The paradox of technology quality and ethical concerns in building trust and behavioral intention in the AI-enabled face recognition payment. Electron. Mark. **34**(1) (2024). https://doi.org/10.1007/s12525-024-00742-y
53. Falco, G., Shneiderman, B., Badger, J., Carrier, R., Dahbura, A., Danks, D., Yeong, Z.K. et al.: Governing AI safety through independent audits. Nat. Mach. Intell. **3**(7), 566–571 (2021). https://doi.org/10.1038/s42256-021-00370-7
54. Knowles, B., Richards, J. T.: The Sanction of Authority: Promoting Public Trust in AI. In: Proceedings of the 2021 ACM Conference on Fairness, Accountability, and Transparency, pp. 262–271 (2021)
55. Shneiderman, B.: Bridging the gap between ethics and practice: Guidelines for reliable, safe, and trustworthy Human-Centered AI systems. ACM Transactions on Interactive Intelligent Systems (TiiS) **10**(4), 1–31 (2020). https://doi.org/10.1145/3419764
56. Yam, J., Skorburg, J.A.: From human resources to human rights: Impact assessments for hiring algorithms. Ethics Inf. Technol. 1–13 (2021). https://doi.org/10.1007/s10676-021-09599-7
57. Koester, N., Salge, T.-O.: Building Trust in Intelligent Automation: Insights into Structural Assurance Mechanisms for Autonomous Vehicles. In: 41st ICIS International Conference on Information Systems, December 13–16, 2020 (2020)
58. Stewart, K.J.: Trust transfer on the World Wide Web. Organ. Sci. **14**(1), 5–17 (2003). https://doi.org/10.1287/orsc.14.1.5.12810
59. Łapińska, J., Escher, I., Górka, J., Sudolska, A., Brzustewicz, P.: Employees' trust in artificial intelligence in companies: the case of energy and chemical industries in Poland. Energies. **14**(7), 1942 (2021). https://doi.org/10.3390/en14071942
60. Gkinko, L., Elbanna, A.: Designing trust: the formation of employees' trust in conversational AI in the digital workplace. J. Bus. Res. **158**, 113707 (2023). https://doi.org/10.1016/j.jbusres.2023.113707
61. Chen, Y.K., Wen, C.R.: Impacts of attitudes toward government and corporations on public trust in artificial intelligence. Commun. Stud. **72**(1), 115–131 (2020). https://doi.org/10.1080/10510974.2020.1807380
62. United Nations: Standard country or area codes for statistical use (M49) (n.d.). https://unstats.un.org/unsd/methodology/m49/

63. Brislin, R.W.: Back-translation for cross-cultural research. J. Cross-Cult. Psychol. **1**(3), 185–216 (1970). https://doi.org/10.1177/135910457000100301
64. International Labour Organization: International Standard Classification of Occupations (ISCO). ILOSTAT (n.d.) https://ilostat.ilo.org/methods/concepts-and-definitions/classification-occupation/
65. Gillespie, N.: Survey measures of trust in organizational contexts: an overview. In: Lyon, F., Mollering, G., Saunders, M.N.K. (eds.) Handbook of Trust Methodology. Edward Elgar (2015)
66. Zhang, A., Moffat, K.: A balancing act: the role of benefits, impacts and confidence in governance in predicting acceptance of mining in Australia. Resour. Policy. **44**, 25–34 (2015). https://doi.org/10.1016/j.resourpol.2015.01.001
67. Ipsos: Public Views of Machine Learning: Findings from Public Research and Engagement Conducted on Behalf of the Royal Society. The Royal Society (2017) https://royalsociety.org/~/media/policy/projects/machine-learning/publications/public-views-of-machine-learning-ipsos-mori.pdf
68. Vu, H.T., Lim, J.: Effects of country and individual factors on public acceptance of artificial intelligence and robotics technologies: a multilevel SEM analysis of 28-country survey data. Behav. Inform. Technol. **41**(7), 1515–1528 (2021). https://doi.org/10.1080/0144929x.2021.1884288
69. Zhang, B., Dafoe, A.: Artificial Intelligence: American Attitudes and Trends. SSRN (2019). https://doi.org/10.2139/ssrn.3312874
70. European Commission: Ethics guidelines for trustworthy AI (2019). https://digital-strategy.ec.europa.eu/en/library/ethics-guidelines-trustworthy-ai
71. O'Shaughnessy, M.R., Schiff, D.S., Varshney, L.R., Rozell, C.J., Davenport, M.A.: What governs attitudes toward artificial intelligence adoption and governance? Sci. Public Policy. **50**(2), 161–176 (2022). https://doi.org/10.1093/scipol/scac056
72. Kline, R.B.: Principles and Practice of Structural Equation Modeling. Guildford Press (2015)
73. Hair, J.F., Black, W.C., Babin, B.J., Anderson, R.E.: Multivariate Data Analysis, 8th edn. Cengage Learning (2018)
74. PytlikZillig, L.M., Hamm, J.A., Shockley, E., Herian, M.N., Neal, T.M.S., Kimbrough, C.D., et al.: The dimensionality of trust-relevant constructs in four institutional domains: results from confirmatory factor analyses. J. Trust Res. **6**(2), 111–150 (2016). https://doi.org/10.1080/21515581.2016.1151359
75. IBM: IBM Global AI Adoption Index 2023: enterprise report (2023). https://filecache.mediaroom.com/mr5mr_ibmspgi/179414/download/IBM%20Global%20AI%20Adoption%20Index%20Report%20Dec.%202023.pdf
76. Featherman, M., Pavlou, P.A.: Predicting e-services adoption: a perceived risk facets perspective. Int. J. Hum. Comput. Stud. **59**(4), 451–474 (2003). https://doi.org/10.1016/s1071-5819(03)00111-3
77. International Organization for Standardization: Artificial Intelligence. ISO (n.d.) https://www.iso.org/sectors/it-technologies/ai
78. IEEE Standards Association: Autonomous and Intelligent Systems (AIS) Standards. IEEE (2025) https://standards.ieee.org/initiatives/autonomous-intelligence-systems/standards/
79. Smith, N., Gillespie, N., Rinta-Kahlia, T., Lockey, S., Pool, J., Curtis, C.: How can government demonstrate trustworthy use of AI in public services? A case study. Inf. Syst. J. (forthcoming)
80. Cheng, X., Su, L., Luo, X., Benitez, J., Cai, S.: The good, the bad, and the ugly: impact of analytics and Artificial Intelligence-enabled personal information collection on privacy and participation in ridesharing. Eur. J. Inf. Syst. **31**(3), 339–363 (2022). https://doi.org/10.1080/0960085X.2020.1869508
81. Ministry for Foreign Affairs of Finland: Finland to enhance Europeans' digital skills—elements of AI online course to be launched in EU countries (2020). https://um.fi/current-affairs/-/asset_publisher/gc654PySnjTX/content/suomi-vahvistaa-eurooppalaisten-digitaitoja-ja-osaamista-elements-of-ai-verkkokurssin-lanseeraukset-eu-maissa-alkavat
82. Ministry of Education and Culture: Media Literacy and Education in Finland. Finland Toolbox (2024) https://toolbox.finland.fi/life-society/media-literacy-and-education-in-finland/

83. Lockey, S., Gillespie, N.: Understanding trust in artificial intelligence: a research agenda. In: Mayer, R., Mayer, B. (eds.) A Research Agenda on Trust: Interdisciplinary Perspectives, pp. 11–24. Edward Elgar, Cheltenham (2024). https://doi.org/10.4337/9781802200942
84. Parker, S., Ballard, T., Billinghurst, M., Collins, C., Dollard, M., Griffin, M., Johal, W., Jorritsma, K., Kowalkiewicz, M., Kyndt, E., Lusher, D., McLennan, C., Miller, T., Neal, A., Paterson, J., Vetere, F., Walsh, T.: Quality work in the future: new directions via a co-evolving sociotechnical systems perspective. Aust. J. Manag. (2025). https://doi.org/10.1177/03128962251331813
85. Pereira, V., Hadjielias, E., Christofi, M., Vrontis, D.: A systematic literature review on the impact of artificial intelligence on workplace outcomes: a multi-process perspective. Hum. Resour. Manag. Rev. **33**(1), 100857 (2023). https://doi.org/10.1016/j.hrmr.2021.100857
86. Rinta-Kahila, T., Someh, I., Gillespie, N., Gregor, S., Indulska, M.: Algorithmic decision making and system destructiveness: a case of automatic debt recovery. Eur. J. Inf. Syst. **31**(3), 313–338 (2021). https://doi.org/10.1080/0960085X.2021.1960905
87. Lockey, S., Gillespie, N., Holm, D., Someh, I.A.: A review of trust in artificial intelligence: challenges, vulnerabilities and future directions. In: Proceedings of the 54th Hawaii International Conference on System Sciences, pp. 5463–5472 (2021)
88. Gillespie, N., Lockey, S., Ward, T., Macdade, A., Hassed, G.: Trust, Attitudes and Use of Artificial Intelligence: A Global Study 2025. The University of Melbourne and KPMG (2025). https://doi.org/10.26188/28822919.v1

Steven Lockey is a Research Fellow at Melbourne Business School. His primary research focus is on the development and repair of trust in organizational contexts. He also examines attitudes and expectations about the use of emerging technology in the workplace and in society. Steve has published in journals such as *Business Ethics Quarterly*, *Computers in Human Behavior*, *AI and Ethics*, and the *International Journal of Medical Informatics* and presented his work at international conferences including the Academy of Management and the Hawaii International Conference on System Sciences. His research has been cited by the Australian and UK governments and in over 80 media articles.

Nicole Gillespie is Professor of Management and holds the Chair in Trust at Melbourne Business School and The University of Melbourne. She is an International Research Fellow at the Centre for Reputation at Oxford University and a Fellow of the Academy of Social Sciences in Australia. Her research focuses on understanding trust in challenging contexts with current projects examining trust in AI, human-AI collaboration, digital disruption, and trust repair. She has a strong track record of leading industry-engaged research including commissioned research for the OECD, the World Economic Forum, and the UK Institute of Business Ethics.

Chapter 11
Insights into AI's Influence on Enterprise Software and Systems: Lessons from Varied Contexts

Shaoyang Fan and Javad Pool

Abstract This chapter explores the impact of artificial intelligence (AI) on enterprise software and systems through six case studies. The case studies include Midjourney, Zillow, Canva, the Australian Government's Department of Human Services (Robodebt), CareMonitor, and Capillary. The case studies have been chosen to highlight both successes and failures in projects relating to the use of AI in enterprises. For each case, we provide a summary of the company's use of AI and its impact in order to analyse the various factors that led to the success or failure of the project. The chapter concludes with a summary of key observations from varied contexts.

11.1 Midjourney: Navigating Generative AI

11.1.1 Introduction to Midjourney

Midjourney, established by David Holz in February 2022 in San Francisco, has become a leading force in the creation of AI art. The development of a platform that converts textual prompts into visually engaging works contributes to human creativity and represents a significant shift in how industries approach art and creative processes. Its novelty on the tech side lies in the use of Discord,[1] and the "/imagine"[2] command facilitates an innovative and user-friendly experience,

[1] https://discord.com/

[2] To initiate the creation process with Midjourney, simply type "/" followed by "imagine," and add your specific prompt. The generation process typically takes about a minute. Upon completion, the Midjourney bot automatically produces four unique images derived from your input as the standard output.

S. Fan (✉) · J. Pool
The University of Queensland, Brisbane, Australia
e-mail: shaoyang.fan@uq.edu.au; j.pool@uq.edu.au

S. Sadiq (ed.), *Enterprise AI*, https://doi.org/10.1007/978-3-032-01940-0_11

making art creation accessible to a diverse audience, including artists, designers, and enthusiasts worldwide.

11.1.2 Deployment of Generative AI in Creative Processes

Midjourney achieved extraordinary success in 2023, generating US$200 million in revenue and reaching a valuation reportedly exceeding US$10 billion according to market analysts [1, 2]. With its community of more than 19 million users [2, 3], the platform demonstrates the transformative impact of Generative AI in the creative landscape. This development rests on three key elements: the application of Generative AI, the integration with Discord's established community platform to enhance user accessibility, and the incorporation of user feedback.

Firstly, the principle of operation for Generative AI applications is based on generating new images from prompts after being trained on patterns and relationships found in millions of images scraped from the open Web [4]. This technology became central to Midjourney's ability to democratise art production. It allows users to convert verbal descriptions into visual art without requiring extensive drawing or editing skills. This has opened vast creative opportunities, establishing Midjourney not just as a tool but as a transformative methodological innovation that stimulates new ways of thinking and empowers the human imagination [4].

Secondly, the decision to utilise Discord, an established community platform, has significantly contributed to Midjourney's ease of use [5]. This strategic choice ensured that the platform was readily accessible and facilitated seamless interaction and engagement among a broad user base [6]. The embedding in Discord further enhanced the user experience, fostering a sense of community among artists and creatives.

Lastly, user feedback has been instrumental in Midjourney's ongoing development and success [5]. Midjourney empowers users by providing multiple outputs in response to prompts [7, 8]. This grants the freedom to choose images that best reflect their individual vision, prioritising user preferences for a satisfying and engaging experience. With active incorporation of feedback, the team behind Midjourney has managed to update and iterate its models frequently. As a result, the platform continuously evolves to better meet user needs and preferences.

Together, these three pillars have underscored Midjourney's substantial impact: Generative AI, the use of Discord, and the incorporation of user feedback. They have evidenced its financial success and pivotal role in heralding a new era of AI-enhanced creativity.

11.1.3 Implications for Enterprise Software and Systems

Generative AI has enabled remarkable success stories like Midjourney's rapid growth and market penetration [1, 2]. However, deploying such technology in enterprise contexts presents complex opportunities and challenges. Generative AI's transformative potential comes with inherent risks that enterprises must carefully consider. Research reveals that successful AI platforms often grapple with ethical dilemmas around copyright infringement, artist consent, and content moderation [9]. This pattern offers critical lessons for enterprises: the same technology that drives innovation can simultaneously create complex governance challenges that require proactive management strategies.

Enterprises can learn from Midjourney's approach by implementing robust, context-specific AI governance frameworks. For example, Midjourney confronts the risk of political misinformation through content filtering and user reporting systems [10, 11]. Similarly, a company using Generative AI for marketing must guard against creating misleading product claims or brand-damaging deepfakes. This requires not just general guidelines but also function-specific protocols and built-in technical safeguards tailored to each use case. In practice, this means establishing human review queues for AI-generated ad campaigns. It also means implementing automated content verification systems that cross-reference claims against product specifications. Companies should also deploy technical constraints that prevent the AI from generating content on prohibited topics similar to Midjourney's blocking of sensitive political figures [11]. Additionally, enterprises should establish continuous monitoring systems that track AI outputs for drift in quality or appropriateness [12]. This ensures that governance measures evolve alongside the technology's capabilities.

Midjourney's use of Discord for community engagement and user feedback elevates the potential for enterprises to better engage with both customers and employees. Community platforms enable companies to establish direct lines of communication with users and also foster a sense of community belonging. This approach proves valuable for customer support, product development, and marketing. Businesses can collect real-time feedback, conduct user acceptance testing, and enable audience interaction in a more dynamic environment. This real-time visibility into customer sentiment and behaviour ensures better product offerings and greater customer satisfaction [13].

Incorporating user feedback intentionally during the development and refinement of products and services underscores the importance of user-centred design in enterprise software. This customer involvement in product development approach ensures that products are technologically advanced while also aligning with the genuine needs and preferences of end-users [14]. Using user feedback can result in more intuitive interfaces, improved user experiences, and solutions that truly address user issues for enterprise systems [15]. This promotes continuous improvement and adaptation, ensuring that software solutions remain relevant and effective over time.

These approaches outline an effective strategy for enterprise software development and system design. The combination of Generative AI, community engagement platforms, and user-centric development enables enterprises to create adaptable, innovative solutions for business operations. This framework improves operational efficiency while maintaining ethical standards in AI implementation.

11.1.4 Summary

Midjourney's key innovation lies in combining Generative AI with extensive community engagement through Discord and strategic user feedback integration. This strategy provides significant takeaways for enterprise software development, particularly in building responsive, user-driven systems. By capturing real-time user preferences and feedback via a community platform, Midjourney demonstrates how businesses can develop AI-powered solutions that truly serve user needs. Additionally, Midjourney's experiences with copyright and ethical challenges underscore the importance of responsible AI implementation, providing practical lessons for enterprises navigating similar issues in their AI initiatives.

11.2 Zillow: Navigating Complex Terrain of Advanced AI

11.2.1 Introduction to Zillow

Zillow has led the real estate technology sector since launching its Zestimate tool in 2006.[3] US homeowners have the option to utilise Zestimate for a rapid assessment of their property's worth. In 2018, Zillow launched direct property purchases through a service known as iBuying. This service uses automated valuation algorithms and predictive analytics to determine fair prices for houses on the market. Sellers can get a quick cash offer instead of going through the usual sales process. Companies like Zillow then fix up these properties and sell them for a profit. Zillow's goal was to speed up property sales by using data to make quick decisions.

[3] The Zestimate uses machine learning trained on millions of US home sales to predict house prices. The system looks at location, market conditions, and house features to work out an estimated value.

11.2.2 Zillow's iBuying Venture: A Cautionary Tale

After losing US$881 million in 2021 [16], Zillow closed its iBuying venture later that year. The fundamental problem was their algorithmic prediction system, which consistently overvalued houses. This mistake led to Zillow overpaying for properties they later sold at substantial losses. The company's heavy reliance on these flawed AI predictions for large-scale purchasing decisions created two major issues. First, it led to systematic financial losses, which the volatility of the COVID-19 pandemic's market made even worse [16]. Second, it raised ethical concerns about whether such AI-driven mass purchases could manipulate market prices and disrupt traditional real estate practices [17].

Zillow's experience with iBuying demonstrates a critical lesson about AI in real-world applications: Even sophisticated algorithms can make systematically wrong predictions when their underlying assumptions do not match market realities. Although Zestimate worked well for years in providing home value estimates, using similar prediction models for actual purchasing decisions proved disastrous. The transition from estimation to transaction highlighted how AI systems need different levels of accuracy and risk management depending on their use case. Companies must carefully evaluate whether their AI models are truly suitable for high-stakes financial decisions.

Furthermore, Zillow has been accused of manipulating the market through their iBuying strategy. A viral TikTok video with nearly 500,000 likes [17] claimed that Zillow bought several properties within a neighbourhood to inflate housing prices, creating challenges for typical buyers seeking affordable homes. When AI systems failed in iBuying, people lost trust in the company. In fact, other iBuyer companies have even faced legal challenges. In 2022, Opendoor, an iBuying company similar to Zillow, reached a settlement of US$62 million with the US Federal Trade Commission (FTC) because the company was accused of misleading home sellers by claiming that sellers could earn more money through iBuying than through traditional methods [18].

After its iBuying setback, Zillow went back to what it does best and looked for more practical ways to use AI to address market needs. For example, the company created an AI-powered natural language search feature that allows people to search for homes using conversational language [19]. This makes it easy for users to find homes by simply typing everyday phrases, and Zillow ensures the tool's effectiveness by scanning millions of listings. The company now focuses on useful AI tools that solve real problems, improving its service and taking fewer risks. This shift shows that Zillow now wants to use technology in a more prudent manner that aligns with the actual needs of home buyers and sellers.

11.2.3 Implications for Enterprise Software and Systems

A primary lesson from Zillow's iBuying venture is the critical need for robust AI risk management. During the COVID-19 pandemic, their AI for home buying struggled to keep up with the rapid changes in the housing market, leading to significant losses. This real-world example showed that companies need better ways to manage AI risks in changing markets.

Businesses can reduce market unpredictability by using the NIST AI Risk Management Framework (AI RMF 1.0) to handle AI-related risks more efficiently [20]. This model provides a clear method to identify, assess, and control AI risks. AI RMF 1.0 helps companies detect problems and implement safety measures when building AI systems that can adapt to market changes. This highlights why companies need to assess the risks in AI systems affected by external factors. The framework also helps companies develop testing processes to identify problems early.

The viral TikTok video in the Zillow case underscores the critical importance of building and maintaining public trust through transparent operations and clear communication about automated decisions. The FTC's action against Opendoor further emphasises that enterprises must go beyond mere technical compliance to ensure their AI systems operate ethically and transparently. Regular audits on models is important for preventing unintended consequences in AI deployment [21]. In addition, maintaining comprehensive documentation and implementing robust compliance checks helps organisations navigate the complex landscape of automated decision-making while upholding both legal obligations and public trust [22, 23].

Companies must continuously update their AI systems with new data while recognising that some events are inherently unpredictable. Zillow struggled to predict house prices correctly for multiple reasons. The market was moving rapidly and had become increasingly complex. Additionally, the COVID-19 pandemic represented a Black Swan event [24] that fundamentally disrupted historical pricing patterns. This highlights the inherent limitations of AI in rapidly changing environments, especially during unprecedented events that lie outside the training data. This shows why enterprise software and systems need to continuously refine AI models using various relevant data sources to improve predictive ability [25].

AI models require rigorous validation, especially when used for major financial decisions. The failure of Zillow shows that an AI system's strong performance in one area (estimating home values) does not guarantee success in another (making purchase decisions). Their experience demonstrates that companies need different validation standards depending on how they use AI. For estimation and analysis, companies might accept a margin of error. But for automated purchasing decisions, they need extensive testing with real-world data and careful monitoring of model assumptions. They should regularly audit their AI systems to identify and rectify flaws in their decision-making processes.

11.2.4 Summary

Zillow's iBuying venture failure offers crucial lessons for companies using AI in their business. When Zillow moved from estimating house prices to actually buying them, their AI system's flaws during the COVID-19 pandemic led to systematic overvaluation and significant losses. This experience shows companies need to carefully validate AI systems before using them for automated decision-making. Zillow's successful pivot to AI-powered search tools also demonstrates how companies can find appropriate ways to use AI that match their capabilities and reduce risks.

11.3 Canva: Harnessing AI for Design Innovation

11.3.1 Introduction to Canva

Canva is an online graphic design platform founded in Australia in 2012. In 2023, Canva launched a suite of Generative AI products to expand its design capabilities and user engagement. According to Canva's Marketing & AI Report [26], users have used these AI tools more than four billion times. This helped Canva grow to 170 million users in 190 countries, with yearly earnings of about US$1.7 billion in 2023 [27].

11.3.2 Canva's AI-Powered Transformation of Graphic Design

Canva has integrated AI technologies to make graphic design accessible to a global audience [28]. The Smart Design Assistant, built on machine learning, provides personalised design suggestions to users across all skill levels. Through natural language processing, Canva enhances its search functionality, enabling users to locate design elements and templates efficiently. In addition, computer vision technology powers advanced image editing features, including background removal and object detection, simplifying complex design tasks.

However, the integration of AI technologies into Canva's platform presents several challenges. A primary concern is maintaining the equilibrium between automation and human creativity. Canva addresses this by developing AI systems that augment rather than replace the creative process [28, 29]. This approach allows users to retain creative control while benefiting from AI's capabilities.

Another challenge involves ensuring fairness, inclusiveness, privacy, and security in AI models. As a platform serving millions of users globally, Canva's AI-powered features must prevent biases that could disadvantage specific user groups. The company implements a responsible data strategy, using over 120 million pieces of international, localised content[4] [28]. To ensure representative data across its global user base, Canva sources content from diverse demographics and employs bias detection algorithms [30]. The company prioritises data security and user privacy [31]. It implements robust data protection measures, including encryption and controlled access. Canva conducts regular security audits and maintains compliance with privacy regulations such as the General Data Protection Regulation (GDPR) [32].

To support global expansion, Canva has invested in infrastructure and algorithms for effective AI scaling [33]. The company migrated from traditional Online Transaction Processing (OLTP) databases to modern Online Analytical Processing (OLAP) systems[5] with scalable storage and computing capabilities. Canva replaced scheduled worker services with an ELT pipeline using OLAP databases for calculations, enabling the processing of billions of usage events in minutes. These infrastructure improvements have simplified the codebase, reduced maintenance requirements, and improved system reliability, decreasing incident frequency from monthly occurrences to once every few months while simplifying troubleshooting and recovery processes [33].

Through these developments, Canva's AI application has enhanced user engagement and satisfaction. By automating complex design tasks and personalising the user experience, Canva streamlines the design process while encouraging creative exploration. The resulting operational efficiencies have enabled rapid diversification of product offerings and market expansion.

11.3.3 Implications for Enterprise Software and Systems

Canva's achievements can be largely attributed to its user-focused AI development strategy. By focusing on AI features that address specific user needs and pain points, Canva has simplified workflows and provided users with actionable insights. Enterprises should emulate this strategy, prioritising AI solutions that not only automate tasks but also genuinely support user objectives. In fact, a crucial aspect of integrating AI into software systems is to strike a balance between automation and human control [35]. Canva demonstrates that while AI can automate repetitive tasks and offer guidance, it should ultimately serve as a powerful tool that complements human capabilities rather than replacing them.

[4] It refers to Canva's strategy of managing a vast repository of materials that cater to both global and specific regional audiences. "International content" is designed to be universally applicable across various regions and cultures, often using neutral language and imagery to appeal to a broad audience. In contrast, "localised content" is tailored to meet the specific linguistic, cultural, and regulatory requirements of a particular locale or market.

[5] OLTP databases are designed to manage and process a high volume of day-to-day transactions quickly and efficiently. In contrast, OLAP systems are optimised for complex queries and data analysis on large volumes of historical data, enabling insights into trends and performance [34].

Ethical considerations are central to Canva's approach with a focus on biases, data privacy, and fairness in AI. Canva's approach can serve as an instructive example to enterprises that venture into AI about how they can observe the major principles of developing AI responsibly, such as the mitigation of biases, data privacy and security, transparency and accountability, and continuous monitoring and improvement with diversified and representative data. By adopting these principles and responsible AI practices, companies can learn from Canva how to build user trust with users, ensuring that the ethical development in the deployment of AI technologies are prioritised. This means that for organisations to successfully navigate the complex AI ethics landscape, they must establish a clear ethical direction, foster a culture of accountability and transparency, and maintain ongoing dialogue with stakeholders [36, 37].

Deploying AI at scale, as Canva has done, requires significant investment in infrastructure and algorithms. This underscores the crucial need to create scalable systems capable of managing varied datasets and accommodating a growing user base all while ensuring consistent performance. Businesses should emphasise scalability and flexibility in their AI approaches to achieve global reach.

11.3.4 Summary

Canva's integration of AI offers a road map for enterprises looking to leverage AI technologies. By following a user-centric design approach, balancing automation with human creativity, adhering to ethical AI practices [31], investing in scalable infrastructure [33], and prioritising a robust data strategy [32], enterprises can effectively integrate AI into their software and systems, achieving similar success as Canva in improving accessibility and user empowerment.

11.4 Robodebt: Lessons from an Automated Debt Recovery System Failure

11.4.1 Introduction to Robodebt

Robodebt, introduced by the Department of Human Services (DHS) of the Australian Government in 2016, was an automated system designed to uncover inconsistencies in the income information submitted by welfare beneficiaries to Centrelink and the Australian Taxation Office (ATO).The system utilised an algorithm to compare welfare recipients' reported fortnightly income with averaged annual income data obtained from the ATO. When a disparity was identified, the system automatically issued a debt notice to the individual concerned. However, the

Robodebt implementation used a flawed methodology: it averaged individuals' annual income to estimate their fortnightly earnings.

Robodebt had harmful effects, particularly on vulnerable populations including low-income earners, unemployed people, and people with disabilities. The system caused widespread distress and financial hardship [38]. Legal challenges and public outcry increased pressure on the government. In November 2019, the government acknowledged the system's weaknesses and suspended it [39]. The government subsequently committed to repaying over AUD 720 million related to more than 470,000 incorrectly calculated debts [40].

11.4.2 Robodebt: Lessons from the Impact of Automation

The government designed the Robodebt scheme as an extension of existing welfare compliance policies [41]. The scheme aimed to improve the accuracy and speed of debt recovery and reduce welfare fraud. However, the scheme's severe negative impacts show important lessons about designing and deploying automated systems. Although Robodebt did not use artificial intelligence, its failure provides important lessons for AI system development. As an example of large-scale Automated Decision-Making (ADM), Robodebt's collapse shows the dangers in any automated system. These include flawed logic, poor data handling, and weak human oversight. These problems become more serious with complex AI systems.

The system's core operational flaw demonstrates these risks clearly: averaging annual incomes to determine fortnightly earnings [38]. This approach assumed that people earned the same amount throughout the year. The system failed to account for variable earnings among casual and seasonal workers. This led to incorrect debt calculations.

The system also limited human oversight, reflecting broader institutional pressures within the Department of Human Services. Officials designed it to increase efficiency and reduce costs. This reflected the department's ongoing need to generate budget savings through compliance measures [41]. However, the system could not handle the complexity of individual income patterns that required human judgement. As Priergaard demonstrates, this approach was part of a decades-long pattern where compliance policies were expanded "layer by layer" to meet annual budget pressures, with each iteration seeking greater automation to reduce operational costs [41]. This poor oversight contributed directly to the crisis.

The scheme also had legal and procedural failings. The income-averaging approach rested on questionable legal grounds [42] and automatically issued many debt notices without proper legal foundation. The system was implemented without sufficient pre-launch testing or a robust and accessible appeal mechanism. This caused distress including financial hardship and mental health issues among affected people [38]. The combination of flawed methodology, insufficient oversight, and underestimation of legal and ethical implications brought the system down. It cost the government hundreds of millions of dollars in refunds and compensation [40].

The Royal Commission into the Robodebt Scheme conducted an extensive investigation in response to the scheme's widespread failings [43]. Its report confirmed the systemic issues outlined above and recommended crucial reforms to prevent such mistakes recurring. Key recommendations emphasised the need for robust legal frameworks, adherence to legal counsel, and comprehensive training for personnel involved in such systems. The Commission also called for stringent legal checks, enhanced ethical training, and improved data management practices. The goal is to establish an effective, transparent, and fair social security system that rebuilds public trust and safeguards citizens' rights and welfare.

11.4.3 Implications for Enterprise Software and Systems

The Robodebt scheme serves as a warning for enterprises designing and implementing software and systems, particularly when systems make automated decisions. This case highlights several key lessons for organisations deploying such systems.

First, companies must test and validate their algorithms thoroughly before deployment. Data used to train algorithms needs critical review. All underlying assumptions and decision-making logic require examination. Systems need regular audits to catch problems early [21]. Companies should monitor performance continuously and maintain clear complaint processes. They must also develop contingency plans to handle system failures quickly.

Second, Robodebt demonstrates the critical need for human oversight and intervention in automated systems. Automation can enable efficiency and cost reduction, but balancing machine-driven processes with human judgement is essential [44]. Systems need to be designed to allow human review and intervention at critical decision points.

Third, the legal and ethical implications of automated decision-making must be comprehensively addressed. Companies should ensure that fairness, transparency, and accountability guide their approach and that they comply with applicable laws and regulations. This requires close collaboration with legal advisers and all stakeholders, including regulators and civil society organisations, to ensure that system designs meet society's values and expectations [23].

Finally, the Robodebt experience demonstrates the need for effective communication and transparency when deploying automated systems. Enterprises must ensure clear communication with users and stakeholders about the system's purpose, functioning, and limitations. This includes being clear about the logic that supports decisions and providing easily accessible mechanisms for individuals to seek clarification or contest outcomes [45].

The Robodebt case serves as a stark reminder of the risks involved with automated decision-making systems. As companies develop and deploy such systems, they must do so with the highest care and responsibility, ensuring that accuracy, fairness, transparency, and accountability are central to system operation.

11.4.4 Summary

Australia's Robodebt program was designed to automate debt collection in social security but stands as a significant warning about deploying automation in sensitive domains. Algorithm flaws led to incorrect debt calculations and automated collection notices, causing financial hardship and mental distress for vulnerable groups. This failure highlights the need for extensive testing, human oversight, legal and ethical considerations, transparency, and robust safeguards when implementing automated decision-making systems in any industry.

11.5 CareMonitor: Transforming Healthcare with AI-Powered Remote Patient Monitoring

11.5.1 Introduction to CareMonitor

CareMonitor, an Australian medtech start-up established in 2018, uses AI to enhance healthcare services by integrating data from clinical management systems, medical devices, and direct patient inputs into a unified view. This integration supports risk stratification tools, care plan templates, and continuous monitoring of vital signs through intelligent algorithms and data analysis. A key feature of the platform is its telemedicine capability, which facilitates real-time audio and video communications for remote consultations, in order to better manage chronic diseases and reduce unnecessary hospitalisations. Founder and CEO Deepak Biswal highlights the convenience of the platform, noting that since patients spend a large amount of their time outside of hospitals, CareMonitor is particularly beneficial for those with complex chronic diseases that account for a significant proportion of healthcare costs [46].

CareMonitor's success extends beyond individual patient care to large-scale health initiatives. The platform managed more than 100,000 COVID-19 patients in Australia. This was achieved through partnerships with major healthcare providers, including Western Sydney Primary Health Network, Medibank Private Health Insurance, and major Catholic hospitals [46, 47]. The platform provides hospital-level care directly to patients' homes through devices that offer medication reminders and vital test monitoring, such as HbA1c tests for diabetes management. This leadership in remote healthcare delivery was recognised by the Innovation Challenge of the Australian Digital Health Agency in June 2020 [48].

11.5.2 Why CareMonitor Stands Out in Digital Health

CareMonitor's strength lies in its comprehensive integration capabilities and advanced technology stack [49]. The platform ensures native connectivity across healthcare providers by merging disjointed electronic medical records and health systems [50]. This promotes effective team-based care, enhancing provider efficiency and patient outcomes [49]. The platform provides real-time access to clinical information, enabling healthcare providers to make informed clinical decisions and collaborate more efficiently [50, 51].

Building on this technological foundation, CareMonitor allows patients to monitor their vital signs at home and receive treatments there [52]. The platform works by collecting vital signs from patients through connected devices and transmitting these real-time data to remote clinicians for continuous monitoring and analysis. The hospital-at-home programs are designed to reduce pressure on hospitals by enabling patients to receive monitoring and treatments at home, thereby freeing up hospital beds and clinical staff for more acute cases, while offering more comfortable and personal care experiences [52]. These programs are designed to reduce the number of times patients need to return to hospital, potentially saving money through decreased readmission rates and helping people with ongoing health conditions manage them at home [52]. This approach optimises resource use throughout the healthcare system while maintaining high standards of care.

CareMonitor extends these benefits to a broader population through its scalable architecture and strategic partnerships with leading health networks. Partnerships with organisations like the Western Sydney Primary Health Network and Medibank create measurable improvements in patient care delivery [46, 47]. The Western Sydney partnership enables integration with existing regional healthcare workflows, providing CareMonitor access to undeserved patient populations while ensuring clinical protocols meet local standards. The Medibank collaboration extends monitoring services to privately insured patients across Australia, creating a feedback loop where insurance claims data helps validate the platform's effectiveness in reducing hospital readmissions. These partnerships provide CareMonitor with real-world clinical validation and help refine the platform's algorithms based on diverse patient populations and healthcare settings. The platform's ability to manage thousands of patients simultaneously—demonstrated during the COVID-19 response—while maintaining quality care standards proves its scalability in high-demand scenarios. This scalability model applies beyond healthcare to any enterprise system requiring rapid scaling while maintaining service quality.

As a result of these integrated approaches, the transformation CareMonitor has brought to healthcare delivery exemplifies digital technology's potential to revolutionise traditional services. By combining patient-centric engagement, cutting-edge AI capabilities, and strong partnerships, CareMonitor has created a model for accessible, efficient, and effective healthcare [49].

11.5.3 Implications for Enterprise Software and Systems

The transformative impact of CareMonitor on healthcare delivery yields important principles for enterprise software development in diverse industries. Their journey demonstrates key strategies that can guide organisations in delivering adaptable, user-centred software solutions that meet evolving requirements.

The first key strategy contributing to CareMonitor's success is data integration and accessibility. The platform eliminates data silos and facilitates smooth information exchange between systems, providing decision-makers with comprehensive information. For enterprises, isolated data repositories within organisations hinder decision-making and operational efficiency. They can adopt cloud data integration to enable seamless data sharing and collaboration across departments and platforms and improve decision-making [53].

CareMonitor's hospital-at-home model demonstrates how digital platforms can extend traditional service boundaries. This principle applies beyond healthcare: Remote education platforms, virtual customer service, and distributed technical support all benefit from similar approaches. The platform's success in delivering hospital-level care remotely while maintaining quality standards shows how organisations can create efficient service delivery models that build user trust through effective remote management. This aligns with research showing that trust management is critical for cloud-based and distributed systems, where traditional face-to-face trust mechanisms are absent [54]. As Noor et al. emphasise, establishing trust in distributed environments requires robust frameworks that can assess credibility, ensure transparency, and maintain accountability across remote interactions—principles that are fundamental to successful digital service delivery models like CareMonitor's.

Equally significant is CareMonitor's emphasis on scalability and adaptability. The ability of the platform to accommodate varying user numbers and evolving business requirements highlights the importance of building flexible enterprise solutions. This architectural approach ensures long-term viability in dynamic markets, where businesses must rapidly adapt to changing conditions and growing demands. For enterprises, this can be achieved through AI-driven cloud computing with dynamic resource allocation and auto-scaling mechanisms [55], which is particularly crucial for platforms like CareMonitor that must maintain performance reliability while serving variable user populations across diverse operational environments.

CareMonitor's success underscores the value of developing solutions that directly address industry-specific challenges. Their focused approach to healthcare problems, from reducing hospital readmissions to enabling remote care, demonstrates how deep industry understanding can drive innovative solutions. This strategy can be replicated across sectors, where software solutions must be tailored to unique industry requirements while maintaining adaptability and user focus.

11.5.4 Summary

Through comprehensive data integration, CareMonitor enables effective remote patient care, featuring risk stratification, care plan templates, telemedicine, and intelligent monitoring capabilities. The platform has demonstrated its effectiveness by managing large-scale health initiatives, including successful recovery monitoring of patients with COVID-19. This success comes from CareMonitor's seamless data integration, patient-centric design, AI capabilities, scalability, and strategic partnerships with leading healthcare networks.

11.6 Capillary Technologies: Redefining Loyalty in a Digital Age

11.6.1 Introduction to Capillary Technologies

Capillary Technologies, founded in 2012, provides cloud-based software for retailers. The company helps retailers increase sales and build customer loyalty by analysing customer behaviour across digital and physical stores. Their solutions include CRM software, loyalty programs, and retail analytics.

Traditional loyalty programs were often designed as short-term sales promotions rather than long-term relationship builders [56]. In contrast, Capillary takes a strategic, long-term approach by collecting data from multiple retail channels, including in-store systems, e-commerce platforms, and social networks. AI and machine learning algorithms process this data to identify purchasing patterns and customer preferences. Retailers use these insights to create targeted marketing campaigns and personalised shopping experiences.

Capillary supports over 400 retail brands in 30 countries. Their systems process more than 1.95 billion customer interactions each year [57]. Major global retailers across fashion, electronics, grocery stores, and restaurants use Capillary's solutions [58, 59].

11.6.2 Capillary Technologies' Rise as a Market Innovator

Capillary Technologies has become a key contender in the loyalty management sector by implementing several strategic moves. The company adopted a cloud-based software-as-a-service (SaaS) model. SaaS allows businesses to access software applications over the Internet rather than installing and maintaining them on local servers, reducing costs and complexity [60]. This model provides flexibility and efficiency for enterprise brands deploying loyalty programs [61]. Furthermore, the company allocates 50 to 75% of their yearly tech investments to AI development [61]. Capillary's AI loyalty solutions combine personalisation, segmentation, and predictive analytics to create programs that outperform traditional methods through better customer insights and targeted experiences [62].

Building on their technological foundation, Capillary has strengthened their position in the market through strategic acquisitions, such as acquiring Persuade in 2021 [63] and Brierley in 2023 [64]. These acquisitions broadened Capillary's service range and added consulting expertise to their technical offerings. The company has also hired specialists across various departments to strengthen their loyalty program knowledge.

By integrating technology with strategic advice, Capillary's suite of products—comprising Loyalty Plus, Engage Plus, Rewards Plus, and Insights Plus—offers a customer-focused solution [65, 66]. Loyalty Plus helps brands develop and manage tailored loyalty programs [65]. Engage Plus facilitates customer interactions across multiple channels [67]. Rewards Plus provides a rewards network to motivate customer actions [68]. Insights Plus offers analytics for decision-making [69]. Collectively, these tools enable brands to create unified and customised loyalty experiences at every point of consumer engagement [65].

Capillary's quadruple growth in the United States from 2021 to 2024 [61] has led to increasingly complex infrastructure challenges. By adopting advanced performance observability platforms to track application and infrastructure performance, Capillary enables rapid troubleshooting and enhances effective communication with customers [70]. At the same time, Capillary consolidated their monitoring and alerting infrastructure, which streamlined troubleshooting processes [70]. This approach delivered a 75–80% improvement in problem resolution times and continually improved quarterly customer satisfaction scores [70].

11.6.3 Implications for Enterprise Software and Systems

Capillary's successful experience in transitioning from traditional methods in the loyalty management field to a technology-driven model provides valuable insight and inspiration for the enterprise software and systems domain. One key aspect is the shift from traditional, agency-led models to cloud-based SaaS platforms. This transformation enables businesses to benefit from flexibility, scalability, and cost efficiency while gaining access to real-time data and insights [60]. Enterprises can apply this model by prioritising cloud-first architectures that integrate seamlessly with existing systems and support rapid deployment of new capabilities.

Furthermore, AI and ML are playing an increasingly critical role in current technology trends, acting as key drivers of innovation and competitive advantage. Capillary dedicates a substantial share of its incremental technology investments to AI and ML, which not only enhances its platform capabilities but also strengthens its position as an industry leader. This strategy aligns with findings that link AI expertise to increased market value [71]. For instance, following the open-source release of Google's TensorFlow, companies with AI-intensive operations experienced a notable surge in market valuation [71]. Enterprise software providers can adopt a similar strategy by focusing on core technologies that differentiate their offerings and deliver measurable customer value.

Another critical factor in Capillary's success is their strategic acquisitions and focus on attracting top talent. These acquisitions have helped the company expand their service portfolio and integrate consulting expertise into their technological offerings. Capillary's acquisitions of Persuade and Brierley demonstrate how enterprises can build comprehensive solutions that address customer needs holistically rather than through isolated point solutions. Furthermore, to successfully create value, an acquiring company must not only purchase technology but also improve and integrate it into its own processes [72].

To manage the growing complexity of infrastructure demands, Capillary has implemented advanced performance observability platforms and streamlined operational processes. This proactive approach offers a valuable lesson for growing enterprises, as problem-solving competencies are crucial for a company's survival in today's business landscape, allowing organisations to effectively identify, analyse, and solve problems that could impact the customer experience [73]. Combining such technological solutions with operational efficiency can lead to improved problem resolution times and higher customer satisfaction [73].

These strategic approaches are applicable across industries where customer experience, data analytics, and scalable technology platforms are critical success factors. Enterprise software companies, in particular, can apply Capillary's model of combining cloud infrastructure, AI capabilities, strategic acquisitions, and operational excellence to build sustainable competitive advantages in their respective markets.

11.6.4 Summary

Capillary Technologies transitioned from traditional loyalty programs to AI-powered cloud solutions. The company invests 50 to 75% of their tech budget in AI and achieved four-fold growth in the USA between 2021 and 2024. Capillary's experience demonstrates how companies can use cloud platforms, strategic acquisitions, and AI investment to compete in digital markets.

References

1. CB Insights: With $200M in revenue, Midjourney could be worth $10B. https://www.cbinsights.com/research/midjourney-revenue-valuation/ (2023). Accessed 5 June 2025
2. Demand Sage: Midjourney Statistics 2025: Users & Revenue Data. https://www.demandsage.com/midjourney-statistics/ (2024). Accessed 5 June 2025
3. ElectroIQ: Midjourney Statistics By Revenue And Facts (2025). https://electroiq.com/stats/midjourney-statistics/ (2024). Accessed 5 June 2025

4. Tsidylo, I.M., Sena, C.E.: Artificial intelligence as a methodological innovation in the training of future designers: Midjourney tools. Inf. Technol. Learning Tools **97**(5), 203 (2023)
5. Discord: How Midjourney Built a Business on Discord. https://discord.com/build-case-studies/midjourney (2024). Accessed 5 June 2025
6. Midjourney: Discord Overview. https://docs.midjourney.com/docs/midjourney-discord (2025). Accessed 5 June 2025
7. Zapier: How to use Midjourney. https://zapier.com/blog/how-to-use-midjourney/ (2024). Accessed 5 June 2025
8. Midjourney: Getting Started Guide. https://docs.midjourney.com/docs/quick-start (2025). Accessed 5 June 2025
9. Naik, T., Gostu, H., Sharma, R.: Navigating ethics of ai-powered creativity in midjourney. In: 2024 3rd International Conference for Innovation in Technology (INOCON), pp. 1–6. IEEE, Piscataway (2024)
10. Duffy, C.: Top AI photo generators produce misleading election-related images, study finds. https://edition.cnn.com/2024/03/06/tech/ai-images-election-misinformation/. Accessed 24 Apr 2024
11. O'Brien, M.: AI image-generator Midjourney blocks images of Biden and Trump as election looms. https://www.pbs.org/newshour/politics/ai-image-generator-midjourney-blocks-images-of-biden-and-trump-as-election-looms. Accessed 24 Apr 2024
12. Patchipala, S.: Tackling data and model drift in ai: Strategies for maintaining accuracy during ml model inference. Int. J. Sci. Res. Archive **10**(2), 1198–1209 (2023)
13. Famoti, O., Omowole, B.M., Okiomah, E., Muyiwa-Ajayi, T.P., Ezechi, O.N., Ewim, C.P.-M., Omokhoa, H.E.: Enhancing customer satisfaction in financial services through advanced BI techniques. Int. J. Multidiscip. Res. Growth Eval. **5**(06), 1558–1566 (2024)
14. Kaulio, M.A.: Customer, consumer and user involvement in product development: a framework and a review of selected methods. Total Qual. Manag. **9**(1), 141–149 (1998)
15. Fotrousi, F., Fricker, S.A., Fiedler, M.: The effect of requests for user feedback on quality of experience. Softw. Qual. J. **26**, 385–415 (2018)
16. Parker, W.: Zillow's Shuttered Home-Flipping Business Lost $881 Million in 2021. https://www.wsj.com/articles/zillows-shuttered-home-flipping-business-lost-881-million-in-2021-11644529656. Accessed 23 July 2024
17. Poulter, A.: Zillow responds to viral Tik Tok video claiming housing market manipulation. https://finance.yahoo.com/news/zillow-tiktok-video-real-estate-housing-211403123.html. Accessed 29 Nov 2024
18. Commission, F.T.: Opendoor Refunds. https://www.ftc.gov/enforcement/refunds/opendoor-refunds. Accessed 29 Nov 2024
19. zillowgroup: Zillow's new AI-powered natural-language search is a first in real estate. https://investors.zillowgroup.com/investors/news-and-events/news/news-details/2023/Zillows-new-AI-powered-natural-language-search-is-a-first-in-real-estate/. Accessed 24 Apr 2024
20. Tabassi, E.: Artificial intelligence risk management framework (AI RMF 1.0) (2023)
21. Bharadhwaj, H., Huang, D.-A., Xiao, C., Anandkumar, A., Garg, A.: Auditing AI models for verified deployment under semantic specifications. arXiv preprint arXiv:2109.12456 (2021)
22. Koenigstorfer, F., Krieger, F.F.A., Thalmann, S.: Bridging AI development and compliance: design principles for the documentation of AI (2024)
23. Golpayegani, D., Hupont, I., Panigutti, C., Pandit, H.J., Schade, S., O'Sullivan, D., Lewis, D.: AI cards: towards an applied framework for machine-readable AI and risk documentation inspired by the EU AI act. In: Annual Privacy Forum, pp. 48–72. Springer, Berlin (2024)
24. Taleb, N.N.: The Black Swan: The Impact of the Highly Improbable, 2nd edn. Random House Trade Paperbacks, New York (2010)
25. Sjödin, D., Parida, V., Palmié, M., Wincent, J.: How AI capabilities enable business model innovation: scaling AI through co-evolutionary processes and feedback loops. J. Bus. Res. **134**, 574–587 (2021)

26. Canva: Canva report findings: AI is transforming the roles of marketers and creatives. https://www.canva.com/newsroom/news/ai-report-findings/. Accessed 29 Nov 2024
27. Chanticleer, A.F.R.: Canva's new revenue number supports $39b valuation, IPO the real test. https://www.afr.com/chanticleer/canva-s-new-revenue-number-supports-39b-valuation-ipo-the-real-test-20231005-p5e9xv. Accessed 25 Apr 2024
28. TechCrunch: From graphic design to visual workflows, Canva's new AI core is changing its business. https://techcrunch.com/2023/12/28/canva-ai-core-growth/. Accessed 25 Apr 2024
29. Adams, C.: How generative AI unlocks creativity in all professions. https://www.canva.com/newsroom/news/canva-generative-ai/. Accessed 25 Apr 2024
30. Canva: AI Safety at Canva. https://www.canva.com/policies/ai-safety/. Accessed 25 Apr 2024
31. Team, C.: Introducing Canva Shield: Safe, fair and secure AI. https://www.canva.com/newsroom/news/safe-ai-canva-shield/. Accessed 25 Apr 2024
32. Canva: Security at Canva. https://www.canva.com/security/. Accessed 25 Apr 2024
33. Canva: Scaling to Count Billions. https://www.canva.dev/blog/engineering/scaling-to-count-billions/. Accessed 25 Apr 2024
34. Reddy, G.S., Srinivasu, R., Rao, M.P.C., Rikkula, S.R.: Data warehousing, data mining, olap and oltp technologies are essential elements to support decision-making process in industries. Int. J. Comput. Sci. Eng. **2**(9), 2865–2873 (2010)
35. Cavalcante Siebert, L., Lupetti, M.L., Aizenberg, E., Beckers, N., Zgonnikov, A., Veluwenkamp, H., Abbink, D., Giaccardi, E., Houben, G.-J., Jonker, C.M., et al.: Meaningful human control: actionable properties for AI system development. AI Ethics **3**(1), 241–255 (2023)
36. Jobin, A., Ienca, M., Vayena, E.: The global landscape of ai ethics guidelines. Nat. Mach. Intell. **1**(9), 389–399 (2019)
37. Pirozzi, M.: The stakeholder perspective in the generative artificial intelligence scenario and the AI-stakeholders. PM World J. **XIII**(Issue VIII), 1–27 (2024)
38. Rinta-Kahila, T., Someh, I., Gillespie, N., Indulska, M., Gregor, S.: Managing unintended consequences of algorithmic decision-making: the case of robodebt. J. Inf. Technol. Teach. Cases **14**(1), 165–171 (2024)
39. Victoria State Government, L.A.: Learning from the failures of Robodebt – building a fairer, client-centred social security system. https://www.legalaid.vic.gov.au/learning-from-the-failures-of-robodebt. Accessed 25 Apr 2024
40. News, S.: Federal government to repay 470,000 wrongly issued robodebts worth $720 million. https://www.sbs.com.au/news/article/federal-government-to-repay-470-000-wrongly-issued-robodebts-worth-720-million/w9f7r3t4k. Accessed 25 Apr 2024
41. Priergaard, J.: Not my debt: the institutional origins of robodebt. Aust. J. Public Adm. **84**(1), 142–158 (2025)
42. Carney, T.: Robo-debt illegality: the seven veils of failed guarantees of the rule of law? Alternative Law J. **44**(1), 4–10 (2019)
43. Commission, T.R.: Royal Commission into the Robodebt Scheme. https://robodebt.royalcommission.gov.au/ (2023). Accessed 25 Apr 2024
44. Narne, S., Adedoja, T., Mohan, M., Ayyalasomayajula, T.: AI-driven decision support systems in management: enhancing strategic planning and execution. Int. J. Recent Innov. Trends Comput. Commun. **12**(1), 268–276 (2024)
45. Kim, S.S., Watkins, E.A., Russakovsky, O., Fong, R., Monroy-Hernández, A.: " help me help the ai": Understanding how explainability can support human-ai interaction. In: Proceedings of the 2023 CHI Conference on Human Factors in Computing Systems, pp. 1–17 (2023)
46. Powell, S.: Medical services take a leap into remote areas. https://www.afr.com/work-and-careers/management/medical-services-take-a-leap-into-remote-areas-20221118-p5bzdd. Accessed 25 Apr 2024
47. Pulse, T.: Dropping out of mobile apps has health consequences. https://thepulse.org.au/2020/11/05/dropping-out-of-mobile-apps-has-health-consequences/ (2020). Accessed 25 Apr 2024
48. Caremonitor: Our ADHA Innovation Challenge Win. https://caremonitor.com.au/news/australian-digital-health-agency-innovation-challenge-winner. Accessed 25 Apr 2024

49. CareMonitor: Digital Healthcare Software. https://caremonitor.com.au/ (2024). Accessed 5 June 2025
50. CareMonitor: Community EMR Solutions. https://caremonitor.com.au/community-emr (2024). Accessed 5 June 2025
51. Service, A.W.: CareMonitor Case Study. https://aws.amazon.com/solutions/case-studies/caremonitor/. Accessed 25 Apr 2024
52. CareMonitor: Hospital in the Home: The Future of Care. https://caremonitor.com.au/home-hospital (2024). Accessed 5 June 2025
53. Patel, J.: Bridging data silos using big data integration. Int. J. Database Manag. Syst. **11**(3), 1–6 (2019)
54. Noor, T.H., Sheng, Q.Z., Zeadally, S., Yu, J.: Trust management of services in cloud environments: Obstacles and solutions. ACM Comput. Surv. **46**(1), 1–30 (2013)
55. Nama, P., Pattanayak, S., Meka, H.S.: AI-driven innovations in cloud computing: transforming scalability, resource management, and predictive analytics in distributed systems. Int. Res. J. Modernization Eng. Technol. Sci. **5**(12), 4165 (2023)
56. Dorotic, M., Bijmolt, T.H., Verhoef, P.C.: Loyalty programmes: current knowledge and research directions. Int. J. Manage. Rev. **14**(3), 217–237 (2012)
57. Marcom, C.: Sabre announces agreement with Capillary Technologies. https://www.capillarytech.com/blog/pressrelease/sabre-announces-agreement-with-capillary-technologies/. Accessed 30 Nov 2024
58. Technologies, C.: Caring Pharmacy Taps Capillary Technologies to Drive Customer Loyalty In Malaysia. https://www.acnnewswire.com/press-release/english/41561/caring-pharmacy-taps-capillary-technologies-to-drive-customer-loyalty-in-malaysia (2018). Accessed 30 Nov 2024
59. Capillary Marcom: Capillary raises $45Mn to build the best Loyalty Management Company Globally. https://www.capillarytech.com/blog/pressrelease/capillary-raises-45mn-to-build-the-best-loyalty-management-company-globally/ (2024). Accessed 30 Nov 2024
60. Aslam, F.: The benefits and challenges of customization within saas cloud solutions. Am. J. Data, Inf. Knowl. Manage. **4**(1), 14–22 (2023)
61. Capillary Marcom: Capillary Technologies Grows 4x in the USA; Set to Dominate the Loyalty Technology Market with its SaaS offering. https://www.capillarytech.com/blog/pressrelease/capillary-grows-4x-in-usa-dominates-loyalty-technology-market-with-saas-offering/ (2023). Accessed 5 June 2025
62. Bharat Menon: Generative Loyalty: Transforming Loyalty Programs with aiRA. https://www.capillarytech.com/blog/generative-loyalty-ai-meets-customer-loyalty (2024). Accessed 5 June 2025
63. Nagaraj, V.V.: Capillary Technologies Ramps up Loyalty Game with Acquisition of Persuade. https://www.businesswire.com/news/home/20210906005216/en/. Accessed 30 Nov 2024
64. Marcom, C.: Capillary Acquires USA-Based Brierley Partners. https://www.capillarytech.com/blog/pressrelease/capillary-acquires-usa-based-brierley-partners/. Accessed 30 Nov 2024
65. Capillary Technologies: Loyalty TV - CapillaryTech. https://www.capillarytech.com/loyalty-tv/ (2024). Accessed 5 June 2025
66. Let's Talk Loyalty: Capillary Technologies. https://letstalkloyalty.com/capillary-technologies (2024). Accessed 5 June 2025
67. Capillary Technologies: Customer Data Platform Software - USA UK India Dubai Malaysia. https://www.capillarytech.com/products/customer-data-platform-software/ (2024). Accessed 5 June 2025
68. Capillary Technologies: Customer Loyalty Rewards Platforms UK, Germany, Singapore, USA, India. https://www.capillarytech.com/products/customer-loyalty-referrals-rewards-platforms/ (2024). Accessed 5 June 2025
69. Capillary Technologies: Customer Insights Platform. https://www.capillarytech.com/products/customer-insights-platform/ (2022). Accessed 5 June 2025
70. New Relic: Capillary Technologies relies on New Relic to drive seamless CX for global retail customers. https://newrelic.com/customers/capillary-technologies. Accessed 5 June 2025

71. Rock, D.: Engineering value: the returns to technological talent and investments in artificial intelligence. Available at SSRN 3427412 (2019)
72. Savovic, S., Zlatanovic, D., Nikolic, J.: Technology acquisitions as a supporting tool for improving companies'innovative potential. Ekonomski horizonti **23**(1), 3–17 (2021)
73. Antić, Z., Bogetić, S.: The importance of problem-solving competencies in achieving customer satisfaction. J. Eng. Manage. Compet. **14**(1), 21–32 (2024)

Shaoyang Fan is a Data Engineer at the ARC Training Centre for Information Resilience (CIRES) and incoming Senior Data Scientist at The University of Queensland. His research focuses on microtask crowdsourcing, data quality, and bias in human-in-the-loop systems. He works closely with Professor Gianluca Demartini on crowd-powered data curation pipelines that support responsible AI. Shaoyang holds a PhD and a Master of Science in Information Technology from UQ and a Master of Science in Econometrics from the University of Manchester. His interdisciplinary work bridges data science, human computation, and ethical machine learning.

Javad Pool is a Postdoctoral Research Fellow at The University of Queensland. He completed his PhD in Information Systems at UQ Business School, with a focus on data privacy and the effective use of information systems, specifically in the digital health context. By employing a combination of qualitative and quantitative research methodologies, Javad has conducted studies in a wide range of organizational and technological contexts, including healthcare, artificial intelligence, digital health, and social media. His work includes the development of inductive and theory-driven models, contributing to the existing body of knowledge on the effective use of information systems and health informatics research. His research endeavours to better understand and address socio-technical challenges within information systems use, including data governance, privacy risks, cybersecurity, data breaches, data protection, and responsible AI.

GPSR Compliance
The European Union's (EU) General Product Safety Regulation (GPSR) is a set of rules that requires consumer products to be safe and our obligations to ensure this.

If you have any concerns about our products, you can contact us on

ProductSafety@springernature.com

In case Publisher is established outside the EU, the EU authorized representative is:

Springer Nature Customer Service Center GmbH
Europaplatz 3
69115 Heidelberg, Germany

www.ingramcontent.com/pod-product-compliance
Lightning Source LLC
Chambersburg PA
CBHW060415260326
41837CB00004BA/98
9783032019394